A Walk Through the Past

PEOPLE AND PLACES

of Florence and Lauderdale County, Alabama

By William Lindsey McDonald

Cover by Dorothy Carter McDonald   Indexed by Robert E. Torbert

To My Youngest Grandson,

Michael McDonald Backensto

*... with prayers that your tomorrow will
be as wonderful and fulfilling as has
been my yesterday.*

In Recognition
EZRA LEE CULVER

Who sponsored a part of the funding for the original publication of
this book so as to "enable our younger generation to learn about
our country."

ABOUT THE AUTHOR

William Lindsey McDonald is a product of the hills of North Alabama. Mainly of Celtic blood, four of his direct ancestors can be traced to Scotland and others from England, Ireland, Wales, and Northern France (Black Dutch.) One, a Chickasaw Indian, was born in 1813 on Koger Island in West Lauderdale County. Seven forefathers fought in the American Revolution, one in the War of 1812, and two in the Civil War (one Confederate and the other a Yankee.)

The author is a retired Army Reserve Colonel with thirty-eight years of service, including World War II (European Theater) and the Korean War. His reserve duty included a sixteen-year assignment on the staffs of the Provost Marshal General and the Assistant Chief of Staff for Personnel at the Pentagon. He also served thirty-eight years with the Tennessee Valley National Fertilizer Development Center. He is a retired United Methodist minister with thirty-eight years of service in rural churches in Lauderdale and Colbert Counties. He served as Chairman of the Florence Historical Board from 1968 until 1989 at which time he was appointed City Historian.

McDonald is a member of the National Honor Society of Phi Kappa Phi, and was graduated form Florence State Teachers College in 1952. He also was graduated from the Army's Command and General Staff College, the Military Police School, the Army Finance School, The Industrial College of the Armed Forces, and seminary studies in the United Methodist Church.

He is a journalist for the Times Daily and the East Lauderdale News of Florence and Rogersville, Alabama. He has published articles in magazines, newspapers, and periodicals over many years. He is the author of fourteen books. Two of his most popular, Paths in the Brier Patch and The Old North Field are about growing up in Alabama. The others are about the history of the area.

William McDonald is married to Dorothy Carter McDonald, a retired artist and teacher in the Florence City School System. They have two daughters: Dr. Nancy Carter McDonald of Montgomery, Alabama, and Suzannah Lee McDonald Backensto (Mrs. Eric), of Birmingham, Alabama, There are five grandchildren: Carter McDaniel Buttram, Lindsey Katherine Middleton (Mrs. Scott), Andrew William McClellan, Amanda Suzannah Carey McClellan, and Michael McDonald Backensto. The newest addition to this family is a great-grandson—William Albert Middleton.

CONTENTS

ACKNOWLEDGMENTS

First, I am most grateful to Robert Torbert for editing the complete manuscript and for preparing the index. Also, I am obliged to Donna Haynes Rogers for her excellent proofreading and to Milly Wright for reading and making suggestions to the original draft. A special thanks goes to my Son-In-Law, Eric Backensto, for keeping my aged computer up and running during the preparation of the pages that make up the book.

There is a long list of people whose works and papers I have referred to, and for this privilege I am most grateful: Milly Wright, Charles Wilder Watts, Jill Knight Garrett, Oscar D. Lewis, Joshua Nicholas Winn III, Dr. Mary Jane McDaniel, Dr. Bernaar Cresap, Dr. Kenneth R. Johnson, the Reverend Hiram Kennedy Douglass, Elizabeth McDonald, Reynold B. Burt, Richard C. Sheridan, Mary Threet Sharp, George Alfred McCroskey, John L. McWilliams, James Jackson VI,. W. Rutland Cunningham, Charles E. Moore, William C. Scott, Jr., Fred Johnson, Ninon Holder Parker, Dallas M. Lancaster, Mary Lancaster, William Q. Hill, Dan Wallace, Turner Rice, Harold T. Damsgard, Doris Metcalf, Kathleen A. Darby, Faye A. Axford, Judge J. J. Mitchell, Judge William B. Wood, Dawson A. Phelps, Wayne Gray, Marianne Bernauer, Ronald Pettus, Earl Daniel, Eva Dendy, Dr. Ben Earl Kitchens, Dr. Darrell A. Russel, Theo Williford, Sr., John Nelson McDonald, Sr., Orlan K. Irons, Sam Wade and Lois E. Henderson.

Last but not least, my wife, Dorothy, has been a constant help over these last three years of writing this book. As I completed each chapter, she graciously reviewed it for grammar, style, and punctuation. For her patience, encouragement, and counsel I am forever grateful.

FOREWORD

"History is the essence of innumerable Biographies."
(Essays, by Thomas Carlyle)

This book tells the history of Florence and the towns, villages, communities, and crossroads in Lauderdale County, Alabama. Most of the characters in this story are the hard working pioneers, settlers, and slaves who cut the trees, cleared the land, and established our towns and county. These were the folk who never expected their names to appear in print.

Time-wise, I have been laboring over the writing of this history for more than three years. Yet, the truth of the matter is that I have been researching, interviewing, and collecting material for this volume for more than sixty years. It began when my Grandmother Lucy Lindsey would tell of her early days in Florence.

She had a magic way with words and a first-hand touch with generations all the way back to the American Revolution. This was through her own Grandmother who came to Alabama during pioneer years in a caravan that was led by her Grandfather who had served under General LaFayette in the Siege of Yorktown.

It has been my privilege over these many years to interview such men as Kit Butler, a former slave who "knew the exact spot where Chief Doublehead was buried." Another personal interview I shall not soon forget was in 1965 with a descendant of Levi Colbert at Colbert's Ferry, Oklahoma. Also, in my growing up years I knew and talked with a few old veterans of the Civil War. I am blessed to have had ancestors who were early settlers at Green Hill, Cow Pen, Waterloo, Wright, Cloverdale, Central Heights, Murphy's Chapel, Zip City, the Bend of the River, and Florence. It also has been an honor to have served Churches throughout the county where I knew and conversed with such wonderful people as Patrick White, Harvel White, Green Berry Lindsey, Jeff Smith, Jim Frye, Henry Darby, Drucilla Crow Harrison, Alice Tidwell, Roma Harrison Parker, Keron Lindsey, Homer Haygood, Frank Henken, B. Lee

Springer, Gilbert Thornton, and former slave, Lucy Reeder, and Robert Armistead, a son of former slaves.

I have inherited several private collections, including the papers of my Great Grandfather Franklin Pierce Johnson. His eldest daughter, my Great Aunt Magnolia Johnson Cole, was a storehouse of knowledge about early life in Florence. Among life's most treasured blessings have been my personal friendships with local historians, including a number who are now deceased.

All of these connections and experiences, and years of travel and research, have gone into the creation of this story of People and Places in Florence and Lauderdale County, Alabama. It truly has been for me a labor of love.

PART I – STORIES ABOUT THE EARLY HISTORY OF FLORENCE

This journey through the early life of Florence begins with its day of origin on March 12, 1818, and ends with the creation of the Tennessee Valley Authority on May 18, 1933. These were the formative years of a town on the Tennessee which grew from a small river port to a progressive Renaissance city at the dawn of the Twenty-First Century. These stories reflect the people, places, and events which help to tell how it all began.

1. THE CITY OF FLORENCE

"...A city that is set on a hill cannot be hid."
(Matthew 5:14)

March 12, 1818, is recognized as the official birthday for Florence. On that eventful day, a document known as the Articles of Association was signed by the trustees of the newly organized Cypress Land Company which was formed from two rival groups – the Tennessee Company and the Alabama Company. This occurred in the office of the federal surveyor for northern Alabama, General John Coffee. The purpose for this occasion was to establish a new town that would become the county seat for the newly created Lauderdale County. As they affixed their signatures to this historic document, the seven trustees of the Cypress Land Company became the founding fathers of Florence, Alabama[1].

Their next action was the purchase of 5,515.77 acres of land at the foot of the Muscle Shoals for $85,235.24, or $15.45 per acre. This large tract provided all possible sites for a new town between Campbell's Ferry (near the location of the 20th Century Wilson Dam) and the mouth of Cypress Creek. The company managed a first payment of $21,308.81, which amounted to twenty-five percent of the amount of the purchase. John Coffee, assuming the role as leader of the trustees as well as the principal developer for the new town, set out to supervise the work of the surveyors.

This site for the county seat was originally called "North Port."[2] After the town was named Florence, its docking and shipping area along the riverbank continued to be called North Port for a number of years. Affixing these "north-south-east-west" designations to river ports seems to have been popular in the development of towns along the water routes. On the opposite side of the river from Florence would be located another early town to be called South Port. Its name was later changed to South Florence.

Some thirty miles or so down the river – just inside the Mississippi line – another early river town would be designated as East Port.

The port at Florence was at the foot of the Muscle Shoals, meaning that it was as far up the river as most boats could go except during heavy floods which usually occurred in late winter and early spring. Thus, the newly established town quickly evolved into a commercial center for groceries and foreign goods received from New Orleans and other places. Supply wagons would pick up these shipped-in goods and transport them to towns north and east of the Muscle Shoals as well as to points in Middle Tennessee.

Actually, the site that would become Florence was seen as a potential place for a town a number of years prior to the acquisition of the land. Coffee and his mentor, General Andrew Jackson, were already well acquainted with this part of North Alabama.[3] They and others were quick to recognize its potential advantages. Jackson's letter to Coffee, written in August 1817, pointed out ideal sites on both sides of the river "where the military road crosses the same."[4]

Florence was built on a hill overlooking the Tennessee River. It would be difficult to find a town anywhere with a better setting. The geology of the site shows that Florence is almost surrounded by a palisade of ancient rocks from an elevation of about 450 to 500 feet. Parts of this outcropping can be seen in a number of places. The high plateau of the city is mindful of the fortified towns of the Old World. These heights offered a protection from the devastating floods that had been occurring along the Tennessee River for eons of time. The tableland offered an almost level area for the business district and its elevation helped insure against some of the diseases that were associated with the lower lands in the Tennessee Valley.

Ferdinand Sannoner and Hunter Peel were employed by the Cypress Land Company as surveyors. Sannoner, a native of Italy, had served as a military surveyor under Napoleon. Although legend has it that Sannoner was responsible for laying out Florence, a study of the papers of John Coffee reveal that the man most responsible for designing the city was none other than the General himself.[5] The founding fathers were so pleased with the new town that Sannoner was given the honor of proposing its name. Recalling the beauty of the Renaissance city of Florence, Italy, which was built around the River Arno, he suggested the name "Florence" for the new town overlooking the Tennessee River in Alabama.

Coffee's plan for the main section of the town consisted of dividing the area into blocks of almost two acres in size; these, in turn, were divided into four equal half-acre lots. The land surrounding the city was carved into parcels ranging from a few acres to small-size farms.[6]

The streets of the town were laid out somewhat askew. Its lines vary about 26 degrees running north to south and east to west. One can readily see that its planners were guided by the presence of the river below the town. Seemingly, with the twentieth century automobiles in mind, the principal streets were provided a width of 115 feet; all other streets were allowed the width of 99 feet. It is unfortunate that some of these streets were later narrowed by town fathers who did not share the long-range vision of the original planners. It has been pointed out that Florence's original streets were named for stately trees and scenic rivers rather than for battles and men of war as was popular among some towns of that era.

Another unusual feature when compared to most cities is the almost total disjointment in the roads from one section of town to the other. This was not a problem in the early days since East Florence did not develop until the 1880s, and the neighborhood known as North Florence did not come into being until about the turn of the twentieth century. Also, when Florence was laid out its planners provided a circular road around its perimeter – as though guided by an ancient military handbook. The April 21, 1825, edition of the Florence Gazette reported that within this area enclosed by Circular Road "... are 262 town lots from one-half to 31 acres in size with an average value at lowest calculation $300, making a total of $78,600."

Provisions were made for the future needs of Florence as a county seat, commercial and industry center, and for its religious and educational life. Two lots were set aside for Court Square which would become the site for a courthouse, clerk's offices, and jail. Also, the trustees reserved two lots for a hotel, which they referred to as a tavern. These facilities were to be constructed at company expense. It was reported later that $23,000 had been spent for the courthouse, jail, and offices; cost of the tavern was listed at $3,500. The generous Cypress Land Company was careful to reserve lots for a future college, a cotton factory, a livery stable, a ferry to cross the Tennessee River below the town, and for three downtown churches – the Methodist, Baptist, and Presbyterian. For some reason the Presbyterians were required to pay for their land.[7]

The first land sale ran from July 22 through July 26, 1818. This event had been well publicized which resulted in a large attendance. The second sale was held five years later – in July, 1823. Purchases, however, were not limited to these advertised dates. Records show that 180 people acquired lots over the first five years, many of them buying on credit instead of paying cash. Unfortunately, within a year following the first land sale, the country was hit by an economic recession known as "The Panic of 1819." As a result, a number of the people who had purchased Florence lots on credit defaulted on their payments. Thus, the Cypress Land Company was caught up in a cash flow situation. They helped matters by reducing their land holdings so as to include only the site of Florence and the immediate area around it.[8]

As far as human dwellings go, Florence was almost an isolated hilltop in the wilderness at the time of the 1818 land sale. Just above Florence near the present Wilson Dam was Campbell's Ferry which served as a river crossing for three wilderness roads. One followed today's Butler Creek Road and the Middle Road to the ferry site. This original Indian path intersected with the Jackson Military Road near present St. Florian and crossed the Pulaski Pike a few miles southwest of St. Florian. Thus, travelers on these three trails were funneled to Campbell's Ferry. It is believed that this ferry was established around 1804 by a Captain Campbell who had at one time commanded a garrison of soldiers near the Tennessee River.[9]

Early records show that there was a residence east of Cypress Creek known as Colonel Puler's place which was designated as a courthouse until an adequate building could be erected. Puler's home was perhaps located near what would later be called the Gunwaleford Road, or in the area of Palisade Drive, or in the vicinity of Handy School along Fish Trap Road or Irvine Avenue.

James Sample, native of Pennsylvania, had a one-room frontier store at the intersection of Court Street and the Jackson Military Road which later was known as "Mitchell's Corner." Sample's family lived in a nearby log cabin believed to have been located near the present Pope's Tavern and Museum on Hermitage Drive. At the centennial celebration of Florence in 1918, one of its oldest citizens, James Simpson, told the story of how it was at the time of the first land sale:

> "My father came from Nashville here in 1818 and when he came to the little store which was located on the corner of Court Street and Military Road, as it was then, a little log store, he got out and went in there and said, 'How far is it to Florence?' the storekeeper said, 'If you come to the middle of my store you will be in the middle of town.' That was in the early part of 1818. The store belonged to Mr. James Sample, who had been living here just long enough to build the little storehouse and a cabin to live in."[10]

Benjamin Price and his wife, Jane, were living just east of the future town of Florence before the creation of the Alabama Territory in 1817. In an interview with the Clifton Mirror, a Tennessee newspaper published June 23, 1905, their daughter, Catherine Sinclair, talked about her parent's pioneer home in North Alabama. She recalled that Indians were their only neighbors and that her father had to go to Giles County to buy salt.

Florence was not the typical frontier town that slowly evolved over a period of time. It saw considerable growth at the beginning. One source reported in 1820 that there were two log houses, a log jail, a tavern, a blacksmith's shop, and probably one hundred inhabitants.[11] In 1821, Anne Newport Royall, America's first traveling lady correspondent, wrote: "Many large and elegant brick buildings are already built here, (although it was sold out, but two years since,) and frame houses are putting up daily. It is not uncommon to see a framed building begun in the morning and finished by night. Several respectable mercantile houses are established here..."[12]

Although not typical in growth, Florence was similar in appearance to other developing towns in what was known as the "New West" beyond the Appalachians. The streets were muddy in winter and dusty in summer. Plank sidewalks, later to be replaced by brick, eased the task of reaching the shops, businesses, and hotels. A letter to the editor, signed by a "Mr. Prosper Hope," appeared in the April 21, 1825, edition of the Florence Gazette. The writer, who obviously used a pen name, made these observations about local conditions:

> "Cannot be denied streets are in very bad order – composed of stumps, ditches, and very frequently filth; Town spring kept in most disgusting condition; Low class of people in town; Great number of grog shops; Wells in public square ought to be filled in..."

Actually, the earliest business section began at the river's edge where there were commission warehouses and, for a brief time even a hotel.[13] The town spring was just below the crest of the hill south of Spring Street (now Veterans Drive) between Court and Pine Streets. This was a watering hole for man and beast, a public walk, and a campground for out-of-town people doing business at the county seat.

The business district continued up Court Street some five blocks to the intersection of Tennessee Street just north of Court Square where the original courthouse was located. Although there were a number of fine brick buildings as noted in 1821 by the Washington correspondent Anne Royall, the town was interlaced with wooden structures as well.[14] The townsfolk referred to the intersection of Alabama and Court Street as "Fant's Corner," where the early Charles W. Fant Wool Factory was located. The most popular downtown area was the intersection of Limestone and Court Street where the Eagle Hotel was located. Here people gathered to read the newspapers and to hear from the outside world through guests arriving by boat and stagecoach. The Exchange Hotel was near the intersection of Court and College Streets. An early Florence post office was located in a section of this hotel.

As the business district expanded northward, hotels and taverns began to locate in and around the intersection of Tennessee and Court Streets. William Garrard's two-story frame house on the northwest corner of this intersection was converted into an inn or tavern. Other hotels appeared along Tennessee Street both east and west of this corner. Later, the post office was moved to this area where provisions were made for patrons to receive their mail without dismounting from their horses. The area on Court Street north of this intersection was slower in developing as part of the business district. For a number of years Peytona Livery and Trade Stables on the southwest corner of Mobile and Court Streets served as a general dividing line between the business and residential areas. In between this stable and the Garrick Campbell Hotel could be found a blacksmith shop, wood shop, and other businesses.[15]

The town's first postmaster, appointed December 14, 1818, was John Craig. John was a brother to Samuel Craig who operated Craig's Inn, a stagecoach stop near the crossing of the Jackson Military Road over Shoal Creek near Florence. Three Craig brothers – John, Samuel, and David – natives of North Carolina were among the early investors in Florence lots. These brothers had connections with Andrew Jackson. However, by 1827, there were disturbing reports of violations in the post office. The General John Coffee Papers in the Tennessee State Archives has a copy of a letter to Coffee from Judge John McKinley in Washington, dated December 15, 1827, which reads:

"The Postmaster General was very prompt however in his determination to remove him (Craig) from this office under existing circumstances."

Obviously, the political influence of the friends of Andrew Jackson came once again into play. Seven days later, James H. Weakley replaced John Craig to become the city's second appointed postmaster. Until recent years, the local postmaster appointments were often influenced by the political world.

Florence's first residential area was in the section now called West Florence. One of the first of the finer homes was built on South Pine Street as an investment by the Cypress Land Company.[16] It wasn't long before the "porticoed mansions," for which Florence became noted, began appearing along North Court, North Pine, and North Seminary Streets.

The planners provided lots for a college, or seminary, in this area. Florence's earliest churches were located nearby. Close to the center of this cultural and religious area, an entire block was set aside for a park or "pleasure ground." Since 1924, this has been known as Wilson Park. However, there had been a movement by the people to name it Sannoner Park in honor of the man most responsible for its inclusion in the early plans for the city.[17] The area north and east of Seminary Street and Wood Avenue would later develop into residential districts as the population of the town increased. Yet, there were a few large homes on this side of town, surrounded by sizable lawns and grounds, within a few years after the town was established.[18]

Just east of town, and outside the town itself, two acres were reserved for the burying grounds. Now called the Florence Cemetery, this is one of Florence's most historic places. Many of the area's first settlers rest within its gates.

The act establishing Florence as a corporate city was approved January 7, 1826. The city limits were generally described as the Tennessee River on the south and Poplar Street to the east, then following a line southwestward around the town to its point of beginning at the river.[19] Twelve aldermen were elected and Alexander Hamilton Wood became the first mayor. Wood, a veteran of the War of 1812, became the patriarch of one of the most influential families in the history of Florence.

Although Florence has yet to reach the great dream as envisioned by its early developers and planners, it has continued through its steady and healthy growth to become the largest of the cities at the Muscle Shoals. It also is rated as a leading commercial, educational, and medical center of North Alabama.

Downtown Florence has survived a number of devastating fires over the years, including the Civil War period when several blocks were burned by occupying forces. The coming of the large malls and shopping centers in the latter part of the twentieth century have, in effect, tended to relocate the business center to the outskirts of the town. But due to the foresight of the town's leaders and business people, the old has not been relegated into the ruins of abandoned buildings. Today, the downtown area continues to be a living part of the heritage of a historic and progressive city that was built upon a hill overlooking the great Tennessee River below.

2. THE FOUNDING FATHERS OF FLORENCE

"Remove not the ancient landmark which thy fathers have set."
(Proverbs 22: 28)

The Cypress Land Company, named for the scenic creek which enters the Tennessee River in Lauderdale County, came into being by the merger of two rival groups who were interested in establishing a town at the foot of the Shoals. One faction, "The Tennessee Company," was made up of a number of prominent men from Nashville, including John Overton, John Childress, General John Coffee, James Jackson, and General Andrew Jackson. The other group, "The Alabama Company," listed among its leaders a number of investors from Huntsville: LeRoy Pope, Thomas Bibb, Waddy Tate, John McKinley, and James Madison, who incidentally was not the same Madison who served as the Fourth American President.

The newly established Cypress Land Company elected seven trustees from among both former factions. These seven men, by the act of signing their names to a document at Huntsville, Alabama, on March 12, 1818, inscribed themselves in history as the "Founding Fathers of Florence." At this occasion they were some seventy miles distant from the site of the proposed future town. Perhaps one or more of them would never see the city they established that day.

The leader of these seven trustees – and, thereby the venerable patriarch of Florence – was General John Coffee, a veteran of the War of 1812 and Indian Campaigns. As history associates the name of Washington with this nation, so is the name of John Coffee connected with the City of Florence. Coffee was born June 2, 1772, in Prince Edward County, Virginia. John and his widowed mother settled on the Cumberland River a few miles from Nashville in April of 1798. This event in his early life could well have been described over 1800 years earlier by a poet named Pinder who wrote: "A dream about a shadow is man: yet, when some god-given splendor falls, a glory of light comes over him and his life is sweet."[1]

In Nashville, Coffee became a life-long friend and close associate of the powerful Andrew Jackson. This connection led Coffee into the military from which he emerged as a national hero. It was at this place along the Cumberland River where he met and was married to Mary Donelson, a niece of Rachel Jackson, the wife of the future President of the United States. Mary was also a granddaughter of Colonel John Donelson who was among the first to recognize the potential advantages of establishing a town at the Muscle Shoals in Northwest Alabama. Beginning in March, 1817, Coffee began his career as surveyor general of public lands which he held until his death some sixteen years later. At first his supervision covered only the public lands in the northern part of the Mississippi Territory. This was extended a year later to include all public lands in the Alabama Territory. This office placed Coffee in complete control of surveying in Alabama. Consequently, many of the towns in North Alabama were laid out under his leadership.[2]

In 1818, Coffee purchased land for a plantation just north of Florence on Cox Creek near the present intersection of Cox Creek Parkway and Cloverdale Road. He named this place "Hickory Hill," and moved his family here in early 1819. In February, 1823, he transferred his general land office from Huntsville to East Tennessee Street in Florence. Coffee died July 7, 1833, at the age of sixty-one years and was buried in the Coffee Cemetery on the grounds of his plantation.[3]

James Jackson was also one of Florence's best-known and most influential founding fathers. As with John Coffee, the name of Jackson is perpetually linked with the history of the seat of Lauderdale County. Also in like manner, James Jackson very early moved his family to this area where he established one of the great plantations of the Tennessee Valley. Known as The Forks of Cypress, this fertile farm some five miles north of town became internationally famous as the home of a number of the world's great race horses.[4]

James Jackson was the seventh son and eleventh child of James and Mary Steel Jackson. He was born October 25, 1782, at Ballybay, County, Monaghan, Ireland. In 1799, he came to Philadelphia from Germany where he and an uncle had fled because of their involvement in the Irish Rebellion.[5] In 1801, Jackson moved to Nashville.[6] It wasn't long before he began an association with Andrew Jackson and John Coffee that would lead him to the banks of the Tennessee River in North Alabama. It was in Nashville where Jackson met and was married to Sarah Moore McCullough, a descendant of three colonial Caroline governors, including Sir John Yeamans, founder of Charleston. James Jackson served in both Alabama houses and in 1830 was elected president of the state Senate.[7] This prominent founding father of Florence died August 17, 1840, and is buried in the Jackson Cemetery near the ruins of the Forks of Cypress mansion.[8]

John McKinley gained regional status as an Alabama legislator and national recognition as a United States Senator and, later, as Alabama's first Associate Justice of the United States Supreme Court.[9] McKinley's name is also engraved in the history of Florence as one of its founding fathers. Born May 1, 1780, in Culpeper County, Virginia, his family moved to Lincoln County, Kentucky, where as a young man, he studied law. About 1819, he migrated to Huntsville, Alabama. By 1821, he had moved his family to Florence where his residence was located near the intersection of South Court and Spring Streets (now Veterans Drive.) The various descriptions of his home are interesting. Anne Newport Royall, the Washington reporter, while visiting the area in 1821 wrote: "Major McKinley lives in Florence...and his dwelling contains more taste and splendor, by one half, that I ever saw in my whole life put together...Everything in the house had, to me the appearance of enchantment. I never was in such a paradise before."[10]

Yet another description of this "mansion" was given in 1918 by James Simpson in his recollections of early Florence: "Judge John McKinley was one of the pioneers of Florence. I recall him very well up to about 1840, I reckon it was. His residence was just a plain house down on the left of Court Street..."[11]

Judge McKinley died July 19, 1852, and was buried in Louisville, Kentucky. A number of years afterwards, the remains of other family members who were interred in the McKinley Cemetery near the ruins of his Florence home were removed to Louisville. LeRoy Pope, known as the "Father of Huntsville, Alabama," was also one of the seven "Founding Fathers" of Florence. Born in Westmoreland County, Virginia, in 1765, he was married to Judith Sale, daughter of Cornelius and Jane Dawson Sale of Amherst County, Virginia. In 1790, the Popes joined a colony of friends who were migrating to Georgia. They later became early settlers of Madison County, Alabama. As early as 1809, LeRoy Pope purchased the land where the future city of Huntsville would be developed. It was Pope who actually selected the site for the town and gave it the name of Twickenham, which in 1811 was changed to Huntsville. LeRoy Pope became a wealthy planter in Madison County and the first president of the Planters and Merchants Bank of Huntsville. There are legends that associate Pope with an early tavern at Florence. However, other than his purchase of one lot in the city and a tract of land east of Florence at Shoal Creek, no other records have been found to substantiate his involvement in the business life of the town or county. He died June 17, 1844, in Huntsville.[12]

John Childress died September 10, 1819, some eighteen months after affixing his name to the document that gave him status as a founding father of Florence. At the time of his death he was District Marshal for West Tennessee. John and his brother, Thomas, were early associates of James Jackson as Nashville merchants. As early as 1805, these three gentlemen, with others, were offering to purchase delivered loose cotton at $15 per hundred weight and $17 per hundredweight if baled and delivered to them.[13]

Later, John became associated with John Donelson and James and Andrew Jackson in efforts to buy up the choicest lands offered in the 1818 Huntsville land sales. Among John Childress' acquisitions were two Florence lots. One was located at the intersection of Tennessee and Poplar Streets and the other at the corner of Alabama and Cherry Streets. Thomas, brother of John Childress, became a resident of Florence and built a large frame house at the northwest corner of Court and Tuscaloosa Streets.[14]

According to a newspaper, dated December 23, 1824, Thomas purchased the Florence Hotel. He had previously been the proprietor of the Bell Tavern in Nashville.[15] Paralee, a daughter of Thomas Childress, was married on February 6, 1823, to James J. Hanna, son of Sarah Hanna who was a sister to James Jackson.[16] For many years the home that Thomas Childress built in Florence was known as the Hanna Place.

Dabney Morris was another member of the elite group of seven "Founders of Florence." Very little is known about him. There are records at Nottoway County, Virginia, that show Morris and his wife, Sally, as residents of that county. These documents also reveal that Morris was an associate of Colonel James Madison, a tobacco merchant of Prince Edward County, Virginia, who invested in more than twenty lots at Florence.

Last – but far from being least – among the seven "Founders of Florence," was Thomas Bibb, a wealthy planter of Limestone County, Alabama. He was born in 1784, at Amelia County, Virginia. His mother, Sally Wyatt Bibb, was related to Martha Washington. Thomas Bibb's family moved to Georgia around 1790 where he became associated with LeRoy Pope who became a fellow-trustee of the Cypress Land Company. Bibb was married to Pamelia Thompson of Elbert County, Georgia. In 1826, Bibb built Belle Mina, one of the outstanding mansions of Limestone County, Alabama. Thomas Bibb became the second governor of Alabama following the untimely death of his brother, William Wyatt Bibb, who was Alabama's first governor as well as the only governor of the Alabama Territory. Thomas Bibb died in 1839 and is buried in Limestone County.[17]

One wonders if these seven men fully appreciated the importance of signing their names to a document that day in March, 1818. Most likely a few of them viewed their action only as a business venture in the buying and selling of land in the wilderness. Yet, in the annals of history this event is recorded as the birthday of Florence, and their names on the document have earned for them the honor of being the founding fathers of the city.

3. FERDINAND SANNONER: PLANNER WITH GENIUS

"Talent is that which is in a man's power!
Genius is that in whose power a man is."
(Lowell)

Ferdinand Sannoner, who was granted the honor of choosing the name for the City of Florence, was, according to tradition, somewhat of a genius with a talent to see beyond the surrounding wilderness of the early eighteenth century. His visions seemed to have been caught up in the needs of the next two centuries and beyond.

The papers of John Coffee plainly show that the responsibility of laying out the town of Florence was on the shoulders of the General himself.[1] Yet, legends have been handed down from the very earliest citizens of the town about how its broad streets and other unique and attractive features clearly bear the mark of the young engineer, Ferdinand Sannoner.

Sannoner was born in the year 1793 at Leghorn, Italy, in the Duchy of Tuscany. His father, John Angelo Sannoner, was of German origin. This family is believed to have immigrated to Italy from lower Saxony.[2] Ferdinand Sannoner received his degree from the French Polytechnic Institute at Paris. It has been written that at the age of sixteen he had mastered several languages and by his eighteenth birthday had received the classification as "an engineer of high standing." In 1811, this young man was employed by the Department of the Arno at Florence, Italy, as a "surveyor of first class." Later, he was in the service of Napoleon as a surveyor in France.[3] These two assignments on the Continent must have been invaluable learning experiences for a young engineer who was getting ready to carve out towns in the virgin forests of the New World.

Sannoner was twenty-three years of age when in 1816, he was attracted by the call to come to America. Advertisements in French newspapers appealed to "English-speaking engineers" to help survey and map America's rapidly expanding frontiers. Landing in New York, Sannoner was immediately sent south to the Alabama Territory to work under the supervision of John Coffee, the Surveyor General.[4]

In April, 1818, Coffee assigned Sannoner and Hunter Peel as surveyors for the new town at the foot of the Muscle Shoals that would be given the name of Florence. Both men received part of their wages in real estate. Sannoner's lot was located on South Pine Street near McFarland Bottom. He later acquired other property, including most of the present Walnut Street Historic District. He built his home on the south side of East Tuscaloosa Street between Market Street (now Wood Avenue) and Walnut Street.[5] He was married to Frances Holt of Huntsville. They moved to Florence in 1824 when the land office was moved here from Huntsville. Sannoner remained with the Cypress Land Company for a number of years. During this time he also served as clerk for Lauderdale County. It is believed that he helped in the surveying of a number of towns in the Tennessee Valley, such as Triana, Cotton Port, Marathon, Bainbridge, Marion, and Havanna.[6]

At some time prior to 1831, two of Sannoner's brothers, F. J., and John Baptiste, joined him at Florence. John Baptiste Sannoner died at the age of thirty in 1831, and is buried in the Florence Cemetery. According to tradition, this brother had operated a small bar and, due to failing health, was forced to close his business.

Ferdinand mortgaged his own property to purchase his brother's bar. Later, Ferdinand and his other brother, F. J. Sannoner, operated a bakery and delicatessen shop on Tennessee Street.[7] Ferdinand and Frances Sannoner, who were members of the First Methodist Church, lost an infant son, Rodolphus Henry Sannoner, in October, 1835. He was buried alongside his Uncle John Baptiste Sannoner, in the Florence Cemetery. In 1857, the Sannoners moved to Memphis, Tennessee, where Ferdinand died two years later and was buried in an unmarked grave. Frances outlived her husband by several years. They were survived by five sons and a daughter: James, John, Sam, Ferdinand, Rory, and Penelope.

In December, 1973, the Florence Historical Board and the Florence Chamber of Commerce placed a marble memorial at the burial site of Sannoner at Memphis' historic Elmwood Cemetery.[8] Thus, a grave that had remained unnoticed for more than a century was properly recognized as that of the engineer who will always be identified with the legacy of a town on the hill above the Tennessee River to which Ferdinand Sannoner so appropriately gave the name of Florence.

4. OUR AFRICAN-AMERICAN HERITAGE

"We carry within us the wonders we seek without us:
There is all Africa and her prodigies in us."
(Sir Thomas Browne)

The story of the African-American at the Muscle Shoals is an interesting and important fabric woven into the heritage of a place and its inhabitants. This race of people arrived in the very beginning of the exploration of the area. They came with the first settlers. The Alabama Territorial Census of 1818 shows 267 blacks in Lauderdale County along with 1,698 whites.[1] It was the labor of both that carved this place out of the wilderness and gave its communities a formidable way of life.

Possibly, the first African-American to visit Florence was a servant on board the fleet of boats, under the command of Colonel John Donelson, which passed through the Muscle Shoals on March 12, 1780. More probably, the first blacks at the Muscle Shoals were the slaves of the Cherokee and Chickasaw Indians who were in the area before the coming of the white settlers. As example, a roll used for the removal of the Chickasaws from their homes in Mississippi and Alabama in the 1830s shows a population of 4,914 Chickasaws and 1,156 slaves.[2] John Melton, an Irishman who lived among the Cherokees at Melton's Bluff, employed slaves at his inn near the river. This Indian village was located on the high bluffs along the Tennessee in Lawrence County almost directly across from the mouth of Elk River in Lauderdale County. It is not known when John Melton arrived in the area. However, historians point out that the village was established by the Cherokees following their battle with the Chickasaws in 1769.[3] Toward the later part of Melton's life he moved across the river where he had acquired a large farm near the present site of Rogersville.[4] It is reasonable to assume that most of his slaves went with him. Perhaps the remains of these African-Americans, along with old John Melton, rest in some forgotten cemetery in East Lauderdale County.

Chief George Colbert, who owned the ferry at the crossing of the Natchez Trace over the Tennessee River near Florence, employed a number of slaves. Lem Colbert was one of these African-Americans who operated this ferryboat which connected Colbert County to Lauderdale County. Lem was born in 1795 at Colbert's Ferry when it was located at Waterloo.[5] Elvira, who took Shoals for her family name, was a proud black who also claimed her roots at Colbert's Ferry. In 1838, she and the other slaves went with the Colberts over the cruel Trail of Tears to the territory west of the Mississippi. Elvira Shoals lived to be over 100 years of age. In her declining years she recalled many stories about her early life at the Muscle Shoals.

In a newspaper interview, Elvira thought it possible that she and Lem Colbert may have lived at least on one occasion on separate plantations.[6] George Colbert owned a number of land holdings, including one in West Lauderdale County called the "Reserve." Although Lem Colbert and Elvira Shoals were not the first of their race at the Muscle Shoals, it is believed they were the first African-Americans to leave their names to its legacy.

The population of both races increased significantly after Alabama became a state. In 1820, there were 3,556 whites and 1,407 blacks in Lauderdale County. By 1860, these numbers had grown to 10,639 whites and 6,781 blacks.[7] It is believed that most of the early black population of Lauderdale County either came from – or were descended from – a people who had inhabited the central grasslands or the coastal plains of the rain forest in West Africa. These were agricultural tribes with strong family loyalties and religious beliefs.[8] The African-Americans brought much of their rich culture with them.

A large majority of the local African-American population prior to the Civil War were in servitude for more than two generations, or almost half a century. Yet, a few of the blacks lived as free men and women. Two of these were barbers at Florence: John H. Rapier, Senior, and John Goins. No man was more highly respected than Rapier. Born a slave in 1808, John was emancipated in 1829 by the last will and testament of Richard

Rapier, a local white merchant and prosperous owner of boats that plied the Tennessee, Cumberland, Ohio, and Mississippi Rivers. Richard hired John out of Nashville and grew to love him as if he were his own son. By his will, Richard Rapier set aside $1,000 with instructions for his executors to purchase John and then arrange for his freedom. It also took an act of the Alabama legislature to bring about John Rapier's emancipation.

As the Florence barber, John earned about $1,000 a year during the antebellum period when the national per capita average was only about one-tenth of that amount. He was so influential around Florence that when his first wife, Suson, died during childbirth in 1841, John had her buried in the white section of the Florence Cemetery along with her two infant children, Jackson and Alexander. John had married Suson shortly after his emancipation. She was born as a free black in 1811 at Baltimore, Maryland. At the time of John Rapier's death in 1869, he was a comparatively wealthy man. He owned a number of valuable lots in Florence, as well as three city lots in Toronto, Canada, and had earlier been making payments on a hundred acres of wilderness land in Canada.[9]

At the time of the Civil War most of the people in Florence and Lauderdale County did not – and had never – owned slaves. Some sixty percent of the local slaves lived on farms, or with town residents, who owned less than fifty slaves. Thus, only twenty-three plantations in Lauderdale County were working more than fifty slaves in 1860. The largest slaveholder was John Peters who lived west of Florence on the Gunwaleford Road. In 1860, his plantation included 340 slaves for whom he had built 108 houses.[10]

A number of writers have noted that in general, the smaller the number of slaves the better the relationship between the owner and his slaves.[11] There were notable exceptions to this in Lauderdale County. For a number of generations following emancipation, some descendants of former slaves remembered the names of "the good" as well as "the bad" plantation owners. Some of those who were remembered as having taken good care of their servants and as having treated them with kindness were among the larger planters.[12] Beautiful stories have been handed down through these families that tell of close relationships that existed between the blacks and their masters.

Edmund, known as "Uncle Champ," was the butler at the Sweetwater Plantation east of Florence. He risked his life to protect the young ladies in his master's household during a night raid by the soldiers of U. S. General William T. Sherman in 1863. Sam, also of Sweetwater, went to war with young William Patton. When Billy was killed at Shiloh, Sam managed to return the body of his young master to his home for burial.[13]

Parson Dick, the butler at the Forks of Cypress, was so loved by his master's family that his portrait hung in the hall as long as the Jacksons owned the mansion. This story is one of intrigue. Parson Dick mysteriously disappeared during the latter part of the Civil War. His portrait mysteriously disappeared after the war. Some fifty years later mysteriously reappeared in one of the restored mansions at historic Williamsburg, Virginia.[14]

Some forty years following the Civil War, a former slave by the name of Mose worked on the William Wesley Carter farm east of Florence. Mose told about "Emancipation Day" when a Union Army Lieutenant and three soldiers came to announce their freedom. His old master, he said, stood beside these soldiers to assure the blacks that they need not leave their homes until they found work and new places to live.[15]

Large numbers of blacks at other plantations, however, were left without homes or employment. Many of these people who had been slaves in West Lauderdale County moved into the area west of Florence, especially around the abandoned racetrack along Gunwaleford Road and the banks of Cypress Creek. Thus, West Florence, which had been the town's first residential district, also became the first of the historic African-American communities in the city following the act that brought freedom to the slaves.

From the very beginning the black community in Florence has produced exceptional personalities, a number being recognized at the national level. This distinguished line of leaders from the black community began with the early history of the area. Their leadership and influence has been recognized throughout the succeeding generations. One former town slave, Dred Scott, gave his name to a famous United States Supreme Court Decision which became influential in the events leading to the Civil War and the Emancipation Act which brought about the freedom of all slaves. Dred Scott was born about 1795, in Southampton County, Virginia.

In 1818, his owners, Peter and Elizabeth Blow, moved to Madison County, Alabama. In 1820 they moved again, this time to the new town of Florence to operate a hotel. In 1827, they established the Blow Inn at the intersection of West Tennessee and Pine Streets. Here Dred Scott worked as a hostler and became well known in the streets of Florence. The Blows sold the establishment in 1831, to Mary Lucinda Pope for $2,000, and moved to St. Louis, Missouri. They sold their servant, Dred Scott, a year later to Dr. John Emerson, a military physician. Scott traveled with Dr. Emerson and lived with him at various times in Illinois and in the Wisconsin Territory. This became the basis for the famed Supreme Court Case which resulted in the Dred Scott Decision of February 1857. It is interesting that two sons of Peter Blow, Henry and Taylor Blow, assisted Dred Scott with the legal aspect of the long and extended court battles. These two brothers had grown up in the same household with Dred Scott. It was Taylor Blow who later purchased Dred Scott, his wife, and two daughters, and then arranged for their emancipation.[16]

Tom Brannon was heralded across the South and most of the nation when he engineered the capture of the infamous Natchez Trace outlaw, John A. Murrell. Known as the "Great Western Land Pirate," Murrell was involved in stealing and selling slaves as well as other high crimes. With his own hands he killed some four hundred men.[17] Brannon was born near Nashville. As a young boy he was purchased by Abraham Ricks, a cotton planter near La Grange Mountain in what was to become Colbert County, Alabama. Later, Brannon became a house servant for the James Irvine family on North Pine Street in Florence. Here is where he was first approached by John Murrell in 1831. Three years later, in

1834, Tom Brannon quite cleverly arranged with the local militia for Murrell's capture at a tavern west of Florence near the Waterloo Road bridge over Cypress Creek.[18]

Florence's black community produced two prominent politicians following the Civil War: James T. Rapier and Oscar DePriest. A son of the freedman Florence barber, John Rapier, James was born in Florence in 1837. He attended school in Nashville, Tennessee, and Buxton, Canada. Among his many accomplishments, Rapier helped draft Alabama's 1868 constitution and organized the state's black labor union. In 1872, James Rapier was elected to the United States House of Representatives.[19]

Oscar DePriest was born in Florence on March 9, 1871. His father and mother were Alexander R. and Mary Karsner DePriest. His early family had been connected with the Lauderdale County plantation of Judge Sidney Posey who was also a Methodist minister. Posey's wife was Harriet Calista DePriest, daughter of Dr. Horatio DePriest of Columbia, Tennessee. Alexander and Mary DePriest moved to Kansas in 1877. Oscar DePriest, descended from former slaves, was elected to the United States House of Representatives from Chicago, Illinois, in 1928. DePriest became the first of his race to be elected to Congress in the twentieth century. He also became the first African-American to be elected to that august body from a northern state.[20]

The renowned Father of the Blues, William Christopher Handy, was born at Florence on November 16, 1873. His parents were former slaves who had been set free by the Emancipation Proclamation. His father and grandfather were Methodist preachers. Handy's grandfather, the Reverend William Wise Handy, had run away from his master in Princess Ann, Maryland. He was later caught and sold into Alabama. At some point in time he was owned by the McKiernans of Colbert County, Alabama, who were related to the James Jackson family of Florence. Because of this connection, W. C. Handy maintained a close relationship with the descendants of James Jackson all of his life.

W. C. Handy's maternal grandfather was Christopher Brewer who had been given his freedom by John Wilson who owned a large plantation near the present community of St. Florian. However, Brewer preferred to stay near his former master as a trusted servant. On the night of April 30, 1865, a local gang of thieves dressed in Yankee uniforms tortured and burned John Wilson to death. In trying to protect his old friend and master, Christopher Brewer was shot and left for dead by the same robbers, although he did recover from the injury.[21]

The City of Florence has restored the birthplace of W. C. Handy. A statue of this famous musician stands in the town park. Annually a musical celebration, the W. C. Handy Festival, is held at the Muscle Shoals. People come from all across the country and from many parts of the world to pay tribute to this famous son of Florence – William Christopher Handy.

The Muscle Shoals area has long enjoyed an excellent and warm relationship among all of its citizens. It would be difficult to find a city and county anywhere with a richer or more noble black heritage than Florence and Lauderdale County in Alabama.

5. SOME EARLY FLORENCE MERCHANTS

"... the crowning city, whose merchants are princes ..."
(Isaiah 23:8)

Old Amos Wilkes, without doubt, was Florence's first merchant. He was doing business with the local Indians as early as 1810. His blacksmith shop and trading post were located near what is now the intersection of Darby Drive and Berry Avenue in the eastern section of the city.[1]

Perhaps the next earliest merchant was James Sample. In 1817 a year before the birth of Florence – he brought in his merchandise and built his log storehouse at the intersection of the Jackson Military Road (now Hermitage Drive) and North Court Street.[2]

Sample was also a brick mason, a contractor and a brick maker. His brick factory was near the intersection of Wood and Morrison Avenues. The red clay for the brick production was mined at the present location of the President's House on the University of North Alabama campus. Long after the brick factory ceased to exist there was a large pond of standing water at the site of this clay pit. Sample, a native of Pennsylvania, was married first to Parthenia McVay. Following her death, he was married to her sister Susan. Parthenia and Susan were daughters of Hugh McVay, an early settler of Lauderdale County, who served as Alabama's Governor in 1836. The Samples built the house now called "Wakefield" on North Court Street, one of the first brick homes in Florence. By January of 1822, the town was growing so fast that the brick industry was hard pressed to meet demands.[3] Thus, Sample closed out his general store to devote full time to making bricks and building houses. In 1852, after acquiring considerable resources, he purchased a plantation near Tupelo, Mississippi, where he died in 1864.

It wasn't long afterwards that Sample's old store site became the location of Robert Lewis Bliss' General Store. Bliss didn't remain here long. He soon established a larger business, "The Florence Apothecary and Drug Store," at the southeast corner of Tennessee and Court Streets; this structure was called the Bliss Block. Robert Lewis Bliss, Senior, was born in 1804 in Bristol, England, and died in Florence, April 4, 1872. His wife, Susan Collins, was a native of Cookestown, Ireland. A son, Robert L. Bliss, Junior, became one of the founders of the First National Bank of Florence which was organized in the Bliss Building. He served as its first president.

The large and portly bachelor, Captain Richard Rapier, was not only one of the earliest merchants, he was also among the first developers of the barge trade that made antebellum Florence an important river port. He was here as early as 1818. His "Rapier and Company," was located on the northeast corner of Court and Tennessee Streets. In a short while Rapier and John Simpson formed a partnership and expanded into the cotton business. They built a number of large warehouses near the river. Rapier died around 1826 and was buried on the grounds of his home at the southwest corner of Seminary and Mobile Streets. A century later his remains were unearthed by construction crews who were excavating the site for a large building. This created much excitement around town. No one seemed to have remembered the story of this merchant and barge prince who had been an important figure in the early economic development of Florence.[4]

Following Rapier's death the firm of Rapier and Simpson was taken over by John Simpson. The story of the Simpsons at Florence is in large measure an epic that tells of the success of a family of Irish immigrants in the wilderness of Alabama. John Simpson arrived in 1818 as a clerk for James Jackson. Born August 17, 1790, in Tyrone County, Ireland, he was married to Mary Patton, native of Belfast, Ireland. Simpson frequently made trips to Philadelphia with packhorses to bring back goods for his store. Sometimes he would arrange to transport his merchandise by wagons from Philadelphia to Pittsburgh. From there he would use flatboats to barge down the Ohio River and then up the Tennessee to Florence. Two of his brothers, Hugh and Thomas, soon joined him at Florence. It wasn't long before these three Irishmen amassed considerable wealth – so much so that they began investing in extensive cotton-producing lands in West Lauderdale County.[5] After several productive years as a Florence merchant, one of the brothers, Thomas, was appointed a land agent in Demopolis, Alabama, by President Andrew Jackson. Following the loss of his eyesight, Thomas and his wife, Elizabeth, returned to Florence where they lived the remaining years of their lives.[6]

Two of John Simpson's sons – William and John Junior – succeeded their father under the name of Simpson, McAlister, and Company. Following the Civil War, this large enterprise became the McAlister and Irvine Company.[7] Located at the corner of College and Court Streets, this firm served as the banking house of the county for many years. John Wightman McAlister, a native of Ireland was born in 1810 and died in 1888. He and his wife, Narcissa Foster, lived in the landmark now known as Pope's Tavern.

The Irvines, who were prominent attorneys, were among the number of Irish immigrants to establish mercantile houses in Florence. In addition to his connection with McAlister, James Irvine was list as being in partnership with a kinsman, George Boggs. A newspaper of 1839 listed Irvine and Company as sellers of Kentucky whiskey.

The senior James Irvine was born about 1797 in Londonderry, Ireland. He is believed to have been at Nashville and possibly in Athens prior to becoming a resident of Florence. Irvine was married to Emily Wrenshall Boggs, a first cousin to Julia Dent, wife of U. S. General Ulysses S. Grant. In 1831, the Irvines built their stately home on North Pine Street. This landmark is known today as "Hickory Place." Their son, James Bennington Irvine, acquired the large mansion directly across Pine Street from the home of his parents. This was the former home of John Simpson and is now "Coby Hall," a part of the University of North Alabama campus. During the Civil War, James Bennington Irvine was a captain in the Fourth Alabama Cavalry. He left a diary that gives accounts of his confinement in a Yankee prison as well as interesting sketches of a number of local skirmishes.

Hugh Thomson, a clerk for the Simpson, McAlister, and Company, came into a large inheritance from his native Ireland. Using this resource he first tried farming in West Lauderdale County. Not being successful at this, he returned to Florence and established a merchandise house. About the year 1848, Thomson moved to New Orleans where he died a year later in a terrible cholera epidemic.[8]

James and Thomas Kirkman are listed by one historian as "the second merchants who came ... to Florence."[9] This firm later became a partnership with Thomas Kirkman and Robert Andrews, and eventually with Thomas Kirkman and Neander Hickman Rice.[10] The Kirkmans, natives of Ireland, arrived at Florence in 1821. James Kirkman moved to New Orleans and died there. Thomas Kirkman accumulated large land holdings in the area and was a breeder of fine racehorses. He was married to Elizabeth McCulloch, the stepdaughter of James Jackson, who established the Forks of Cypress near Florence where he imported and bred award-winning thoroughbreds.

Robert Andrews, a native of Lancaster, Pennsylvania, arrived in Florence at an early age. He was born in 1810 and died in 1848.

Andrews was a planter as well as one of the proprietors of the prosperous firm " Kirkman and Andrews." He was married to Martha Jackson, a daughter of James Jackson. Following Andrews' death, Martha was married to the well-known Presbyterian minister at Florence – Dr. William H. Mitchell. A son of Robert and Martha Jackson Andrews was Captain Robert Andrews, Jr., who was born in 1842 and died in 1918. He was commanding officer of Company E, 27th Alabama Infantry Regiment, Confederate Army, during the Civil War. Robert Andrews, Junior, was married to Melissa Adair daughter of William Adair of Lauderdale County. He served the county as registrar in chancery, and Florence as one of its most beloved mayors.

Neander Hickman Rice was born about 1815 in Kentucky. He was in Lauderdale County as early as 1839, and was married to Penelope Sannoner, a daughter of Ferdinand Sannoner, the surveyor who was given the honor of naming the new town of Florence. Following Penelope's death in 1846, Rice was married to Lucy Lester, daughter of German Lester.[11]

Another Irishman, Walter "Waddie" Glenn, whose store was located on Court Street, was one of the first hardware dealers in town. Glenn was born in Ireland in 1780, came to Florence in 1818, and died in 1866.[12]

Bayles E. Bourland's first store was in Florence. However, he soon moved to Rogersville. He later filled a number of important positions: County Surveyor, Justice of the Peace, Representative in the State Legislature, and Superintendent of Public Schools. Bourland was killed by lightning in 1868 while seeking shelter under a tree beside a road during a thunderstorm.[13]

Florence merchant John M. Davis tried shifting his business to Lexington, Alabama. This didn't work out and he was soon back where he started. He remained at Florence until his business was ruined by the Civil War. Discouraged and broke, he returned to his native Kentucky where he was able to begin his business anew.[14]

Martin and Samuel Harkins, natives of South Carolina, operated one of the largest general stores in the city. Both of these men at different times served the county as sheriff.[15]

Pearson and Corrin were partners together for a few years. Later this merchandise house was listed only as the Pearson Store. Percifer F. Pearson was a prosperous city merchant for some twenty years. However, he lost his business as a result of excessive gambling and the use of alcohol. He eventually became a homeless beggar and at his death was buried through the kindness of the people of Florence.[16]

The Irishman James J. Hanna was associated with Henry Anderson as wholesale grocers. Hanna, born in 1800 in Ballybay, Ireland, was a nephew of James Jackson, one of the city's founding fathers. He was married to Paralee Frances Childress, niece of

John Childress, another founder of Florence. James and Paralee Hanna made their home on the northwest corner of North Court and Tuscaloosa Streets. Hanna's partner, Henry Anderson, later moved to Mississippi.[17]

Ezra Webb, Junior, was advertising his groceries as early as February 22, 1827. Originally from Louisville, Kentucky, he returned to that city sometime later. Webb was also involved in a number of steamboat lines doing business on the Ohio and Mississippi Rivers.[18] Webb's business was at the intersection of Alabama and Court Streets. This site was at one time the location of a wholesale grocery under the name of Campbell and Hancock. Other merchants who advertised in the 1827 issue of the local newspaper included William L. Yarbrough's Color (paint) Store, and Thomas Huling's Grocery. Six months later, three other merchant houses were advertising their goods: George Boggs, Junior, Abraham Fox, and the firm of Buchanan and Sproule.

Henry A. Bragg and Marshall Clark were in the dry goods business at Florence for many years. Clark died in 1853 at the age of 51 years. Bragg later moved to Memphis.[19]

In April, 1829, a Virginia native, Peter Saffarans, purchased a number of acres alongside the Jackson Military Road on the outskirts of the city. A tinsmith by trade, he managed to accumulate enough money by 1838 to become a downtown merchant. But the economic crash the following year destroyed his business. He died in 1840 leaving very little in the way of resources for his family. However, his brave widow Mary gathered up what she could and opened a milliner's establishment, enabling her to support and educate a large family.[20]

Another merchant who succumbed to the economic depression of the late 1830s was Waddy Tate. Dr. Tate was a prominent resident of Limestone County. During the early land sales Tate bought property in Florence for the Cypress Land Company. This accounts for his name being recorded on a number of deeds in the county records.[21]

Alexander Hamilton Wood was a merchant and a manufacturer of furniture who became well known for his Windsor chairs. His father, Basil Wood, was secretary for the statesman Alexander Hamilton. Basil's father, Leighton Wood, came to America to manage the vast family estates. During the American Revolution, Leighton Wood sided with the colonies which cost him his share of the family fortune. His descendants were left to their own initiatives. Seeking a place of opportunity, two brothers, Alexander and William Richardson Wood, were advised by Andrew Jackson to settle in the new town of Florence. They arrived in 1821, and in 1826 Alexander Wood, veteran of the War of 1812, became the town's first mayor. Mayor Wood's two-story frame house was located at the northeast corner of Pine and Tuscaloosa Streets. It was torn down in 1892 to make way for the Trinity Episcopal Church. The sons of Alexander and Mary Esther Evans Wood added their own names to the history of Florence. Sterling Alexander Martin Wood became a brigadier general in the Confederate Army. Major Henry Clay Wood was a leading insurance agent and cotton broker. Judge William Basil Wood was the prime mover and promoter of the city until his death in 1891.[22]

Joseph Biggers, born in 1788, was an early jeweler. His daughter, Margaret, was married to a son of Ferdinand Sannoner, one of the original surveyors of Florence. The inventory of Biggers' estate in 1850 listed stocks, bonds, slaves, gold and silver.[23]

A local newspaper in 1840 carried an advertisement for Willett and Trisler, cabinetmakers. It also called attention to Dr. William C. Crow's "Old Drug Store," located next to Pope's Tavern which was near the courthouse. Dr. Levi Todd, who lived in the mansion now called "Mapleton" located on "Coalter's Hill" overlooking McFarland Bottoms, ran an advertisement for his "Todd's Southern Anti-Bilous Pills," being dispensed in his store on South Court Street. Todd was said to have been a cousin to Mary Todd, wife of Abraham Lincoln. A number of smaller businesses listed for the 1840s included Wilson and Rice, Pickett and Rankin, and William H. Rogers.[24]

The successful Lauderdale County planter and future Governor of Alabama, Robert Miller Patton, was also a longtime Florence merchant. He moved from Huntsville to Florence in 1829.[25]

Joseph Milner opened his Milner's Drug Store on North Court Street in 1853. He was born in 1824 in Leeds, England. His father, James Milner, arrived at Florence in 1848 to become associated with the Cowpen Woolen Factory near Green Hill in Lauderdale County. Joseph, however, detoured by way of California and did not join his family until after his adventure in the famous gold rush. Joseph was married to Margaret Woodall. Their home on North Seminary Street, behind the First United Methodist Church, was an area landmark for over a hundred years. Their son, James Milner, became proprietor of Milner's Drug Store following the death of his father in 1894. Two of Joseph Milner's daughters, Mary and Jossie, were beloved elementary school teachers in the city.[26]

Perhaps one of the town's most popular merchants was Zebulon Pike Morrison, undertaker and builder. He built a number of outstanding area landmarks including Wesleyan Hall on the University of North Alabama Campus. His well-kept death and burial documents are now a part of the genealogy room in the Florence-Lauderdale Public Library. He served in the city government for forty years, first as an alderman, and from 1880 until 1890 as its mayor. Morrison Avenue is named in his honor.

A number of years following the Civil War, his business was located in a building on the north side of Tombigbee Street between Court and Seminary Streets. He was married to Bridget Blessing, a native of Canada. Her father, Thomas Blessing, was an engineer who helped construct the first Muscle Shoals Canal during the 1830's. Bridget and Zebulon "Uncle Pike" Morrison lived on the southeast corner of Wood Avenue and Mobile Street.

It would literally take a number of volumes to list all the merchants who have contributed to the commercial growth of Florence. By 1857 the population of the town was 1,444, with about fifty business establishments. A number of these were merchants whose names and locations have been lost in the passing of time.

6. SOME EARLY PHYSICIANS AND THE MODERN ELIZA COFFEE MEMORIAL HOSPITAL

"Honour a physician with the honour due unto him ..."
(Ecclesiasticus)

For almost one hundred years after Florence was settled there was no public hospital. Yet, the town was never without a doctor. They came with the first wave of pioneers. While visiting Florence in 1821, Washington correspondent Anne Royal wrote:

"It is unaccountable why such a number of physicians should flock to this country. Every town is flooded with them. They are strung along the roads like so many blacksmith's shops. You can neither walk nor ride, but you have a physician on each side, one in front, and one in rear. There are seven in Florence – seven more went away, for want of room..."[1]

Perhaps the lady from Washington invoked her "poet's privilege," and exceeded realism in trying to tell a good story. Yet, there are documents to show that as early as 1823, there were four physicians located in the town. Some thirty years later there continued to be four physicians in Florence. Also listed in 1857 were two dentists; one was Benjamin Abraham who was located in the city although he was serving the entire county.

Dr. John Robertson Bedford arrived here with General John Coffee. It is said that he was the first medical doctor in both the county and its county seat. The Bedfords were credited with being the fourth family to settle in Florence.[2] He was a son of Thomas Bedford, Junior, and Anne Robertson of Nashville, Tennessee. Dr. Bedford's father and grandfather were veterans of the American Revolution in Virginia.[3] John R. Bedford was married to Isabella Matilda Smith. Her father was the legendary Bennett Smith of North Carolina, said to have had a lifestyle much like the great land barons of the Old World. Dr. Bedford's town house was near

College Square on East College Street. His plantation, "New Mount Hope," was near the intersection of Cox Creek Parkway and Chisholm Road where he and other family members are buried.[4] Two interesting physicians who were here in the 1820's were Dr. Llewelyn Powell and Dr. Western Territory Rucker. Powell was married March 17, 1827, to Sarah E. Harrison. He later moved to Louisville, Kentucky. Rucker was married to Frances Savage on April 15, 1823. Sixteen months later, Dr. Rucker wrote a letter to Andrew Jackson, which was signed by Dr. John H. Woodcock and others, inviting the Hero of New Orleans to a public dinner in Florence.[5] Jackson accepted and the gala affair was held in a downtown hotel on August 28, 1824.

John H. Woodcock's local medical practice was short-lived. By 1836 he was in Mobile, Alabama. His home on West Tennessee Street later became the residence of Florence druggist, Robert Lewis Bliss. Magnolia Gardens 1, a high-rise apartment house, now occupies this entire block. Woodcock was described by a neighbor as "a tall fine looking man, bold and reckless in the expression of his views."[6]

Among other early physicians were Young A. Gray, Dickey Peacock, H. V. Posey, Levi Todd, and a gentleman named Craine.[7] It is believed that Captain Y. A. Gray of the 11th Alabama Cavalry, C.S.A., was a son of Dr. Gray. This young man was living in the household of E. Childress in 1850 and listed his occupation as a clerk. In the Florence Cemetery is a lonely and faded marker dedicated to an infant son of Dr. H. J. Posey. This child died in 1841.

Dr. Levi Todd, physician and merchant, was noted by an early writer as having "had all the noble qualities of the Old Kentucky gentlemen."[8] Soon after the Civil War, his cousin, Dr. George Rogers Clark Todd – a brother to Mary Todd Lincoln – practiced medicine for a short time in Florence. George Todd was not able to return to Kentucky because of his reputation for mistreating Federal prisoners, especially those who were natives of Kentucky.

An announcement was made by Dr. George Hill in the August 4, 1827, edition of The Florence Register that he was located one mile west of the New Meeting House on the west side of the Waterloo Road. His reference to the "New Meeting House." was perhaps the modest Methodist Church, twenty-four by thirty feet in size, which had been erected that year near the corner of Tuscaloosa and Locust Streets. It was later moved to the corner of Tuscaloosa and Seminary Streets.

James T. Hargraves enjoyed saying that he was from Port Tobacco, Charles County, Maryland, although the 1850 census listed his place of birth as Georgia. He came to Florence in the late 1830's and located on Court Street. A young physician, Thomas Maddingly, was living in the household with Dr. Hargraves in 1850. During the Civil War Hargraves was so harassed by Union soldiers that he moved into the home of John Simpson. Following the war he gradually gave up his medical practice except for a few families, although he continued to make exceptions for the poor. As long as he lived, Dr. Hargraves never refused calls from people he knew could not afford a physician.[9]

Neal Rowell practiced medicine in early Florence for a number of years before retiring to West Lauderdale County where his wife had inherited a fine plantation called Alba Wood. A native of Wood County, Virginia, Rowell was married to Martha Ann Cheatham, daughter of Christopher Cheatham, one of the county's earliest settlers. Cheatham operated a ferry at Alba Wood in the community of Smithsonia.[10]

Dr. William Koger was another physician from Virginia who moved to West Lauderdale County to establish a large plantation. He became a close neighbor to Dr. Neal Rowell. Koger was married to Martha Westmoreland who was also from Virginia. Their Virginia-style manor house is one of West Lauderdale County's most prized landmarks. In recent years the Koger Cemetery was destroyed by vandals. However, in 1997 in was partially restored by Craig Williams as an Eagle Scout project.

Another neighbor to the Kogers and Rowells was the physician, Jonathan Beckwith, who was also a planter. Dr.

Beckwith, born in Fredericksburg, Virginia, was married to Dolly Winston who was a first cousin to Dolly Madison, wife of the Fourth President of the United States. It has been said that in her youth, Dolly Winston was a frequent guest in the Madison home.[11]

Dr. Gabriel Bumpass and Dr. Oen Boyce Sullivan were early physicians in Waterloo. Bumpass, who organized the town in 1819, became one of the first men to practice medicine in Lauderdale County. Sullivan arrived at Waterloo in 1844.

William H. Harrington was a chemistry professor at La Grange College near Leighton, Alabama, before establishing his medical practice at Florence in 1834. During the 1840 presidential race between William Henry Harrison and Martin Van Buren, Dr. Harrington created an allegorical painting that was widely used by the Whig Party. A number of years later, this Florence physician killed a man in self-defense on a downtown street. Not being able to cope with this terrible tragedy he moved to New Orleans where it is said that he began his life anew.[12]

Dr. James D. Belote was practicing medicine in Florence at the time of the 1850 census. He listed his age as 28 years, and his place of birth as Tennessee. Other early physicians mentioned in various documents were Dr. Bruce and Dr. Cowles. They must not have remained here long since very little is known about them. The story of these early physicians of Florence and Lauderdale County will ever be woven into the fabric that makes up the history of this area. Perhaps no profession has affected the lives of more people – then and now.

Florence's Eliza Coffee Memorial Hospital came into being in 1919. Its original location was in a building on East Tuscaloosa Street that had been erected by the Florence Land, Mining, and Manufacturing Company as an apartment house. The hospital was named for Eliza Croom Coffee, daughter of Captain Alexander and Camilla Madding Jones Coffee following a gift of $10,000 made by the widow, Mrs. Coffee. These facilities were later relocated to West Florence. Its grand opening was celebrated on September 1, 1943. However, the first public hospital for Florence was located in the Malone Home on the southwest corner of Hawthorne and

Meridian Streets. Dr. Lewis W. Desprez, who lived nearby on North Wood Avenue, was one of its attending physicians. This house was used briefly as a military hospital during the Civil War.

Previous to these public facilities, Dr. Alva Albertus Jackson established a private hospital sometime after his arrival in town in 1912. The first location was on North Court Street in the historic Governor Edward A. O'Neal Home. He later moved these facilities to the corner of East Tombigbee and Cherry Streets. The founding of the Eliza Coffee Memorial Hospital was, perhaps, the most significant accomplishment ever undertaken by the governing bodies of Florence and Lauderdale County.

7. EARLY JUDGES AND LAWYERS

"Hear my law, O my people ..."
(Prayer Book)

From the beginning, Florence has been a town of successful and resourceful attorneys, judges, and court officials. Some of them, especially in the early days, were merchants, planters, and preachers as well. This city built on a hill overlooking the Tennessee River has always had good laws, fair and just leaders, law-abiding citizens, and men and women who have dedicated themselves to the court systems of the land.

William S. Fulton, born in 1795, became Lauderdale County's first judge in 1819. A native of Cecil County, Maryland, he served as General Andrew Jackson's private secretary during the Seminole Indian Campaign. In 1817, he began the practice of law in Nashville. By 1819, Fulton had moved to Florence to establish its first newspaper, The Florence Weekly Gazette. In 1825, he was married to a local young lady, Matilda F. Noland. Some four years later, Fulton was appointed Secretary of the Territory of Arkansas. He remained in this office until 1835, at which time he was appointed Territorial Governor. After Arkansas became the twenty-fifth state in 1836, William S. Fulton was elected one of its first United States senators, serving until his death in 1844.[1]

David Hubbard, born in Rutherford County, Tennessee, was elected solicitor in 1823. During the 1830s Hubbard became one of a number of speculators who took advantage of the lands left behind by the Indians who were forced out of Alabama and Mississippi in the sad and tragic exodus called "The Trail of Tears." Heading up the Chickasaw Land Company, the second largest of these land agencies, it is reported that he personally acquired more than 20,000 acres.[2]

George Coalter of Kentucky was admitted to the bar in Maury County, Tennessee, in 1808. As one of Florence's earliest practicing attorneys, he built a fine mansion, "Coalter's Hill," on

South Pine Street now known as "Mapleton." Here he housed his private library containing 160 volumes – quite a number for a small frontier community in Northwest Alabama. Coalter served as a colonel in the local militia as well as state senator. He was one of the unfortunate promoters of Havannah, a land speculators' dream that somehow never made it as a successful pioneer town in West Lauderdale County.[3]

John McKinley fulfilled what has been said to be every lawyer's ambition – to go all the way to the U. S. Supreme Court. Many years before being appointed to that august body, he was a working attorney in the courts of Lauderdale County. As has already been noted, Judge John McKinley was one of the founders of the City of Florence.

William B. Martin was remembered as "a lawyer of great shrewdness, wit, and power before a jury."[4] A native of Blount County, Tennessee, he was the son of Warner and William Bailey Martin. William's brother, Joshua Martin of Limestone County, served as Governor of Alabama 1845 - 1847. Another brother, Peter Martin, became Attorney General of Alabama in 1832. William's uncle, Henry Bailey, was South Carolina's Attorney General from 1836 - 1845. It is said that William, the Florence attorney, fell victim to "the influence of liquor," and died an early death.[5]

Peter Anderson and James Irvine were law partners. Anderson, called "an attorney after the English style," relocated later to Holly Springs, Mississippi, and from there to New Orleans. James Irvine, native of Ireland, was a prominent Florence merchant as well as planter and attorney. He served as trustee of the Florence Wesleyan University, President of the Board of Muscle Shoals Canal Commissioners, and board member for the Florence Bridge. His son, James Bennington Irvine, was also one of the city's leading attorneys.[6]

Judge Sidney Cherry Posey was born in May, 1803, in the Pendleton District of South Carolina. His family was among the earliest settlers of Madison County, Alabama. As a young man Posey taught school in Tuscumbia to meet expenses while training to become a lawyer. After being admitted to the bar in 1832, he moved to Florence to begin his practice. He was married the following year to Harriet Calista DePriest, a daughter of Dr. Horatio DePriest of Columbia, Tennessee. Harriet was known to her Coffee relatives in Florence as "Cousin Kit." According to the Coffee Papers, Posey and Kit must have kept their courtship rather private up until a few days before the wedding. It caught almost everyone by surprise, although it was reported that all the young people in town were present for the elaborate ceremony. Posey was an ordained Methodist minister. At various times he served as a circuit court judge. Also, during different periods he represented his county in both houses of the state legislature. A member of the convention when Alabama withdrew from the Union, Posey voted against secession. When war commenced he supported the Confederacy and lost one of his sons in that terrible conflict.[7] The Judge died in 1868 and was buried in the historic General John Coffee Cemetery north of town among the graves of his wife's kin.

During the few years before his death, Judge Posey formed a law partnership with Colonel Josiah Patterson who later relocated to Memphis, Tennessee. While in Florence, the Pattersons lived in the house at the corner of Hermitage Drive and North Seminary Street now known as Pope's Tavern. One of their sons, Malcolm R. Patterson, was governor of Tennessee from 1907 until 1911.

Colin S. Tarply, native of Tennessee, began practicing law at Florence in 1830. In a few years, however, he moved to Jackson, Mississippi.

Sam L. Probasco, native of Ohio, was considered "an excellent lawyer" at the time of his early death in 1846.[8] The 1850 census shows that an attorney, James A. Baker and his young family were living in the Probasco household with Sam's widow, Catherine. Benjamin W. Edwards, a young and promising attorney, died September 3, 1836. He was a native of Pulaski, Tennessee.[9]

Another promising young lawyer who died in the prime of life was Charles Savage. He was a son of Colonel Samuel Savage one of the first land buyers in Lauderdale County. This family came from South Carolina and acquired a large plantation in West Lauderdale County.[10]

John T. Harraway was a native of Rogersville in Lauderdale County. A one-time editor of the Florence Inquirer, he became judge of the circuit court. Although it was said that he was not necessarily a good speaker, he, nevertheless, proved to be an excellent writer. He died in 1845.[11]

John Edmund Moore was born in 1815 in Rutherford County, Tennessee. In 1847 he was elected to the General Assembly of Alabama. Four years later he elected to the circuit court, a position he held for twelve years. He died in Green County, Alabama, during the Civil War while serving as a military judge in the Confederate Army.[12]

The July 18, 1846, edition of the Florence Gazette listed law partners L. P. and R. W. Walker. Leroy Pope Walker's practice in Florence was brief. Born in Huntsville in 1817, he was admitted to the bar in 1837. After leaving Florence and returning to Huntsville he became a prominent political figure. He was the Confederacy's first Secretary of War in 1861. In, September of that same year he was appointed brigadier general in the Provisional Army. After failing to secure field duty he resigned. Near the close of the war he presided over the military court in North Alabama as a colonel. He died in 1884 and is buried in Huntsville. His brother and law partner, Richard Wilde Walker, moved to Florence from Huntsville in 1844. He was soon elected solicitor of the Fourth Circuit. In 1863 he became a Confederate Senator. After the Civil War, Richard Walker moved back to Huntsville and soon became a Justice of the Alabama Supreme Court.[13]

William H. Price, a young lawyer with great promise, was one of the first to volunteer for service in the Confederate Army from Alabama. He rose to the rank of major and was killed in the Battle of Perryville in 1862.[14]

Theophilus A. Jones also entered the Confederate Army at the beginning of the Civil War and was rapidly promoted to the rank of colonel. Returning to Florence following the war, he resumed his practice of law in the local courts. He died in 1873.[15]

Robert Tennent Simpson was born in Florence in 1837. A graduate of Princeton and Cumberland University, he practiced law in South Alabama and Arkansas before returning to Florence. He fought as a captain in the Confederate Army. Following the war he served in the Alabama General Assembly and, later, as a state senator. In 1904, he was elected as Associate Justice of the Alabama Supreme Court and remained in that office until his death in 1912.[16]

Hugh McVay, Governor of Alabama in 1837, was an attorney, having been admitted to the bar in Madison County prior to 1817. However, it is not known if he actually practiced before the courts in Lauderdale County.

Edward A. O'Neal, Governor of Alabama from 1882 - 1886, practiced law at Florence prior to the Civil War. His son, Emmet, Governor of Alabama from 1911 - 1915, was a law partner with his father prior to his entry into the political arena.[17]

Another Alabama Governor from Lauderdale County – George Smith Houston – was a practicing Florence attorney for a brief period. Born in Williamson County, Tennessee, in 1811, he moved to Lauderdale County with his parents in 1821.[18]

William Basil Wood, who became one of the most prominent leaders in the history of Florence, was born October 31, 1820, in Nashville, Tennessee. He came with his family to Florence in 1821. A graduate of La Grange College, he was admitted to the bar in 1843. As Colonel of the 16th Alabama Infantry Regiment during the Civil War, he was in the Battles of Wild-Cat, Fishing Creek, Murfreesboro, and Chickamauga. He led a brigade in the Battle of Truine, and was recommended for promotion to the rank of brigadier general. However, he was transferred to General James Longstreet's Corps where he was assigned as President of the Military Court. After the war he served as circuit court judge. Judge Wood was also an ordained Methodist minister. He, more than any other leader, was responsible for the relocation of La

Grange College to Florence as Wesleyan University in 1855. In 1872, he – more than any other North Alabamian – was responsible for bringing about the transfer of the college facilities by the Methodist people to the State of Alabama; this institution eventually became the University of North Alabama. Judge Wood was also credited, more than any other local citizen, with the initial promotion and activities that brought about the industrial boom of the late 1880s that gave birth to East Florence. Wood was also one of Lauderdale County's early historians. One of the town's major thoroughfares, Market Street, was renamed Wood Avenue in his honor. The Judge died April 3, 1891. Carved on his gravestone in the Florence Cemetery are these words: "Citizen, Soldier, Christian. A leader in family, state, and church. After the storm and toil of life, he, beloved, rests in peace."[19]

Sterling Alexander Martin Wood, born in Florence in 1823, became a law partner with his brother, William Basil Wood, in 1845. Sterling was elected to the Alabama Legislature to represent Lauderdale County. He also served as district solicitor, an office he held until appointed a captain in the Confederate Army in 1861. He resigned after the Battle of Chickamauga as a brigadier general for unclear reasons. However, following this engagement, his commanding officer, General Cleburne, while praising other brigade commanders in his general report, omitted mention of Wood. Going to Tuscaloosa where his family had taken refuge from the enemy, Wood began practicing law in that city. Here, he soon was elected again to the Alabama Legislature, and in 1889 - 1890, taught law at the University of Alabama. He died at Tuscaloosa in 1891 and is buried there.[20]

This list is only the beginning of a long roster of attorneys who, at one time or another, were a part of the court scenes in Florence and Lauderdale County. After the Civil War, and for the scores of decades to follow, others came to fill their offices and continue their legacy.

8. THE FIVE GOVERNORS

"He that would govern others, first should be the master of himself."
(The Bondman, printed in 1624)

Florence and Lauderdale County have given the State of Alabama five governors. This compares with four from Madison, one from Morgan, one from Colbert, and three from Limestone County (which includes George Smith Houston who is also claimed by Lauderdale County.)

Hugh McVay, Lauderdale County's first to be seated as an Alabama governor, was a native of South Carolina. He was born in 1766, and was first married to Polly Hawks who gave him nine children. After living briefly in Kentucky and Tennessee, Hugh and Polly and family moved in 1807 to a part of the Mississippi Territory that was soon to become Madison County, Alabama, where he was admitted to the bar. It was in Madison County where he first entered politics – as a representative in the Mississippi Territory and, later, in the Alabama Territory.

Following Polly's death in 1817, McVay moved to Lauderdale County to became one of the county's earliest settlers. He built his modest three-room log house near the head of Cox Creek in the Mars Hill community. Some of the logs used in the restoration of the W. C. Handy Cabin and Museum were taken from McVay's historic home.

McVay's second marriage was to Sophia Davidson of Memphis, Tennessee. During one of her husband's frequent absences as a state legislator, Sophia left home with a man claiming to be her cousin. This incident resulted in one of the first divorces recorded in the county. McVay was one of the organizers of the Factory Methodist Church which met at the site of the Wright and Rice Iron Factory. This mission of Florence's First Methodist Church later became Moore's Chapel, located across the road from the historic Mars Hill Church of Christ. Hugh McVay represented Lauderdale County in the state Constitution Convention at

Huntsville in 1819. The following year he was elected to the state legislature where he served until his retirement in 1844. As President of the Senate in 1837, McVay was elevated to Governor of Alabama for a short duration when Governor Clement Clay resigned to become a United States Senator. McVay died in 1851 and is buried near his Mars Hill home site.[1]

Robert Miller Patton was Alabama's twentieth governor and Lauderdale County's second citizen to ascend to that high office. Born in Virginia in 1809, Patton moved to Madison County, Alabama, with his parents in 1818, where his father, William Patton, native of Londonderry, Ireland, became a founder of one of the first cotton mills in the state – the Bell Factory. Robert Patton was married to Jane Locke Brahan, daughter of General John and Mary Weakley Brahan.

Robert and Jane Patton moved to Florence in 1829, at which time he entered the mercantile business. Following General Brahan's death, the Pattons purchased his large estate, located east of the city, known as the Sweetwater Plantation. They completed the mansion that Brahan had started which is listed among the outstanding Georgian brick houses in the area. Robert Patton became one of Lauderdale County's most successful planters. Patton was elected to the state legislature in 1832, and served almost continuously until Alabama seceded from the Union. At the beginning of the Civil War, he was president of the Senate. He opposed secession, but once the war began he gave his full support to the Confederacy.[2] Three of his sons and two sons-in-law were in the Confederate Army. One son was killed at Shiloh. Another son died in Selma from wounds received in a nearby battle.

Robert Patton was an elder of the Florence First Presbyterian Church and superintendent of the Sunday School for more than fifty years. During the Civil War, the pastor of this church was arrested by the occupying Union Army and sent away to prison for about three months.[3] During the absence of the minister, Patton gave notice that the morning services and the Sunday school would be continued with their usual regularity. This period of time was especially remembered by Dr. Robert A. Young, President of Florence Wesleyan University, who wrote in his book Reminiscences: "Old Governor Robert Patton was a ruling elder in the Presbyterian Church. He could manage an enormous cotton plantation, could count interest on a note until two o'clock in the afternoon, could govern the State of Alabama, but nobody expected him to preach... Every wit and humorist of the town attended, and each Sunday morning heard a sermon from one of the leading politicians of the State. At one service he aired the whole volume of his sacred learning to prove that John the Baptist was not John the evangelist, but a different individual."[4]

Patton was elected Governor of Alabama in 1865. He labored under great difficulties to finance the government under the most extreme times and was credited with saving thousands of destitute people from starvation. Although he tried to cooperate with the federal authorities, he was removed from office by military order in July 1867. After the war, he was active in establishing several Southern railroads. As a member of the Board of Trustees of the University of Alabama he was involved in bringing about the rebuilding of those facilities which had been burned by the Union Army during the war. Robert Miller Patton died in 1885 and was buried in Huntsville.[5]

Gravelly Springs, a popular watering hole on the old Natchez Trace, was the boyhood home of Lauderdale County's third son to become Governor of Alabama. He was George Smith Houston, of Athens, Alabama, who became the state's twenty-fifth governor in 1874. Houston was born January 17, 1811, in Williamson County, Tennessee. His grandparents, John and Mary Ross Houston, migrated from County Tyrone, Ireland, to the Carolinas in 1790. The Governor's parents, David and Hannah Pugh Houston, relocated to Virginia, and from there moved to Tennessee.[6]

In 1821 they settled in Lauderdale County, at which time they acquired a large plantation called "Wildwood.," Here they built a brick mansion about two miles east of Gravelly Springs near the modern crossing of the Natchez Trace Parkway over the Waterloo Road. They installed what may have been the first indoor plumbing in the area; a large open-top reservoir on the roof discharged water by gravity to the kitchen and bathroom below.[7] This manor house became the headquarters for Union Major General William James Harrison Wilson during the winter of 1865. In his memoirs, Wilson wrote: "I established headquarters at the house of Miss Houston, a sister of Governor Houston of Alabama. The family was an old and distinguished one ... Curiously enough, Mr. Boggs, a first cousin of General Grant, with his wife and a charming young daughter, had taken refuge with their kinswoman in the large and commodious mansion near the springs which gave their name to the place..."[8]

The "Mr. Boggs," referred to by General Wilson, was related by marriage to George Houston. In 1861, Houston was married to Ellen Irvine of Florence. Ellen was Houston's second wife; she was a daughter of James and Emily Wrenshall Boggs Irvine. Emily Irvine's mother was a first cousin to General Ulysses S. Grant of the Union Army. Houston's first marriage was to Mary Beaty of Athens who died in 1856.[9]

Houston studied law under Colonel George Coalter of Florence and afterwards completed his work at a school in Harrodsburg, Kentucky. His first years as an attorney were in Florence before moving to Athens in 1835. While in Lauderdale County he was sent to the Alabama Legislature and was twice elected as circuit solicitor. In 1841, he was elected to the United States Congress where he served until the outbreak of the Civil War. At the close of the conflict, he was elected to the United State Senate, but was not allowed to take his seat because of Alabama's role during the war. He served as Governor of Alabama from 1874 until 1878. The next year he was once again elected as United States Senator from Alabama. However, on December 31, 1879, he died – a short time before he could take his seat.[10]

Edward Asbury O'Neal and Emmett O'Neal, father and son, were the twenty-seventh and thirty-sixth governors of Alabama. They were the fourth and fifth citizens from Lauderdale County to hold this high office.

Edward O'Neal's father – also named Edward – migrated from Ireland to South Carolina. He was married to Rebecca Wheat, a descendant of Huguenot immigrants. The O'Neals became early settlers of Madison County, Alabama. They had two sons – Basil Wheat O'Neal and Edward Asbury O'Neal. Basil went to Texas and became a planter.

Edward Asbury O'Neal was a graduate of La Grange College where he held top academic honors. Afterwards, he studied law in Huntsville with a well-known attorney. In 1838, he was married to Olivia Moore, the eldest daughter of Dr. Alfred Moore.[11] Two years later, they moved to Florence where Edward began his practice of law. Upon entering town, they passed by a house under construction on North Court Street. Olivia liked what she saw and persuaded her husband to purchase it – and this became their home for the remaining years of their lives. Located in the Sannoner Historic District, the O'Neal Home is a Florence landmark.

Edward A. O'Neal's political life began in 1841 when he was elected solicitor of the fourth judicial circuit. After a few years as a public servant, however, he resolved to return to his private practice. At the outbreak of the Civil War, he entered the Confederate Army as a captain and was immediately sent to Virginia. Here, he fought in a number of major battles with the Army of Northern Virginia. As a colonel, he led his regiment in the Peninsula Campaign, was wounded at Seven Pines, and again at Boonsboro in the Maryland Campaign. Before the Battle of Gettysburg, General Lee recommended O'Neal for promotion to brigadier general.[12] Although this commission was evidently issued, it was never delivered to O'Neal, although he did receive a state appointment to that grade. Later, O'Neal and his regiment served as guards at the Andersonville Prison in Georgia. In the spring of 1864, the 26th Alabama was with General Joseph Johnston around Atlanta. In the fall of that year they moved through North Alabama with General John Bell Hood. They were headed toward the disastrous Battles of Franklin and Nashville where O'Neal's regiment was almost destroyed.[13] One of the O'Neal sons, Alfred, was a cadet at West Point when Alabama seceded from the Union. He immediately resigned to return to his native Alabama where he entered the Confederate Army. Rising to the rank of major, Alfred was captured at Petersburg, Virginia, and spent the remaining months of the war in a Yankee prison.[14] Another son, Edward Asbury O'Neal, Junior, was appointed a second lieutenant in the Confederate Army at the age of seventeen years. Assigned as aid-de-camp on the staff of Major General Robert Emmett Rodes, young Edward served with distinction until the close of the war.[15]

Olivia Moore O'Neal, at home with her children, endured many frightening experiences during the war years. Because of her husband's high military rank, her home was especially singled out by occupying and raiding forces. According to family sources she had to flee to Russellville for refuge on at least one occasion.[16] A collection of Olivia's letters to her husband is preserved at the University of North Carolina Library. These documents tell of the hardships at Florence during the war years. In May, 1863, she writes about Colonel Florence Cornyn's raid: "I was very much alarmed. The shells flew across my yard, and one went through one end of my smokehouse. I ran over with my children to Mr. Simpson's and got in their cellar. "[17]

In another letter, dated June 5, 1863, Olivia tells about a drunken Yankee soldier entering her front door and threatening to burn the house. In this same correspondence she describes how Dr. Robert A. Young, President of Florence Wesleyan University, came to her rescue as she and her children were being harassed by soldiers.[18]

In 1882, Edward Asbury O'Neal was elected Governor of Alabama, and succeeded himself in 1884. He died November 7, 1890, and is buried in the Florence Cemetery.

Emmett O'Neal, born in Florence on September 6, 1853, was too young to serve in the Confederate Army with his father and two brothers; however, he followed in his father's footsteps to become Alabama's thirty-sixth governor in 1911. Emmett was a graduate of Florence Wesleyan University and the University of Alabama. After being admitted to the bar, he entered into a law partnership with his father and maintained that relationship until Edward A. O'Neal was elected governor in 1882.

In 1881, Emmett O'Neal was married to Elizabeth Kirkman, daughter of Samuel Kirkman of Florence. In 1900, the O'Neals purchased the antebellum mansion, "Courtview," which is located at the head of Court Street, and which overlooks the downtown business district. This historic landmark is now a part of the campus of the University of North Alabama. In 1911, when news was received that O'Neal had been elected Governor of Alabama, a torchlight parade of citizens approached Courtview from Court Street. The governor-elect greeted them from the high portico of his home and made one of his famous impromptu speeches.

A terrible tragedy occurred at Courtview some three years after the O'Neals acquired it from the family of Sterling McDonald. On the day after Christmas in 1903, the O'Neal's teenage daughter, Elizabeth, was standing in front of an open fire. The hem of her long gown brushed against the smoldering coals at the hearth and caught fire. Elizabeth was badly burned. She died in a Memphis hospital on February 19, 1904.[19]

Governor Emmett O'Neal died September 7, 1922, and is buried in the Florence Cemetery. The O'Neal Bridge across the Tennessee River at Florence, opened in 1939, was named for him.

Thus, ends the story of five Alabama governors who at one time or another resided in Lauderdale County. Added to this saga could be accounts of other sons at other times who became governors in other places. William S. Fulton, who lived a few years in early Florence, became Governor of the Arkansas Territory in 1835. Malcolm Patterson, Governor of Tennessee from 1907 until 1911, lived as a young boy in what is now Pope's Tavern, a city museum located on Hermitage Drive. Perhaps, this list could even be expanded to tell about a student at Florence Wesleyan University – Sul Ross – who became Governor of Texas in 1887 and 1889.

These men, too, have added their names to the list of sons and former residents of Florence and Lauderdale County who became leaders of sovereign states in our nation's history.

9. RELIGION AT THE SHOALS

"... increase in us true religion, nourish us with all goodness, and of Thy great mercy keep us in the same."
(Prayer Book, 1662)

The average frontiersman was busy carving his home out of the wilderness. He lived in rude surroundings and, in general, there was a shortage of women. These factors contributed to what has been called "a frontier unreligious atmosphere."[1] Thus, in most cases it took a few years for organized religion to catch up with the new settlements.

In many areas of the South, the great numbers of Scots and Scots-Irish were responsible for the Presbyterian Church becoming one of the earliest forces to reach the settlements, especially in East Tennessee. The Baptists, known as the pioneer faith in Kentucky, quickly followed the initial movements into the Mississippi and Alabama Territories. Despite slow growth in earlier years, the Methodists became the leading denomination in establishing preaching appointments through their system of circuit riders.[2]

The area that became Lauderdale County generally followed this trend, with the Baptists leading the way. Gabriel Butler, an elder of that faith – whose name appears on the 1810 Doublehead's Reserve list of tenants – may well have built the first Baptist place of worship in Lauderdale County. In fact, his original brush arbor on Blue Water Creek was perhaps the first place of worship of any of the various faiths in the county.

In 1818, two preachers from Maury County, Tennessee, A. Cunningham and J. Hunter, established the Mill Creek Baptist Church in East Lauderdale County with eleven charter members. In 1823, this congregation organized the Blue Water Baptist Church with eleven charter members. D. Lancaster was installed as pastor. He was born in 1782 in Edgecomb County, North Carolina. In 1821 he moved to Lauderdale County and was ordained the same year.

Two Baptist Churches, Butler's Creek and Little Cypress Creek, were organized in June 1818, by the same Presbytery which organized the Mills Creek Church. It was reported that there was no Baptist minister living on the north side of the Tennessee River in this region at that time. A year later, H. Garrard arrived from Kentucky and took charge of Butler's Creek Baptist Church. About the same time, J. Burns came from Tennessee to become pastor of the Little Cypress Baptist Church. The Big Cypress Creek Baptist Church, originally a mission of the Little Cypress congregation, was organized in 1821 by Elders Burns and Garrard. William Smart, native of North Carolina, was ordained as pastor.

There were a number of other early congregations of this faith in the county. Anderson Creek Baptist Church was established in 1822 with fourteen members under the care of A. Jones and R. R. Shelton. Pleasant Grove Baptist was organized in 1824 by Elders J. Harden and D. Lancaster. Four years later, the membership of this church increased to 104 under the leadership of J. Harden. Antioch Baptist was founded by Harden in 1824, but existed only a few years. The Shoals Creek Baptist Association was constituted in 1825 with churches scattered throughout the county and across the line into Tennessee. In 1831, there were seven Baptist churches in Lauderdale County with a total of 450 members.[3]

When Florence was laid out in 1818, its founding fathers reserved a lot for the Baptists and Methodists at the corner of Locust and West Tuscaloosa Streets. Some seventy years later, on May 27, 1888, the First Baptist Church of Florence was organized by the Reverend W. H. Smith of Huntsville and the Reverend J. C. Hudson of Florence. The seven charter members were: Hudson and wife, Dr. Levi F. Duckett and wife, Florence Rooke, Dr. L. C. Allen, and Julian Field. The building site for this church, fronting East Tombigbee Street, was donated by the Florence Land Company. In 1954, a new church structure was erected on Wood Avenue, which is adjacent to the earlier building on Tombigbee Street.[4]

The Presbyterians and Methodists came through this part of the state perhaps earlier than the Baptists, but unlike the Baptists did not tarry to establish a church or, as far as is known, to preach a sermon. Joseph Bullen, a Presbyterian missionary, passed over the Natchez Trace around 1799, on his way to the Chickasaw Nation. The Methodist circuit rider, Tobias Gibson, made three trips on the Trace from 1799 to 1803 going to and from his assignment in the lower Mississippi Territory. Another Methodist preacher, Lorenzo Dow, crossed the river here on October 26, 1804. Three years later, Jacob Young, Methodist minister, camped in what is now Lauderdale County while waiting for George Colbert's ferry.[5]

The Presbyterians became the "Mother Church of Florence," preceding all other denominations in the city. It is believed that the First Presbyterian Church was organized in 1818 by a visiting minister from Huntsville, the Reverend Gideon Blackburn. In that same year a lot was purchased from the Cypress Land Company for the Presbyterians by Hugh Campbell for $1,600. A temporary log structure was perhaps built here soon after the purchase was made. The first permanent structure, known as "The Old Meeting House" was erected in 1824.[6] Major renovations were made in 1898 - 99, and in more recent years. Essentially, this same structure continues to serve the local Presbyterians on the same lot that was purchased in 1818. It is one of the area's most revered landmarks.

The Cumberland Presbyterian Church was organized in 1810, following the great Kentucky revival of 1799 - 1802. Over the years, a number of both Presbyterian faiths have been located throughout the county. Three Methodist circuit riders arrived at the settlement near the mouth of Blue Water Creek in June, 1818. This congregation eventually became the Center Star United Methodist Church, the oldest congregation of this faith in Lauderdale County. However, as early as 1816, two Faires brothers, Alexander and Richard, began holding religious services in the vicinity of their farms in Northwest Lauderdale County. In the summer of 1818, they were instrumental in the organization of Wesley Chapel United Methodist Church.

The Florence First United Methodist Church was organized in a small log house on West Tuscaloosa Street on Sunday, September 8, 1822. A local preacher, John Cox, was the first minister. Its eight charter members were: John and Frances Cox and their three children, Mary, Thomas, and James; the Reverend John Kerr from Ireland; Dr. Shadrack Nye, local newspaper editor; and Joseph Paddleford. Religious services soon thereafter were held in the front room of Thomas Farmer's shoe shop on West Mobile Street. In 1826, a sanctuary measuring twenty-four by thirty feet, was erected on the southwest corner of West Tuscaloosa and Locust Streets. In 1827 this small structure was rolled on logs up Tuscaloosa Street to the corner of Seminary and Tuscaloosa. Over the years there have been three structures at this site. The present sanctuary was completed in 1924.

It wasn't long after the arrival of the first circuit riders until the Methodists had circuits and congregations in every town and almost every crossroads in Lauderdale County. Two of the largest circuits were the Shoals and Cypress. At one time the Shoals Circuit was made up of more than twenty preaching places. In 1824 the Cypress Circuit had a membership of 127 whites and 31 blacks. Within four years it had grown to 598 whites and 76 blacks. The Cypress Camp Ground was located north of the Underwood community on Little Cypress Creek near its confluence with Ijams Branch. In the summer of 1828 one hundred people professed their faith at this camp meeting, including fifty-eight who united with the Florence Church. A number of these were added to the rolls of the Presbyterian Church.

In 1835 Florence became headquarters for Methodism in this part of Northwest Alabama and sections of nearby Tennessee counties. This continued for some twelve years. However, in 1856, the Florence District again was established by the Annual Conference, with William H. Browning as Presiding Elder. In 1997

Florence continues to serve as the Methodist center for this area with more than fifty churches listed on its rolls.

In 1824, the Reverend William Spenser Wall held the first Episcopal Church worship service in Florence. This was in a log house where he was teaching school. He was born in Pittstown, New York, in 1790. Wall established what was to become Florence's second school in 1823. Trinity Episcopal Church was organized in 1836 on the southwest corner of College and Cedar Streets. Eleven people were baptized on April 27th and 28th of that same year. Following a fire in 1893, this church was relocated to the northeast corner of Pine and Tuscaloosa Streets. Additions were made to the building complex in 1967.[7]

The Church of Christ, sometimes-referred to in early records as the "Restoration Movement," began holding services in Lauderdale County in 1823 when Ephraim D. Moore moved here from Tennessee. Moore, native of North Carolina, was born in 1782. A veteran of the War of 1812, he served with Andrew Jackson in the Battle of New Orleans as a mess cook. Moore was a farmer and teacher when he settled on Little Cypress Creek in a village which became known as Brandon Factory.[8]

The first Church of Christ congregation in Lauderdale County was located near Brandon Factory. It is believed that Ephraim D. Moore became its founder in 1823 or 1824. Moore was joined a few years later by another minister, James E. Matthews. The earliest name for this congregation was "Republican." Later, it was referred to as "Old Cypress." Originally, services were held in the homes of its members as well as in the Methodist Church located on nearby Chisholm Creek. About 1884 the Methodists relocated to Brandon Factory. At this time the Church of Christ congregation moved up the hill from Chisholm Creek and became Stony Point Church of Christ. This is the oldest congregation of this faith in Lauderdale County.[9] Among its earliest members were: Dr. Edward Gabriel Bumpass, founder of Waterloo; General Leroy Pope Walker, who later became the Confederacy's first Secretary of War; Dr. John H. Hancock, a prominent physician; Dr. Pugh Houston, brother of Alabama Governor George Smith Houston; and John

Chisholm, Junior, who died in 1847 and was buried in the nearby Chisholm Cemetery on Chisholm Highway.

The next congregation, Liberty Church of Christ, was established at Barton, a community now known as Gravelly Springs. Services were held in the homes of its members as well as in the Poplar Springs Methodist Church located nearby. The Liberty Church erected its own building in 1848, at which time there were eighty-five members. During the winter of 1865, Major General James H. Wilson established a training camp at Gravelly Springs. His troops demolished most all of the church buildings in this area, including Liberty, so as to provide lumber for barracks and stables.

Prior to the Civil War, there were four organized Churches of Christ in Lauderdale County. One was the Blue Water congregation, perhaps a forerunner of Antioch Church of Christ in East Lauderdale County. Another in this area was the congregation at Lexington. Liberty was the only congregation with its own building. The others were meeting in private homes known as "house churches."[10]

Census records indicate there were no Church of Christ ministers living in Lauderdale County in 1860. Perhaps the last minister here prior to the Civil War was James Young who moved away in 1850. There was a large increase in the number of Churches of Christ in this area following the Civil War. Much credit for this remarkable growth is attributed to the leadership of Theophilus Brown Larimore who established the Mars Hill College for young ministers at the present campus of the Mars Hill Bible School in 1871.[11]

One of newest congregations of this new era following the war was Hopewell Church of Christ. Located in a grove of old cedars near the present-day intersection of Cox Creek Parkway and the old Jackson Highway, this was the original home of Hopewell Methodist Church, one of the early churches of that faith in the county. The devastating effects of the Civil War resulted in the closing of services for its white membership. The black members, however, moved to the nearby Middle Road as the

Hopewell African Methodist Episcopal Church. This abandoned building was purchased by the Hopewell Church of Christ May 31, 1868. It is believed that this congregation was absorbed into the Mars Hill Church of Christ soon after Larimore established his college at Mars Hill.

The oldest Church of Christ in the central Florence area is the Wood Avenue Church on the northeast corner of Wood Avenue and Tuscaloosa Streets. Its earliest services were held in the home of Susan Thrasher on the northeast corner of Court and Tuscaloosa Streets in 1886.[12]

Near the close of the twentieth century, the Churches of Christ in Lauderdale County have more congregations of that faith than any other county in Alabama.[13] In 1985, they were listed as having the second largest membership among all faiths in the Muscle Shoals area.[14]

The first African-American church in Alabama was established in 1806 as the Stone Street Baptist Church in Mobile.[15] A number of antebellum plantations had their own worship services for slaves. Sometimes white ministers were in charge of these services. Most often, as at the Forks of Cypress Plantation near Florence, the ministers came from the slave community.

Among the earliest organized black congregations in Florence was Church Springs Church. This congregation originally made up of fourteen slaves and freemen, who had been members of the town's First Methodist Church, began having their own worship services as early as 1837. During the early 1840's a brick shed was purchased for them by the Trustees of the Florence Methodist. The Reverend Robin Lightfoot, who became a martyr during the Civil War, was the first minister for this black congregation. In 1879, the Church Springs Church was organized as the Greater Saint Paul African Methodist Episcopal Church. They purchased the abandoned Fant Wool Factory at the southwest corner of Court and Alabama Streets in 1895. Bricks from this building were used in the walls and foundations of their new church. This sanctuary was used until 1968, when St. Paul's was relocated to Cherokee Street in West Florence. Almost all faiths can be counted among the local black churches of the twentieth century. A survey made in 1985 indicates, however, that the largest number of black congregations are affiliated with the Missionary Baptist.[16]

Priests of the Catholic Church may have been at the Muscle Shoals long before the coming of the other Christian faiths. When excavations were made on Jackson Island during the construction of Wilson Dam, crosses were found among the Indian artifacts. This discovery adds to legends that priests in black robes ministered to the local Indians and the earliest white settlers here. However, no documentation for this has been found. [17]

There are existing records of a number of visits by Catholic priests in the early part of the nineteenth century. In 1824, and on later occasions, Father Robert Abel of Bardstown, Kentucky, came here on brief trips. At that time there were about 200 adherents to this faith living at the Muscle Shoals. In 1830, they were ministered to by Fathers Mathias Loras and Gabriel Chalou who were touring the diocese on horseback. Visits of this nature, however, were infrequent.[18]

Our Lady of the Sacred Heart in Tuscumbia, dedicated in 1869, was the first Catholic parish at the Muscle Shoals. For a number of years people in Florence traveled to Tuscumbia to attend services. Construction of the Muscle Shoals Canal, beginning in 1875, brought in a number of workers who were of the Catholic faith. These and other new arrivals led to Florence being listed as a mission of Tuscumbia in 1879, with Father John B. Baasen, pastor. A year later it became a mission of the parish at Saint Florian. However, it soon reverted back to the Tuscumbia parish, with the Reverend Cyprian Creagh as missionary. The home of Joe Beckman was used as a chapel for the celebration of Mass.[19]

Sometime prior to 1889 a small frame church was built on land donated by Mrs. Lena Peters. This was near the home of Joe Beckman on a hill in East Florence known as "Laughton Heights." Its name was later called "Catholic Hill." This is the same area where the present parish is located. Either John Stumpe or his brother Henry, both of Saint Florian, built this church under the supervision of the Reverend Polycarp Scherer, a missionary from Tuscumbia. In 1898, the Reverend Gammelbert Brunner became the first resident pastor in Florence. In the same year construction of a larger frame church began. Completed in 1902, this church served the parish for the next seventy-five years. A two-room frame building for use as a school was also built. In 1898, the first Benedictine teachers, Sisters Perpetua and Aloysia, of the Sacred Heart Convent in Cullman, came as teachers. During World War II, a mission parish for the local black community was established under Father Isidore Fussnecker. A new brick school was erected in 1948, with another addition completed in 1962. In 1959, a rectory and activities building was erected. The present church was completed in March 1974.[20]

In 1872, following the settlement of Saint Florian by a colony of German Catholics, a small frame church was erected here. Two years later the church was moved across the road. Additions were made in 1878 and 1889. The Reverend Miahael Merz was its first resident pastor. Work on the present Saint Michael's Church began in 1914, and by 1918 it was essentially completed. Stones used in its foundation were cut from nearby Shoal Creek. Stained glass windows ordered from Bavaria were added later. A parochial school was operated by this parish for many years.[21]

The Industrial Revolution that swept across the nation in the 1880's made its dramatic appearance at Florence in 1887. More industry was located in the city from 1887 until 1910 than during all the other years of its history, before or after. During a three-year period, its population increased by 500 percent. This influx of people resulted in the organization of a number of new churches in the area.

Practically all of the major Christian faiths are now a part of the city and county. Others locating here since earlier years are: Free Will Baptist, Church of the Nazarene, Salvation Army, Unitarian Universalist, Seventh-Day Adventist, Church of Jesus Christ of Latter Day Saints, Lutheran, Jehovah's Witness, Full Gospel, Christ Chapel, Christ's Church, Church of Christian

Mission, Faith Tabernacle, Assembly of God, Churches of God, Churches of God in Christ, Churches of God in Prophecy, Community Churches, Independent Methodist, Pentecostal, Apostolic, and a number of congregations listed as nondenominational.[22]

Prominent Jewish families moved to the Shoals area about the time of the East Florence and Sheffield Industrial Booms, establishing themselves as merchants and community leaders. Their first place of worship was in Sheffield as early as August, 1887. In 1906 they were organized as B'Nai Israel, and in 1908 they erected a temple at Eighth and Atlanta Avenues. Jacob "Jake" Spielberger was its first president. He moved to Florence from Birmingham in 1888. Ten years later he relocated to Sheffield. The other officers were: M. Coplan, Vice President; A. J. Miller, Secretary; Joe P. May, Treasurer. The three trustees were: Max R. Block, H. A. Weinbaum, and Isaac Kreisman. The first wedding in this temple was for Sam Israel and Bessie Kreisman in January, 1912. Sam was a native of Ponadel, Lithuania, located in one of the Baltic States which was later absorbed by Russia. Bessie was a daughter of Adolph Kreisman, a business leader in Florence and Sheffield. In 1953 Florence was made the center for the Jewish faith in the Shoals area when Temple B'nai Israel was erected on Hawthorn Street.[23]

It would be difficult to find a city or county anywhere, comparable in population, which is more blessed with churches and with a greater variety of faiths. A number of years ago a visitor from Ohio, while touring this area commented: "it looks as if there is a church on every corner and at every crossroad."[24]

10. THE LOCAL COTTON INDUSTRY

"...Others look each year to the same fields, and hear the drone of the same gins, to capture a quaint beauty found nowhere else in the world."
(Paths In The Brier Patch by the author)

During most of its first one hundred years Florence was known as a cotton mill town. In fact, at the outbreak of the Civil War it boasted the largest textile mill in the state. A similar orientation can generally be said about the early days in surrounding Lauderdale County. Cypress, Little Cypress, Sweetwater, Shoal, and Cow Pen Creeks were good locations for these early water-powered factories. The developers of Florence were quick to point out these advantages in their advertisement for the 1818 land sales: "...It has the Tekatanoah (Cypress) on the west, on which mills are already erected and in operation. The small but beautiful creek of Sweetwater winds along near the outskirts of the town ... the neighborhood of Florence abounds in sites for factories of every description..."[1]

Sweetwater Creek in East Florence, near where it crosses Huntsville Road, was the location of one of the earliest cotton mills in the Muscle Shoals. Plans were made by Edward Ward, James Jackson, and General John Coffee in 1822 to build this factory for lease to Daniel Rider and William McRobb. However, prior to its completion, the equipment was procured by Samuel Bolton who sold it to Warren Isham in 1825. Seven years later it became the property of General John Brahan of the Sweetwater Plantation.[2] Although never a successful operation, this Sweetwater Mill became a forerunner of the large textile enterprises to be located here during the East Florence Boom which began during the latter part of the nineteenth century.

Cypress Creek, known by its Indian name "Tekatanoah," was the location of another early cotton industry. Its strong flow of water and its rapid descent over a fall line about two or three miles west of Florence made this an ideal factory site. James Martin and

Levi Cassity established the Cypress Mill here in 1839. Martin, a Kentuckian whose father was born in Ireland, arrived in Florence about three years following the first land sale. Cassity, native of Bath County, Ireland, was here by 1826 according to the records of the First United Methodist Church. Purchasing a small operation built three years earlier, Martin and Cassity began spinning yarns which were used in weaving cloths in the local homes. This was later upgraded to a production of skeins of yarns which were distributed to weaving mills. By 1844 the size and output of this facility had been increased considerably. Unfortunately, however, the entire factory was destroyed by an arsonist.[3]

Following Cassity's death, Martin secured two new partners – Samuel D. Weakley and Alexander D. Coffee. They built a new and larger factory known as the Martin-Weakley Mill. In addition to spinning yarn, they were now able to weave cloth. During the 1850's the firm was again expanded to include three cotton factories and three grist mills – one for flour and two for corn meal. By 1860 these mills, called the Globe Factory, employed 310 workers including women and children. Their average wages amounted to $2.50 a week. They operated 8,000 spindles and 200 looms to produce 1.5 million yards of osnaburg cloth as well as large quantities of yarn annually.[4]

The Globe Factory was burned in May 1863 by a Federal brigade commanded by Colonel Florence M. Cornyn of the 10th Missouri Cavalry. In 1866, James Martin and sons advertised in a local paper for forty good, able-bodied men to assist in rebuilding one of these mills.[5] Known as the Cypress Mill, its chief executive officer in 1878 was Dr. Albert H. Jones of Florence. There were 3,000 spindles, 60 looms, and 50 employees. The dam at this site, called "Number Three Dam", was twelve feet in height. This restored factory operated for about twenty years after which time some of its machinery and a large number of its employees became a part of the operations in Colbert County known as the Mountain Mill. This cotton factory, located south of Barton, was relocated to East Florence in 1893 to become the Cherry Cotton

Mill. The flour and corn mills at the Cypress Mill site were later sold to Frank Perry and became known as the Perry Mills and Dam.

There were a number of early cotton factories in the county. The largest of these was the Lauderdale Factory situated across from Happy Hollow on Shoal Creek about nine miles from Florence. Built in 1845 it employed 50 men and 100 women to produce 812,500 yards of osnaburg and 110,000 dozen cotton yarns annually while operating 2200 spindles and 70 looms.[6] A few miles west of Zip City on Little Cypress Creek was a small cotton mill operated by Darby, Benham, and Company. Its proprietors were Henry Jackson Darby and Colonel James Benham. Darby was married to Mary Sue White. Benham was married to Ursula McDonald, daughter of William and Ursula Hough McDonald, early landowners and settlers of Lauderdale County. This mill was probably one of those destroyed by the Union Army in 1863. Following the Civil War, a larger operation, the Brandon Factory, was located a short distance downstream on Little Cypress Creek near the present White's Lake. During the late 1880s this became the Embrey, Son, and Young Factory. The nearby Kernachan Mill was made a part of this enterprise. Altogether, there were 2,500 spindles and 30 looms used in the production of cotton yarns and jeans for the New York market. Prior to the Civil War there was a small cotton operation on Cowpen Creek near Green Hill called the Foster, Simpson, and Company Mill. This plant is believed to have been destroyed by the Union Army.

The location of three cotton factories and a textile mill in East Florence during the latter part of the nineteenth century and the early years of the twentieth century revived Florence's status as a "cotton mill town." The largest of the cotton mills was the Cherry Mill on Sweetwater Creek. The other two were the Ashcraft Cotton Mill located near the old Florence Canal and the Broadus Factory which operated a brief time near the present Wilson Dam Reservation. The textile factory, known originally as the Gardiner-Warring Knitting Mill, came here from Utica, New York, in 1927. It was located in the Sweetwater business district.

The demise of these textile mills in the early part of the twentieth century brought about the end of the cotton mill image that had long been a part of the town. Too, it signaled the closing of an age of the high smokestacks. A new appearance was now in the making – that of a bedroom town where people own their homes in its lovely subdivisions and generally travel elsewhere to earn their living.

11. OTHER EARLY MILLS AND FACTORIES

"I'll build me a mill on Barren Fork;
And a house, up high on the hill."
(Dwight M. Wilhelm)

There were a number of wool cording mills and factories in the local area. One known as the Fant Factory, and sometimes as the Florence Factory, was established in 1858 on the southwest corner of Court and Alabama Streets. Its proprietors were Charles W. Fant, Samuel Porter, George Washington Foster, and Benjamin Franklin Foster. The two Fosters were brothers. Fant was married to Louisa Foster, daughter of George Washington Foster. The Fosters were planters and manufacturers, owning a number of mills throughout several North Alabama counties. This woolen factory was housed in a building that had been erected during the 1820s by Ezra Webb for his store and warehouse. The firm also built a structure over the public spring between South Court and Pine Streets for supplying water to their steam-driven machinery. Their invasion of a public water source proved to be unpopular with the citizens. This was corrected when the Memphis and Charleston Railroad announced their plans to build a depot near the south end of Court Street which would require water from this source.[1] Thus, cut off from their water supply, the Fant Factory closed its doors in 1859. Their abandoned building was used as a Confederate hospital following the fall of Forts Henry and Donelson in February 1862. It was eventually torn down in 1895 to make way for the Greater Saint Paul's African Methodist Episcopal Church which was located for many years on this downtown intersection known as "Fant Corner."

In the spring of 1845, James Martin and Levi Cassity acquired the Johnson Wool Carding Mill. This early wool factory, located on Cox Creek near Mars Hill, was established about 1834 by William P. Johnson. Martin and Cassity made it a part of their textile complex on Cypress Creek. In April, 1845, they ran an advertisement advising that persons bringing cotton and wool from south of the river would be allowed to cross the Florence Bridge "free of charge."[2]

The Darby, Benham, Company Cotton Factory on Little Cypress Creek near Zip City also had equipment for carding wool. A number of women and girls were employed as weavers. One was Clarissa Adeline Fowler, daughter of Lorenzo Fowler, the nearby miller. Clarissa became the bride of Joseph C. Terrill on November 6, 1860. Another weaver was Margaret Wood, daughter of Samuel Wood. Martha Burks and Sarah Gillum were seamstresses.

George M. Bretherick's Wool Mill was located on Bretherick Creek about two miles from the Lauderdale Cotton Factory on Shoal Creek near Happy Hollow. This was the former site of the J. C. F. Wilson Saw Mill. Bretherick carded wool here for seven cents per pound, or if the customer preferred, he extracted one/fifth of the total pounds carded as a toll.[3] Bretherick, native of England, was a former foreman at the Darby, Benham, and Company Textile Mill on Little Cypress Creek.

The best known, and perhaps the largest of its kind in the area, was the Cow Pen Factory; located on Cow Pen Creek near Green Hill it was founded in 1850. In 1860 its proprietors were Isaac and Samuel Milner, Judge William Basil Wood, and John Wren. At one time or another Dr. James W. Stewart of Florence and John Spinks Kennedy of the Green Hill Kennedys were associated with this mill. Raw wool was procured from Alabama, Mississippi, and Kentucky. Sixty-eight men and 16 women were employed in 1860 to produce 117,600 yards of cloth using 45,000 pounds of wool as a raw material.[4] This factory produced Confederate uniforms during the early years of the Civil War. It was burned by the Federal Army in the spring of 1863.

A number of small family-owned wool carding mills were located throughout the county. They were generally attached to a gristmill so as to use the same water-powered machinery. One such wool carding and gristmill was operated by John Scruggs McDonald in the Brandon Factory community on Little Cypress Creek during the 1870's. McDonald's brother, Thomas Anderson

McDonald, operated a blacksmith shop which was a part of the same complex.

Practically every creek with any sizable flow passing over the slightest fall line had its gristmills. Mills in areas where there were no creeks used horse power for grinding corn and flour. The 1850 census listed a total of 25 gristmills in the county. Their owners usually enjoyed a certain amount of prosperity and influence in the community.

Sherwood White's Grist Mill on Second Creek in East Lauderdale County was one of the earliest. On April 21, 1825, Judge John McKinley advertised that his overshot gristmill was for sale. It was located on Sweetwater Creek near the intersection of Sweetwater Avenue and the present Patton Street.[5] Ferdinand Sannoner's 1852 map of Florence shows Patrick Andrew's Mill on Sweetwater Creek near the present crossing of Veterans Drive. Patrick and his wife Mary purchased a large acreage extending all the way from the mouth of Sweetwater Creek to just south of the Huntsville Road. Andrews was the proprietor of the Florence Hotel.

Clopper's Grist and Saw Mills were on Cypress Creek about three miles from Florence. This firm is credited with producing the lumber for many of the early homes in Florence. In 1825 the assignees of William Schlatter advertised the sale of these mills together with 400 acres of adjoining land.[6] This later became the site for the Cypress or Globe Cotton Mills.

Early sawmills were dependent upon waterpower as well as much physical labor. Often slaves were hired out to the local proprietors. On September 3, 1830, Wallace and Mussleman advertised any quantity of sawed lumber for delivery into Florence from their sawmill on Shoal Creek "at low prices and on long credit."[7] Fifteen saw mills were listed in Lauderdale County at the time of the 1850 census.

James Sample became a wealthy man by producing bricks in early Florence. This operation, too, employed "hired" slaves as well as indentured servants. Tom Brannon, a slave of James Irvine, and Randle Campbell, who belonged to Hugh Campbell, were brick makers. One of the indentured workers was the younger brother of the infamous Natchez Trace outlaw John A. Murrell.

The 1850 census lists several tanneries in the county. The largest of these was in Rawhide, which is now the town of Cloverdale. Ruins in this area indicate that Native Americans were tanning hides here before the coming of the white settlers. Jonathan Paulk established his tannery here in the 1850's. These tanneries at Cloverdale were among the targets of a federal raid in 1863.

Hugh Simpson's Tan Yard was located on the old Waterloo Road near the present campus of the University of North Alabama. This operation was purchased in 1850 by a firm known as Stewart and Walston. Dr. James W. Stewart was a well-known physician. His home was on the hill near the present Dixie Avenue overlooking what is now Wildwood Park Drive near North Florence. Walston is believed to have been one of the sons of Turner Walston, an early settler in the Oakland community.

There were a number of foundries and machine shops in the area at the beginning of the Civil War. The Wright and Rice Foundry was located at the present site of the Mars Hill Church of Christ on Cox Creek about four miles from downtown Florence. Erected in 1835 by William P. Johnson, it was purchased in 1853 by James Wright and William T. Rice. Thirty men were employed in 1860. Steam engines, saw mills, cotton gins, farm implements, and industrial machinery for local textile mills were manufactured as well as various assortments of forgings and castings. This foundry was rapidly converted into a defense plant during the Civil War, producing shells and munitions for various types of weapons.[8] For this reason, its destruction was one of the primary missions of an invading Federal task force in May 1863.

Another early iron furnace associated with this area was the Wayne County Iron Works located just across the state line in Tennessee. Built in 1833 by Samuel Vanlier, it produced pig iron and castings that were hauled by wagons to the river port in

Florence. It also supplied iron for several of the local gun factories in Lauderdale County. This operation closed down about 1837.[9]

There were a number of early gun factories in the county, mainly around Green Hill. The best known of these was owned by David Kennedy and his son Hiram. Jacob "Drummer Jake" Stutts of Green Hill shipped his long rifles by boat on the Tennessee River. Other smaller shops were the McDonalds, Keys, Richardsons, Davidsons, Myricks, and Higgins. Alexander Higgins later moved his small gun factory and blacksmith shop to Waterloo.[10]

These early factories, foundries, and mills made up the basic economic structure of the county. Most of them were destroyed during the terrible Civil War. However, as the South began to recover, a number were rebuilt as other new plants moved in as part of the East Florence Boom during the 1880's and 1890's.

12. BOATS, STAGECOACHES, AND TRAINS

"Row, brothers, row, the stream runs fast,
The rapids are near and the daylight's past."
(Canadian Boat Song)

From its beginning and until the fading of the steamboat, Florence was first and foremost a port on the Tennessee at the foot of the treacherous Muscle Shoals. The earliest use of its port facility was as a docking place for flatboats and keelboats used mainly for transporting bulky freight. The main disadvantage of the flatboat was that it was for downstream traffic only. The keelboat was constructed so that it could be rowed or poled upstream, although the task was slow and laborious. Lambs Ferry, south of Rogersville and near the head of the Shoals, also served as an early port for these primitive river crafts.

Tradition has it that Captain Richard Rapier from Nashville was among the first to bring a large keelboat, referred to as a "commercial barge," up the river to Florence. This was in 1818. He moved here a year later and soon joined with John Simpson to establish the firm of Rapier and Simpson.[1]

Steamboat days at the Florence port began in March, 1821, when the "Osage" arrived from New Orleans loaded with various kinds of freight ranging from coffee and sugar to iron, nails, and bags.[2] Not until 1828, did the first of these steam-driven vessels pass over the Shoals above Florence. However, this proved to be an isolated and a not often repeated event. Upon completion of the Muscle Shoals Canal in 1887, boats could at last make their way from the lower Tennessee to the upper Tennessee. However, even then it was difficult for the larger crafts because of the size and shape of the canal.[3] Actually, it was not until the completion of Wilson Dam in 1925 that the two rivers – the upper and the lower – converged as one mighty Tennessee River that could be navigated from its mouth near Paducah, Kentucky, to its head near Knoxville, Tennessee.

The history of steamboats on the Tennessee River is almost two separate stories because of the barrier at the Shoals. One history involves river traffic from Decatur to Knoxville. The other relates to the saga of boats between Florence and Paducah, Kentucky.[4]

About twenty steamboats were in service on the lower Tennessee by 1830. This traffic had increased to 49 riverboats by 1901; by then there were 271 steamboat landings listed between Florence and Paducah. A significant change in the lifestyle of the area occurred when the mail was routed by boats from Paducah to Florence from 1830 until 1887.[5]

Waterloo and Riverton, Alabama, Eastport, Mississippi, and Clifton, Tennessee, were nearby deep-water ports below Florence. In 1897, "The Mayflower" advertised an eight day excursion between St. Louis and Waterloo for $ 8.00.[6] "The Florence" was the local pride and joy of riverboats between St. Louis and Clifton, Tennessee; when the river was high it extended its run all the way to the town of its namesake. This boat replaced "The Tyler" which charged its passengers $10 for a round trip including meals and a berth.[7] Only during high water seasons could the larger vessels venture up the river to Tuscumbia and Florence. Light-draft shuttle boats were used between the nearby deep-water ports and the local ports at the Shoals. The most popular of these shuttles following the Civil War was "The J. T. Reeder." Wagon trains were sometimes used between Florence and Waterloo. It was not unusual for some Waterloo residents to ride "The J. T. Reeder" to Florence and walk all the way back home.[8]

Public transportation by land during most of the antebellum period was by stagecoaches. At best this was a rough and hard way to travel. Although most of these conveyances were fitted for six passengers, they would often be overloaded by as many as could be squeezed into its seats.[9]

The roads and highways were at times almost impassable, especially during wet and muddy seasons. Stages often became bogged down, requiring the assistance of its passengers to push and tug. Rest stops were almost always inadequate with primitive accommodations. Generally, the same could be said for food and lodging.

John Dunn was one of the earliest local stagecoach entrepreneurs, beginning perhaps as early as 1817.[10] His stages served the area between Florence and Huntsville. He was also a planter whose home faced what later became the Savannah Highway a few miles west of Florence. His impressive two-story log mansion was built earlier by J. L. D. Smith whose wife was a niece of James Jackson, owner of the Forks of Cypress Plantation located on the opposite side of Cypress Creek. The Dunn family cemetery, once located in a grove of old cedars near the house, has been lost to posterity.

Perhaps the last of the stages to include Florence as a stopping place was owned by P. F. Patrick. His line ran between Memphis and Huntsville as late as 1849.[11] Among the drivers listed in the 1850 census were Varest Pool and William Cullum. The old stages were now bowing out to the luxurious steamboats and the faster and more convenient railroad connecting nearby Tuscumbia with other places.

The railroad crossed the Tennessee River into Florence following the rebuilding and strengthening of the bridge by the Memphis and Charleston Railroad in 1860. A passenger and freight depot was erected by this company at the foot of Tennessee Street near the Indian Mound. This area often flooded during extended spring rains. During the great March 1897 flood a steamboat actually unloaded its passengers at the railroad station.[12] This depot was destroyed by fire in 1906.

A major spur of the railroad connected East Florence to the trunk line at Sheffield in 1888. Following the fire in 1906, all rail activities were shifted to East Florence which became the center of railroad services for the city. In 1888, rail tracks were completed between East Florence and Columbia, Tennessee. This eventually became a part of the Louisville and Nashville Railroad. The last of the passenger trains was operated by this line. Known locally as "The Doodle Bug," it consisted of one passenger car and one freight car. During the 1920's a one-way trip to Tuscumbia cost twenty-five cents.

A small railroad bed was laid at Waterloo to nearby timber-producing forests in Tennessee in the early 1900s. An unsuccessful attempt was made during the East Florence Boom to build a small railroad line from that industrial area to the iron ore fields in Tennessee. The Railroad United Methodist Church just across the Alabama line in Wayne County, Tennessee, is located near this once proposed railroad bed.

On November 27, 1901, the first of the modern automobiles appeared on the streets of Florence. It was driven by a Decatur salesman. This created quite a sensation as the driver "showed out" by entertaining the crowds as to his skills.[13] Little did they know that this was the beginning of a new age. Soon the steamboats would all but disappear from the nearby river. Soon the busy East Florence railroads would be ghost tracks leading to nowhere.

13. EARLY SCHOOLS

*"What greater or better gift can we offer the
republic than to teach and instruct our youth?"*
(Cicero)

From the outset the people of Florence and Lauderdale County began in earnest to provide a means of education for their children. They had left behind their old institutions. Now it became necessary to build schools and academies in a land being carved from the wilderness. The original plans for Florence reserved two whole city blocks for educational institutions. One of these blocks was on East College Street at the present location of the City Utilities Storage Yard and Warehouse. It was known as "College Square" in the early life of Florence. The other block is now the location of the Florence Post Office.

No one knows for sure the name or the location of the first school in Lauderdale County. Generally, the earliest attempts to establish these learning places were associated with churches or with ministers of the Gospel. A log schoolhouse was built about 1816 near present-day Wesley Chapel United Methodist Church a few miles from the Central Heights community. Its teacher was Alexander Faires, a local preacher in the Methodist Church. According to legend this log structure replaced an even earlier school.[1]

In December 1820, General John Coffee and his neighbor, Dr. John Bedford, established a school about halfway between their plantations for the benefit of their children and others in the neighborhood. This was near a spring alongside the modern Cox Creek Parkway. It became the first structured place of learning within what is now the city limits of Florence. Among its earliest teachers were Robert Burton, Willie Conner, and Chillon White. However, the instructor remembered most fondly was James Lorance who is listed in the 1830 census as Lucious Lorance. In fact, this facility became known as the Lorance School. There are five graves of the Lorance family, including the wife of Lucious

Lorance, in the historic General John Coffee Cemetery. The Lorance School was in operation until about 1875. A former student who lived on Cypress Creek told about walking over a footbridge to attend the Lorance School.[2] The second school in Florence was in the basement of the home of Judge John McKinley located about 300 feet south of the intersection of South Seminary Street and Veterans Drive. The McKinleys moved here in 1821. They imported their children's teacher from France. According to legend the young McKinleys were encouraged to converse only in French at the dinner table. Soon afterwards, a Miss James from Pennsylvania opened a school for children over the age of ten years. This was in a small building near the corner of Pine and Mobile Streets. The teacher had heard through a friend of Mrs. John McKinley that the new town had a great interest in education.

The Reverend William Spencer Wall, the first to minister to the Episcopalians in Lauderdale County, established a Florence school on South Cedar Street in 1824. He was succeeded by a Professor Vigus, who was followed in 1834 by a Professor Breeze.

In 1824, General John Coffee was instrumental in founding a female academy in Florence. About thirteen prominent families sent their daughters to this academy, including James Jackson and General Coffee. It is believed that Jackson contributed one-half of the cost of operating this school.[3] Mr. and Mrs. Daniel Berry were the first teachers here and the institution was often called "The Berry School." Tuition for the preparatory class was $16.50 a semester, whereas for the seniors it was listed at $27.50. The local boarding fees for girls who stayed in town amounted to about $10.00 a month. This charge excluded weekends at which time the young ladies were expected to return to their homes.

In 1825 Neil Pollock taught piano lessons for the daughters of John Coffee. Four years later, a Professor King was teaching singing and W. C. Nolke had a dance studio in Florence.

In 1830 a Mrs. Crocker was providing private instructions in both painting and the French language. In 1830 a Professor Tinnon organized a school on the northeast corner of Tennessee and Seminary Streets. Tinnon at one time owned Patton Island.[4]

An early map of 1844 identified it as "Tinnin's Island." Tinnon later sold it to Governor Robert Miller Patton of the Sweetwater Plantation. Later, Lucious Lorance became a teacher in the Tinnon School. About 1833 a Professor Oliver from Philadelphia conducted a school in a log house on the southeast corner of North Pine and Tennessee Streets. Oliver's School for young boys was in session during the same period as the school taught by Professor Breeze on South Cedar Street.

From 1834 to 1843 the Locust Dell Academy, a school for young girls, was located in a locust grove where Willingham Hall now stands on the University of North Alabama campus. One of area's best known schools, it was owned and supervised by Nicholas Marcellus Hentz, a former professor at the University of North Carolina as well as an accomplished painter, entomologist, and author. He was assisted by his wife, Caroline Lee, the noted novelist and poet. She also taught the fundamentals along with classes in painting, violin, piano, organ, harp, and composition. It was said that Professor Hentz was possessed with an "unreasoning jealousy"[5] which probably prompted the departure of this talented family from Florence.

The Florence Male Academy, a high grade school known as "Prepdom," was established at the northeast corner of West Tombigbee and Cypress Streets sometime prior to 1835 where it served the town for more than twenty years. This lot was originally reserved by the founding fathers of the city as the future site for both the Methodists and Baptists although it was never used for that purpose. The nearby Cedar Street School was relocated to become a part of Prepdom. The Reverend James L. Sloss, known as "The Father of Presbyterianism in Alabama" taught at Prepdom. He served as the first installed minister of the First Presbyterian Church of Florence from 1830 until his death in 1841.[6] The Reverend Elijah Slack, supply pastor for the First Presbyterian Church in 1843 and 1844, taught at Prepdom while in Florence. Another prominent teacher was Thomas Neville Waul who was commissioned a brigadier general in the Confederate Army during the Civil War. Born January 5, 1813, in South Carolina, Waul was admitted to the bar soon after he left Florence. Later he moved to Texas where he recruited Waul's Texas Legion in 1862. Other professors were: Buchanan, McCauley, Howard, and Harris. In 1855, when La Grange College was moved to Florence to become Florence Wesleyan University, the facilities of Prepdom became the Preparatory School for the University with Dr. Septimus Primus Rice as its director. During the Civil War this facility was used as a high grade school. From 1868 until 1873 a private high school was in session at old Prepdom under Professor W. D. Willis.

A primary school for small children was located in 1837 on the southeast corner of Mobile and Pine Streets. This was one of several small schools in the area during this period. A Scottish lady, Mrs. Henderson, taught in her small house near the corner of what is now Wilson Park. Other local teachers during this era were a Miss Stevens and a Mrs. Woodall.[7]

Following the state legislative act of 1853 establishing public schools, the city authorities in Florence erected a one-room brick school on East College Street. This lot, known as "College Square," had been reserved by the Cypress Land Company in 1818 for a future college. A local drive to organize this school was under the leadership of "Bats" Baugh, the county circuit court clerk. Later, another room was added. The educators who served this school were: Miss George, Miss Julia Young, William M. Price, W. R. Shoemaker, Miss Lizzie Reed, Leroy Garner, Walter Glenn, Miss Betty Cain, Miss Priscilla Hodgins, Mrs. Bettie Waters, and Captain A. D. Ray. Ray was later elected County Superintendent of Education. Dr. Price became a beloved Florence physician. Mrs. Waters is memorialized by a beautiful stained glass window in the First United Methodist Church. This red brick schoolhouse was torn down about 1890 to make way for the R. M. Patton School.

One of the first schools for slaves was established in a brick cow shed by Judge John McKinley and his wife. Its teachers were said to have been local African-American ministers. This school faced the public spring that at one time existed between South Court and South Pine Streets south of Veterans Drive. This building also housed a church for slaves as early as 1840.

Following the Civil War, Mr. and Mrs. Myers came here from the North to teach the children of former slaves in this place.

During the 1830's another slave school was located in a small log cabin that stood on the corner of Court and Alabama Streets. Supported by the townspeople, its teachers were a Mr. and Mrs. Northcross, who came here from Philadelphia. It is said that its students were children of the servants who lived in town.

The site of the nearby McKinley home at the intersection of South Court Street and Veterans Drive is rich in the legacy of education for African-Americans. It is believed that this was the location of Professor Young A. Wallace's school for Negro children as early as 1870. For a number of years students met here in a large two-room frame building which was later supplanted by a two-story frame building. Following a fire, this structure was replaced by a brick building which became the John F. Slater School, the first school for African-Americans built by the City Board of Education. Sadly, the Slater School offered only elementary education until around the turn of the twentieth century. On December 8, 1958, a fire consumed this landmark. Its students were temporarily housed in the nearby Patton School until a new Burrell-Slater High School was completed on the northwest corner of Cherokee and West College Streets in 1960.[8]

The site for this Burrell-Slater High School was the former home of the Burrell Normal School, a two-story brick high school erected in 1903. Prior to Burrell Normal, however, it was known as the Carpenter School. It was originally founded as a secondary school for African-Americans by the American Missionary Association of New York City with financial help from the local citizens.

Part of the Burrell Normal School was dedicated to teacher training for African-Americans with Professor B. T. Cox as its first President. He was succeeded in 1907 by Dr. G. N. White from Chicago.[9]

This school was named for Jabez Burrell of Oberlin, Ohio, who had assisted with the financing of the Burrell Academy in

Selma, Alabama. When this South Alabama facility was destroyed by fire in the late 1890's, it was decided to relocate to a place where the need was greater. Florence was blessed by this decision.

The operation of this school was taken over during the late 1930's by the Florence City Board of Education and the name was changed to Burrell High School.[10] Following the integration of schools this facility became the Burrell Slater Area Vocational School.

About five years following the ravaging era of the Civil War, Miss Ann Stevens, a native of Ireland, began teaching school on Pine Street. A year later, in 1871, a school was held on North Court Street with Miss Mattie Ray as its teacher. During this same time, the renowned Church of Christ minister and educator, Theophilus Brown Larimore, established Mars Hill Academy for boys and girls. This school, which was in operation for seventeen years, is now the Mars Hill Bible School, one of North Alabama's most prestigious educational institutions. It opened its doors in 1947 under the sponsorship of the Churches of Christ.[11]

The historic landmark known as the J. J. Mitchell Place on North Wood Avenue functioned as a school in 1872. Miss Susan Leigh was its teacher. She had been a member of the facility of the Florence Synodical College under Dr. William H. Mitchell.

During the 1890's the Florence Institute was established on the second floor of the early City Hall on Short Court Street. Its professor was Alex S. Paxton, an honored graduate of Washington and Lee University. During this same period a North Pine Street school was in session with two teachers: Misses Janie and Emily Thompson. Its pupils were from West Florence. During this same time a private kindergarten and primary school served this section of town. Its teacher was Miss Helen Ware.

The year 1890 saw the beginning of what would become the Florence City School System. Its first superintendent was James W. Morgan, Jr., appointed in 1891. Buildings were rented for temporary classrooms while construction began on the Patton

School. In August 1891 a census revealed that the city had 893 white students and 582 African-Americans.

The R. M. Patton School, located near what is now the Dr. Hicks Boulevard entrance to the Florence Cemetery, was the first school erected by the new Board of Trustees (later the City Board of Education.) This three-story brick school was named for former Governor Robert Miller Patton of the Sweetwater Plantation east of Florence. Patton, while serving in the Alabama Legislature, was instrumental in the passage of the Public School Act of 1854.[12]

During this early period elementary schools were established in both North Florence and East Florence. Initially they were known as the Fifth and Sixth Ward Schools. In March, 1921, the new Gilbert School replaced both the Fifth Ward School and the Coffee Grammar School which was housed in the high school. The North Florence school was named for Henry C. Gilbert, Superintendent of Education for the years 1892 to 1904. Charles M. Brandon, an executive in the Cherry Cotton Mill, headed the movement to establish the new Brandon School which was completed in 1899. It replaced the Six Ward School.

Also in the East Florence district was the Pine Ridge School. It served the children of African-Americans who were employed in the local industry as well as those working on the construction of Wilson Dam during the early 1920's.

Two or three miles east of the city limits on Hough Road was another Patton School. This one was carved from land owned by Governor Patton. It was located on a small triangle of three acres between the Sweetwater Plantation and the farm belonging to William Wesley Carter and his wife Nancy Jane Ramsey Carter. Mrs. Ben Fuqua and Miss Myrtle White were its early teachers. This was a county school.

One of the most beautiful stories in the annals of education at the Muscle Shoals is that of the Maud Lindsay Free Kindergarten in East Florence. Established in 1898 for the children of working mothers, it has brought acclaim from across the nation. Its first teacher was Miss Maud McKnight Lindsay, daughter of former

Alabama Governor Robert Burns Lindsay of Colbert County. This institution continues to serve the people of Florence and is one of the area's most treasured landmarks.

The old Colonel John Trumbull Burtwell home on Pine Street was converted into the Florence High School in 1914. This antebellum two-story frame house had a double-deck front porch at the entrance with four columns on each level. The Burtwell home was the scene of a celebrated wartime wedding when Ann America Burtwell was married to Confederate Major Eugene Louis Frederic de Freudenreich Falconnet of royal descent from Switzerland. The principal of this first high school in Florence was H. B. Norton. This make shift facility in an elegant old home served the town until 1916, just prior to the opening of the first Coffee High School in 1917.

Coffee High School was named for Camilla Madding Coffee and her husband Captain Alexander Donelson Coffee. Camilla gave the land for this original school in memory of her husband who was a son of General John Coffee. This campus faced Hermitage Drive at the intersection of North Walnut Street. In 1939 the Kernachan Estate, consisting of thirty-two acres bordering Royal Avenue and Hermitage Drive, was purchased for the modern Coffee High School which opened its doors on August 29, 1951.[13] The old Coffee High School building became the Appleby Junior High School when the upper grades moved to the new location. It was named for F. T. Appleby who served as superintendent of the Florence schools from 1917 to 1932. The Appleby Junior High School absorbed the Florence Junior High School which was built in 1936 on the lot adjoining the original Coffee High School.

The W. C. Handy School, named for Florence's famed "Father of the Blues," opened its doors in 1951 for grades one through six. Its principal was Welton Reynolds who was later the principal of the J. W. Powell School. Reynolds was instrumental in the preservation and restoration of the historic birthplace of W. C. Handy which was made a part of the W. C. Handy Cabin and Museum. The W. C. Handy School facility now serves as the W. C. Handy Head Start School for the city.

Weeden School was named for John D. Weeden of the Sweetwater Plantation who gave the land for this school during the 1920's. It became a part of the city school system in 1951 when this section of town was annexed to Florence. Three years later construction began on the newly combined Weeden Elementary and Junior High School at the head of Fifth Avenue.

Harlan School in North Florence was constructed at the same time as the Weeden School. It was named for Sam C. Harlan, member of the Board of Education from 1921 to 1929. Harlan was one of the executives of the Florence Wagon Works in East Florence.

In 1959 the children who had been attending the Patton School were moved to the new J. W. Powell School in the Edgemont area of town. It was named for Josiah Whitaker Powell, native of Lowndesboro, Alabama, who served as Florence Superintendent of Education from December 1932 until his retirement in June 1958. The H. G. Richards School on Riverview Drive was built in 1961. It was named for Dr. Henry Grady Richards who served about forty years as principal of the Gilbert School in North Florence. This facility was also referred to as the Riverview Elementary School. It now houses the administrative offices for the Florence City School System.[14]

The Forest Hills School is located in the Forest Hills subdivision near the Chisholm Highway north of Florence. It was completed in 1963 on land donated by Dr. W. W. Alexander and F. R. Stovall.

Henry A. Bradshaw High School, built on land purchased from the John Finley Estate northeast of Florence, was named for the City Board of Education's attorney, Henry A. Bradshaw. The first session in 1966 was made up of the tenth grade class. This led to the first graduation exercise in 1968.[15]

The Rufus G. Hibbett School opened its doors in 1980. This facility, which serves the North Florence area, was built on land near the historic Cypress Mill Road. The school honors a beloved educator who served as Superintendent of Florence City Schools from 1958 to 1966.[16]

It would have been difficult anywhere to find schools with a higher academic standing than the two area Catholic Schools. The St. Michael's School at St. Florian, was established the year following the arrival of the German immigrants during the early 1870's. Miss Annie Mertz was its first teacher. These educational facilities at St. Florian now house a private institution known as the Riverhill School. The Saint Joseph School in Florence was held in a two-room frame building as early as 1902. The modern brick school was erected in 1948.

As previously stated, at least one county school located near the Central Heights community predated the first schools established in Florence. Esther James, wife of a Baptist minister, established a one-room school in Rogersville during the early 1820's. Among the early teachers at Waterloo was Miss Carrie Sullivan, daughter of Dr. O. B. Sullivan. Among the others who taught here were Donald J. Edwards, Homer L. Reeder, Miss Callie Faires, and John Lincoln Hall, Sr.

One-room schools, academies, and seminaries began appearing in towns, communities and remote crossroads from the time the earliest settlers arrived. An academy is identified as a school above the elementary level. A seminary in those days was the name used for a school for the education of girls. One of these was the Oak Grove Seminary on the Savannah Highway about thirteen miles from Florence. Bettie M. Smith was the teacher here in 1860.[17]

An early academy was located near Gravelly Springs. A celebrated graduate of this school was George Smith Houston, Alabama's 25th Governor. He received his basic education here in the early 1820's. By 1920 there were 92 schools located throughout Lauderdale County. Sixteen of these were for African-American students: Bethel, Center Star, Cloverdale, Good Hope, Green Hill, Hewitt, Hopewell, Killen, Little Zion, Mt. Zion, Oakland, Pisgah, Shiloh, Walker Hill, Waterloo, and Coffee Rosenwald. Another Rosenwald School was established sometime after 1920.

This was the Anderson Rosenwald School located near McGee Town on the Old Savannah Highway. These Rosenwald Schools for African-Americans were part of a program established in 1917 by Julius Rosenwald of Illinois.

The Lauderdale County schools listed for 1922 were: Alabama (located near Cow Pen) Anderson, Atlas, Antioch, Arkdell, Beulah, Bumpas Creek, Burcham Valley, Brush Creek, Bethel Grove, Center Star, Confluence, Cloverdale, Cedar Grove, Cross Roads, Dabney, Dukes, Ebeneezer, Elting, Fairview, Fords Mill, Grassy, Greenhill, Graham, Gravelly Springs, Howard, Harmon, Hopewell, Hammond, Haraway, Jacksonburg, Jackson, Kilburn, Killen, Lovelace, Lexington, Liberty, Kendell, Mars Hill, Mt. Zion, Myrick, McNairy, Macedonia, Mt. Pleasant, McGee, New Georgia, New Hope, Mt. Olive, Oliver, Olive Hill, Oakland, Pleasant Valley, Poplar Springs, Powell, Panther Creek, Pruitton, Portertown, Palestine, Rhodesville, Ray, Romine, Rocky Knoll, Rogersville Public, Sego, Sherrod, Smithsonia, Stony Point, Shaws, Sweet Gum, Striplin, Springfield, St. Florian, Threet, Union Hollow, Union, Underwood, Weeden, Wilson, Woodland, Wright, Waterloo, and Whitehead.[18]

The consolidation of the county school system, which began during the 1920's, resulted in the phasing-out of these small community schools. Students are now bused to modern centralized educational centers located in various sections of the county.

14. COLLEGES AND UNIVERSITIES

"L' education nous faisait ce que nous sommes."
(Helvetius)

The founding fathers of Florence provided two sites for future colleges. One was on East College Street. In 1891 this became the location for the R. M. Patton Grade School. The second site was reserved for a seminary. In those days a "seminary" was commonly identified either as an institution of learning for young ministers or as a female academy. Thus, this site fulfilled its original intention when it became the place where young ladies were taught. Dreams for places of higher learning by the early town planners influenced the naming of two major avenues: College and Seminary Streets. When the colleges and universities did come, it is of interest that all of them which located within the city were either founded or sponsored by religious faiths.

The "seminary" on Seminary Street became a reality in 1855 when the Florence Synodical College was founded by the Presbyterian Synod of Nashville. This prestigious school stood where the present Florence Post Office and Federal Building is now located. The roots of this college go back to an earlier school known as the Florence Female Academy. It was established in 1847 by Professor S. S. Stevens who was a native of Pennsylvania.[1]

One of the founders of the Florence Synodical College was Dr. William H. Mitchell. Born in the County of Monaghan, Ireland, Mitchell arrived in Florence in 1851 to become pastor of the First Presbyterian Church. In 1856, he was appointed president of the Florence Synodical College, a position he held until his death in 1872.[2]

Two stately buildings housed this institution. One faced Seminary Street. It was surrounded by columns, resembling an ancient Greek temple. The other of Georgian architecture faced Tombigbee Street. These structures were built by Zebulon Pike

Morrison who served as the mayor of the town for many years. Among his employees were Charles Gray and Washington Farris, African-American slaves. These men, whom he leased from local citizens, were outstanding brick makers and masons.[3]

The Florence Synodical College closed its doors in 1893. However, a private school was held in the Georgian-style building facing Tombigbee Street during the next two years. Afterwards, the Reverend A. H. Todd conducted a college in this facility until 1897.[4]

La Grange College was Alabama's first chartered four-year liberal arts college to open its doors to students. It was moved to Florence in January 1855. Within a matter of a few months it was chartered as Florence Wesleyan University. This was without question the most important singular event in the history of the town and its people. Through the process of a number of evolutionary changes, this early Methodist pioneer college has emerged as the University of North Alabama.

La Grange College was founded as a liberal arts institution by the Tennessee and Mississippi Conferences of the Methodist Church. It was located on Lawrence Hill a few miles south of Leighton, Alabama. Its doors were opened January 11, 1830. Its first president was Robert Paine, a young thirty-one year old Methodist preacher. A native of North Carolina, he proved to be a strong leader and educator. Following Dr. Pain's ordination as a Methodist bishop in 1847, the college fell upon hard times with mounting debts and decreasing enrollment.

Dr. Richard Henderson Rivers, the fifth president of La Grange, was persuaded by a number of Florence citizens to move the college to Florence. An endowment of $50,000, a new building on twelve acres of land near the heart of the business district, plus a home for the president were among the incentives offered.

The move was made on a cold day in January 1855. Wesleyan Hall, the school's new home, was still under construction. Therefore, classes were held temporarily in the Masonic Temple located at the southwest corner of Court and Tombigbee Streets. According to one source, 160 students were enrolled at Florence

Wesleyan University that first year. Tuition was listed at $25 for a ten-month semester. There was a $5 charge for chemical fees that had to be paid only one time. Students were boarded in private homes of good families at $12 per month, including everything but lights.

Wesleyan Hall, completed in 1856, housed the Florence Wesleyan University for fifteen years – until 1871. It was built by Zebulon Pike Morrison who had erected the buildings for the nearby Florence Synodical College. Wesleyan Hall is listed on the National Register of Historic Places and is considered to be one of the area's most valuable landmarks.

The tragic Civil War marked the beginning of the end of Florence Wesleyan University. Many of its students and faculty marched away to the battlefields. However, Dr. Robert A. Young, who became president in 1861, plus a few faculty members, managed to carry out an abbreviated program until the war's end. Dr. Young later published his recollections of the war years in Florence. He told of General William T. Sherman's occupation of Wesleyan Hall and how, when the General went away, he gave the President a letter to protect the college from destruction by other invading armies. Young was also instrumental in protecting the helpless citizens of the town when it was invaded by Union Colonel Florence M. Cornyn in May 1863.

Florence Wesleyan University was not able to survive the economic disaster brought about by the four years of war and its aftermath. Its facilities were deeded to the State of Alabama in 1872 to become the first state supported normal school south of the Ohio River. The admission of girls in 1874 also made it the first co-educational teacher training institution in the state. Dr. Septimus Primus Rice, an alumnus and former faculty member of La Grange College and Florence Wesleyan University, became the first president of the Florence Normal School.

In 1888 the name of Florence Normal School was changed to State Normal College, and changed back to Florence Normal School in 1913. It was changed again in 1929 to Florence State Teachers College, and in 1957 it became Florence State College.

In 1968 it was changed to Florence State University, and on August 15, 1974, this institution became the University of North Alabama.

It was during the era of Reconstruction when the Mars Hill College was founded by the Church of Christ minister, Theophilus Brown Larimore. Established initially in 1871 as the Mars Hill Academy, it later became Mars Hill College and operated as a college until 1887. This institution was primarily for the training of young preachers and Christian workers among the Churches of Christ.

In the modern setting of the 20th Century, the higher educational mission of the Churches of Christ continues through the International Bible College. Located in the Industrial Park, its campus is only a short distance from Mars Hill Bible School. It was founded as a four-year Bible college in February 1971 with Charles R. Coll, Senior, as its founding president. He became its first chancellor in 1990 at which time Dennis Jones succeeded him as president. In 1996 there were 156 students enrolled, including 17 international students from 15 foreign countries.[5]

The Baptists built their college in North Florence during the days of the East Florence Land Boom. It was located on seven acres of land at the intersection of Seymore and Sherrod Avenues, about one and one-half miles from downtown Florence.

The initial efforts to establish this institution were planned by Dr. J. B. Hawthorne, a popular Baptist minister from Atlanta, Georgia. This school operated briefly as the Southern Female University and later as the Florence University for Women. However, in its earliest days it was sometimes referred to as "Hawthorne's College."[6] One sources says that Dr. Hawthorne's first classes may have been held in the historic Mitchell Malone Home on the southwest corner of Hawthorne and Meridian Streets.[7] This was across from his large Victorian home constructed about 1888.

Much to everyone's surprise, the Reverend Hawthorn returned to Atlanta soon after construction began on the Southern Female University in North Florence. This building was completed in late 1890 at which time efforts were made to organize the college.[8]

The Reverend L. B. Bass, native of South Carolina, was named president of the Southern Female University. Its doors were opened in September 1891 with sixty-three young lady students from a number of states.

Because of the failing economy, the promises made to the University by the local officials did not materialize. In spite of the fact that they were located near the new city water works, water was not made available to the University. The streetcar line was extended only to the North Florence business area and not, as hoped, to the campus. Paved streets were not extended to the campus. These were among the problems faced by Dr. Bass when he announced in 1892 that the University was moving to Birmingham.[9]

In the spring of 1908, the Florence University for Women was organized in the abandoned Baptist facilities in North Florence. There were two presidents. One was W. W. Hatton, who also presided over the Southern Female College in LaGrange, Georgia. The other was O. W. Anderton who moved to Florence to prepare for the opening of the new institution. During the academic year of 1910 - 1911, there was a faculty of 16 members and an enrollment of 112 female students.[10]

This promising University came to an abrupt end on March 2, 1911, when its facilities were completely destroyed by fire. Many of the students returned to their homes. The seniors transferred to a college in Kentucky where Dr. Hatton's brother was president.[11]

Bailey Springs University, located about nine miles north of Florence near St. Florian, was another college for young ladies. Its facilities were the former hotel and outlying buildings of the once popular Bailey Springs Health Resort. The University opened its doors in 1893 and received its charter a year later. Its founders were Charles H. Tatus, Dr. Henry A. Moody, and William P. and Ella B. Ellis. Dr. Moody, a prominent physician who had practiced at the resort, became its one and only president.

This school had hardly begun operation when the panic of 1893 - 94 struck the country. Its student body was reduced to 8 preparatory students and 28 collegians. Only one young lady was graduated in 1894. Because of its isolated location, Bailey Springs University was never financially successful. Its doors were finally closed by 1900.

15. THE MUSCLE SHOALS CANAL

"Construction of the Muscle Shoals Canal was a great
nineteenth century accomplishment."
(Professor Joshua Nicholas Winn III)

It was the attempt to dig a canal around the treacherous Muscle Shoals that for the first time made this geographic feature on the Tennessee River a recognizable name across the nation. It was a gigantic effort by man to remedy an almost impassable obstruction created through eons of time by the forces of nature.

From the earliest attempt to navigate the mighty Tennessee River during the latter part of the seventeenth century, it was known that a formidable obstacle existed that made passage from one end to the other almost impossible. This river barrier became known as the Muscle Shoals. The fall of the river between Bear Creek below Florence and Brown's Ferry near Athens, a distance of approximately eighty miles, was around two hundred feet. The worst section of this fall line occurred above Florence where in a distance of about thirty-seven miles the river dropped over one hundred and thirty seven feet. In its most dangerous parts the water plunged in one mile distances as much as fifteen feet. The roar of these many cascades could be heard up to ten miles away.[1] The shoals in this fall line were caused by reefs of rocks upon which sand and gravel accumulated. In and among these pools and reefs were whirlpools, sinks, and numerous islands of all sizes.

Actually there were six shoals within the eighty-mile stretch of the river near Florence. Below Florence were the Waterloo Shoals, Bee Tree Shoals, and the Colbert Shoals. These were mostly sandbars. Above Florence were the Little Muscle Shoals, Big Muscle Shoals, and the Elk River Shoals. These were far more hazardous as the shallow bed was formed of almost all solid rock and the rapids were filled with boulders and islands of all sizes.[2]

Ferdinand Sannoner's surveying of this local problem was among the first undertaken.[3] In 1824 Secretary of War John C.

Calhoun recommended improvements on the river at the Muscle Shoals. Three years later Congress appropriated $200 for an additional survey. This was made the following year by Captain William Tell Poussin. Another survey was made two years later under the direction of Lieutenant Colonel James Kearney.

Plans were completed by the United States Corps of Engineers to circumvent the entire hazardous barrier from the mouth of Bear Creek to Brown's Ferry. Politics entered the picture, however, as the state did not want the federal government to have control over this program. Thus, the U. S. Government granted 400,000 acres of land to Alabama to be sold and the proceeds used in financing the canal. This proved to be the first major mistake. Sales of land failed to raise sufficient funds. Therefore, plans were downsized so as to build only around the "Big Muscle Shoals." This was the second blunder. The "Big Muscle Shoals" was near the center of the river barrier; hence, during low water seasons it could not be approached from below or above. Had the revised plans called for improvements in the lower series of shoals below Florence it would have been more practical. This would have allowed a progressive series of work over time as money became available to eventually bypass the entire eighty miles of barriers.[4]

Construction of this first of the two Muscle Shoals Canals began early in 1831. It was completed and opened in 1836 at a cost of $644,594.71. There were seventeen locks, 110 feet long and 32 feet wide. Each had a lift of five feet. Because of the limited approach to both ends of this canal there were few boats that used it. Alabama sought additional appropriations but to no avail. Finally, the entire system was abandoned in 1838.[5]

Thus, the first attempt to build a canal around the Muscle Shoals was a failure. However, all was not lost. This was the area's first big public works. Large amounts of money were spent here and numbers of people arrived from other places as part of the work force. Many of these families remained to establish their roots in Florence and Lauderdale County.

Failure of the canal project became a financial advantage for the local railroad. The Tuscumbia, Courtland, and Decatur Railroad was chartered in 1832. Freight and passengers could be transferred at either Decatur or Tuscumbia from boats to the railroad, or from the railroad to boats. This, in effect, became a means of bypassing the impassable Shoals. In 1851 this railroad was absorbed by the Memphis and Charleston Railroad Company which greatly enhanced its competition with the waterways.[6] During the tragic Civil War this railroad became a major military target. By the war's end most of its trestles were gone and its rails uprooted and twisted around nearby trees.

A renewed interest in the Muscle Shoals Canal following the Civil War became in reality a new beginning. It came as an economic rescue from the ravages of the terrible Reconstruction Era. The federal government was now ready to step in and do something about the river barrier at the Muscle Shoals. The state had had its chance and had failed.

In 1867 the United States Congress authorized an overall survey of the Tennessee River from Chattanooga to Paducah. This set the stage. Local preliminary surveying and planning began in 1871 under Major Walter McFarland of the Corps of Engineers. Major construction commenced in 1875.

McFarland was succeeded by Major William Rice King who placed Lieutenant William Louis Marshal in charge of the local work. Marshal's innovative ideas proved so successful that in 1908 he was promoted to Chief of Engineers.[7] King was eventually succeeded by Lieutenant Colonel John W. Barlow. His home on a hill near Killen became an area landmark. This hill is sometimes referred to as Barlow Hill.

The earlier canal was widened. The original seventeen locks in Lauderdale County, a distance of a little over fourteen miles, were reduced to nine with a total lift of 85 feet. Three additional locks were added on the south bank – one at Riverton and two across from Elk River. One of the new canal's engineering marvels was an aqueduct over Shoal Creek. This metal trough, 700 feet long and 60 feet wide, was a means of solving a major problem involving one of the major creeks that flowed into the canal.

A railroad track was built alongside the canal. A locomotive known as "the Little Train" towed the boats through the canal. The observation coach pulled by this engine was known as "Black Maria."[8]

Jesse and Frank James, with Wild Bill Ryan, robbed the paymaster from the Blue Water Creek Construction Camp on March 11, 1881. This official had gone to Florence to pick up the weekly payroll. On his return to camp the James gang took the entire $5,000 he was carrying.

Lock Six near Killen was the headquarters for the Muscle Shoals Canal. This beautifully landscaped reservation became a popular visitor's paradise. Author and English Professor Joshua Nicholas Winn, III, who was reared at Lock Six, often referred to it as "the garden spot of the world."[9]

One of the most interesting stories about the Muscle Shoals Canal involves its relationship with the Panama Canal in Central America. Major General George Washington Goethals who was credited with building the Panama Canal received his apprenticeship in Florence. He was sent here in 1888 as a first lieutenant to speed up work on the Muscle Shoals Canal. He attained results fast by initiating two shifts a day and by personally supervising the night work. His genius was noted at the national level by the design of the Riverton Lock. The initial plans called for two lift locks there at a height of 13 feet each. Goethals replaced these two with a one-lift lock that was 26 feet in height. This became the highest lift lock in the nation at that time. It also became a model for the series of locks that were used in Panama. Late in life Goethals remarked that his work on the Muscle Shoals Canal loomed far larger in his memory than the canal in Panama.

The second Muscle Shoals Canal was successful. The main part, including all the operations in Lauderdale County, was completed and opened for river traffic on November 10, 1890. In 1911, the Colbert Shoals Canal was proclaimed a success. The entire river barrier known as the Muscle Shoals had now been conquered by the genius of man.

Yet, man had made another serious error. From lack of foresight, the new canal was not designed for the new age of tugboats and barges. It would take three dams – Wilson, Wheeler, and Pickwick – to finally and forever bypass the river barrier called the Muscle Shoals.

16. THE TERRIBLE YEARS OF THE CIVIL WAR

"...then was war in the gates: "
(Judges 5:8)

While pacing the floor at Wesleyan Hall on a November day in 1863, U. S. General William Tecumseh Sherman muttered his famous three words: "War is hell." Few at the Shoals would have understood this lament at the beginning of the war. At its tragic ending, however, these words had become a lesson learned by the hardest of ways.

The firing of the guns at Fort Sumpter on April 12, 1861, marked the war's beginning. The surrender of Confederate General Joseph Johnston two weeks after Appomattox near Durham, North Carolina, marked the agonizing end. Yet the suffering was far from over. The people of Lauderdale County would never forget that "war is hell."

There were no important battles in Lauderdale County. However, there were numerous skirmishes and military clashes throughout the war years. There were countless raids upon its citizens. Both armies lived off the land, meaning that food, fodder, animals, firewood, and other items were confiscated from the farms and homes. There were arrests and burnings. There were revenges, pillages, atrocities, and murders. Florence was occupied numbers of times by the enemy with frequent turnovers as armies came and went. War in the Tennessee Valley was in every way a certain kind of hell.

The Muscle Shoals, that almost impassable barrier in the winding Tennessee River, was in itself as a mighty army for the Confederacy. Its formidable rapids and shallows guarded the eastern reaches of Alabama and Tennessee from the invading Yankee Navy. Bragg for a time could freely maneuver his army without fear of an approach of the enemy from the west. But Northwest Alabama from the outset was in a vulnerable position. War came quickly to its doors.

1861

Lauderdale County's delegates, Judge Sidney Cherry Posey and Henry Cox Jones, refused to sign the articles of secession at the called State Convention in January 1861. Their action represented the view of many prominent North Alabamians. However, when war came the people were quick to close ranks against the threat of an invasion from the North.

War fever in Lauderdale County preceded the declaration of war. A military committee was formed by leaders such as Florence attorney James Irvine and Lauderdale County planter and industrialist George Washington Foster. Eleven days prior to Fort Sumpter military units were parading in the streets of Florence. Men, young boys, and even a few elderly seniors, streamed into Florence, Center Star, and other designated places to enlist. Some journeyed to Courtland and nearby Tennessee and Mississippi counties where there were musters for enlistment. They joined units such as the 4th, 7th, 9th, 16th, 26th, and 27th Alabama Infantry Regiments which were organized that first year. Others were formed later, including the 35th Alabama Infantry, the 4th, 9th, 10th, and 11th Alabama Cavalry, as well as a number of Tennessee commands from nearby counties. War meetings were held in Wesleyan Hall. On April 27 the aging lady of Hickory Hill, widow of War of 1812 General John Coffee, unfurled a banner which had been stitched by the ladies of Florence. The officers and men gallantly marched away amid shouts and tears of patriotism. A number of older men who had been left behind were quick to meet at the Masonic Temple to form a Home Guard.

Meanwhile, Fort Henry was erected at the mouth of the Tennessee River and Fort Donelson at the mouth of the Cumberland. These were to block the passage of the Union gunboats. A committee at the Muscle Shoals was organized for the security of the river and its towns. Samuel D. Weakley of Florence was its chairman.[1]

1862

This was the year when war actually came to the gates of Florence and Lauderdale County. It arrived first by water.

General Ulysses S. Grant knew the strategic importance of the Tennessee and Cumberland Rivers. Fort Henry fell on February 6th. Ten days later Fort Donelson surrendered. Two days following the capture of Fort Henry two gunboats, the U.S.S. Lexington and the U.S.S. Contestago, were at the Florence port. They had captured three Confederate vessels downstream. Three steamers at Florence were immediately set on fire by the Confederates to prevent their capture. Gunfire rang out from the opposite bank. A landing force from the gunboats pulled a considerable amount of supplies from the burning vessels. A delegation of townspeople appeared at the dock and pleaded that the town and the new railroad bridge not be destroyed. The bridge was an important military target. Union Lieutenant Commander S. L. Phelps of the U.S.S. Contestoga heeded their pleas.

The Federals did not find the Confederate Dunbar. It had escaped up the mouth of Cypress Creek. To prevent its capture it was scuttled near Cheatham's Ferry Ford. Its gunwales could be seen by those crossing Cypress Creek. From that day to this, this ford has been called "Gunwale Ford," and the road over it became "Gunwaleford Road." The Dunbar was later raised by the Confederate Navy and during a time of high water in January 1863 was floated over the Shoals to the upper reaches of the Tennessee River.[2]

More than 500 sick and wounded were cared for at Florence following the fall of Forts Henry and Donelson. Two makeshift hospitals were used. One was the old Elliott Hotel located near the northeast corner of Dr. Hicks Boulevard and Court Street. The other was the abandoned Fant Woolen Mill located on the southwest corner of Alabama and Court Streets. R. F. M. Lindsey was in charge of both places. Thirty-three of these wounded died and were interred in the Florence Cemetery. After the war their graves were relocated to a section of the cemetery known as "Soldiers Rest. Other facilities were later used as military hospitals. One is today a city museum known as "Pope's Tavern." The other was the Reverend Mitchell Malone House on the southwest corner of Hawthorne and Meridian Streets.

West Point graduate and Massachusetts born Confederate Brigadier General Daniel Ruggles was in charge of defense of Florence at this time.[3] As part of Albert Sidney Johnston's Army, his troops dug the first of the breastworks overlooking the river from the hill on present Veterans Drive. This is now the site of the Florence Coliseum.

Lauderdale County lost four bridges in March due to heavy floods. One crossed Shoal Creek. The other two were over Bluewater Creek.[4]

The Florence Bridge was burned prior to April 17th. This was one of those strange twists of irony that sometimes happens in wartime. The townspeople had persuaded the Union gunboat commander to spare it in February. Now, a little over three months later it was burned by one of their own. Confederate Colonel Benjamin Hardin Helm of the 1st Kentucky Cavalry was the bridge burner. He was married to the half-sister of President Abraham Lincoln's wife Mary. Florence was now essentially cut off from the south side of the river and the lower part of Alabama.

Distant sounds of battle, almost as if it were thunder, could be heard in Florence on April 6th and 7th.[5] This was the ill-fated Battle of Shiloh. During the same weekend, the 3rd Michigan Cavalry staged a raid in the vicinity of Rawhide (Cloverdale.) A large number of prisoners were taken, including Captain John W. Chisholm of the 9th Alabama Infantry.[6] This marked the beginning of raids that now would become frequent throughout the war, especially in the homes where it was known that the men were away.

West Point graduate and Kentucky born U. S. General Ormsby MacKnight Mitchel, who had seized the Memphis and

Charleston Railroad at Huntsville, began extending his lines toward Florence and Tuscumbia on April 12th. This command was a part of Don Carlos Buell's Army of the Cumberland. One of Mitchel's most feared Colonels, Russian born John Basil Turchin, was placed in command of Tuscumbia. His military supplies were unloaded at the Bainbridge Ferry east of Florence. Brigadier General Turchin, who became notorious for his disregard of persons and property, died in 1901 in a hospital for the insane. By this time soldiers of both gray and blue were now coming and going throughout the area. Lamb's Ferry at Rogersville became a frequent military crossing for both armies. Perhaps the first to cross here was Colonel J. C. Scott and his 1st and 2nd Louisiana Cavalry on May 1st. He was followed three years later by Brigadier General John Adams and his Mississippi Brigade. The first of the many skirmishes at Lamb's Ferry occurred on May 10th between units under Mitchel against Colonel John A. Wharton's Texas Rangers. Another brisk fight occurred four days later with the advanced forces under Union Brigadier General James Scott Negley who was also with Buell's Army. Negley burned the ferryboat at Lamb's Ferry and pushed on to Cheatham's Ferry at Smithsonia below Florence where he also destroyed its ferryboat.

General Negley arrived in Florence on May 16. He arrested a number of local manufacturers extracting heavy bonds in exchange for their release. He also levied taxes on those identified as "prominent secessionists." In spite of these actions, the General was remembered years afterwards for his kindness. A kinsman, Major Albert Negley, became a local businessman during the East Florence Boom of the late 1880's. He also served a number of years as City Engineer for Florence.

The summer of 1862 was a time of a protracted occupation of Florence. On June 23rd, Union Major General Don Carlos Buell arrived with some 30,000 troops. The area north of Wesleyan Hall and east of the North Wood Avenue Historic District was made into an extensive camp for his Army of Ohio. Although Buell was remembered as an amiable enemy, this could not be said of one of his subordinates, Brigadier General William "Bull" Nelson, who was especially feared by the townspeople. He was promoted to Major General while in Florence and transferred to Nashville. Two months later in Louisville, Kentucky, he was shot down by a fellow officer whom he had slapped in the face.

Within two weeks following Buell's arrival, the city treasurer reported that soldiers had entered his office and scattered his records. At the same time, city officials announced that no more tax money could be paid in Confederate currency.

About this time a "floating bridge" was erected across the river at Florence. Another of Buell's subordinates, Major General George Henry Thomas, crossed over this bridge on his way from Tuscumbia to Athens. Thomas, known later as the "Rock of Chickamauga," was a graduate of West Point and an aristocrat from Virginia. Because of his Yankee connection his sisters disavowed him until the end of their lives.

It was Buell's Provost Marshal, Colonel John Marshal Harlan, who arrested the popular Presbyterian minister, Dr. William H. Mitchell, on Sunday, July 27. As usual, Dr. Mitchell's prayer that morning was for Jefferson Davis and for the success of the Confederate Armies. Mitchell was sent to a military prison in Alton, Illinois, where he remained for several months.[7] Colonel Harlan became an Associate Justice on the United States Supreme Court. Several generations later one of his descendants with the same name filled this office on the same high court.

Another Buell subordinate, Brigadier James Abram Garfield who would become the 20th President of the United States, made another unpopular arrest. William H. Casey of Cloverdale was sent to a prison in St. Louis, Missouri. One thousand bales of his cotton were confiscated. Casey was a grandson of Revolutionary War General Levi Casey.

One of the most terrible of the local atrocities occurred in Florence after General Buell's Army went away. Apparently in retaliation for Dr. Mitchell's arrest, a local African-American minister, the Reverend Robin Lightfoot, was apprehended at the present site of the Wood Avenue Church of Christ. He was then marched to the present campus of the University of North Alabama where he was hanged on a tree near Stewart Spring. Some believe this was carried out by a partisan unit known as Dunc Cooper's Battalion.

While Buell was in Florence there was a lot of activity in West Lauderdale County. Eastport, Mississippi, across from Waterloo, by now had become a major Union supply depot. Transport ships were seen daily on the river between the two towns. This brought about an incident involving the old men of Waterloo. One day they formed a local militia and fired on the U.S.S. Cottage from Lucy Hill. In retaliation, the angry gunboat captains shelled the town. On July 22 it was reported that a storehouse and other property at Waterloo were burned. Josiah Higgins and nine others were arrested and sent to a federal prison in Alton, Illinois. They were later transferred to St. Louis, Missouri, where Higgins was released following the death of his friend and neighbor, Captain John Thomas Humphry, who had been arrested on August 7th. His death resulted from a deadly smallpox virus.[8]

After Buell moved his army from Florence, the town was raided on Tuesday, July 29 by a large Confederate force, believed to have been "Rebel guerrillas." A Memphis paper reported that the entire city was sacked. Warehouses, quartermaster's stores, and a commissary, all being used by the Union Army, were burned. They also captured a small garrison of U. S. troops along with a Federal supply boat, the U.S.S. Colona. The Confederate force then proceeded down the river to Chickasaw and Waterloo where warehouses were burned. These facilities were being used by the U. S. Army to store cotton that had been confiscated from local farmers. It was reported that five gin houses and 110 bales of cotton were destroyed at Waterloo.[9]

Philip Dale Roddey of Moulton, Alabama, began to appear on the local scene in 1862. He would soon earn the name as "the Defender of North Alabama." He had organized a cavalry company the previous year.

In December 1862, he recruited the 4th Alabama Cavalry and served during the balance of the war mainly in North Alabama under both Generals Bedford Forrest and Joseph Wheeler. He lived off the land. As a result of his men's preference for buttermilk, they were labeled the "Buttermilk Brigade." Roddey was promoted to Brigadier General on August 3, 1863. In December 1862 Roddey, having driven off Colonel Thomas William Sweeny's 52nd Illinois Infantry at Cherokee, crossed the river into Florence. Here he made quite a name for himself by repairing boats for the Confederate Navy. While Roddey was in Florence, the local newspaper, The Florence Gazette, resumed publication. It had been idled since the spring when the first of the federal commands had entered the city.

By the end of 1862 the entire Muscle Shoals area was feeling the effects of war. A local resident, John E. Moore, wrote to the Confederate Secretary of War: "It is unnecessary to relate to you the innumerable instances of pillage and robbery which the people of North Alabama have already been subjected. Suffice it to say that they have been almost ground into the very dust by the tyrants and thieves.[10]

Another letter, signed by sixteen prominent men including Judge Sidney Cherry Posey, was mailed to Richmond: "... The citizens of Florence ... would respectfully make known to you that they have been greatly oppressed by the ravages of the Federal army during the past year; their property destroyed, wantonly and vindictively; the privacy of their homes invaded; citizens carried off, ill-treated, and imprisoned ... We appeal to you for protection."[11]

Two Companies of the U.S. First Alabama Cavalry were formed in November and December 1862. The earliest mention of these "volunteers from Alabama" appeared in special orders issued July 12, 1862, by General Buell at Huntsville. Almost 2,100 men enlisted in this regiment, including 712 from Alabama. Seventeen were from Lauderdale County.[12]

Major General Don Carlos Buell, of Welsh descendant, was ordered to Kentucky in September 1862. His superior, Major General Henry Wager Halleck, was called to Washington following his slow maneuver to secure the rail junction at Corinth. One of Grant's biographers wrote about Halleck's transfer: "Unable to command successfully one army, he was ordered to Washington to command all the armies."[13]

Northwest Alabama now had new adversaries: Ulysses Simpson Grant and Greenville Mellon Dodge. Grant replaced Halleck. Dodge would have the most contact with the people at the Shoals. A native of Danvers, Massachusetts, he was promoted to Brigadier General on March 21, 1862, and to Major General as of June 7, 1864. In his activities around this part of the Tennessee Valley he held the position as Commander of the District of the Mississippi. One of Dodge's most feared subordinates was Colonel Florence M. Cornyn whose regiment became known as the "Destroying Angels." By his orders the La Grange Military Academy near Leighton was burned on April 28, 1863.

1863

The new year began with exciting river crossings. No troop movement is more dangerous or more vulnerable than this. Confederate Major General Edmund Kirby Smith, commander of the District of East Tennessee, crossed at Florence the first week in January. A graduate of West Point and native of Florida, Smith was almost the last of the Confederate Generals to surrender after Appomattox.

Smith's activities were followed by an alert that Confederate Major General Earl Van Dorn would probably attempt to cross the Tennessee River in the neighborhood of Eastport or Florence. Five federal gunboats – the Lexington, Fairplay, St. Clair, Brilliant, and Rob – reached Florence on February 22nd. The river was high enough to enable three of these to pass over the Shoals to the Brainbridge Ferry. They were too late! Van Dorn had crossed on February 16th at two places: Brainbridge and at Seven-Mile Island.[14]

Before dark on February 22nd, Florence was suddenly invaded by cavalry troops. This became the first of two Florence raids made over a four-month period by Colonel Florence M. Cornyn from Corinth. He was at the head of a task force consisting of two cavalry regiments – the 10th Missouri and the 5th Ohio – two batteries of mounted howitzers, and two attached cavalry companies including one from the First Alabama. A small detachment of Confederates, consisting of about thirty men from Baxter's Battalion was driven out of town. Six of these Confederates were taken prisoners. Cornyn's orderly was killed and several of his troops were wounded. The Colonel made his headquarters at the home of Dr. William Chisholm near the northwest corner of Mobile Street and Wood Avenue. His men were camped in and around the public square. Fencing from nearby homes was used for firewood. The town was plundered. The camp was strewn with flour, bacon, preserve and pickle jar, ladies' dresses, infant's clothing, and other personal items. Fines ranging from $500 to $5,000 were assessed against a number of townspeople. Fifty bales of cotton, 60 slaves, and a large number of mules and horses were confiscated.[15]

Preparation for the military expedition in North Alabama which became known as "Streight's Raid" began in March. Transports on the river were used to assemble the Union troops at Eastport, Mississippi.[16] Again, this caused much excitement around Waterloo which lay across from Eastport. A number of gunboats made their way to Florence on March 13th and again on the 25th.

Roddy, now back in North Alabama, detailed fifty men to the task of building flatboats for use in crossing the river. He assigned Colonel Josiah Patterson's Fifth Alabama Cavalry to the defense of Florence. Patterson liked the area so well that he returned after the war to live for a while in what is now Pope's Tavern and Museum. A son, Malcolm Patterson, was elected Governor of Tennessee in 1907.

Leroy Finch, commander of all Federal gunboats on the Tennessee, reported on April 1st that he had made a trip to Florence and had found the enemy in considerable force. The next day a dispatch from General Dodge reported that three gunboats –

Lexington, Silver Lake, and Robb – had shelled Florence and destroyed factories west of the town. Sadly, the people of North Alabama learned that Eastport, Mississippi, had been burned on April 19th, two days before Colonel Abel Strieght departed for his ill-fated ride across Sand Mountain. Strieght was captured along with 1,465 of his command near Rome, Georgia, on May 3rd.

During the month of April, General Van Dorn moved back toward Florence, forcing General Dodge out of the immediate area. In less than a month, Van Dorn would die at the hands of a jealous husband in Spring Hill, Tennessee.

During the latter part of April, Colonel George Gibbs Dibrell arrived in Florence with two cavalry regiments, the 8th and 9th Tennessee. Two detachments were assigned to nearby river crossings to raise the sunken ferries. One was at Bainbridge east of Florence and the other was at Garner's Ferry west of town. Dibrell placed his Huggins Artillery Battery at the Old Fort on Veterans Drive overlooking the river. This unit fired across the river into South Florence. However, there were no Yankees there! Its alarmed citizens waved white sleets and table clothes. Yet, the sound of this action was said to have convinced Dodge to retreat from near Tuscumbia. Dibrell remained six weeks to provide protection for Florence. In a letter written after the war, he remembered its citizens "as kind and hospitable a people as ever lived."[17] He also wrote that "the noble people of that hospitable town provided a hospital for sick – of whom we had quite a number – and cared for them in the best style. We had nine or ten deaths while there."[18] The hospital Dibrell spoke of is now a city museum known as Pope's Tavern. Local ladies served as nurses here. One of its attending physicians was a Yankee spy. Dibrell was later promoted to the rank of brigadier general. He was a native of Sparta, Tennessee. Colonel Dibrell's restoration of the Bainbridge and Garner Ferries was timely. This allowed his commanding general, Nathan Bedford Forrest, to cross the Tennessee River on April 27th on his way from Spring Hill, Tennessee, to Courtland.

The "Destroying Angels" raided Florence again in May. Colonel Florence M. Cornyn departed from Corinth on the 26th with his task force of 1,381 men. His mission was to burn and destroy all the industry and farming resources of Northwest Alabama. And, with few exceptions, he succeeded. The Colonel brought with him Lieutenant Risden DeFord who had grown up around Florence as the son of a Methodist circuit rider. He knew the area and Cornyn used him well. Almost every factory and mill were burned. A number of business houses in downtown Florence were torched, including the Masonic Temple on the southwest corner of Court and Tombigbee Streets. Dr. Robert A. Young, president of Florence Wesleyan University and pastor of the First United Methodist Church, confronted Colonel Cornyn in the parlor of Dr. William Chisholm's home on Wood Avenue. He persuaded the Colonel to spare the town. The narrative of both men has been preserved.[19] Dr. Young was a busy man during this occupation by the enemy. On another occasion he rushed to the home of Olivia O'Neal, wife of confederate Bragadier General Edward Asbury O'Neal, to rescue the family from harm. The O'Neal home was being threatened by a drunken soldier.[20] Olivia O'Neal fled with her family to Russellville to escape further harassment by occupying forces.

The Official Records of the Union Army reported that sixty of the defending Confederates were killed or wounded and that eight officers and 100 men were captured.[21] Cornyn reported the destruction of seven cotton mills and some 200,000 bushels of corn. He also boasted that he had taken 400 horses and mules and about 300 slaves of both sexes and all ages.[22]

This leader of the "Destroying Angels" would never lead another raid into Florence. After returning to Corinth charges were brought against him by one of his subordinates, Lieutenant Colonel William D. Bowen. Bowen, who had been assistant on the LaGrange raid, was upset with Cornyn's conduct as an officer, and especially for his action in burning the college. During the court martial proceeding Cornyn was assassinated by Bowen in an adjoining room. Bowen was later acquitted.[23] In October General Dodge crossed the river at Florence, moving his entire command to Pulaski. Here he was placed in charge of rebuilding bridges along the Nashville and Decatur Railroad, a major supply route between Nashville and Atlanta.

Meanwhile, units under General Sherman were repairing the Memphis and Charleston Railroad south of the river. Sherman's headquarters was at Corinth. Following Major General William Starke Roscran' defeat at Chickamauga, Sherman was ordered to move his corps to Chattanooga. On October 31st he began crossing the river at Waterloo with the aid of gunboats, a ferryboat, and two transports that had been rushed to Eastport. Prior to crossing the river, Sherman made his temporary headquarters in the home of Dr. O. B. Sullivan. Soldiers were everywhere! Sulivan's wife had to step over those sleeping on the floors. They threw out her valuable piano to make more room.[24]

Sherman arrived in Florence late in the day on November 3rd where he united with a fourth division under his foster brother, Brigadier General Hugh Boyle Ewing. The forth division set up camp in and around the city. Sherman made use of the home of General Samuel Weakley, located near the intersection of North Court and North Pine and Tuscaloosa Streets, as his residences. He established his headquarters in Wesleyan Hall. Before he went away, he presented the University President with a document that would insure it against possible destruction during the remaining years of the war. It is believed that Sherman was influenced in this action by one of his staff officers, Colonel Daniel McCook. McCook, a native of Carrollton, Ohio, graduated from Florence Wesleyan University in 1858. He died July 17, 1864, after being wounded at Kennesaw Mountain. He was made a brigadier general the day before his death.

There was a small detachment of Roddey's cavalry on the north side of the river watching Sherman. This unit was made up of 100 men under Major Dick Johnson. Although Johnson succeeded in capturing over 30 prisoners and 50 horses at Gravelly Springs and Waterloo, Sherman's main concerns were with the harassing actives of the bushwhackers along the Waterloo Road.

While in the area, Sherman's men committed a number of raids against the citizens. One involved a nighttime intrusion at the

Sweetwater Plantation east of town. The terrified Patton family witnessed the bravery of one of their servants, Edmund, who blocked the stairwell so that the soldiers could not harm the young ladies of the household.[25]

Waterloo witnessed another crossing by federal troops on November 6th and 7th. This was the 2nd Division of the 16th Corps commanded by Brigadier General Thomas William Sweeney, a native of County Cork, Ireland. Sweeny then joined Dodge in Tennessee.

Once more the Tennessee River became the dividing line between the two armies in North Alabama. Confederate pickets under Roddey patrolled the south banks from his headquarters in Decatur. The northern bank was watched by Union cavalry units under Dodge at Pulaski.

1864

The New Year began with both Roddey's and Dodge's cavalries precariously close at hand. Yet, the town celebrated what has become its most historic wedding, as well as the one best remembered. It was solemnized on January 12 in the parlor of the Burtwell home of North Pine Street. The bride, Ann America, called "Micki" by friends, was a daughter of John Thrumbull Burtwell and his wife, Cornelia. Confederate Major Louis Frederic de Freudenreich Falconnet was the groom. Micki was one of the young nurses at the local military hospital now called Pope's Tavern. The Major, descended from the royal family of Switzerland, was in command of Roddey's scouts. The officiating minister was Dr. William H. Mitchell, pastor of the First Presbyterian Church and president of the Florence Synodical College.

General Dodge at Pulaski had received information about the wedding as early as January 9th. Suspecting that there would be a number of high-ranking officers present, he dispatched Lieutenant Colonel Jesse J. Phillips and his 9th Illinois Mounted

Infantry to Florence. Phillips was not a stranger in town, having been here a number of times. He had been Colonel Cornyn's assistant during the May 1863 raid. In fact, Phillips had been one of the bride's former suitors. His cavalry reached the outskirts of town just as the wedding ended. The bride and groom escaped by way of an awaiting carriage and then a prearranged boat waiting to ferry them across the river and safely into Confederate lines. It is said that a piece of the wedding cake was sent to the Yankee commander under a flag of truce.

Colonel Phillips, not to be outdone, was later married to a young lady in Athens. Following the war, the Falconnets visited his ancestral home, Chateau Bremgarten, in Bern, Switzerland. Eventually they settled in Tennessee where Falconnet continued his employment as an engineer in the construction of railroads. Their small son, Hunter, is buried in the Bedford Cemetery at the top of the hill overlooking the intersection of Cox Creek Parkway and the Industrial Park Road. Falconnet died in 1887. Micki's death occurred a number of years later.[26]

There were a number of local skirmishes in January involving the Fourth Alabama Cavalry. The first of these incidents occurred January 23 on the grounds of the Sweetwater plantation. A detachment of Colonel William A. Johnson's Fourth Alabama Cavalry attacked a unit of the 92nd Illinois Infantry under the command of Captain Matthew Van Burkirk. Fifteen of Johnson's men were killed and three captured including two officers. Two days later a fierce skirmish occurred just east of the present intersection of Cox Creek Parkway and Hough Road on the grounds of the widow Ann Hough's plantation. Here a column of the Fourth Alabama was attacked by a unit of the 72nd Indiana under the command of Captain James E. Robinson.[27]

The third of these early 1864 skirmishes occurred January 25 near the present entrance to the Indian Springs Subdivision on U. S. Highway 72. Here the main force of Johnson's Fourth Alabama Cavalry was engaged with the 2nd U. S. Cavalry under Colonel A. D. Miller. Dodge had sent Miller to intercept Johnson who had been sent by Roddey into Lauderdale County to secure food and fodder. The fighting lasted two hours. Johnson lost seven men. Miller's losses included 15 killed and 25 wounded.[28]

Colonel Phillips was back in Florence on the 29th searching for small Confederate parties as well as partisan units said to be along the river between Florence and Waterloo. While in the Bend of the River, he burned George Washington Foster's Mill at Woodland. He afterwards camped for the night on the grounds of the Hood Plantation a few miles west of Florence.[29]

Another incident occurred in what is now the Kendale Gardens Subdivision in February. Captain A. J. Kelly of Colonel Duncan Cooper's Rangers, a partisan outfit, crossed the river here with ten men. Seeing three Federal soldiers in the door of a nearby house, Kelly ordered an attack, not knowing that twenty additional Yankees were concealed inside the dwelling. During the melee Kelly and all but one of his party were killed.[30]

During the first week of April, approximately 7,000 Union infantrymen landed at Waterloo and made their way through the county toward Huntsville and Chattanooga. One of the brigades passed through Florence.[31]

One of the most daring raids of the war occurred in April. It became known as "The Capture of the White Horse Company." This nighttime skirmish occurred five or six miles west of Florence on the large plantation of John "Jack" Peters. Company G of the 9th Ohio Volunteer Cavalry, known as the "White Horse Company," was on a foraging expedition, and had made camp in and around Peters' main house and nearby barn. Colonel James Jackson, Junior, and Colonel Samuel Ives, both Lauderdale County natives, formed a joint task force consisting of about 100 men from their respective commands, the 27th and 35th Alabama. They crossed the river at Seven Mile Island, and attacked Company G, 9th Ohio Cavalry, before daybreak on April 12. The fighting was fierce but brief. The Confederates suffered the loss of one man. Two Federal cavalrymen were killed and thirty-five captured. All of the enlisted men were sent to the Andersonville prison in Georgia; nineteen of these prisoners died within seven months following their confinement.[32]

The regimental commander of the 9th Ohio was Colonel William D. Hamilton. About two weeks following the capture of the White Horse Company, he was sent to Florence with the entire 9th Ohio by orders of General Sherman. Their mission was to patrol the Tennessee River in this area of North Alabama. They were ordered to live off the land. Colonel Hamilton made his headquarters at the Hood Plantation west of Florence which was then the home of Captain Alexander Donelson Coffee. Some of Hamilton's men were encamped on the grounds of plantation near the community known as Three Points. Others were located at Cheatham's Ferry which is now called Smithsonia. One company was at the Bainbridge Ferry east of Florence. Two were in Center Star, one at the Benjamin Taylor plantation and the other camped on the grounds of the nearby home of David Williams. Other units were located at the mouth of Elk River near Rogersville. The Colonel was remembered by the citizens of the area as being a kind and just individual. However, the reign of his occupation proved to be extremely harsh as his troops raided the farms and homes, taking from them what little was left of the necessities of life.[33]

The 7th Illinois under Colonel Richard Rowett was also in the area at this time. Their mission was to patrol the river from the mouth of Elk River to the mouth of Cypress Creek. Two or three of Rowett's companies were encamped at Bailey Springs, one at Waterloo, and the remaining were located between Waterloo and Florence. On April 25th, the units at Bailey Springs were moved to Mars Hill where they set up camp at the site of the Wright and Rice Iron Foundry.

On April 14th, a letter written from Tuscaloosa reported that Florence "is constantly infested either by Yankees or Tories. It is hardly an exaggeration to say that every good horse in the county has been taken off, and a very large proportion of the slaves. "[34]

A skirmish occurred north of Florence on May 7th between Colonel Richard Rowett's 7th Illinois Regiment and the cavalry under Brigadier General Roddey. Roddey had crossed the river both above and below Florence with about 5,000 men. The skirmish lasted two hours. Rowett reported that after losing a great many men, he fell back on the Cloverdale Road and was pursued as far as Cloverdale. However, he managed to escape into the area of Lawrenceburg, Tennessee.[35]

The skirmish at North Florence was followed ten days later with another two-hour encounter at Center Star. This engagement was between Colonel William A. Johnson's Fourth Alabama Cavalry and a task force of the 7th Illinois and 9th Ohio under Colonel Richard Rowett. Rowett reported that he drove Johnson back across the Tennessee River after capturing 35 prisoners.

General Dodge relocated his headquarters from Pulaski to Athens in late February, giving him better control of the riverfront. More frequent patrols appeared in Florence throughout the spring and summer. Eliza Weakley, who lived just north of the downtown business district, noted a number of these raids in her diary.[36] General Roddey, protector of North Alabama, kept surveillance from the south bank of the river. Often the two opposing patrols clashed.

On August 10, a skirmish occurred in Florence with a patrol from the 12th Tennessee (Union) Cavalry, commanded by Colonel George Spalding. This was one of a number of Tennessee units recruited by the Union Army. Also, in the local area at various times were Tennessee commands serving in the Confederate Army.

There were four other clashes in early September. One occurred on September first with the 9th Ohio Cavalry. The second skirmish was on September 10 involving Lieutenant Colonel John B. Minnis' 3rd Tennessee (Union) Cavalry. Two days later there was another clash with the 9th Ohio, followed on September 17 with the 3rd Ohio Cavalry.[37]

September 22 became a memorable day for the citizens of Florence. It would be talked about for generations. General Forrest, by now one of the most popular military figures in the South, was given a hero's welcome by a crowd of men, women, and children. This happened in spite of an earlier threat by

Sherman to burn Tuscumbia and Florence if Forrest chose to use this place as a launching base for future raids into Tennessee.[38]

The famed cavalry commander crossed the Tennessee River near Woodland on September 21 and made camp that night about two miles west of Florence. The next day he led his long column up Court Street amid shouts of the people. Upon reaching Mitchell's Corner (Court Street and Hermitage Drive), these mounted troops turned east and headed toward Shoal Creek where they were joined by Roddey's brigade. (To travel east in those early years, the route ran north on the Jackson Military Road, then south on Circular Drive to present Royal Avenue where it became Huntsville Road in what is now East Florence.) Now with a force of 4,500 men, Forrest headed toward Athens, and then into Tennessee with a mission to destroy Sherman's vital lines of communications.

Federal cavalry from both Pulaski and Athens were alerted of Forrest's presence. Colonel Spalding, now commanding the Fourth Cavalry Division of the Cumberland, was sent from Pulaski toward Shoal Creek with the 10th and 12th Tennessee (Union) Cavalry. On September 22nd, he ran into Colonel Jacob B. Biffle and his 9th Confederate Tennessee Regiment at James M. Powell's Grist Mill on Blue Water Creek, three miles southeast of present Loretto, Tennessee. The next day Spalding captured three wagons and five men at Green Hill, Alabama, and quickly turned back to Pulaski to sound the alarm.

Lieutenant Colonel Minnis at Athens was ordered here with his 3rd Tennessee (Union) Cavalry consisting of some 300 men. Approaching Rogersville from Lexington on September 23, he found himself cut off at the Huntsville Road which was filled with Forrest's cavalry heading east. Turning northeast, Minnis quickly forded Elk River near the Salem community in Limestone County to give the alarm from Athens.

Meanwhile, events were taking shape in Atlanta that would affect the Muscle Shoals. John Bell Hood was promoted to the rank of full general on July 18, 1864. At this time he took over the command of the Army of Tennessee from General Joseph

Eggleston Johnston. Then a strange thing happened in the annals of warfare. Hood headed west as his opponent, General William T. Sherman, moved his army eastward across Georgia. Hood's grandiose plan was to capture Nashville, invade Kentucky, cross the Ohio River, and march through Virginia. This would hopefully bring him to the side of his hero, General Robert E. Lee, who so desperately needed him around Richmond. It was a bold and dangerous gamble.

Hood began moving into North Alabama in late September with intentions of crossing the Tennessee River at Guntersville. However, federal gunboats were patrolling the river from Chattanooga to Brown's Ferry. His secondary objective was Decatur, but he found a strong federal garrison there along with two wooden gunboats on the river. Thus, Hood continued his line of march to Tuscumbia.[39] Florence was now to be the place for the dangerous river crossing. Its location at the foot of the Muscle Shoals offered considerable protection from the gunboats on the upper river.

Hood's Army was made up of 27,000 infantry and artillery, plus 2,000 cavalry under Brigadier General William H. Jackson. General Joseph Wheeler's cavalry was still in Georgia. It now became imperative to terminate Forrest's raid in West Tennessee. He was now the Army of Tennessee's new chief of cavalry and was ordered to join Hood at Florence.

While Forrest's main force was terminating its Johnsonville raid, one of his brigades, commanded by Brigadier General Abraham Buford, began pulling back from its activities around Athens and Huntsville. Sending a part of his brigade to the opposite bank of the Tennessee River at Rogersville, Buford continued toward Florence. Arriving on October 3, he ferried his captured supplies and all of the remaining regiments of his command to the south bank of the river.

Two days later Forrest camped his troops in Happy Hollow near the Shoal Creek crossing of the Jackson Military Road. He sent his captured cattle and oxen to Colbert's Ferry and his captured wagons to Smith's Ferry near Smithsonia. The General

119

personally directed much of the work in ferrying these military spoils across the river. He assigned a part of the 4th Alabama, under Lieutenant Colonel F. M. Windes, to guard the Huntsville Road. The Jackson Military Road entrance to Florence was assigned to Colonel C. R. Barteau and part of his 2nd Tennessee (Confederate) Cavalry. The remaining units of the 2nd Tennessee, along with the 7th Tennessee, were detailed as a rear guard at the ferries below Florence. Realizing that the enemy was now close at hand, Forrest ordered his men to swim their horses across to Seven Mile Island. By October 6, the major part of his cavalry was safe on the south bank of the Tennessee.

General Thomas at Nashville dispatched Major General Lovell Harrison Rousseau in pursuit of Forrest. By October 7, he was at Blue Water Creek above Green Hill on the Jackson Military Road near Elias McDonald's blacksmith shop. Brigadier General Richard W. Johnson was between Green Hill and Happy Hollow. Brigadier General John Thomas Croxton's brigade had reached Happy Hollow the previous day. Here, at the Shoal Creek crossing, a furious skirmish was fought on the 6th between Croxton's brigade and units of the Confederate 2nd Tennessee under Colonel C. R. Barteau. At this time, Major General Cadwallader Colden Washburn of the U.S. XVI Corps was approaching Waterloo from Waynesboro with part of his three divisions.

Union Brigadier General James Dada Morgan reached Rogersville on October 4 where he camped for the night. He reached Florence two days later as the Confederate 4th Alabama Cavalry and 2nd Tennessee (Confederate) slowly retreated to the Martin and Weakley Cotton Mill on Cypress Creek west of town. Colonel Windes and his 4th Alabama Cavalry continued westward toward Woodland at the Bend of the River.

Meanwhile, parts of the Confederate 7th Tennessee, retreating from heavy skirmishes at Happy Hollow, joined Barteau at the Martin and Weakley Mill. On October 8, Barteau dispatched Lieutenant Colonel George H. Morton with most of the Confederate 2nd Tennessee to guard the ford near the Forks of Cypress plantation. Barteau remained at the cotton factory with a combined force of about 500 made up of the Confederate 7th and 16th Tennessee Regiments.[40]

One of Rousseau's cavalry brigades crossed Cypress Creek upstream from the Forks of Cypress and attacked Morton's Confederate 2nd Tennessee from behind. However, Lieutenant Colonel Morton led a charge through the Union lines and escaped, although greatly outnumbered. This fight is sometimes referred to as the Battle of Jackson's Ford. Following his escape from Jackson's Ford, Colonel Morton joined Barteau who was now fighting a much larger Union force. This engagement, sometimes called the "Battle of Cypress Mill," was near the crest of the hill on the Old Waterloo Road overlooking the cotton mill on Cypress Creek. After much fighting which continued until after dark, Barteau was slowly pushed westward on the Waterloo Road.

Now facing some 12,000 Union soldiers, these small Confederate units which were on the north side of the river began retreating toward Waterloo on October 9. Deploying rear guards at several creek crossings to delay the enemy, these Confederates began splitting into smaller groups. These companies and squads now made their way to the river. They were able to join their other comrades at Cherokee by plunging with their horses into the Tennessee River. Forrest once again had escaped the enemy!

General Rousseau now camped his men in the Old Confederate Fort, which is now the location of the present Florence-Lauderdale Coliseum. After destroying all the ferryboats between Florence and Waterloo, he moved back toward Nashville while General Morgan's infantry returned to Bridgeport.[41]

October 30, 1864, became another memorable day. It marks the capture of Florence by Confederate General John Bell Hood to secure the crossing of his army on its historic march into Middle Tennessee.

Hood had arrived in Tuscumbia that same day with almost 30,000 troops. His chief engineer, Lieutenant Colonel Stephen W. Presstman, began preparations to link his pontoons across the river. But first it was necessary to secure beachheads on the north shore which was under the control of Union Brigadier General John T. Croxton's First Cavalry Brigade. Hood decided to launch two river assaults. The frontal attack was planned for Florence and the flanking movement was to be from upriver at Bainbridge, where the modern Kendale Gardens subdivision is now located.

Brigadier General Randall L. Gibson was in command of the frontal assault. Lieutenant Colonel R. M. Lindsay led this attack under a barrage of artillery fire from Cobb's Artillery Battalion on the high bluffs at the south bank. Florence was quickly captured. The townspeople were elated! Eliza Weakley noted in her diary: "... the ladies ran down the street yelling and clapping their hands."[42]

Major General Edward Johnson commanded the flanking assault with two brigades which crossed the river at Bainbridge. Brigadier General Jacob Hunter Sharp with his Mississippi Brigade spearheaded this operation. All went well until he ran into Croxton near the modern entrance to Indian Springs subdivision on U. S. Highway 72 East. Croxton had been driven from Florence by Lieutenant Colonel Lindsay's frontal assault. After suffering a loss of about 40 killed, wounded, and captured, Croxton retired during the night to the vicinity of Happy Hollow on Shoal Creek.

Once the area was secured, Lieutenant Colonel Presstman began erecting the pontoon bridge. He used the piers and remaining structure of the burned-out Florence Railroad Bridge as anchors for his pontoon boats. Fortunately, Hood's pontoon train had been rescued and sent ahead by General Beauregard. It had been left them behind after crossing the Coosa River.[43]

Now at Happy Hollow on the east bank of Shoal Creek, General Croxton established his outposts so as to watch and report the movements of Hood's Army. He immediately began dispatching patrols in the direction of Florence. One encountered a unit from Gibson's Louisiana Brigade on the Huntsville Road near the site of the earlier skirmish at the modern entrance to the Indian Springs subdivision. The Federals suffered heavy loses including most of their horses. A few days following his capture of Florence, Lieutenant Colonel Lindsay encountered another Union patrol at

Bailey Springs. They were quickly dispersed by one volley from Lindsay's rifle.

Croxton was effective in causing damage to Hood's pontoon bridge. He made a daring raid on this structure during the first week of November. It took Presstman two days to make repairs. Before daylight on November 4, Croxton floated five of his cavalrymen down the river in an unsuccessful attempt to cut the cables holding the pontoons together. A second attempt on November 10 was successful; three of these raiders were captured. High floods and floating debris had broken the pontoons on the previous night.[44]

It was not until November 13th before Hood, along with Major General Benjamin F. Cheatham's Corps, made it across the river. On the next day, following more heavy storms, the river rose eighteen feet. Finally, on November 20th, Lieutenant General Alexander Stewart's Corps became the last of Hood's Army to make the perilous crossing. General William H. Jackson had crossed his 2,000 cavalrymen by swimming the river near Woodland in West Lauderdale County.

Hood established his headquarters in Wesleyan Hall and his residence in the large antebellum mansion now known as Coby Hall. Both are now a part on the campus of the University of North Alabama. The elegant homes in the Sannoner Historic District on North Court Street were used by his general officers and staffs. His divisions were camped in and around the city, including the Sweetwater Plantation east of town.

Forrest joined Hood on the morning of November 14 and established his headquarters in Courtview, now a part of the campus of the University. In the evening Forrest was serenaded by the Tennesseans in Hood's Army. Following this honor, Forrest gave a speech which was followed by remarks from General Hood. On November 15, Forrest assumed command of all cavalry in the Army of Tennessee.

During Hood's sixteen-day delay at Tuscumbia and Florence, almost all military actions with the enemy occurred in and around the Jackson Military Road crossing at Shoal Creek. This place was known then as Baugh's Ford. It is now called Happy Hollow. These skirmishes, and others here during the war years, identify this area as perhaps the most fought-over field of battle in Lauderdale County.

Union General Croxton's brigade, located in the vicinity of Shoal Creek, was reinforced on November 6th by Brigadier General Edward Hatch's 5th Division. As division commander, Hatch was now in control of all the Union forces opposing Hood at Florence. During the next fifteen days, Hatch used Colonel Datus E. Coon's 2nd Brigade as his reconnaissance force. Coon was later brevetted as a brigadier general. Following the war, this Iowa newspaperman returned to Alabama and became active in the Republican Party during the Reconstruction Period.[45]

Colonel Coon's first encounter here occurred at the time of his arrival on November 6th. His 2nd Iowa Cavalry managed to push Roddey's pickets two miles and forced them to the west bank of Shoal Creek. However, the federals dared not follow, as a heavy line of pickets could be seen on the high bluffs overlooking Happy Hollow. Instead, Coon dispatched some of his troops up Shoal Creek with orders to burn the flourmill, a part of the Lauderdale Cotton Factory complex. Here they ran into about 300 Confederates who were guarding the mill. The ensuing skirmish lasted about an hour. Leaving the 2nd Iowa Cavalry at Happy Hollow to watch the enemy, Coon moved back about five miles with the main part of his brigade.

At 1:00 p.m., on November 7th, Coon drove back the Confederate pickets from the high bluff on the west bank of the creek. This fierce fighting lasted about an hour. However, because of high water, Coon was not able to cross the ford with his entire command. Consequently, his second attempt to destroy the flourmill was a failure. After this skirmish, Coon withdrew to Stutts Cross Roads near Green Hill and camped for the night. On the following day, detachments were sent back to Happy Hollow which resulted in a third hour-long skirmish.

General Hatch ordered another reconnaissance at Happy Hollow on November 9th. Coon again found well-posted pickets on the west bank of the creek, although he succeeded this time in capturing the flour and gristmills. He then made camp at the nearby John Watkins farm located behind the modern Lone Cedar Church of Christ Cemetery. The Watkins place was the former stagecoach inn of Samuel Craig, a personal friend of Andrew Jackson. It was an ideal campsite.

Two days later, there was a fourth engagement at Happy Hollow between Coon's brigade and Gibson's pickets. The 6th Illinois Cavalry, commanded by Major Charles W. Whitsit, formed a line of battle extending from the Cow Pen Road to the bank of Shoal Creek opposite the millrace. Whitsit's charge was covered by artillery fire from the Jackson Military Road. The Confederate pickets and reserves were driven back. The 1st Battalion, 2nd Iowa Cavalry, led by Major Gustavus Schnitzer, managed to get across the rain-swollen creek about a quarter of a mile below Baugh's Ford and became engaged in heavy fighting. Because he was now out of range for artillery support, he was ordered to withdraw to the east bank of the creek. During Schnitzer's two creek crossings, his cavalry came under fire from the Confederate artillery entrenched on the high bluffs on the west bank. On November 15th Colonel Coon moved his brigade from the Watkins place to the farm of John Wilcoxson which was closer to Green Hill. Next day he crossed Shoal Creek at Wolf Ford and went down Butler Creek Road toward Wilson's Crossroad (now St. Florian.) About a mile from Wilson's Crossroad he ran into Roddey's Cavalry. The Confederates retreated back toward Florence after the loss of several men who were taken prisoners. Coon, now convinced that Forrest had joined Hood at Florence, crossed back to the east bank of Shoal Creek at the Savannah Ford and made camp about three miles from the Cow Pen Woolen Mill. Over the next two days Colonel Coon sent reconnaissance forces in and around the areas of Butler Creek and Cloverdale Roads. On November 19th, his patrol drove back the Confederate pickets on Butler Creek Road. Coon was quick to realize that these pickets were part of Forrest's Cavalry commanded by Brigadier General Abraham Buford.

Retreating rapidly, Coon was almost cut off at the confluence of Big and Little Butler Creeks.

Meanwhile, the 9th Illinois reconnaissance patrol on the Cloverdale Road ran into Confederate Brigadier General James R. Chalmers' wagon trains. Several wagons and prisoners were captured, along with secret documents which revealed in detail Hood's plans for his campaign in Tennessee. During this skirmish the 9th Illinois Cavalry lost thirty men, most of whom were taken prisoners.

Thus ended the last of the 1864 skirmishes at Happy Hollow. Knowing now that Hood was ready to make his move, General Croxton ordered Colonel Coon to unite with his command in Lexington.

Hood moved out of Florence on November 21st. The ground was frozen hard. Snow began falling about noon and lasted until after dark. Three routes were taken. Major General Benjamin F. Cheatham's Corps took the Cloverdale Road toward Waynesboro, camping the first night at Rawhide (now Cloverdale.) Lieutenant General Alexander P. Stewart's Corps left Florence on the Jackson Military Road through Green Hill toward Lawrenceburg. Lieutenant General Stephen D. Lee's Corps traveled over a series of connecting roads (now the Chisholm Highway) between the other two corps. Riding in front of these three corps were the three divisions of General Nathan B. Forrest's cavalry.

Hood was heading now into one of the most disastrous military campaigns of the Civil War. His army was brutally cut to pieces and all but destroyed at Franklin and Nashville. The remnant of his army began its flight for survival. Leaving Columbia on the morning of December 20th, they took the Pulaski Pike (Hough Road) out of Pulaski, waded Sugar Creek north of Anderson, straggled through Lexington, and crossed Shoal Creek northeast of present Killen. Hood was madly racing toward the Tennessee River, his only chance of escaping the pursuing Union Army.

Bainbridge Ferry, now the modern Kendale Gardens subdivision east of Florence, was chosen as the place to cross the river. The shallow shoals, both above and below this point, offered some protection from Federal gunboats.

General Phillip Roddey's pontoons had been floated over the Shoals from Decatur. Some of these rickety boats carried fancy names, such as Emma, Julia, and Beckie Sharp. Yet, most of these vessels were nothing more than wooden scows. Lieutenant Colonel Stephen W. Presstman and his engineers began placing these pontoons across the river on Christmas Day. Working tirelessly they had their improvised bridge in place for the first wagons to cross early on December 26th.

In the meanwhile, General Cheatham's men began constructing earthworks to protect the pontoons. This action enabled the artillery to fire on two approaching gunboats which had crossed over the Shoals from Florence. These boats were commanded by Admiral S. P. Lee who had been ordered to cut off Hood at the river. Shells from Colonel Melancthon Smith's artillery were sufficient to turn Lee around to head back down the river. According to Union General James H. Wilson, Admiral Lee had come within a mile of Hood's pontoons.

Cheatham's Corps, along with General Stephen Lee's Corps, crossed over the pontoons on December 26th. They were followed the next day by the men under General Stewart. Forrest's cavalry crossed that night. One of his men wrote: "...we could hear the firing as we went over. It was a scary passage. The night was very dark, the black, rushing, rearing current only a few inches under us..."[46] Finally, Walthall's rear guard began arriving around daybreak on December 28th.

Thus, safely on the south bank of the Tennessee River, General Hood had saved his army. Bainbridge had missed by a mile and perhaps by only a few hours from becoming one of the Civil War's bloody fields of slaughter.

1865

The defeat of the Army of Tennessee brought about complete chaos at the Muscle Shoals. The resulting demise of law and order set the stage for a reign of terror against helpless citizens by numerous gangs of outlaws. Records of these acts of torture among the flames of wartime passion are almost unbelievable. Actually, these ruthless groups had been active for most of the war years, but by the beginning of 1865 all restraints were gone as they plundered, raped, maimed, and killed.

In the cold winter of 1865, West Lauderdale County became an armed camp. Gravelly Springs was established as a training center for some 22,000 cavalrymen in preparation for the upcoming Spring invasion of South Alabama and Georgia. This became the largest cavalry force ever assembled in the western hemisphere. This corps was under the command of Brigadier General James Harrison "Harry" Wilson, who was only 27 years of age. A native of Shawneetown, Illinois, he was graduated from West Point in 1855, ranking sixth in his class. At the close of the war, Wilson was promoted to the rank of major general.[47] During the Spanish American War, he served with former Confederate General Joseph E. Wheeler in Cuba.

Gravelly Springs was ideally situated for Wilson's training camp. It was near the steamboat ports of Waterloo and Eastport, Mississippi, and the railroad line at Iuka. The hills around Gravelly Springs met the "high ground" advantage that commanders usually prefer. On these hills were excellent flat plateaus for the training of men and horses. There were numerous limestone springs and creeks available for the camp's water supply.

The officers, men, and horses began arriving in early January. There were five division areas. Brigadier General Edward M. McCook's division was at the Waterloo landing. The four divisions in the Gravelly Springs area were those of Brigadier Generals Edward Hatch, Emory Upton, Joseph F. Knipe, and Eli Long.[48]

Wilson had intended to live off the land. However, he soon found that the entire area had been devastated by earlier Union occupations as well as by the constant raids by gangs of local outlaws. With few exceptions, there was simply no food left for his men to confiscate. However, they tore down almost every barn and outhouse, including a number of churches. The lumber from these structures was used in the erection of barracks, administrative offices, and stables. The Canaan United Methodist Church was spared because of its use as a military hospital. Evidence in the structure of this church show that it was at one time or another in the center of a skirmish.

The initial plans following the training period called for this cavalry corps to cross the Tennessee River on March 2. However, the river was at flood stage. It was not until March 22, when Wilson with 13,480 men on horses and armed with Spencer carbines rode away into fame. Because of a shortage of horses, it was necessary for the General to leave behind one dismounted division at Eastport.

Wilson's Raid became the largest and most successful Civil War cavalry campaign. He accomplished his mission to destroy the heart of the remaining industrial area of the South. He also succeeded in burning the University of Alabama and Selma, and in capturing the fleeing Confederate President Jefferson Davis and his Vice President Alexander H. Stevens.[49] The war was over for the people at the Muscle Shoals. But the suffering had not ended. The defeated Southern states had other battles to fight. These consisting of rebuilding homes, farms, towns, infrastructures, and governments. It would not be easy. The subsequent hard years of Reconstruction would leave its impact upon the memories of a number of generations that were yet to be born. The people who made their home at the Muscle Shoals were more blessed than many other sections of the country. On the horizon were a number of good men who would lead them through the valley of despair into the new age of industrial revolution.

17. A TIME OF OUTRAGE

"Satan was now at hand."
(Milton in Paradise Lost)

Few places in modern times have endured the sufferings imposed upon it by lawless men as did the people of Lauderdale County during the last months of the Civil War. Monstrous gangs descended upon helpless individuals, families, and communities. These outlaws left a legacy of hideous crimes with scars that can never be erased from the history of the Muscle Shoals.

Lauderdale County during the Civil War was much like the backcountry of the Carolinas during the Revolutionary War. Although its representatives voted against secession, in the main its people united behind the Confederacy once it became clear that war was inevitable. Yet, there remained considerable diversity in political ideology. Neighbors and even families were sometimes divided. There were numbers of instances where brothers fought in opposing armies, and even situations were fathers and sons wore different uniforms. These differences flamed by passions of war became in themselves inducements for violence.

Lauderdale County was even more vulnerable to lawless actions because of its closeness to Hardin and Wayne Counties in Tennessee where there was much Union sentiment. For example, the people of Wayne County voted 905 to 409 to oppose secession from the Union.[1] Clifton, in Hardin County, became the base for a number of notorious gangs who frequently raided across the line into Alabama.[2] By the end of the war, ruthless desperadoes were hiding in the hills and hollows of Lauderdale, Wayne, Hardin, and nearby counties as they raided, plundered, raped, burned, and murdered.

Generally, these gangs were classified as either Bushwhackers, Guerrillas, or Tories. Bushwhackers or Guerrillas were paramilitary forces. For most of the war they performed a valuable service to the Confederacy by harassing the enemy's flanks and rear echelons, or by destroying their vital supply and communication lines. Tories, a term used in the Revolutionary War for those who supported the Crown of England, became the name for those in Lauderdale County who supported the Union. Near the end of the war, as law and order in Florence and Lauderdale County disappeared, it became difficult to identify the former loyalties of some of these gangs as they randomly plundered in greed and lust.

As early as May, 1862, Union Major General Ormsby MacKnight Mitchel reported from Huntsville that "Guerrilla warfare has been inaugurated along my entire line, and we are attacked nightly at bridges and outposts..."[3] Union General William Tecumseh Sherman, while passing through Lauderdale County in November 1863, reported that "the country was full of guerrillas."[4] He suspected that several prominent men of Florence had connections with these irregular forces. There were a number of these "guerrilla" forces operating in this area. Because they were irregular partisans, practically no records existed following the war to identify who they were or how many men were in each organization. Three of the most active were known as Boyle's 56th Alabama Partisan Rangers, Carter's Scouts, and Dunc Cooper's Battalion.

Cooper's Battalion was commanded by young nineteen-year-old Colonel Duncan Cooper. A subordinate, Captain A. J. Kelly, called "Hick Kelly," was known as the "brains of the outfit." A native of Columbia, Tennessee, Kelly was effective in attacking isolated Federal patrols and pickets. He was labeled a "thief" by local families who were loyal to the Union because of his raids among them. Hick Kelly was killed while attacking a Union patrol near the modern Kendale Gardens area in February, 1864. He was only twenty-one years old at the time.[5]

Federal officers branded a number of local leaders as "guerrillas," although they were bona fide Confederate officers. One was Colonel Jacob B. Biffle, commanding officer of the 19th Tennessee Cavalry, which was more often referred to as the 9th Tennessee. As one of Confederate General Nathan Bedford

Forrest's men, Biffle was often in Lauderdale County. Men who belonged to Biffle's Regiment were especially targeted by local Tory outlaws. When caught they were brutally tortured and murdered.

Like Forrest, who was his mentor, Biffle paid little attention to the traditional standards of warfare. A native of Wayne County, Tennessee, and veteran of the Mexican War, the Colonel was not able to return to his home after the Civil War because of so much bitterness against him. He became a rancher in Texas where he was shot and killed in 1876 by one of his hired hands. They were in a dispute over how to cook venison.

Captain Samuel P. Emerson of Company B, 6th Kentucky, was a regular Confederate Officer branded as a "partisan" by the Union Army. Emerson was sent to Lauderdale County to break up a notorious desertion ring. The focal point for this clandestine operation was in a small community now known as Stout, Tennessee. Located a few miles north of Waterloo, it almost straddles the border between Wayne and Hardin Counties. A price, called a "ransom," was paid here for soldiers who agreed to desert the Confederate Army and be sworn into the Union Army. Thus, the Stout community was known in those days as "Ransom Town," and sometimes as "Turn Over." Emerson soon established a network of informants, most of whom were women. When a deserter was captured, Emerson would either hang him immediately or take him to his home community and there carry out the execution.[6]

Another well-known Confederate officer branded by the Union as a "guerrilla" was Captain William Burton "Bert" Hayes, Company H., 21st Tennessee Cavalry. Union Brevet Major General Edward Hatch of the U. S. Fifth Cavalry Division called Hayes "one of worst" of the guerrillas who surrendered to him in 1865.[7] There are many legends about the unorthodox activities of Bert Hayes in support of the Southern cause. This was especially so in West Lauderdale County. However, as pointed out by one historian, no official charge was ever made against him by the Federal government, nor was his family molested by Union sympathizers during or after hostilities.[8] A native of Wayne County, Hayes was shot and killed three years after the war at his home in Hardin County.

Tories were at times also called "bushwhackers" in some accounts of the war. At first these "Union sympathizers" targeted homes where the soldiers were away in the Confederate Army. Many of these defenseless families became so destitute that funds were allocated for their necessities of life by the local government. However, as the war wore on, these gangs became bolder. There were instances where they terrorized entire communities.

One diarist, a Confederate soldier whose home was in Gravelly Springs, defined them in this manner: "The Tories, as we called them, made frequent raids in our county, robbing and plundering the citizens and picking up any lone rebel who might be so unfortunate as to fall in their hands. These men were mostly Tennesseans who wore the blue as a cloak for their deviltry and for the protection of the Federal Army... They tortured citizens who were supposed to have money in every conceivable way, branding, burning, or whipping, as they thought most likely to induce them to give up their money. I dreaded them more than I did the Yankees, for if captured by soldiers I knew the worst that could befall me would be a term in prison, but if caught by these fellows I didn't know what would become of me."[9]

There were a number of Tory gangs. One, led by Elias Thrasher, was mentioned in a report by a Union officer. Called "The Man Thrasher" by U. S. Brigadier General Granville Dodge, Thrasher and his followers were said to have committed many atrocities, including murder by torture. Most of these crimes were in the area of Gravelly Springs. Thrasher's boyhood home, a log house on Chisholm Highway near the Jacksonburg community, was listed in 1983 as a local landmark. His father, William Thrasher, built this house in 1818, and in 1820 moved it to its present site. Legend has it that three Confederate soldiers were killed at different times in Thrasher's front yard.[10]

Elias was a Lieutenant in Company B, 2nd Tennessee Mounted Infantry, U.S.A. Most of his gang were members of this unit, including such notorious characters as Tom and Dennis Clark, French Hollis, Bill Bridges, Lumb Phillips, Paul Kiddy, Green and Albertie Gallion, Jim Martin, and Bill Carter. Apparently, no criminal charges were made against Thrasher by the Federal government. Following the war, he resided for some time in Bridgeport, Alabama, where he lived for the remaining years of his life. However, his death occurred in Lauderdale county where he is said to be buried in an unmarked grave.[11]

"Mountain" Tom Clark was the most feared of all the Tories. His full name was Thomas M. Clark. Sometimes he went by the name of "Bill Woods." He grew up near the home of Elias Thrasher on the Chisholm Highway near the Jacksonburg community. These two were closely associated in a number of crimes committed in the local area.

There were two Tom Clarks in this neighborhood. They were both given nicknames for identification purposes. Tom Clark, the Tory criminal, was called "Mountain Tom." His neighbor was known as "Chinubee." The term "Mountain" denoted Clark's birthplace in the mountains of East Tennessee.

The full extent of the atrocities committed by Clark and his men will probably never be known. At the time of his hanging, Clark confessed to having murdered eighteen people plus a small infant.[12] The most often repeated story about his crimes involved the murders of John and Matthew Wilson.

John W. Wilson, along with his brothers Samuel and Matthew, were prosperous planters of Lauderdale County. The plantations of John and Matthew were later divided into smaller tracts which were sold to German-Catholic immigrants to become the present community of St. Florian. John Wilson's home faced the old Jackson Military Road across from the intersection of the present Church Road in St. Florian.

On Sunday night, April 30, 1865, Wilson's home was raided by members of two Tory gangs – those of Tom Clark and Elias Thrasher. Wilson, an elderly man, was sick in bed. He was being cared for by his grandson, Turner Landers Foster, and nephew,

Matthew Harvey Wilson. The Tories were after money. They slowly burned John Wilson until he died in horrible pain. Matthew was killed outright. The grandson was also shot, but he survived and made his way to the home of Robert M. Patton on the nearby Hough Road.[13]

Two others on the Wilson plantation were shot that night. One was Christopher Brewer, a former slave who had received his freedom from Wilson prior to the war. Brewer, who survived the ordeal, was the maternal grandfather of the famous "Father of the Blues," William Christopher Handy of Florence. The plantation overseer, George Twiddy, also survived his wound. However, on the following day, one of the gang members returned and killed him.

Upon learning that Wilson's grandson had escaped, three members of Clark's gang followed him into Florence where he had taken refuge with his aunt, the wife of John W. McAlister. They were driven off by gunfire. During their attempt to capture Foster, the outlaws fired three shots at Narcissa McAlister who was observed near a window on the second floor of the house.[14]

A number of prominent citizens in the downtown area were also terrorized during this raid. Joseph Milner, a druggist, was stripped and tied to a tree in his front yard. Although severely beaten, he survived to carry the scars as long as he lived. A Jewish merchant, Simon Fortcht, was strung from a tree until forced to tell where his gold was buried in the garden behind his home. Dr. James T. Hargraves, the town's foremost physician, fled from his home before they arrived, but they burned it nevertheless. Among others who were harassed were: William Henry Wade, local builder and millwright, two merchants, Alex W. Falk and James Hancock, and John "Dutch" Kachelman who sold fresh vegetables to the townspeople from his lush gardens on the ancient Indian Mound on South Court Street.

The citizens of Florence were desperate. In February, 1865, they had appealed to the Federal Army stationed at Gravelly Springs for help. Company D, 4th Iowa Cavalry under Captain Abraham Lot was dispatched to capture these renegades.

Although he learned the names of a few of these outlaws, he was only able to capture a straggling soldier of the 9th Indiana Cavalry. This man, who had been stealing and committing other crimes, escaped from Lott's guards to continue his spree of hate in the area.[15]

General Roddey had briefly returned to North Alabama in January, 1865, to protect the people. His depleted command was of little help, although he did execute several bushwhackers under martial law near Moulton.[16]

By May the situation had become so grave that the Federal Army sent detachments into the area in attempts to apprehend the criminals and to restore law and order. One unit was Company H, 6th U. S. Tennessee Cavalry.[17] This was a fortunate assignment. Its commanding officer was Risden D. DeFord who was well acquainted with this place. His father, William, was a Methodist preacher who had served churches in Lauderdale County before the war. A number of individuals were tried and convicted. One of these was Clemens "Clay" Hammond, a son of John and Sarah Hammond who lived near Anderson. Clay received ten years at hard labor "for guerrillaing and robbing."[18] Legend has it that DeFord hanged twenty-one outlaws while in Florence.

The other command sent here was a unit from the 8th Michigan Cavalry under Captain John H. Riggs. The most publicized arrests and executions were made by Captain Riggs.[19] These involved John Campbell and Charles Oliver who were with Tom Clark when John Wilson was tortured and murdered. Campbell was a son of Garric and Ann Campbell, owners of a popular inn on North Court Street known as the Campbell House. Oliver's parents were Daniel and Jane Rose Oliver, Florence residents who were listed in the census as farmers. Testimony against these two Tories indicated that they had committed murder not only for the sake of plunder but for personal gratification as well. Several citizens testified that Campbell and Oliver had raped defenseless women, treating them in a most brutal way when they resisted. A mulatto girl swore that Oliver knocked her down with his pistol and then raped her. She exhibited the bruise on her head which had not healed.[20] Both men were found guilty, after which they confessed to these and other crimes. They were executed by a firing squad commanded by Lieutenants J. S. Cline and Michael Doyle. This occurred under a sweet gum tree on the Jackson Military road just north of where it intersects with Royal Avenue.[21]

In late May, following the expiration of Captain Rigg's assignment, Lieutenant Colonel W. L. Buck was sent to Florence with a task force of 200 men. Thus, with the aid of the U. S. Army, these roving gangs of criminals were subdued as law and order was finally restored throughout the county.

For a number of years following the war, there are accounts of outlaws being apprehended and convicted. In March, 1868, John Garner, described as a "an old villain," was sentenced to prison for five years. A local newspaper, in an article about his trial, closed its story with these words: "... and our citizens are happily rid of a great rascal, for a while at least."[22]

"Mountain" Tom Clark was shot and severely wounded by Lee Howell on October 29, 1866. This occurred at the Baugh Cotton Factory on Shoal Creek near Happy Hollow. Clark had killed Lee's father, Alan Howell, during the war. Clark recovered from this wound. It is believed that he afterwards fled to Jackson County, Alabama, where his family had lived during his youth.[23]

On September 3, 1872, word was received that a number of thieves who had committed robberies in Athens were on their way to Florence. That night they broke into a number of local homes, including several of whom Clark had terrorized in 1865. The following day, these thieves were overtaken on Pettypool Hill, a few miles west of Gravelly Springs by City Marshall William E. Blair and his three deputies: William Barks, William Joiner, and W. B. Warson. Among the three thieves arrested was Tom Clark who was disguised in a woman's dress. One of the others was identified only as "F. R." because of a tattoo on his right arm. The last name of the third thief was listed as Gibson.

These men were returned to Florence and placed in the Lauderdale County jail. As the news of the arrest of Tom Clark spread, a mob appeared at the jail. Around midnight the Sheriff and eight guards were overpowered. The three prisoners were taken by the crowd to a vacant lot on Tombigbee Street between Court and Pine Streets. Here they were hanged from a limb on a sycamore tree.

Not wishing to place these men in the city cemetery, a grave was dug near East Mobile Street across from the cemetery. Here two of Clark's companions were hastily buried. However, at the last minute someone remembered that Clark had once boasted that "no one ever ran over him." According to legend they placed his remains in the middle of East Tennessee Street in front of the main entrance gate to the cemetery. They reasoned that from that time on everyone who passed this way would, in fact, run over "Mountain" Tom Clark.[24] A historical marker now identifies this site. The mere mention that "old Tom Clark will get you" was enough to put fear into the minds of children for many years after his death. The history of the "time of outrage," when blood-thirsty criminals roamed the hills and hollows of Lauderdale County, serves to remind future generations that civilization is indeed built upon the principles of law and order.

18. TIME OF RECONSTRUCTION

"O God ! that bread should be so dear..."
(The Song of the Shirt - Hood)

Mary Ellen Johnson preferred not to talk about it.[1] Her mother, Sarah Catherine McCuan, had been left a widow at war's end. Gathering her young son, three unmarried daughters, along with a widowed daughter and granddaughter, she left what had been a good life on a prosperous Limestone County farm that had been laid waste by Union soldiers to seek work in the Cypress Cotton Mill near Florence. Here, they earned hardly enough to call their daily bread. This for them was the beginning of a period in history known as the Reconstruction. Life for most Alabamians and Southerners would never be the same again.

The word "Reconstruction" identifies the dozen or so years following the Civil War. It was a time when concerted efforts were made by the Radical Republicans in the North to establish their own devised solutions as to certain political, economic, and social problems in the eleven former Confederate states. Attempts were undertaken by Federal authorities to restore these state governments to what the North regarded as a "proper relation" to the Union. Their economic adjustments involved efforts to recondition the Southern economic base from agriculture to one that was to become more dependent upon industrialization. The social reconstruction in the South was centered around the status of the newly freed slaves.

Reconstruction was characterized by hunger and want, political unrest, and reigns of terrorism. Its first two years, 1865 and 1866, have been called "the starving time." Thousands of people, both black and white, were issued rations by the Bureau of Refugees, Freedmen, and Abandoned Lands, known as the Freedmen's Bureau, which was created by the U. S. Congress on March 3, 1865.

Some sources show that between 90,000 and 122,000 Alabama men had enlisted in either the Southern or Northern Army. In 1865, the state's provisional governor estimated that 34,000 of these had either been killed or had died of wounds and that 35,000 soldiers had returned home disabled and helpless. Many of those who survived the war returned to find their homes and farms had been destroyed or severely damaged by invading armies. Millions of dollars worth of property had been burned in Lauderdale County alone.

Though guns were now silenced, there was no treaty and only an uncertain peace. Federal troops were patrolling the streets of cities and small towns.

Defranchised as leaders, the possessions of former officers were made liable for immediate confiscation according to the 1862 Confiscation Act. This congressional action also stipulated that the property of all citizens who had supported the Confederacy was subjected to confiscation on sixty days notice. Fortunately, the enforcement of these rabid measures failed. Yet, even without confiscation, many were forced to sell a part or all of their land.[2] All but a few of the large plantations in Lauderdale County were now either idled or transferred to new owners. In May, 1865, the non-existent civil government was suspended and martial law declared in the state. Major General George H. Thomas, however, issued a decree which affected the counties of North Alabama. Realizing that people had to be fed and their health protected, he allowed civil judges, sheriffs, and administrators to continue in office so as to enforce laws that had been in existence prior to secession.[3]

Most of the factories in Lauderdale County had been destroyed. The economy had been crushed and there was no money or any jobs. Mules and horses needed to plow and plant were almost nonexistent. Some remembered that the only good thing was that after four years of warfare, there were now more squirrels in the forests and more rabbits in the fields; these were regularly hunted so as to supplement their lean supper tables.[4] There were no "foreign aids" for the defeated. Almost one-half of Alabama's population had been slaves before hostilities. There were 475,510 African-Americans living in Alabama in 1870. At the time of their emancipation, they became mostly homeless wanderers seeking food, clothing, shelter, and a place to earn a living. They camped in woods, fields, alongside creeks and springs, and sometimes among the ruins of abandoned plantations and farms. One writer described these shantytowns as being on the outskirts "encircling Florence as a band on a wagon wheel."[5] Such became the beginnings of places such as Petersville, old Hough Town, and West and South Florence.

Major General Oliver Otis Howard was placed over the Freedmen's Bureau, an agency of the War Department, when it was established in 1865. Howard was called one of the great paradoxes of American military history. It was said that no field officer ever equaled his record for surviving so many tactical errors of judgment and disregard of orders. He not only was promoted in rank, Howard was honored on one occasion with the thanks of Congress. He appointed Major General Wager Swayne as his assistant in Alabama.

The Radical Republican Reconstruction movement gained momentum on March 2, 1867, when the first of four major Reconstruction acts were passed. Alabama's twentieth governor, Robert Miller Patton, of Lauderdale County, was removed from office by Federal order in July, 1867. He had been elected in November, 1865.

Ten of the so-called "unreconstructed" states were divided into five military districts commanded by Federal generals. Major General John Pope was appointed commander of the Third Military District, which included Alabama, Georgia, and Florida. He retained Major General Swayne as commander in Alabama. A son of U. S. Supreme Court Justice Noah Haynes Swayne, the General was born in Ohio where his family had moved because of their opposition to slavery in Virginia. Swayne took part in the Battle of Shiloh as a major and served as a colonel under Sherman in his march through Georgia.

Lauderdale County played a major role in the political arena during these first years of Reconstruction. In fact, the first meeting of the freedmen in Northwest Alabama occurred in Florence at the Church Street Church between South Court and South Pine Streets. This congregation is now the Greater St. Paul's African Methodist Episcopal Church located on Cherokee Street. James T. Rapier presided over a meeting at this church on April 24, 1867, to select a voter registrar in accordance with General Swayne's directions. A month later, Rapier called a meeting at the Lauderdale County Courthouse to select a Negro to represent the first Republican Convention.[6] Rapier played leading roles, first in Florence and later in Montgomery, in organizing former slaves and in promoting their civil rights under the new laws enacted by Congress during the Reconstruction Period.

Fortunately, Rapier was present at a rural assembly of former slaves. This occurred at night in the woods close to the Pisgah United Methodist Church near Cloverdale. Two white men from Ohio, Dr. E. R. Yeiser and G. W. Street, called this meeting of several hundred Negroes to organize a secret society. Rapier and his father, John, sensed the potential consequences of such a clandestine movement and quickly moved among the audience urging the Negroes to withdraw. Within a short while more than half of the crowd drifted away. Thus, James and John Rapier were successful in defeating the plans of these two white men which could have led to violence and bloodshed.

Rapier did not escape personal danger. In early September, 1868, the Tuscumbia Female Academy burned to the ground. Rapier and others were blamed for this act. Forewarned by a friend, Alexander DePriest, Rapier fled to Montgomery. This friend was the father of Oscar DePriest who later became a U. S. Congressman in Illinois. The three other suspects – Porter Simpson, Benjamin Cooper, and Jake Bell – were captured and jailed. The next morning ropes were tied around their necks and they were then shoved from a bridge. Here, their lifeless forms were left for almost a week with a note of warning addressed to other African-Americans pinned to their clothing.[7]

James Thomas Rapier was born in Florence in 1837, the son of a free Negro barber who had managed to accumulate both property and money. When James was only four years of age, his mother, Suson, died and was buried alongside her two infant children in the white section of the old Florence Cemetery. James T. Rapier was educated in Nashville and in Buxton, Canada, before returning to Florence to assist others in the transition from slavery to freedom. He helped draft Alabama's 1868 constitution, organized the state's first Negro labor union, and, in 1872, while in Montgomery, was elected to the United States House of Representatives on the Republican ticket.[8]

It is believed that the hanging of Rapier's associates in 1868 was carried out by the Ku Klux Klan. This organization was formed in the South during the period of Reconstruction. The Klan and other secret societies used violence and terrorism to intimidate former slaves as well as leaders among the Radical Republican Reconstruction movement. Numbers of acts of terrorism were said to have been committed by the Klan at the Muscle Shoals. Cabins were invaded and innocent Negroes were whipped, robbed, and murdered.[9] During the 1868 fall presidential campaign, a local white leader, Neander Rice, wrote to James Rapier at Montgomery: "John Gracy was shot badly last Saturday and will probably die...and we had a Negro man killed in this county last week...shot in the nighttime."[10] In November, 1868, a Tuscumbia newspaper reported the assassination of Henry Ellis who had been a neighbor to Rapier in Florence.[11] On November 21, 1868, about 125 men dressed in black sheets rode into Florence astride their horses. At this time they killed one Negro man and hanged three others near the business section of town.[12] The full extent of terrorism in Lauderdale County will probably never be known. Reports of these types of violence caused political reaction throughout the country. On April 20, 1871, the Ku Klux Clan Act was passed by Congress which brought about an increased use of Federal troops throughout the South.

Between 1868 and 1870, the ten remaining Confederate states were readmitted to the Union through the program known as Reconstruction. In 1874, George Smith Houston who had grown up in Gravelly Springs was elected governor of Alabama. This ballot essentially returned the Democratic party to power. Houston sat out the war in Athens. He had opposed secession and was considered a Unionist. At this stage of the Reconstruction era, he was looked upon as the right man at the right time and was elected to serve two terms as governor. For all practical purposes, the Reconstruction era ended during Houston's second term. In 1882, Brigadier General Edward Asbury O'Neal of Florence, a staunch Democrat and Confederate, became the twenty – seventh governor of Alabama. There was now no doubt but that the tides of political activity that had affected the lives of almost every citizen in Alabama had now changed.

One of the few good things that came out of Reconstruction was the emphasis on education for the children of the newly freed African – Americans in the South. From 1866 to 1870, over $3.5 million was allocated by the Freedmen's Bureau for this purpose.[13] This was supplemented by missionary projects of several religious groups as well as by philanthropists such as George Peabody, John F. Slater, John Rockefeller, Anna Jeanes, and Julius Rosenwald.[14] A number of local schools for Negroes can trace their beginnings to these programs during Reconstruction.

Northern passions had begun to cool by 1874. For all practical purposes, the plans of the Radical Republicans to reconstruct the South became less and less a national issue. Things were beginning to happen in Alabama and, especially, in Lauderdale County. The economy began to look up in 1875 when construction started on the second phase of the Muscle Shoals Canal. Jobs were now becoming available for both unemployed whites and freed slaves. Then, a few years prior to the completion of the canal came the East Florence Boom. Some fifty or more industries located in Florence during that industrialization era and the population of the town increased by 500 percent. Reconstruction had now become a bad memory that many did not wish to remember.

19. SWEETWATER

*" ... flowing through a scenic valley between majestic
hills is a clear stream of cold and sweet water."
("A Time To Remember, by the author)*

Sweetwater is the local designation for East Florence. It is named for Sweetwater Creek which flows through it. At the head of this stream is a large spring called "Succotania" by the Cherokee people. Legend has it that this was an Indian word meaning "sweetwater." There were two antebellum tracts of land in East Florence, both named "Sweetwater." One, the plantation of Alabama's twentieth governor, Robert Miller Patton, was located at the head of Sweetwater Creek. The second tract was near the mouth of Sweetwater Creek. This was an industrial site surrounding an early mill owned by Henry Smith who lived on a large plantation known as the "Johnson Place," where the old Natchez Trace crossed the Tennessee River west of Smithsonia in West Lauderdale County. It has been said that Smith at one time owned more land than anyone else in the county. Although the Sweetwater tract was one of his smaller holdings, it later made up most of the business and industrial parts of this section of town. This wealthy man frequently signed his name as "Henry Smith of Sweetwater." In the 1850's, following Smith's death in 1846, this part of his estate was advertised for sale as the "Sweetwater Lands."[1]

Sweetwater Creek was noted in early 1818 land sales as a good place for water-powered mills. Around 1822, one of the first cotton factories at the Muscle Shoals was built here. It was located at the crossing of Huntsville Road over Sweetwater Creek.[2]

The saga of East Florence is not only a study of a unique industrial development of the 19th century, but more importantly, it is a story of a people who lived, worked, shopped, and worshipped in an area where everything was within a convenient walking distance. These workers and their families developed a lifestyle almost as that of the ancient clans of the Celtic lands in the Old

World. They were independent, gentle, and proud. These folk exhibited a strong sense of loyalty to their neighborhood, including where they worked and worshipped as well as with the local merchants who served them.

Sweetwater became the manufacturing section of Florence during the Industrial Revolution that occurred in the United States beginning in the early 1880's. This dramatic growth of industry became, likewise, a time of commercial evolution, especially in the economically depressed South brought about by the Civil War and its aftermath.

Both Florence and Sheffield reaped the benefits of this national expansion of activity. The arrival of this new way of life at Florence between 1887 and 1890 became known as the "East Florence Boom." The seeds for this phenomenon can be traced to a visit in 1881 by C. Eugene Gordon, member of a railroad syndicate. Gordon made an effort to organize the property owners so as to make sufficient land available for future development at reasonable prices.[3] Later, Gordon and his brother, Colonel Walter S. Gordon, were successful in organizing the Sheffield Land, Iron, and Coal Company for the purpose of founding the city of Sheffield.[4] Two years following Gordon's visit to Florence, Captain Alfred H. Moses of Montgomery was given a tour of the north side of the river by Judge William B. Wood and George P. Keys. Moses' interest stemmed from publicity regarding a proposed railroad that would run from Paducah, Kentucky, to other key cities in the southeast. Plans called for its main line to pass through Florence, Alabama.

While at the Muscle Shoals, Moses was invited by Colonel Gordon to see what was being planned for the future town of Sheffield. This impressed Moses so much that he advised his firm, Moses Brothers Bank of Montgomery, to make investments there. Captain Alfred H. Moses became one of the primary developers of Sheffield as well as its first mayor.[5]

The business leaders of Florence, headed by Judge William Basil Wood, now devised a plan to bring new industry to Florence. Eugene Gordon was invited back to the city. He soon became the man behind the scene in the development of East Florence. It was said that he was the prime mover in securing large financial investments from other sections of the country. At his suggestion, The Florence Land, Mining, and Manufacturing Company was organized, with Judge Wood as its chairman. In this role, Wood became a key player in the industrial revolution that made its way to East Florence in 1887.[6] Wood Avenue near downtown Florence was named for this popular son of the town's first mayor. W. B. Wood was also a judge, Methodist preacher, and former colonel in the Confederate Army. One of the original members of the board of directors, Mason B. Shelton, a local merchant, made this observation soon after things began to happen in East Florence: "New industrial plants began to erect their buildings and in a short time the wheels of progress began to wake up the sleeping echoes and Florence was on the boom."[7]

One of the first industries to locate in Sweetwater was the Philadelphia Furnace. Originally the W. B. Wood Furnace, it was built by Judge Wood and others on Sweetwater Creek just south of present Veterans Drive. John W. Norton of Pennsylvania was employed as its manager. This furnace had a capacity of 45,000 tons of product a year. Its workers lived in a company-owned village along Veterans Drive and Aetna Street. A large two-story brick commissary served these families. Iron ore was mined in nearby Tennessee counties and coal came from the foothills of North Alabama. This iron furnace was incorporated by the Florence Cotton and Iron Company in 1889. In 1899 it was sold to the Sheffield Steel and Iron Company and upgraded to a production rate of 70,000 tons a year. It remained in operation until 1926. Another iron industry, the North Alabama Furnace, was opened in 1889, and sold the following year to the Spathite Iron Company. Located alongside the old Muscle Shoals Canal, its production capacity was listed at 39,000 tons of pig iron a year.

This plant was not competitive and was shut down in the spring of 1895. The town boasted a third furnace, known as " The Little Lady." It was located on South Wood Avenue.

The Foundry, which processed the pig iron produced at the furnaces, was brought to Florence by Henry W. Theole from Evansville, Indiana, in 1888. He employed John Smith as manager. Thomas J. Phillips, native of Lexington, Alabama, owned an interest in The Foundry as well as in a number of other early Sweetwater enterprises. Known in its first years as the Florence Stove Foundry, it produced stoves, heaters, wash pots, skillets, sad irons for pressing clothes, and dog irons for fireplaces.[8] At one period of time state prisoners were used in this operation. There was a row of company-owned red frame houses for the workers south of The Foundry called the "Theole Row." This industry has survived for more than a hundred years. In the late 1990's it is identified as an independent casting producer for original equipment manufacturers, with the late A. R. Tomlinson as its chief executive officer. In 1987 its annual payroll was $1.5 million with sales amounting to $5 million.

Alongside the railroad tracks in Sweetwater was the Florence Machine Company that advertised its capital investment at $ 10,000. Its officers were: R. M. Martin, President, N. F. Cherry, Vice-President, and S. S. Broadus, Secretary and Treasurer.

The popular wagons produced by the Florence Wagon Works made the name "Florence" a household word across many sections of the nation, especially in Texas and other western states. This industry was moved from Atlanta, Georgia, in 1889 by Dr. A. D. Bellamy. One of his reasons for relocating here was to be closer to the large hardwood forests in North Alabama. At its peak it employed 175 people and had a capacity of 15,000 wagons annually. Its yearly payroll amounted to $120,000, and it was estimated that some $300,000 in goods and services were added to the local economy each year. It became the second largest producer of wagons on this continent, second only to Studebaker. Among its original officers were: Dr. Bellamy, A. B. Mason, E. Lyon, E. M. Vestal, and Cliff Hallman. Hallman, who supervised the workers, lived in a large two-story company-owned Victorian house near the factory. T. B. Ingram and E. A. Melling were traveling salesmen.

In 1910, Samuel C. Harlan, who was born about 1873 near Columbia, Tennessee, was appointed Vice-President and General Manager of the Florence Wagon Works. He was later elevated to the office of President. Under his management the business expanded and Florence wagons were exported to other countries. Harlan remained with the company for nearly thirty years. For some twelve years he served the city as its Commissioner of Finance. The Harlan School in North Florence was named for him. One of Sam Harlan's daughters, Anne, was married to Major General William R. Calhoun. Harlan's youngest daughter, Josephine, was married to Kenneth C. Darby of Florence. Florence banker, Nial C. Elting, who at one time or another was associated with a number of major East Florence industries, became affiliated with the Florence Wagon Works. Other later executives were: E. R. Carter, Mrs. E. R. Carter, Percy R. Jones, William I. Collier, E. W. Henley, and Luther Baker. Dave Beadle, who lived near the factory, assisted Sam Harlan in the supervision of the workers. Horace Kerby was head of the paint department and Alonzo Lindsey was in charge of the wheel shop.

Near the wagon factory was Mooloosa Spring. The origin of its name, pronounced as "Moo-loo-sa," is believed to have been of the Cherokee language. It was located south of Phoenix Avenue toward the river and between Main and Patton Streets. The drinking water for the wagon factory employees was carried from this spring by young boys who were fitted with padded yokes across their shoulders. Shaler Roberts, Senior, who later became one of Florence's most beloved physicians, often spoke of his days as one of these water boys. The factory built a latticed house over this spring and paved its floor with flagstones. Two benches near this structure were carved from large stones removed from the hillside above the springs. The surrounding grounds were used as a local park and as a meeting place for young people. It was said that the Cherokee people valued this spring for its mineral water. Two physicians, Lee Duckett and William Bramlett, prescribed its use for patients. Around 1900, its water was bottled and sold in Florence and nearby towns for its health value.

There were a number of other industries associated with the local forests. Dr. A. D. Bellamy established the Bellamy Planing Mills on May 25, 1901. It was later purchased by Lewellen and Robbins and renamed the Acme Lumber Company, with William McDonald Richardson as manager. A. M. Lewellen had moved his family to this area by flatboat down the Tennessee River. Richardson later established Richardson Lumber Company alongside Sweetwater Creek on Huntsville Road between Sweetwater Avenue and Minnehaha Street. This had been the former location of the Florence Planing Mill and Manufacturing Company. Richardson eventually moved his lumber business to East Tennessee Street closer to downtown Florence. The W. E. Temple Company and Planing Mills on College Street were owned by William E. Temple who came here from Virginia. He constructed a number of buildings in the area, including the 1901 courthouse and the 1903 Florence First United Methodist Church which burned in 1920. His former home, located on North Poplar Street near Our Redeemer Lutheran Church, was restored in 1996. The Temples moved to Hopewell, Virginia, in 1914. The Florence Lumber Company on East Tennessee, continues as one of the early lumber businesses. Uhland O. Redd III, a descendant of one of its founders, is the chief executive officer in 1997. The R. A. Stricklin Lumber Company's address was at 203 South Chestnut Street, which is now the modern entrance to the Florence Cemetery. The Iowa Land and Lumber Company was on Central and Commerce Streets in East Florence. The Leftwich and Benningfield Saw Mill was near the river on Enterprise Street.

Alabama Stave Factory, located near the railroad tracks, produced nine million barrel staves a year with an employment of eighty men. The Biglow Stave Mill produced white oak staves used in whiskey barrels. The Hudson and Bollinger Manufacturing Company was a planing mill. It was located alongside the L&N railroad tracks at the intersection of Commerce and Limestone Streets. There were also the nearby Florence Stave Company and the McGregor Stave Factory. The Nichols Shingle Mills produced 40,000 shingles a day.

The Florence Pump and Lumber Company was located at the corner of Marietta Street and Vulcan Avenue prior to 1894. It produced 350 boxcars of wooden pumps and special work annually. Later, a pump made from cast iron was produced by the local Dempastry Pump Factory. The Florence Furniture Company was located on the bank of Sweetwater Creek on Aetna Street. Next to it was the Wofford Oil Company. The Florence Wooden Ware Works manufactured wooden dishes. It was located on Terrace Street between Sycamore and Plum Streets. The Bennie Bucket Factory faced Enterprise Street near the river. Next door was the Florence Suspender Factory. At one time there was a pencil factory in this part of town.

The boom days restored Florence to its antebellum status as a "cotton mill town." Several large cotton factories had operated in the city and county prior to their destruction during the Civil War. One of the three Globe Factories was rebuilt after the war and operated about twenty years as the Cypress Mill. However, in 1889, all interests in this plant were sold. Much of its machinery and most of its workers were moved to Mountain Mills, south of Barton in Colbert County. In 1893 the owners, Colonel Noel F. Cherry and his brother, W. H. Cherry, relocated Mountain Mills to East Florence where it became the Cherry Cotton Mill. Most of its machinery and employees came along with the factory. So, an "industrial genealogy" traces the roots of the East Florence Cherry Cotton Mill to the pre-Civil War Globe Cotton Factory on Cypress Creek near North Florence by way of the Mountain Mills in Colbert County.[9] The Cherry Cotton Mill began operation in August, 1893. Colonel Cherry was its first chief executive officer. He was followed by Nial C. Elting from Ellensville, New York. Charles M. Brandon was superintendent of the mill, the same office he had held at Mountain Mills. One of the later superintendents was Miles W. Darby who was an officer in the mill for forty-four years. By 1903 this factory had a capacity of 12,000 spindles, and employed some 400 workers classified as spinners, spoolers, twisters, twilters, reelers, doffers, and sweepers. An April 1898 pay record lists a scale of wages ranging from 15 cents to 75 cents a day for most of the workers. Mechanics and other skilled craftsmen received from

$1.00 to $1.50 a day. John Holt was listed as a master mechanic at $1.50 a day. The highest wage was that of Franklin P. Johnson at $2.00 a day. Classified as a supervisor, Johnson had worked at the Cypress Mill, Mountain Mills, and Cherry Mill. He died in 1926 at the age of 72 years. Children as young as six years of age were employed. Many of its workers were ladies who, along with the children, received the lowest of the wages paid. In 1936 the officers were: Jewell T. Flagg, President, Miles W. Darby, Vice-President, Sam C. Harlan, Treasurer, and Frank Longcrier, Assistant Treasurer. From 1893 until 1929 approximately 150,000 bales of cotton were consumed, most of which was grown locally. Sadly, this major cotton mill in East Florence was not able to survive its mounting labor problems and the Great Depression.

The Ashcraft Cotton Mill, located near the intersection of South Cherry and Terrace Streets began as an Ashcraft family enterprise consisting of John T., C. W., Lee, Erister, and Fletcher. Their father, Andrew J. Ashcraft, was also with this business until his death in 1903. This factory which boasted 3,600 spindles and 100 looms was formed in 1899. It was expanded in 1903, boosting its employment to 250 men and women. C. W. Ashcraft was president in 1912. His brother, John T., was vice-president and secretary. Fred Moore served many years as an executive officer. In 1927 its name was changed to Florence Cotton Mill. Nine years later the average wage was $15 a week. Four thousand bales of cotton were consumed annually. Its finished products were shipped all over the United States and Canada. This factory survived the Great Depression, yet was not able to compete with the foreign textile industries following the end of World War II. The Ashcrafts also owned the Florence Cotton Oil Mill and the Ashcraft Roundlap Bale Ginnery. The 1928 phone book indicates that the Florence Seed and Gin Company was located in this general area.

There was a short-lived cotton factory, called Broadus Mill, near where present Veterans Drive intersects with Wilson Dam Road. This area became known as "Old Cotton Factory Hill." S. S. Broadus was its chief executive officer. He also served as treasurer of the Merchant's Bank in Florence. The papers of

Franklin P. Johnson, a supervisor at the Cherry Cotton Mill, show that he was also a consultant for the Broadus Cotton Mill.[10]

The Gardiner-Warring Knitting Company moved here from Utica , New York, in 1927. This came about as a result of a local committee investing in a building and then seeking an industry to move here. Its first manager, Jewett T. Flagg, eventually became its principal stockholder at which time its name was changed to the J. T. Flagg Knitting Company. During the Great Depression this was one of the few large industries in North Alabama to keep its doors open. Following World War II some of the operations were shifted to the former Cherry Cotton Mill facilities under the name of Sweetwater Mills. Around 1969, the J. T. Flagg Knitting Mill was purchased by Genesco of Nashville. Later, most of the local business was transferred to the Florence Industrial Park, north of town. In the late 1970's, after more than fifty years of operation, this once proud East Florence textile plant closed its doors forever.[11]

An advertisement of the 1900's lists the Tennessee Valley Fertilizer Company on Cherry Street with a capacity of 7,500 tons annually. The International Mineral Corporation's oldest continuously operating plant of the 1990's is a part of East Florence. A flourmill was located at this site prior to the Civil War. Its three-story building was acquired in 1897 by Lee Ashcraft who established the Florence Fertilizer Company. This fertilizer plant was purchased by the International Mineral Corporation in 1909. Nearby on the east bank of Sweetwater Creek was The Coleman Cotton Gin and Cleaner Works. Its large complex included a mechanical and engineering section, machine shop, wood shop, and a manufacturing department. In this area was the 1894 Sweetwater Shoe Company which later became the Snyder Shoe Factory. Next to the shoe factory was the Farmers Alliance Cotton Bagging Factory which was closed sometime prior to 1928. Also nearby, was a large building which housed a business known as Wholesale Drugs as early as 1894. A shed for horses was a part of this complex. The F. H. Foster Manufacturing Company had five large buildings alongside the L&N railroad tracks near both

Sweetwater Creek and the Tennessee River; these structures included an iron foundry, a brass foundry, a wood tumbling and Japan room, a working area, and a packing and machine room. Next door to this company was located The Florence Compress, Packet, Ferry and Transfer Company with its water line feeding from the river.

During the late 1920's the Texas Oil Company was located on present Veterans Drive and the Standard Oil Company was on Terrace Street. Nearby was the Walker-Darby Gin. A manufacturer of cotton gins, The Curry Manufacturing Company, was situated alongside the river between Trade and Enterprise Streets. The Florence Milling Company produced 200 barrels of flour a day. The Muscle Shoals Oil Company was on Sweetwater Avenue. Prior to 1894, the Florence Canning Company was at the intersection of Ironside Street and Vulcan Avenue. The Florence Soap Works was also one of these East Hill factories. Alongside Sweetwater Creek near the Huntsville Road was the Chapin Ice and Coal Company which advertised its ability to produce 25 tons of ice a day. In 1902 it united with the H. J. Moore Coal Company to become the Florence Ice and Coal Company. In 1928 it was listed as the Central Ice Company. The Sam Bruce Coal Company was located on Sweetwater Avenue near the Cherry Cotton Mill. The Alabama Coal Mining Company was in East Florence during the 1920's. J. J. Veid established the Florence Steam Laundry on the west bank of Sweetwater Creek near the Huntsville Road. Leslie Hall, a former foreman in the laundry, joined with Harry Harper to form the H & H Dry Cleaning Service in the back of this laundry building.

The Florence Gas Light and Fuel Company, which at one time was known as the Florence Gas Works, operated west of the Florence Steam Laundry near the Old Huntsville Road. This plant, with its main office in Cincinnati, Ohio, organized its Florence plant in 1902, with its first production occurring in March, 1903. The local plant manager was W. James Salter. Approximately 75,000 cubic feet of gas a day was produced for lighting, heating, and cooking purposes. The rates were $2.00 a thousand cubic feet for lighting and $4.50 per thousand cubic feet for heating or cooking. In 1928 it was listed as the Muscle Shoals Gas Company.

As early as 1894, there was a Campbell and Company Electric Light Plant located near Sycamore Street. It operated with two 40 arc light dynamos and one incandescent generator until midnight each day at which time these facilities were shut down until the next morning. Later, the Florence Electric Light and Power Company supplied the city's electricity. At one period prior to the building of Wilson Dam, the power for Florence was purchased from an electric generating plant across the river known as the Sheffield Company. One of the most successful of the Sweetwater businesses was the Pride of Dixie Syrup Company established in 1927 by W. L. Craft in the Weeden Heights area. It later was moved to Sheffield, Alabama, and Bono, Arkansas, to become a national syrup maker.[12]

Altogether, approximately fifty plants, mills, and factories were located in East Florence during the boom years. One reporter observed that these industries stretched some two miles along the north bank of the Tennessee River.[13]

A number of religious faiths were located at one time or another in Sweetwater. The Saint James United Methodist Church was organized in the fall of 1894 by the Reverend Henry L. Booth. There were thirty charter members, many of whom had letters from the Mountain Mills Church. Their original meeting place was on the Huntsville Road before members purchased land and erected a sanctuary on Sweetwater Avenue. Almost a hundred years later this congregation relocated to Cox Creek Parkway. Saint James traces its roots to an antebellum congregation that was a part of the Globe Cotton Mill village on Cypress Creek.

The Central Baptist Church at the corner of the Old Huntsville Road and Aetna Street was organized as the East Florence Baptist Mission in 1896 by the Reverend R. E. Paulk, a county missionary. Originally there were 53 members who met at Aetna Street and Central Avenue. The name was changed to Central Baptist Church in 1919.

The East Florence Church of Christ had its beginning in the home of Laura Ann Robinett and her sister, Sara Jane Robinett, on Minnehaha Street sometime around 1897. The home of Hiram Brewer was also used as a meeting place. The congregation later worshipped in a building that was a part of the Florence Pump and Lumber Company, known locally as the "column factory," which was located near the river between Industry and Marietta Streets. A number of its early members had been affiliated with the Mountain Mills Church of Christ in Colbert County. Following the relocation of this cotton mill to Sweetwater in 1893 – and prior to 1897 – these people walked to the downtown area of Florence to attend the Poplar Street Church of Christ. The first permanent place of worship for the East Florence Church was at the crest of a high hill facing Huntsville Road on the corner of Ironside and Woodard Streets. This frame building was completed in December 1899. C. E. Holt and J. T. Harris were leaders in the organization of this Church. Holt was from Iron City, Tennessee. Two hundred and nine new members were added to the roll in 1900 under the evangelist J. J. Castleberry. In the early 1950's, a new meetinghouse was built on Huntsville Road; this was at the foot of the hill below the earlier frame building.[14] It is a brick structure.

The First Freewill Baptist Church on Florence Boulevard was established as the East Florence Freewill Baptist Church on December 20, 1903, at what is now the intersection of Sweetwater Avenue and Branch Street. Its first pastor was the Reverend G. W. Mitchell. In 1944 a new place of worship was constructed at the intersection of Sweetwater Avenue and Stevenson Street under the ministry of the Reverend E. P. Roden. This congregation later relocated to Florence Boulevard where the opening service was celebrated on May I, 1966.

Faith Tabernacle on Florence Boulevard had its beginnings in a women's prayer meeting on Cherry Hill during the mid 1930's. Its first pastor, the Reverend Cicero P. Melton, began holding preaching services about 1936 under a tall water storage tower near his home. About a year later he erected a small frame-meeting house at 1225 Iowa Street. In 1959 a larger concrete block structure was built at 330 Thompson Street. In 1977 a new and expanded facility was erected next door under the ministry of the Reverend Henry Melton, a son of the first pastor. In May, 1983, the Faith Tabernacle Church was relocated to Florence Boulevard east of Florence.[15] It is now one of the city's largest congregations.

The East Florence Presbyterian Church was established as a mission by the First Presbyterian Church in Florence during the 1890's. Its last service was held in 1923 at which time its facilities were purchased by the Northern Methodist Church. Later the building was torn down and its materials used for a dwelling. On Commerce Street near the railroad tracks was the East Florence Cumberland Presbyterian Church.

The Salvation Army was first located north of the East Florence Drug Store on Royal Avenue. Its modern location is at the intersection of Minnehaha Street and the Old Huntsville Road.

The site of Florence's First Nazarene Church was at the intersection of East Tennessee Street and Royal Avenue. Two African-American churches were located at Pine Ridge, an area of East Hill. One was a Baptist and the other a Methodist.

The Saint Joseph Catholic Church, located on Laughton Heights, began meeting in private homes in 1879. Its first parish was built some ten years later. This area is now called "Catholic Hill."

The early business district of East Florence centered around the drug store and the traffic circle on the Old Huntsville Road. The drug store occupied the west corner of a large brick complex with three storefronts. Erected in 1894, this landmark continues to serve the public more than a hundred years later. The Charles A. Sullivan Drug Store was the first apothecary to be established here, although an earlier one was located in the Theole Row, south of The Foundry. W. H. Cromwell, a Court Street pharmacist, later acquired the Sullivan Drug Store. Cromwell, along with two partners, W. T. Callahan, and M. S. Dalton, were proprietors in the East Florence Livery and Grocery. The N. J. Callahan Livery was also in Sweetwater. Colonel Henry Cromwell was the second generation of his family to operate this East Florence pharmacy. He commanded the local national guard unit during its active service in World War II and the Korean War. Leslie Hall became the next proprietor of this popular drug store. He was succeeded by John Landers. G. M. Mackey's Drug Store was located on the Old Huntsville Road during the 1920's.

Across from the Cromwell Drug Store was the Thomas J. Phillips General Merchandise. He advertised dry goods, notions, clothing, hats, boots, shoes, groceries, flour, salt, hay, and corn. He became president of the nearby East Florence Bank which was established during World War I. Phillips' large Victorian mansion on the hill above the drug store is one of the landmarks of the 1990's. Near this area was the Furlton, Carter and Company Grocery Store.

Hill Auto Company, owned by Fred A. Hill, was on the west side of the traffic circle. This business was said to have been the second automobile service station in Florence. Hill's father, Augustus Henry Hill, is believed to have been Florence's first plumber. Rube Martin was proprietor of a grocery next door to the Hill Auto Company. There was at one time a movie house in this building. Martin and Hill were in the barber business together in 1900. According to family stories, they were the first white barbers in East Florence.[16] E. M. Young's Shoe Shop was near the traffic circle. His son-in-law, Howard Darby, later relocated it to the business area east of the traffic circle.

R. H. Wilson and A. A. Stults operated a grocery on Royal Avenue northwest of the traffic circle. This was the beginning of Wilson Food Center which expanded to North and West Florence.

Alongside the old Huntsville Road east of the traffic circle were a number of businesses. Clay Reynolds had a grocery in a frame building. He was a son of Thomas H. Reynolds, an early merchant and postmaster in East Florence. Before moving to Sweetwater, Thomas H. Reynolds operated a general store at Pruitton. He was a son of Hugh Riah (Uriah) Reynolds of Pruitton who was a son of Hamilton Reynolds, a Revolutionary War veteran who settled near the old Savannah Ford on Shoal Creek. Clay

Renolds kept 300 head of goats on one of the seven hills of East Florence which became known as "Billy Goat Hill." The other hills of Sweetwater were called Cherry Hill, East Hill, Catholic Hill, Chestnut Hill, Granburg Hill, and Old Cotton Factory Hill. M. L. and C. W. Mitchell from Colbert County erected a two story brick building on the Huntsville Road in 1897 for their Mitchell Brothers General Merchandise Store. Taylor Wiley opened a butcher shop in this area. His son-in-law, Lester D. Staggs, Senior, moved this meat market and grocery nearer to the L&N Railroad Depot. In 1997 this business is operated as a cafe by William Staggs, a son of Lester D. Staggs, Senior. West of this store was a cafe operated by Jesse W. McDonald and his son Ervin. In 1900 A. A. Harrison's Bright Star Restaurant was located in this area. Several doors west of the McDonald Cafe was Nick's Barber Shop. Its barbers were G. C. Nichols and Thomas Benton. Earlier, this was the C. O. Baker Barber Shop. As late as 1963, a haircut at Nichols was billed at $1.50.[17]

In 1900 the C. J. Holland Barber Shop was near this location. Miss Vesta Hager's Milliner Store was in this area. Mary Snow had a beauty parlor on both sides of the Huntsville Road at various times. W. A. Kilburn's Grocery and J. M. Kilburn's Saloon were nearby. John Hall's Grocery and D. L. Garrett's Grocery were in this area. J. A. McKenney's General Merchandise was located nearby in 1900. G. S. Mitchell's General Store on Park Street, south of the business district, served the Ashcraft Mill Village.

Paul Tucker ran a cafe and taxi stand next to the passenger depot of the Louisville and Nashville Railroad. His covered porch served as an unofficial waiting station for the streetcar which made its way to Sweetwater from Tuscumbia by way of Sheffield and Florence.

The Piggly Wiggly, managed by Lawrence Ramsey, was located east of the East Florence Drug Store. The second floor of this building complex was a hotel for men who worked on the railroads. They would often arrive by train, spend the night, then leave on departing trains the next day. This may have been the Hager House listed in the 1900 city directory. Charles Holt,

Chester Spann, and Roy Price were partners in the nearby H & P Market. On the second floor of this building was the medical office of Dr. G. W. Olive. Dr. P. I. Price was another physician. Other merchants in 1900 were: Threet and Darby's Grocery and S. P. Williams' Meat Market.

East of the railroad tracks were other businesses. The Houston M. Ramsey Grocery was near the intersection of Old Huntsville Road and Sweetwater Avenue. Established in 1893, his two sons, Odie and Lawrence, operated it until the early 1950's when they sold it to William C. "Jay" Carter. Next-door was the grocery of Leonard Lindsey who came to Florence around 1900 from Manbone Creek near Waterloo. Lindsey's five sons – Carlos, Nelson, Howard, Marvin, and Claud – worked in the store. Next to Lindsey's was the Homer Rickard Grocery. All three of his sons – James "Dusty", Thomas, and Nathan – were affiliated with this business. The Big Nickel Restaurant and Taxi Stand, owned by Bill and Cecil Potts, was located nearby. Later, there were other restaurants in this section of East Florence: Will Porter's Cafe, Carl Gray's Cafe, Lucille's Cafe, and Killen's Cafe. The latter was owned by Willie Killen. One of his sons, Buddy Killen, became a popular music producer in Nashville, Tennessee. During the pre-World War I era a favorite loafing place for men and boys was the Fulton Cafe. Frank Rickard's Cafe was east of Cherry Cotton Mill. The W. H. Holt Grocery and Webb Staggs' Grocery were in front of this mill.

William M. Matthews opened a grocery next door to Ramsey Store in 1906. It was later relocated to the intersection of Minnehaha Street and the Huntsville Road near the foot of Granburg Hill. This had been the 1890 location for the proposed East Florence Opera. The Granburg and McMorray Saloon was near this intersection. Matthews, native of Lexington, Alabama, was a former professor at the State Normal College. His store featured a "Mint Fountain" which served a mixture of carbonated water with Coca-Cola and lemon, grape, and orange juices.[18] Across the highway near Aetna Street was the Spread Eagle Saloon. Next to it was the Silver Moon Restaurant owned by J. S.

Stafford. In 1930 the A & T. W. Stafford Grocery was in this era. Later, W. O. Goodwin established a grocery store in the former Grimes store building. Afterwards, he moved across the road to the Matthews building. Goodwin eventually relocated his store to the area of Weeden Heights.

James and Harriet Kiddy operated a hotel called the Kiddy House on Aetna Street south of the Matthews Store. They later relocated it to East Hill near Blair, Connor, and Cole Streets where it was eventually sold to the Beckman family. One lady who lived as a child in one of its apartments recalled that the drinking water for the guests came from Arnett Spring. She wrote: "I remember there were pine trees all the way down the hill. A lot of people went to the spring to do their laundry."[19] Around 1927 the F. G. Turner Service Station and Grocery was located on Kirkman Street.

In addition to a number of other groceries, there were wholesale houses in East Florence. The J. T. Fargason Wholesale Tobacco and Cigar Company was on the Huntsville Road. The W. B. Simmons Company was on the Huntsville Road between two sections of railroad tracks. The Bob Dabney Wholesale Company was at the intersection of the Huntsville Road and Sweetwater Avenue.

In 1888 a railroad spur was extended to East Florence to encourage the location of new industry in this area. However, following the big fire at the Florence Passenger Station on South Court Street in 1906, the decision was made to relocate this depot to Sweetwater. This railroad connected with the major trunk line that ran through Sheffield and Tuscumbia which eventually became a part of the Southern Railroad System. In that same year tracks were completed from Columbia, Tennessee, to East Florence which soon became the Louisville and Nashville Railroad. For many years these two lines into Sweetwater served Florence and the surrounding area.

A strange silence now prevails where once there were sounds of turning machinery, railroad car switching, and cotton mill whistles. The last of the big boom days vanished before the coming of the twentieth century. However, a number of its plants and factories continued in operation until the Great Depression. A few lingered until the beginning of World War II. Even the tall smokestacks that once silhouetted the skyline have disappeared. Descendants of those who lived and worked here have been uprooted and many live in distant places. Yet, large numbers of these people return each year for what is called the Sweetwater Reunion.

Their story is far more than a history of the industrialization of a town, it is a study of a people and their legacy.

20. NORTH FLORENCE

"...North Florence has always had an identity of its own."
(A History of Lauderdale County,
by Jill Knight Garrett)

North Florence came to life around the junction of three major roads into Florence – Jackson, Cloverdale, and Chisholm Roads. Jackson Road was named for James Jackson in that it passed by his Forks of Cypress Plantation. In pioneer times this was a major route into Florence from Savannah, Tennessee. Cloverdale Road, known originally as Coffee Road, connected with General John Coffee's Hickory Hill Plantation. From there it ran north to Cloverdale to join the Natchez Trace near Cypress Inn, Tennessee. Chisholm Road followed the route of several earlier trails which led northward into the area of Waynesboro, Tennessee. About the time North Florence was developed, four city streets united with these roads at this same intersection. They are: East Royal and West Royal Avenues, Howell Street, and Wills Avenue. Thus, "Seven Points" became a popular synonym for North Florence. Another early name was "Needmore." One story is that for a number of years after North Florence became a community, one of its early merchants was often heard to complain that "we need more people here." This led to the young men of North Florence jokingly calling it "Needmore."[1]

Ferdinand Sannoner's 1818 plans for the town included a Circular Road around Florence. The northern segment of Circular Road intersects with North Wood Avenue at the north boundary of the University of North Alabama campus. It originally continued eastward across this intersection along what is now Nellie Avenue and Grady Liles Drive to Royal Avenue. During the Civil War large breastworks were dug along Circular Drive near this intersection, although they no longer exist.

When Florence was incorporated in 1826, its corporate limits followed Poplar Street to its intersection with the Military Road (present Hermitage Drive), then curved southwestwardly around the town.[2] Prior to 1900 there were few residences north of this corporate limit. Benjamin F. Foster's antebellum home was east of North Wood Avenue between Nellie Avenue and Hawthorne Street.

This large estate was used as a federal camp during the Civil War. An early industrialist, Benjamin was a brother to George W. Foster who owned the nearby Courtview mansion. Northeast of this place is the Malone House on what is now Hawthorne Street. Some historians think that a part of this house was built around 1832 by the Reverend Mitchell Malone, planter and Methodist preacher. It was used as a military hospital by General Don Carlos Buell when he occupied Florence in the summer of 1862.

Across from Benjamin Foster's home on North Wood Avenue is the Jonesboro Place, now known as the J. J. Mitchell Place. This house, built in the 1830s, was originally on a thirty-acre tract. In 1872, Miss Susan Leigh, a former matron of the Florence Synodical College, conducted a private school here.

The Duckett farm was located adjacent to the present North Florence business district. It was later carved into subdivisions. The Ducketts were early settlers from Newberry County, South Carolina. Dr. Lee Fowler Duckett, Senior, was a county physician for more than forty years. His son, L. F. Duckett, Junior, began his medical practice in Florence in 1901. His office was located on the second floor of the North Florence Drug Store along with the medical office of Dr. William B. Turner. In 1928 another physician, Dr. Arnold Jolly, was located on North Wood Avenue.[3]

Although the beginning of North Florence is associated with the early days of the twentieth century, one section alongside Cypress Creek, west of the business district, dates back to a much earlier period. Here stood the Cypress Cotton Mills – established in 1839 and destroyed by the Union Army in 1863. Following the war, one of the mills was rebuilt and remained in operation for about twenty more years. The mill employees lived in two company-owned villages with the main one located at the west end of Cypress Mill Road. A church, school, and commissary were located in this community. The smaller village was on the south side of the Waterloo Road at the location of the modern Wildwood on Cypress subdivision. These two villages were connected by a foot bridge.[4] The original homes of two of the mill owners, James Martin and Levi Cassity, are twentieth century landmarks on Cypress Mill Road.[5]

A scenic feature of North Florence is the nearby Wildwood Park which originally was called "Vineyard Spring," and later "Wildwood Dell." This was once a part of a farm owned by Dr. James W. Stewart a local physician. During antebellum times his home was on the hill near the present Dixie Avenue overlooking Vineyard Spring. The hillside was planted in grapes. The winepress was near the modern Sherrod Avenue Church of Christ. The Stewart farm also included the heights where the present Mitchell-Hollingsworth Annex is located. The valley below this hill is known as Stewart Spring Hollow. Large Civil War earthworks were erected near Dr. Stewart's home as part of the early defense of Florence. These large breastworks ran from the Waterloo Road to a point near Dixie Avenue.[6]

Following the terrible Yellow Fever Epidemic of 1878, an infirmary called the "Pest House" was established on a hillside near the intersection of Wildwood Park Road and the Old Waterloo Road. People with contagious diseases were cared for in this isolated place surrounded by deep woods. A number of its patients were buried in its nearby abandoned cemetery.

On July 7, 1899, the city authorized the purchase of 208 acres of the old Stewart farm for $2,080.[7] The town fathers had planned for its use as a cemetery. However, they were persuaded by the townspeople to enlarge the Florence Cemetery rather than to establish a second burial place. During the early history of North Florence, Wildwood Park was a popular picnic area. The large Vineyard Spring, located near the middle of Wildwood Park Road, was its centerpiece and a meeting place for young people.

In 1891 the Southern Baptist Female University, which in 1908 became the Florence University for Women, opened its doors at the intersection of Seymore Street and Sherrod Avenue. Unfortunately, it burned on March 2, 1911, depriving North Florence of one of its most prized institutions.

Across from the former site of the Florence University for Women is a landmark that dates from the late nineteenth century – the early water tower located on the highest elevation in the city. Listed on the National Register of Historic Places, this tower was completed in October 1890 as part of the new system to supply water to Florence from near the confluence of Cypress and Cox Creeks.[8]

A brick plant in North Florence was built during this time. Clay for the bricks was mined in large pits located in an area between Simpson Street and the L&N Railroad tracks.

The decade of the 1880's brought about many changes to Florence. Its population grew from approximately 2,000 in 1887 to more than 6,000 by January 1, 1889. East Florence was booming as the new industrial section of town. Local building supplies could hardly keep up with construction activities. The need for more housing units was increasing. The city limits on the north side of town were expanded some two miles from the downtown business district.[9] Thus, North Florence became the newest part of town – yet, with an identity of its own. It is said that until World War I, North Wood Avenue which connected this part of town to downtown Florence was almost impassable in inclement weather, a situation which added to the sense of isolation.

Construction activities surrounding the World War I defense plants and Wilson Dam at the Muscle Shoals played a dramatic role in the early settlement of North Florence. By 1920 the population of the entire city was listed at 10,520. This represented an increase of 57.4 percent over the 1910 figure of 6,689. By 1924 there was a rapid expansion of new family dwellings in this area ranging from Sherrod Avenue on the west side to Simpson Street on the east side to Lelia and Prospect Streets on the south side. One of the first subdivisions was Hawthorne Heights located in the area of Hawthorne Street.

No commercial or professional activity is listed for North Florence in the 1900 city directory.[10] Yet, ten years earlier there was at least one commercial building located on North Wood Avenue near the seven points intersection. This frame building, owned by William Brown, was used by Dr. Sam Albright for his dental office. For the next fifteen years, this district slowly began to emerge. At first the growth was slow, increasing at a more rapid pace as the construction of Wilson Dam continued into the mid 1920's.

In early years, the North Florence Gin on North Wood Avenue, owned by the Florence Seed and Gin Company, was the hub of the commercial district. The Ware Darby Gin was located on Chisholm Road. In 1928, the John Hill Gin was listed as a part of this section of town. These gins were benefited by the three major roads leading into North Florence from cotton farms in the county. H. L. Angel's Grocery and B. F. Townsend's Grocery occupied key points at the seven-road intersection. Townsend was one of the few merchants in this area to survive the Great Depression. B. L. Nabors' Grocery was at 1140 North Wood Avenue. A. H. Nelson's Grocery was nearby. The Dowdy Store was located on Cypress Mill Road. Esslinger's Grocery was at the intersection of Sherrod Avenue and Jackson Road. On Chisholm Road was the Parker Store. During the 1930's other groceries listed were: Young's, Moore's, Angel's and Patterson's.[11]

The Patterson and Beckham Dry Goods was located on North Wood Avenue in 1928. The North Florence Department Store was managed by Zula Wyatt who later established the Northside Florist. Fago Plumbing Company was a part of this section of town. The advent of the North Florence Drug Store made it the most popular gathering place in the business district. It was owned and operated for many years by D. S. Haraway. In the latter part of the twentieth century John Landers became its proprietor along with his East Florence Drug Store. The early restaurants were owned by: Charles Colitzas, Raymond Y. McClain, and Robert and Laura Peerson.

Almost simultaneous with the commercial development of North Florence was the appearance of the modern automobile in North Alabama. Thus, the junction of the seven roads at one place made this an ideal location for gasoline and service stations. These included: Smith and DeLano's, Clark's, Carpenter's,

Wilhelm's, the Seven-Seven-Seven, and the Seven Points. An automobile repair shop was labeled "Marks Brothers Garage." Next to it was an abandoned streetcar which remained for a number of years. According to one account, this car was left here at the end of its final run at midnight on February 3, 1933.[12] This efficient public transportation system had connected Tuscumbia, Sheffield, Florence, East Florence, and North Florence. Its first run to Florence occurred in July 1904.

For a number of years the two blocks in the area of Kenneth Court and Park Court near Cloverdale Road were called the circus grounds. The North Alabama Fair Grounds was located along Fairgrounds Road and Chisholm Highway until the advent of Cox Creek Parkway which, in effect, eliminated a portion of the grounds. During the spring and summer seasons baseball games were played here. At one time it was known as the home for the Florence Raiders. The earlier fairgrounds for the city were located in the area of Gunwaleford and Fish Trap Roads in West Florence.

Crystal Plunge, a popular swimming pool, was located on the north side of the North Alabama State Fairgrounds. Its water intake was from nearby Cox Creek. For a number of years this was the only designed pool of its kind for the entire city.

Perhaps more than anything else, it was Gilbert Elementary School which provided the early adhesive for the bonding of a people into a remarkable community of loyalty, sentiment, and friendliness. The institution began in 1891 as the Fifth Ward School following a petition by the residents in the area. William Brown's building on North Wood Avenue was rented at a cost of $5 a month.[13] This was a three-room frame structure which was set back some 200 feet from the main road. In 1921, land was acquired along Sherrod Avenue and Gilbert Court for the H. C. Gilbert Elementary School. This property had been a part of the old Duckett farm. Gilbert had served as City Superintendent of Education from 1892 until 1904. Dr. Henry Grady Richards became principal when the doors of Gilbert School were first opened. He served until his retirement in 1964. Few gentlemen have influenced an entire community more that Dr. Richards.

Three modern schools now serve the North Florence Area: Harlan, Hibbett, and Forest Hills.

There were four churches associated with the early development of North Florence: Methodist, African Methodist Episcopal, Church of Christ, and Baptist. The Methodists began meeting in the frame building located at the back of the businesses along North Wood Avenue which was being used for the Fifth Ward School. In 1909 Brown Reeder, Stephenson Young, W. P. Rice, J. B. McKelvey, and Probate Judge James F. Koonce initiated plans for the construction of a church. Rice donated the property on Wills Avenue and two carpenters, C. T. Hamm and W. T. McKnight, were named to the building committee. J. H. Madry was employed as contractor. The church was almost completed by the end of the year. Although located on Wills Avenue, the decision was made to keep its original name, "Northwood United Methodist Church." A new sanctuary was completed in 1953 and dedicated in 1957.[14]

The Armstead African Methodist Episcopal Church, located on the north west corner of Simpson Street and Chisholm Highway, came into being about the same time as did the Northwood United Methodist. It was named for Lewis Armstead, one of its first trustees. Armstead and fellow-trustees, Coffee and Rowell, were charged with locating and planning the construction of the church. To select a name for the congregation they painted a piece of wood with three colors representing the three trustees. This stick, when tossed into the air, landed with the white side on top. This was Lewis Armstead's chosen color, and therefore the Church was named for him.[15]

The Sherrod Avenue Church of Christ was organized in 1923. They originally met in the Gilbert Elementary School where they were known as the North Florence Church of Christ. The first trustees were: J. A. Hunt, R. D. Moore, and R. W. Sims. J. J. Holt, J. W. Stutts and a Mr. Holt made up the building committee. The first services were held on June 7, 1925. Elder A. Smith Chambers was its first preacher. Within three months, Chambers died as a result of a freak accident involving a gun owned by a friend. Chambers was removing baggage from an automobile when the

169

weapon was accidentally discharged.[16]   John D. Cox, one of the most popular ministers of Florence, served as preacher here for many years.

The Highland Baptist Church was established October 12, 1924. Among its charter members were: Mr. and Mrs. Clyde Barkley, Mr. and Mrs. S. L. Coburn, Mr. and Mrs. C. F. Dillard, Dr. and Mrs. L. F. Duckett, Levi Duckett, Mr. and Mrs. T. L. Hamm, Mr. and Mrs. L. O. Haynes, Miss Mabel Haynes, Mr. and Mrs. G. C. Jones, Mr. and Mrs. Robert Kershaw, Mr. and Mrs. G. O. McClain, and Mr. and Mrs. E. E. White. Some of these families had been meeting earlier as a Sunday school class in the Gilbert School building. Dr. R. L. Motley, pastor of the First Baptist Church, and the Reverend J. E. Barnard, pastor of Central Baptist Church, along with the deacons from these two congregations, served as a Presbytery during the organization of this congregation. Dr. Motley was elected Moderator and Professor H. C. Gilbert, Clerk. A lot was purchased on Simpson Street at a cost of $2,000. A small frame building without flooring was constructed here. It was torn down in 1929 to make way for a larger and more substantial church structure.[17]   During the latter part of the Twentieth Century the Highland Baptist Church has grown to become one of the largest congregations in the Muscle Shoals area. Its modern Church and adjoining facilities cover an entire block at the northeast corner of Simpson Street and Chisholm Highway.

North Florence is a growing and progressive area of Florence. Its people have never lost their love and dedication to what they affectionately call "Needmore." Although it is an impressive and vital component of Florence, it nevertheless remains as a society within a city that has kept its own separate and proud identity. Its rich and interesting history seems to be as a prelude to all the things that are yet to be as it faces the Twenty-first century.

21. WILSON DAM AND THE WORLD WAR I DEFENSE PLANTS

"The gods are on the side of the stronger."
(Anales, by Tacitus)

Wilson Dam became the federal government's crowning material gift to the Muscle Shoals. Seemingly as another benevolent gesture, this was enhanced by TVA's Wheeler Dam and Pickwick Dam built during the 1930's. Navigation, power generation, and flood control were the major justifications for the three. The almost forty-mile stretch in the river at the Muscle Shoals had been an impediment to navigation from the days of the Native Americans. Its approximately one-hundred-and-forty-feet fall line made it a resource for future power generation. Prior to TVA, the Tennessee was one of the worst of the unharnessed rivers in the nation. During high floods it usually left behind millions of dollars in destroyed property in the valley.

Perhaps the first record of the importance of the Muscle Shoals as a resource for power generation occurred in 1793. William Tatham had been sent by the Governor of Virginia to find a suitable site for a fort in the wilderness. Awed by the sound and fury of the tumbling and turbulent waters, Tatham noted in his report that the Muscle Shoals: "... is nature's masterpiece for an immense and powerful city."[1] General Andrew Jackson recommended as early as 1816 that a military depot be located here. General John Coffee unsuccessfully pursued this effort well into the 1820's. In 1824, Secretary of War John C. Calhoun recommended that the river at the Muscle Shoals be improved for navigation purposes.[2]

In 1899, President William McKinley signed a bill, introduced by Congressman "Fighting Joe" Wheeler, that would authorize the building of a dam at the Muscle Shoals. This was in line with the recommendations of the recently organized Muscle Shoals Power Company. However, this organization was not able to find the necessary funding for an undertaking. Three years later, a bill to authorize erection of a dam and power station at the Shoals was vetoed by President Theodore Roosevelt. His reason was that this bill did not protect the interests of the federal government. This led to the passage of the 1906 General Dam Act, which in effect, cleared up the problems related to building dams on navigation streams.[3] Thus, the story of the federal government's interest in the Muscle Shoals preceded the building of Wilson Dam by more than a hundred years.

Just prior to World War I, a German submarine surfaced in New York Harbor. This sent shock waves through the War Department: most all defense requirements for nitrate explosives were geared to the importation of natural nitrates from Chile. There was now an urgent need for the production of synthetic nitrates in this country. Thus begins the story of the World War I defense plants at the Muscle Shoals and the construction of Wilson Dam.

Wild political maneuvering was involved in the selection of the site for this monumental government construction project. A number of cities were in the running, but President Woodrow Wilson selected the Muscle Shoals – a great natural power resource – as the place.

The dam included in the defense project, later designated as Wilson Dam, was erected near the historic crossing of the river known as Campbell's Ferry. This site was referred to as Dam Number Two in the original plans. Dam Number One, a small navigation dam, was built in the canal near the west end of Patton Island. The present Wheeler Dam was later constructed at the proposed site for Dam Three.

It was altogether fitting and proper that the name for Dam Number Two be in honor of the President of the United States who signed the bill that authorized its construction. Following his death in 1924, the citizens of Florence renamed its City Park in memory of President Wilson.

Great things were now in store for the small rural towns of Florence, Sheffield, and Tuscumbia. Plans called for the construction of two synthetic nitrate plants in Sheffield along with two power generating steam plants. In the meanwhile, work was to begin on the building of Wilson Dam, which was planned to supply the long-range power requirements for the nitrate plants. A large work force – which peaked at 19,300 in August 1918 was required. People came from all across the country. Temporary barracks, tent cities, and mess halls sprang up on the Wilson Dam Reservation. All available resources of the nearby towns were taxed almost to the limit. Construction of housing units and apartments began appearing almost overnight. A temporary tent city overlooked the Florence Cemetery from nearby Catholic Hill. There was a boom of new houses and new businesses in North Florence.

John D. Weeden subdivided part of his vast Sweetwater Plantation and Weeden Heights began to appear as an addition to East Florence. Although it remained outside the city limits for many years, Weeden Heights became a popular section of town with its own business district. One of the area's best-known restaurants, called "Casimus' Cafe," was a landmark here for many years. Also in this area were: Barnett's Grocery, McClure's Store, W. O. Goodwin's Grocery, C. V. Beasley's Grocery, and Bill and Auvin McKee's Grocery Store. Florence improved Court Street which became the first paved thoroughfare in the county and city. The population of Lauderdale County increased from 30,936 in 1910 to 39,556 in 1920. The Shoals had never seen anything to compare with the massive defense works brought to its doors by World War I. In an almost unbelievable time of ten months, the nitrate plants were completed. Plant Number One was located in west Sheffield. This was the new German-invented Haber process which had been obtained by the U. S. Intelligence Agency. Plant Number Two, located on the Wilson Dam Reservation in Colbert County, utilized the well-known Cynamide Process. One of the steam plants was completed although the other was never built. Two permanent villages, Numbers One and Two, were built near these plants. Village Three – which became known as the Dam Village – was located near the north end of Wilson Dam. Sadly, Villages Two and Three were sold and the houses relocated during the Eisenhower Administration of the 1950's. Fortunately, Village Three was allowed to remain as one of the most charming housing areas at the Muscle Shoals. Its houses were sold to individuals.

The two Muscle Shoals nitrate plants were completed just in time for the historic signing of the armistice that occurred November 11, 1918. The war in Europe was over and these plants were no longer needed for the defense of our nation. Therefore, the War Department ordered that they be mothballed and placed in standby condition. Thus began a political issue that soon became a national controversy: what, if anything, could be done with these chemical plants at the Shoals? Once again the name Muscle Shoals became a household word from New York to California.

But the federal government's work in Northwest Alabama had not ended. Although the actual work on Wilson Dam began on November 8, 1918, it was not until the cessation of hostilities in Europe that the more serious phases of the work were undertaken. It would take six more years of labor to complete this colossal wall of concrete in the Tennessee River.

Wilson Dam was designed by Charles Marcus Hackett.[6] Its architecture was created to live as an ageless art that will never be outdated. The arches that form the spillways are patterned after ancient ones that have survived for more than 2,000 years.[7] The walls tower 137 feet in height and its length measures 4,535 feet from shore to shore. At the time of its construction it was heralded as the world's largest dam. It, along with the first of the Aswan Dams in Upper Egypt, changed forever the concept of dam construction. At the time of the Muscle Shoals project, the thought of high dams was new, and to some, frightening. As late as 1908, plans for a high structure on the French Broad River were opposed on the grounds that it might break and flood the lower valley.

The technical concepts of the use of high dams was promoted by John Warren Worthington of Sheffield. More than any other person, Worthington is credited with the promotion of the hydroelectric power potential of the Muscle Shoals that led to the building of Wilson Dam. He was born January 14, 1856, near Trussville, Alabama. It was appropriate that, following his death on April 2, 1942, his ashes were spread over beautiful Lake Wilson.[8]

More than 4,000 people were employed to build Wilson Dam. Fifty-six lives were lost, a very heavy price. General Lansing H. Beach, chief of engineers, was responsible for its construction through a number of field grade officers serving as district engineers. The first and foremost of these was Colonel Hugh L. Cooper who was appointed April 1, 1918. However, a month later he was ordered to duty in France. In May, 1920, Cooper was employed as a civilian designer and construction engineer to complete the work.[9] Although his formal education was at the high school level, it has been said that perhaps no living engineer was more qualified for this job than this self-educated genius in hydroelectric energy.

Authorization was received March 3, 1925, to construct the navigation dam on the canal below Wilson Dam. Known as Dam Number One, its purpose was to provide an adequate pool of water so that boats could approach the lock at Wilson Dam. Completed on November 1, 1925, this small dam was twenty-six feet high and 220 feet long. Three fine houses were constructed on Patton Island facing the dam for use by the lock attendants. When Pickwick Dam was completed by TVA in 1938 this dam and its accessories were no longer needed; they were therefore removed from the canal and island.

Construction of Wilson Dam was completed September 12, 1925, at which time power production began on a testing basis. Finally, on June 1, 1927, the locks were opened to commercial navigation.[10] Originally there were two locks here with a combined lift of ninety feet. These were replaced in 1959 when a new, single-lift lock 110 feet wide and 600 feet long with a lift of 100 feet was completed. At the time it was the highest single lock in the world.[11]

Perhaps Wilson Dam and the facilities at the Muscle Shoals were best described by President Franklin D. Roosevelt following his visit here in 1933: "I was not only impressed with the size of the great operation at Muscle Shoals but I can tell you frankly that it was at least twice as big as I ever had any conception of it being."[12]

22. HENRY FORD'S OFFER TO PURCHASE THE MUSCLE SHOALS PROJECT

"The golden touch of Midas and the mines of Solomon represent but a widow's mite when compared with the productiveness of Muscle Shoals."
(The Facts of The Muscle Shoals,
by Martin Clary)

During the early 1920's the people of Florence, Sheffield, and Tuscumbia were caught up in Henry Ford's dreams to turn the Muscle Shoals into one of the great industrial centers of the South. His proposal seemingly came out of the blue – and ended more than three years later just as dramatically. During this brief period, the name Muscle Shoals became once again a household word across America.

The Ford offer was made during the heated debates in the Congress about what to do with the idled defense plants at the Shoals. These facilities had cost the taxpayers about $130 million, a tremendous sum for that period of time. Opinions were divided in Washington, on the radio, and in the press. Public or private enterprise, especially as related to power production and distribution, became the big issue of the day. Many plans and proposals were advanced as to what could be done with the nitrate plants and Wilson Dam.

Ford made his offer in July, 1921, to the Secretary of War. Although somewhat vague in some areas, he offered $5 million for an outright purchase of the two nitrate plants and the steam plant. In addition, he wanted to lease Wilson Dam after it was completed for $I.7 million annually. He also agreed to produce 40,000 tons annually of nitrogen fertilizer for the American farmer at a profit not to exceed eight percent.[1]

On December 3, 1921, Henry Ford and his friend, the great inventor Thomas A. Edison, arrived in Florence in the "Fair Lane," Ford's private railroad car. Here they were greeted by a large enthusiastic crowd. Ford told the people that, if his proposal was accepted by Congress, that it would lead to the replacement of the gold standard which he labeled as "the real cause of all wars." It would be supplanted by the "energy dollar" produced by waterpower and other energy resources. His new dollar, he said, would "break the strangle hold of Wall Street."[2]

But the most exciting "Ford News" came after he returned to Detroit. With great drama, Ford announced that he had been so impressed with what he saw that he wanted to build a "Seventy-five Mile City." It would begin at Seven Mile Island and reach all the way to Huntsville. This modern utopia would be a decentralized, industrialized regional metropolis. It would incorporate plans for industrial and commercial development as well as for housing, recreation, culture, and educational facilities.[3] He also promised an ultimate employment of one million people for the industry to be located at the Muscle Shoals. He was supported by his friend Thomas A. Edison who announced that he was already conducting a research program for improved fertilizers.

Things began to happen overnight! As expected, there was an immediate boom in real estate. Property was bought up by investors. Paved streets, concrete sidewalks and curbs, street lamps, and street signs began to appear in cotton fields around what was to become Muscle Shoals City. New communities, Ford City and Nitrate City, soon appeared in Colbert County. Florence was not to be left out as new subdivisions expanded northward and eastward. Weeden Heights now became a more thriving place for investments. Lots throughout the entire Muscle Shoals were sold to people from near and far. Many of them never saw what they bought. It is said that a few real estate men became so greedy that they spent time in prison. According to legend, one map of Florence showed the courthouse located in an area somewhat removed from its actual site – and closer to land that was being offered for sale.[4]

Washington was, as usual, slow in its deliberations. There was bitter controversy. Finally, in March 1924, the House approved the Ford Proposal by a vote of 227 to 143. However, in the Senate there was a different story. Ultimately, Henry Ford's grandiose plans were defeated due to the untiring efforts of a little man from Nebraska – Senator George Washington Norris. Senator Norris had a vision that included the development of the entire Tennessee River as a resource for all the people, including not only power, but navigation, forestry, and agriculture as well.

Frustrated and disappointed, Henry Ford dropped another bomb! In a surprise announcement in October, 1924, he withdrew his proposal. The people at the Muscle Shoals were devastated. Never had so many dreams been so completely destroyed at the Muscle Shoals! The name of the little senator from Nebraska became almost as a swear word – that is until the coming of the Tennessee Valley Authority some nine years later.

Although not as dramatic as the Ford Offer, there were other proposals made for the utilization of the Muscle Shoals facilities. In 1922, the Alabama Power Company offered $5 million for the entire Muscle Shoals project, including the dam and plants. Five years later, a bid by American Cyanamid Corporation died in Congress without a vote. The Union Carbide, along with an electric power combine, had submitted an earlier proposal. Alabama Senator Oscar W. Underwood submitted a bill in 1924 which would provide for public operation of the Muscle Shoals facilities. Although it passed the Senate, it died in a House Committee. Senator Norris opposed the Underwood Bill because he considered it too narrow.

The amazing story of Henry Ford's offer to purchase the defense facilities at the Muscle Shoals will be remembered as long as people dream dreams. Although it ended in disappointment, it helped to set the stage for greater things to come.

23. LIFE AT THE MUSCLE SHOALS DURING THE GREAT DEPRESSION

*"...In no other region of the United States were there
more families on relief or with lower incomes..."
(The Quiet Crisis, by Stewart L. Udall)*

The decade of the 1930's, known as the "Great Depression," or "Hoover Days," was a time of extreme hardship across the nation. These years from 1930 to 1940 have also appropriately been called "Hard Times" and the "Time of Trouble."[1] By 1933, the Tennessee Valley had become one of the most depressed areas in the United States.[2] Alabama led the way among the Southern states in declining employment rates, dropping among white workers by 5.6 percent and 13.6 percent among the blacks. These figures include farm labor statistics. Non-farm employment declined in the state by 15 percent between 1930 and 1940.

Florence and Lauderdale County were hit extremely hard, especially in the high-smoke-stack-area of East Florence. An alarming number of downtown stores along Court Street closed their doors. The Reeder Hotel was the only business to remain open in an entire block on East Tennessee Street. One of the town's two theaters, the Majestic, was deserted for a number of years.

In 1931, there were 667 families, amounting to nearly 3,500 individuals in both the city and county who were without the basic necessities of life. A survey made in 1932, showed that one-fourth of the population in and around Florence were "without work or other means of support."[3] Hundreds of others had only part-time jobs or were looking for "odd jobs."[4] A few families were forced out of their homes and lived in tents. An entire row of houses along the L&N railroad were built mostly from shipping crates discarded by the Gardiner-Warring Knitting Mill. One former Wilson Dam employee resorted to peddling stove wood in exchange for butter, eggs, and corn meal to feed his family. On cold mornings people could be seen walking up and down the railroad tracks trying to find coal that had fallen from cars for their grates and cook stoves. Absentee rates increased in local schools, especially during the winter months, when children had no alternative but to skip school because they had no shoes. A local newspaper reported that "hundreds of children right in our midst are without sufficient food and clothing. They eagerly eat stale bread or scraps of food which they can get to keep their little bodies alive."[5] A story is told about a nighttime robbery at the H. M. Ramsey Grocery in East Florence. Upon learning the next morning that only some dry beans and white meat had been taken, Houston Ramsey admonished his son for having called the police.

Those people, he said, were not thieves, "they were just hungry folks trying to find something to eat."[6]

The federal government, under President Herbert Hoover, provided little assistance to the states. Welfare programs in Alabama were practically non-existent due to a lack of funds, although there was, in fact, an Alabama Welfare Agency in Montgomery.[7]

One of the first efforts to organize a relief committee was undertaken in 1931 by James Lawrence Goyer, Senior, who lovingly became known around town as "Dr. Goyer." In response to his appeal, the following letter was written on November 5, 1931, by Thomas M. Rogers, Senior, of the Rogers Department Store in Florence: "Dear Dr. Goyer: Agreeable to your suggestion, I beg to submit the following names from which to select a Relief Committee: James S. Kilburn, James B. Simmons, R. B. Dominick, B. A. Rogers, Brown Stewart, J. H. Blair, John S. Kernachan, Judge James F. Koonce, Dr. J. S. Thomas, Mrs. James A. Stoves, Mrs. George Russell, Mrs. H. C. McGee, Mrs. Frank Jackson, Mrs. John L. Hughston, Mrs. A. T. Putteet, Mrs. R. W. Drane, and Mrs. L. E. Bright. I am sure you can make a good selection from these names. In this connection, please be advised that the United States Government through Colonel Hartley Moon, Adjutant General in Montgomery, is offering to sell Army overcoats and blankets for 5 cents and mattresses at 2 cents each to be distributed to the needy through organized charitable agencies. I am sure we should make requisition for some of these supplies and they can be obtained by making application direct to Colonel Moon or through Dr. H. L. Stutts, Probate Judge of Lauderdale County."[8]

A Good Will Center was organized to collect donations and to coordinate the distribution of food and necessities. Many of the local churches, along with civic organizations and individuals, worked through this center to help feed and clothe the needy. A community garden was planted in McFarland Bottom on twenty acres of land provided by C. N. Curry who lived on North Seminary Street. More than $2,500 was allocated by the Red Cross to purchase the seeds. Labor, tools, and fertilizers were contributed by local citizens. The local Standard Oil Distributor gave the gasoline needed for operating the tractor. Mrs. A. J. Martin of North Wood Avenue organized a group of ladies to form a canning committee. The Red Cross stepped in again with a donation of 240 canning jars.[9]

These were extremely difficult times for both the Red Cross and Community Chest. They had exhausted all of their resources in Lauderdale County by mid-winter in 1932. At this time, the Red Cross Headquarters in Washington appropriated $ 11,000 for local relief. Attorneys Henry A. Bradshaw and William H. Mitchell became leaders of the Community Chest in the fall of 1932. They began the year with an appeal for $12,000 from the local area. This was a bold move in that the highest amount ever raised up to that time was $9,300 two years earlier. Two days earnings were pledged by the employees of Rogers Department Store, Florence Times, and Coca-Cola Bottling Company.[10]

The people at the Muscle Shoals have always been proud and independent. Many of them were descended from the Celtic clans of Scotland and Ireland where hard times had been a way of life for hundreds of years. Even among the most needy, they found it extremely hard to ask for help. A supervisor at the knitting mill in East Florence told of interviewing a long line of applicants for an advertised week's work of cleaning out the rust inside a huge boiler, one of the hardest tasks at the plant – especially during hot summer days. One of the job seekers, upon being asked if he had ever "scaled a boiler," admitted that had no experience. "Then, why do you think I would even consider hiring you?," he was asked. The young father of three children replied, "because I intend to bid for this work at half the price offered by your lowest bidder."[11]

Another story is told about a needy family receiving food from the Community Chest. The mother, in appreciation, stitched a homemade quilt and donated it to the Community Chest. They, in turn, sold chances on the quilt to raise more funds for the agency.[12]

The families in the county suffered as well as did the city folk. However, they had some advantages. There were gardens for the dinner table; most of them – except the poorest of the tenants who survived at the mercy of the landowners were able to raise hogs for bacon, chickens for eggs, and cows for milk and butter. Generally, even the most underprivileged of the tenants were not evicted from their homes as were some of the unemployed in the city. State statistics show that between April l, 1929, and March 31, 1930, 17,580 people had moved back to the farm while only 7,836 had moved away. By 1940 there were almost two million people in Alabama who lived on farms while only 856,000 were residents of towns and cities.[13]

In 1932, the cost of producing cotton in Lauderdale County was estimated at 5.5 cents a pound. Farmers often had to sell for less because of the large two-year storage of surplus cotton in warehouses. Some families picked and hoed cotton in exchange for free food. One young man worked a whole season cutting wood to pay for a pair of brogans.[14]

No one who did not live through the terrible Great Depression in Florence and Lauderdale County could ever understand the magnitude of what it did to the land and its people. Those who were a part of that era were a tough generation. They would never forget its hard times and, truly, their world would never be the same again.

24. TVA COMES TO THE VALLEY

"... Franklin Roosevelt came like one of the giants of old."
("Nature's Masterpiece of Power," the author)

In November 1932 the people of America overwhelmingly elected a New York aristocrat, Franklin Delano Roosevelt, as their 32nd President. No people anywhere could have been more excited than those who lived at the Muscle Shoals. Hope had entered their world of despair. This election was a sign of good things to come in much the same way as the small cloud which appeared as a signal to Elijah that his prayers for rain were to be answered. One old fellow in Lauderdale County was heard to shout: "I think I have eaten my last supper of collard greens."[1]

January 21, 1933, became a red-letter day! The new President-elect toured the Muscle Shoals. The people of Florence were ablaze with excitement! Seemingly every inch of Court and Tennessee Streets was packed with throngs of people. Roosevelt's loud and clear voice could be heard over the crowd as he outlined a plan that had been drafted by the Senator from Nebraska, George W. Norris, and the Congressman from Alabama, Lister Hill. It called for the idle facilities at the Muscle Shoals to be utilized in the production of fertilizers for the American farmer. In fact, the Muscle Shoals was envisioned that day as the centerpiece for a New Deal Program that would become the Tennessee Valley Authority.

The President and his entourage left Sheffield to visit Wilson Dam. Afterwards they traveled through East Florence to Court Street in downtown Florence. Roosevelt was seated in the rear of a large open-top automobile. Its yellow, wooden-spoked wheels added to the festivity of the occasion. Anxious people were standing on both sides of the road. Women were crying and waving handkerchiefs. Unemployed fathers held small children on their shoulders so that they, too, could be a witness to a moment in time that would never be forgotten.[2] As the President watched the water flowing through the spillways at Wilson Dam, he turned to

Senator Norris and said: "This should be a happy day for you, George." The Independent Senator from Nebraska replied: "I see my long anticipated dreams ready to come true."[3]

Franklin Roosevelt and close associates were hosted for the night in one of the large government-built homes overlooking Wilson Dam.[4] The other dignitaries from Washington were in the Reeder and Negley Hotels. Early Sunday morning a call was made to Dr. Henry J. Willingham, President of the State Normal College, seeking his suggestion as to which of the local churches the Roosevelt party should attend. The congregation of the First United Methodist Church were totally surprised when these distinguished guests entered the sanctuary. The minister, Dr. Waits G. Henry, quickly invited the visitors to come down to the front of the church where they were formally introduced.[5]

The second piece of legislation signed by President Roosevelt was the Act that created the Tennessee Valley Authority. This historic event occurred on May 18, 1933. The song, "Happy Days Are Here Again," could be heard throughout downtown Florence as thousands of people literally danced in the streets until dawn![6]

Thus, a dawn of hope came again to the Valley and especially to the people at the Muscle Shoals! Chemists and engineers were soon assembled here and in laboratories at the University of Tennessee in Knoxville. Operators, craftsmen, secretaries, purchasing agents, laborers, and others were employed. It wasn't long until the wheels began to turn at the Muscle Shoals. Large electric furnaces began to produce elemental phosphorus for fertilizers. Soon, a new ammonia plant was built to provide a nitrate nutrient for the soil. Over a period of years, this chemical plant evolved into an experimental fertilizer production component of the National Fertilizer Development Center. For many years this TVA program was considered to be the leading and most comprehensive fertilizer research and development center in the world.[7]

On November 21, 1933, construction began on TVA's Wheeler Dam, one of the seven multipurpose dams on the

Tennessee River. Located at the Elk River Shoals, sixteen miles above Wilson Dam, it was named for General "Fighting Joe" Wheeler of Civil War and Spanish-American War fame. Wheeler's large 17,000 acre plantation was located nearby in Lawrence County. The General had also served in the U.S. House of Representatives from this area. Completed on November 9, 1936, this dam measured 6,342 feet in length and only 72 feet in height, making it the lowest of TVA's main river dams.

Construction of Pickwick Dam began on March 8, 1935, and was completed June 29, 1838. Its length is 7,715 feet and its height is 113 feet. Located fifty-two miles below Wilson Dam, it completed the task of covering the dangerous shoals with beautiful Pickwick Lake.

The coming of TVA literally brought new life as it changed forever the lifestyle of the people in the Valley. Hundreds of work-hungry men were employed in its research, operation, resource development, and construction programs. Rural power lines were soon stretched from one end of Lauderdale County to the other. Scenic lakes covered once fertile agricultural lands. A good many farmers and old established families were uprooted from their homes.

The Great Depression was now nearing its end. The beginning of World War II, with all of its local defense efforts, brought about the final demise of that period of hard times in Florence and Lauderdale County.

Perhaps it could be said that the most significant economic event in the history of the Muscle Shoals was the advent of the Tennessee Valley Authority.

A SCRIPT IN TRANSITION

*"Not stones, nor wood, nor the art of artisans make a state; but
where men are who know how to take care of themselves, these
are the cities and the walls."*
(Attributed to Alcaeus by Aristides)

Florence was destined from the beginning of Lauderdale
County to become its chief cornerstone in government. As a city
perched on a high plateau overlooking the Muscle Shoals at the
Tennessee River, it has all the advantages of being the hub and
focal point of a county seat.

Its history begins not with the advent of the nineteenth
century, but in some far-off eon of time as evidenced by the ancient
Indian mound that continues as a sentinel to guard its entrance
gate. Thus, a study of the history of this town would not be
complete without an introduction to its past as found in the story of
the Tennessee River and the earliest inhabitants along its shores.

Lauderdale County from east to west and from north to south
has attracted mankind for thousands of years. Every town,
crossroad, and community within its border have a remarkable
legacy of its people and places.

Part II – The Beginning of Lauderdale County

To walk through Lauderdale County is to encounter events which happened in prehistoric ages. These stories began with the coming of the Tennessee River to Northwest Alabama at some immeasurable period when the world was yet young. People who arrived here thousands of years ago are introduced, along with the historic Native Americans who claimed these lands long before the arrival of the first European families. These accounts of history give the beginnings of the larger towns of the county. They include, as well, the stories of how places such as Zip City, Johnson's Crossroads, Grassy, and Cow Pen came into being. This stroll through the past is an introduction to the hardy pioneers and the hard-working settlers who made Lauderdale County what it is today.

25. THE TENNESSEE RIVER AND THE MUSCLE SHOALS

"Leap down to different seas, and as they roll
Grow deep and still, and their majestic presence
Becomes a benefaction to the towns......."
(Longfellow)

It would seem strange, indeed, to imagine how it would be if there were no Tennessee River running through Northwest Alabama. How difficult for one to even suggest a mental image of the great Muscle Shoals without its bountiful and beautiful shores of man-made lakes and the faint and almost silent sounds of the river beneath their placid surfaces. Yet, there are geological and geographical theories to imply that the presence of the Tennessee, as we know it, is relatively new to this part of Northwest Alabama.[1] A study of a modern map indicates that something surely happened in the long ago to block the southwestward flow of the river at Guntersville. The two forks of the Black Warrior River rise on the far side of the mountain chain from the dramatic turn of the Tennessee River at Guntersville. It takes little imagination to speculate that the ancestral Tennessee in ages past, before the mountains were formed, surely must have joined with these forks to become a part of the Black Warrior River and Tombigbee River systems which empty into the Gulf of Mexico at Mobile.[2] The most ancient section of the present Tennessee River are thought to be the French Broad, Little Tennessee, and Hiwasee. This same concept of primeval times suggests that the bed of the river has been altered along with the geological modifications that have occurred in the earth's surface through which it passed. Thus, it is believed that the head of the Tennessee River is its most ancient bed, and that its final course from Florence to Paducah is its youngest part.[3] The mighty Tennessee Rivers runs some 652 miles and drains an area as large as England and Scotland combined. It crosses both the eastern and western sides of Tennessee, goes all the way across North Alabama and the entire width of West Kentucky. Among the unusual features of this serpentine flow of water is its northern journey from the corner of Alabama and Mississippi to the Ohio River at Cairo, Illinois, a distance of some 200 miles. This makes it and the Mackenzie the only two rivers on the continent to flow north at such a great distance.[4]

That part of North Alabama within the curve of the river – where it doubles back and heads northwestwardly across the state – has been known as "The Great Bend" from Indian times. The entire land within the Great Bend was also referred to in some eighteenth century document as "The Muscle Shals Country."[5] In the early settlement of North Alabama, a smaller bend within the Great Bend, located in West Lauderdale County, has a local identification as "The Bend of the River."

Some theories indicate that the ancestral Tennessee River at some point in time emptied into the ancient Cretaceous Sea. This body of water later receded southwardly, yet leaving an extension, known as the Mississippi Embayment, which reached as far north as the present confluence of the Ohio and Mississippi Rivers.

Equally as enchanting as these river theories are the number of hypotheses that have been published about the Cretaceous Sea during the Paleozoic or Carboniferous era. This primeval body of shallow water extended from Alabama north and northeast to New York and the Great Lakes and west to the Mississippi River and beyond.[6] Over the passing of time this basin was slowly filled with thick layers of sandstone, shale, and limestone. The formation of the Appalachian Mountains, ranging from Northeast Mississippi to southern New York, caused dramatic changes. Debris from these mountains fell into the shallow sea. As the mountains formed, North Alabama began to rise above sea level to become what is known as the Highland Rim. This section of Alabama is also a part of the Appalachian Region which extends across parts of thirteen states from southern New York to northeast Mississippi.

The Appalachian chain raises other puzzles. These mountains appear to stop in Alabama. Yet, geological evidence shows that they, in fact, resume hundreds of miles to the west where they are called the Ouachita Mountains of Arkansas. In more recent years, geological studies have revealed another strange twist: the same chain of mountains known as the Appalachians reappear some 4,000 miles to the south in Argentina. Here they are called the Precordillera which make up the foothills of the Andes Mountains.[7]

Outcroppings of rocks embedded with small sea fossils can be found in places once covered by Cretaceous Sea during the Paleozoic Era. These ancient rocks cover roughly the northern third of Alabama, from the Fall Line – Tuscaloosa, Montgomery, Wetumpka, and Phenix City – north to the state line. The fossils came from creatures which lived on the bottom of the Cretaceous Sea. On one of the highest hills overlooking Anderson in East Lauderdale County is such evidence. Among other local outcroppings is in an area located between Tuscumbia and Red Bay. These same fossils can be observed among the rocks located in the hills and hollows south of Lawrenceburg, Tennessee.

Yet, with all of its lore and lure, the most fascinating feature of the mysterious Tennessee is a section known historically as the Muscle or Mussel Shoals. This peculiarity in the river bed is believed to have had much to do with the area's earliest habitation, including the most ancient of peoples in prehistoric times.[8] Before the building of Wilson, Wheeler, and Pickwick Dams, this almost forty-mile lineament in the river bed was a formidable barrier to navigation, creating, in effect, two rivers – the Upper Tennessee and the Lower Tennessee. In this short span the river fell a distance of a little over 137 feet, creating rushing cascades of water falls along with sucks, sinks, sand bars, shallows, rapids, and a large number of islands of varying sizes. Old timers described the roar of the waters over these shoals as awesome and ominous, and said that it could be heard for miles in all directions.[9]

Most of the rock above and below the surface in Northwest Alabama are of sedimentary origin, and are believed to have been deposited in the warm waters of the primeval Cretaceous Sea.[10] The waters of the river as it searched for a newer route across

North Alabama carved a normal bed with average banks and widths through these softer rocks. However, when it reached the Muscle Shoals, it was not so easy to cut through older or harder rocks which were to form the cascades or obstructions in the river.[11] Thus, the river had to reach out on both sides, creating a width similar in size to its mouth at Puducah.

There are a number of legends as to how Muscle Shoals got its name. The most plausible of these theories relates to the small fresh water shellfish called the mussel.[12] From the earliest times these small creatures found a natural habitat among these shallows and swift currents in the river. Some of the very earliest maps identify this place as Mussel Shoals.

Equally as interesting are the theories concerning the most ancient vegetation in this part of North Alabama. Bones of a prairie chicken found during the excavation of a cave near Florence in 1996 indicate that a part of the Muscle Shoals once had prairie-like vegetation, since these types of birds do not live in wooded areas. Fossilized pollen discovered in this same cave gives rise to a theory that at the end of the Ice Age, this entire area was perhaps covered by an evergreen forest.[13] Yet, when discovered by the earliest white explorers, this section of North Alabama was part of the great hardwood forests of the Appalachians.

In 1889 the Tennessee General Assembly permanently and officially designated the name of the river as the Tennessee. Historically it has been known by a variety of names. De 1'Isle's map of 1701 labels its main course as the "Acansea Sipi." A map in the Archives of Great Britain from about 1760 identifies the upper and lower parts as the "Cusatees River," and called the middle section "Thegalego." Another map from about the same period referred to its entire length as the "Cusatees River," supposedly from the Koasatis tribe of Native American living along the river in East Tennessee. An early French map labeled it as "Riviere des Cheraquis," or, in English, the "Cherokee River." The Popple map of 1733 calls the lower part the "Hogohegee," the middle section the "Callamaco," and the upper regions of the river the "Acanseapi."

One early Tennessee historian said that the Indians knew the river as the "Kallumuchee."[14]

Early mythology of the Tennessee deals with the very nature of what was once a wild and untamed river. One of these accounts was recorded by the family of James Jackson who helped establish Florence. This Indian legend tells of the disembodied spirit of a goddess who lived beneath the mighty roar of the waters that rushed over the Muscle Shoals.[15] A similar account is about a lady's voice that sings, sometimes loud and boisterous, and on other occasions softly, and now and then only a faint humming could be heard. Some say these are Cherokee myths, others attribute them to the Chickasaws or Creeks, or maybe the Koasatis who in the long ago made their homes at the Muscle Shoals.[16]

26. PREHISTORIC PEOPLES AT THE SHOALS

"No whispered rumours which the many
have spread can wholly perish."
(Hesiod)

The first people to arrive at the Muscle Shoals was during the late stages of the last Ice Age. The earliest radiocarbon date shows the presence of human beings in this area some 11,280 years ago, plus or minus 635 years. Archaeological evidence has been excavated at sites of hearth fires discovered in local caves and shelters. Other clues have been noted along the banks of the Tennessee River and its tributaries and near Ice-Age ponds that still exist in West Lauderdale County.[1] A number of skeletal remains discovered in the upper levels of a site under a large overhanging rock on a hillside in Colbert County indicate that these people of the later period of the shelter's use were relative slender as compared to the Shell Mound Indians who were to follow them at a later period. The height of one male was five feet nine inches and one adult female was five feet and one-half inches.[2]

In the summer of 1996, Dust Cave located a few miles west of Florence, was excavated. Evidence shows that prehistoric peoples inhabited this site as early as 10,500 years ago and as late as 5,200 years ago. A fishhook, believed to be the oldest ever found in Alabama, indicates that people were fishing here at least 10,000 years ago.[3]

It is believed that the ancestors of these people migrated from northwestern Asia more than 20,000 years ago. Perhaps they crossed a land bridge between Siberia and Alaska. Other theories suggest that these first inhabitants of the American continent crossed over a solid sheet of ice sometime after the land bridge had disappeared under the sea. Regardless of when or how they arrived, it seems almost certain that they came over a time frame which spanned hundreds of years. Traveling in small groups and pursuing animals and other food they moved south and east and, eventually, into this part of the southeast.[4]

Abundance of year-around food supplies, plus a more moderate weather, were what brought them to this part of the South. As previously noted, the shallows and rapids at the Muscle Shoals became a natural habitat for the small fresh water shellfish called the mussel. Based upon all the evidence that still exists at nearby sites, these prehistoric nomads must have dearly loved these little morsels of raw meat. Mussels could be scooped up and eaten the year around. They presented a dependable staple rarely found in other parts of the country. Also, in the nearby great hardwood forests, especially in the hilly and mountainous regions, could be gathered nuts, roots, berries, fruits, and all kinds of game both large and small. It is thought that the Tennessee Valley was, perhaps, the most heavily populated area in the Southeast at one time or another during the ancient past. Without question, the Tennessee River from the very beginning has had a considerable impact upon those who found their way to its shores.

These first peoples who came to this part of Northwest Alabama are defined as the late Paleo Indians. Some sources refer to these earliest inhabitants as of the "post-Fluted Point", or "Pre-Shell Mound" period, which began about 10,000 B.C. They were principally hunters and gatherers using stone-tipped spears. They usually lived in closely-knit bands of 20 to 40 members and were always on the move. The men were hunters and makers of tools and weapons. Several types of early spear points have been found, including Clovis points that are named for a place in New Mexico where the first one of its kind was discovered. The women gathered food and firewood and were caretakers of the children and makers of clothing from the skins of animals. Evidence shows that their cooking was done in open fires, and most of the time in pits.[5]

The next Muscle Shoals' residents are classified locally as the Shell Mound People or Gatherers. They were of the Archaic Period from about 8000 B.C. to around 2000 B.C. By then the large animals had disappeared and these people depended more on gathering food and hunting small games such as birds and deer and rabbits. These inhabitants were more settled than their earlier ancestors and at first made use of caves and shelters. Later they often built campsites on the shell mounds along the river and streams which, perhaps, had originated as refuse dumps by those who were here before they arrived. These small elevations were added to and heightened over a period of many years by the frequent flooding of the Tennessee and its tributaries which left deposits of sand, soil, and gravel interspersed with the mussel shells. Several families probably occupied the same mound at the same time. The mussel from the Shoals was the main staple for their well-rounded diet which also included wild plant foods and both fresh and dried animal meat. Eventually hot-rock cooking came into being through a process of dropping heated rocks into food that had been placed in a hollowed-out depression in a stone or in their hard-packed clay floors.

These Archaic Period people learned the art of weaving and how better to make tools and weapons by using bones as well as stones. One of the most amazing discoveries about these primitive inhabitants of the Shoals is that their hunting equipment included the highly technical atlatl. This device was designed to add leverage of a man's arm enabling him to hurl the spear a greater distance than he had previously been able to do.[6]

The third inhabitants from about 2000 B.C. until around 800 A.D. were known as the Woodland Period people. They also lived in groups, although it is possible that neighbors in the area were not of the same clan, or had any family connections, or even spoke the same language. They, like their ancestors, were gatherers and hunters, although they had the advantage of the bow and arrow which gave them more skill in warfare and hunting. They were the area's first farmers. Learning how to plant seeds and to care for growing plants, these people grew mostly gourds, squash, and a small type of primitive corn which was no more than one inch in length.[7]

It was during this prehistoric Woodland Period when the Copena Culture appeared at the Muscle Shoals. Burials and artifacts found in many of the local mounds can be identified in a number of ways with this particular stage of advancement in the life of these early people. Copena is a Southern form of the Hopewell Culture identified with the Ohio River Valley that spread along the western edge of the Appalachian Mountains. This shaping of a higher form of civilization is believed to have originated in Illinois and Ohio. From there it moved rapidly into other parts of the country. Those who carried this way of life into the Southwest are identified as the Copena People. This term was coined because of their use of copper and galena.[8]

Prior to the impoundment of the lake behind Pickwick Dam in March of 1938, the village and camp sites, flint work shops, bluff and cave shelters, and mounds in its path were carefully studied, investigated, and either partially or fully excavated. A number of the more interesting sites excavated, or partially dug into, were in and around the Wright community a few miles east of Waterloo. These Wright Mounds offered some excellent evidence of the Copena Culture.[9]

The last of the prehistoric people at the Muscle Shoals were known as the Mississippian Culture. This period covered the time from about 800 A.D. until the explorations of Hernando De Soto in this part of the South in 1537 - 1547. They formed a more advanced society than the Copena and earlier peoples. As with all civilizations on all continents, it was agriculture that enabled man to build permanent settlements, and to devote time to the pursuit of improving his environment and advancing his standard of living.

Archaeologists find it hard to define "Mississippian." It really is a catchall term for behavioral patterns and beliefs shared by scattered societies. They belonged to two general language groups: the Muskhogeans east of the Mississippi River, and the Caddoans who were west of the Mississippi. With them agriculture became more stable as more efficient types of cultivating hoes replaced digging sticks allowing their fields to be expanded. These people lived in towns and large villages and the small clans expanded into a hierarchy form of government headed by chiefs and priests. The tradition of the Muskhogeans who resided in the Tennessee Valley tell of their migration from earlier homelands west of the Mississippi.[10]

The Mississippians are sometimes called "Mound Builders." Their style of mounds were usually flat-topped with pyramidical sides, and remarkably different from the earlier and more prehistoric burial mounds found in the Tennessee Valley. These flat-topped mounds served as bases for religious temples and houses for chiefs or for other important functions.

More than seventy mounds in the immediate area can be identified on maps that were drawn before the coming of Wilson, Wheeler, and Pickwick Dams. In the Pickwick Basin, alone, there were more than forty mounds and at least 150 villages and campsites. One map identifies the numerous archaeological sites in the Pickwick Basin in the late 1930's.[11] Most of these early villages, campsites, and mounds seem to have been of the Mississippian Period. However, a number have been identified with the earlier Woodland and Copena Cultures. One of these is the large flattop mound on the bank of the Tennessee River in Florence.[12]

Every island of any size at the Muscle Shoals was crowded with early mound builders thought to have been of the Mississippian Period. They are referred to locally as "The Koger Island People." Their center was on Koger and Seven Mile Islands located down river from the Muscle Shoals. Some sources refer to them as the "Round Heads of Koger Island." They also built villages along the river and creeks and near arable soil that was more convenient for good farming.[13]

Well before the arrival of the Europeans, the Koger Island folk and the great Mississippi Culture began to decline. These advanced mound builders did not disappear, but their structured societies broke down. The centers of government were gradually abandoned, and its people returned to a more simple way of life. They became, perhaps, the ancestors of some of the historic Native Americans who were at the Muscle Shoals when the first white explorers arrived.

27. THE FLORENCE MOUND, AN ANCIENT CATHEDRAL

"Mankind was never so happily inspired as when it made a cathedral."
(Stevenson)

The Indian Mound at Florence was somewhat of a mystery even to the Native Americans at the Muscle Shoals when the first white settlers arrived and began to ask questions. These Historic Indians knew little about its age, its builders, or its purpose.[1] The mound stands today as a shrine shrouded by an ancient aura that continues to baffle all attempts to define its reason for being and its true place in the history of a forgotten people.

This temple mound is a monument not only to the compelling power of a religion but also to the leadership of the community of believers responsible for its construction. It points to the genius of an early man, whether chieftain or high priest. Although its basic concept was borrowed from an even more ancient culture, its construction at the Shoals came into being as a result of a conceived plan that dictated its location and structured the labor forces that were employed in its fabrication.[2]

There were actually three mounds at this location when the first white settlers arrived; the existing mound is the only one that has survived. The other two were nearby and were smaller in size, their heights estimated to have been about 25 feet. These three mounds below Florence were once partly enclosed by an oblong shaped earthen wall beginning on the downstream side about 600 to 800 feet from the existing mound and bordering the mounds to a point on the upstream side. It is possible that surrounding these mounds and earthen wall complex was a moat that connected with the river. The earthen wall was thought to have been from twelve to fifteen feet in height. Prior to the Civil War a historian noted that the wall had been cultivated until it was difficult to trace except during the times it was being plowed. Then, he said, one could distinguish the yellow clay of which the wall was composed from the dark sand of the surrounding area.[3] Also, parts of this earthen wall were used as land fill for the railroad beds on the north bank of the river more than a hundred years ago.

The immensity of the Florence Mound is almost overwhelming when one considers the methods used in its construction. This quadrilateral mound, the largest mound on the Tennessee River, stands forty-three feet in height. Its base measurements are 310 feet by 230 feet. It has a distinctive flat top that is 145 feet in length and ninety-four feet in width.

Limited research conducted by the University of Alabama in May, 1996, unearthed evidence to indicate that this mound was probably built during the Woodland Tradition between 100 B.C. and 400 A.D. This is about l,000 years earlier than had previously been estimated by archaeologists.[4] Without question, the Florence Mound is the oldest man-made structure at Florence.

During De Soto's explorations in the New World around 1540 his people observed a mound actually being constructed. Dirt, they said, was carried up in one basket at a time, emptied out, and then stamped down with great force until it had the desired consistency.[5] Perhaps this represents a near description of how the local earthen structure was erected, although the Florence Mound was built much earlier.

The Woodland Tradition emerged as a distinctive culture of people in the eastern states, especially along the Ohio and Mississippi rivers. This involved changes in their lifestyle. It also brought about a marked innovation in the ideology of its population.[6]

It is believed that the Woodland People built the Florence Mound as a place of worship. One of the two nearby smaller mounds – no longer existing – perhaps was used as a base for the house where the high priest or chief resided. The second smaller mound may have been for the secondary priests or chiefs. It is also possible that it served as the base for a mortuary where the dead were prepared for burial. However, the existing ceremonial

Florence Mound contains no burials, based upon excavations that were made in 1914. During these examinations, evidence was found in an adjacent field suggesting that a habitation area was once associated with the mound.[7] Some think that a large portion, if not all, of the Muscle Shoals area was regarded by these early people as their "holy ground." Generally, this part of the Shoals was not used for dwellings or towns. Perhaps the priestly hierarchy lived on the grounds outside the wall surrounding the Florence Mound.[8]

The sides of the mound were purposely built so steep that it was difficult for man to climb them. Thus, the entrance to the small wooden temple at the top, where a sacred fire burned, had to be made up the wide steps constructed of logs and dirt on the eastern slope. Here ascended the priests, or perhaps the high priest, in magnificent regalia to greet the rising sun to the east and to call for blessings upon the people and the land. There were special holy days and seasons of celebrations in which the Florence Mound was used as a great cathedral for a mysterious people who made religion the center of their civilization for hundreds of years at the Muscle Shoals.[9] It is a monument to the religion of an ancient people.

Some two miles below the Florence Mound is an archaeological site believed to have been the dwelling place of a people more ancient than those of the Woodland Period. Here, human bones have laid in the earth so long that they have gone through a state of petrifaction.[10] Thus, when one looks below the hill where rests the modern city of Florence, he becomes aware that ancient man established his home here maybe ten thousand years before the arrival of the Europeans.

28. THE MUSCLE SHOALS INDIANS WHO GREETED THE FIRST WHITE SETTLERS

"My fathers talked of the hills and valleys and the land of swift flowing and many waters ...My fathers lived good lives in Alabama."
(Said to the author by a an elderly Chickasaw in an interview at Colbert, Oklahoma, in 1982.)

The term "Historic Indians" identifies the Native Americans who were inhabitants of the Muscle Shoals when the Europeans arrived to take away their lands and to eventually move them to new territories beyond the Mississippi. In general, the Historic Indians knew little or nothing about their predecessors. There were exceptions, of course. When the young Frenchman, Le Clere Milford, visited the Creek tribes on the Chattahooche River in 1776, he was impressed with their system of preserving the stories of their ancestors.[1]

Alabama received its name from the small tribe of the Alabamas who were also known as Alibamus or Alabamons. These people migrated into Alabama during the 1500s from Northeast Mississippi, and stayed around for 200 years. The Alabamas were located in the lower regions of the state. Some say their population never exceeded 4,500, including women and children.[2] Today, the Alabamas, along with a tribe known as the Koasatis, live in the Big Thicket area of southeast Texas. The Koasatis at first had lived along the Tennessee River in northeast Alabama where they were discovered by Hernando de Soto in 1540. However, by 1684 this tribe had already moved into south Alabama where they settled along the Alabama River.[3]

The first known tribe of Historic Indians to live at the Muscle Shoals were called the Euchees, sometimes referred to as the Tohogalega, or Hogaloge.[4] A number of early maps referred to the upper Tennessee River as the "Thegalego," and the lower part as the "Hogohegee." Both of these names were variations of spellings used for these people who lived along its shores.[5]

These early residents at the Shoals spoke a language entirely confusing to other tribes in the Southeast. It is believed they were already at the Muscle Shoals when de Soto crossed Alabama. Little is known about the Euchees. Some anthropologists think they were an isolated fragment of the Siouans who were, as far as is known, the earliest Historic Indians in the South. The Siouans broke away from a northern people who lived in the area of the Great Lakes before the time of Columbus.[6] These Siouans migrated into the southeast. One of their splinter groups, the Euchees, reached as far south as the Tennessee River where they claimed the Muscle Shoals as their home.

The Siouans and the Euchees had an unusual custom of flattening the heads of their children. This was done by placing the baby's head on a board that was hinged or weighted so as to press the skull. Other characteristics of these people were their long hair and tattooed bodies. Some of these practices were later picked up by the neighboring Choctaw people. The Siouans were not well liked by the civilized tribes in the southeast. These people from the north were considered heathenish because their women engaged in professional prostitution.[7]

Next came the Shawnees to oust the Euchees and claim the Shoals. These war-like people seemed to have always been on the move and constantly dividing into smaller fragments. The Shawnees are believed to have descended from what was known as the Fort Ancient Culture that existed in northeastern Kentucky, southern Ohio, and western West Virginia from about 1400 A. D. to about 1650 A.D.[8] They broke away from a group called the Sac in Illinois to settle along the Cumberland River near the present location of Nashville. By this time they were called Shawnees. These were the people of the famed Tecumseh of the early nineteenth century. His father was a Shawnee and his mother a Creek.[9]

In 1715, at the beginning of the twelve-year Creek-Cherokee War, the Cherokee Indians, with aid of the Chickasaw, expelled the Shawnees from the Nashville and Muscle Shoals areas to a new location on the Red River in Kentucky.[10] From that time to the coming of the white settlers, the Muscle Shoals was sparsely inhabited by the Cherokee and Chickasaw. The entire area was claimed by these two civilized tribes as well as the Creek and Shawnees. These four tribes used it as their hunting grounds.[11]

The Shawnees' claim to the Muscle Shoals was based upon having occupied the land prior to being expelled in 1715. The Creek claim, perhaps, originated with the early settlement of the Euchees who were ousted by the Shawnees. These Euchees, after 1715, moved south to eventually become a part of the Creek Nation.[12] Even during the eighteenth century a few of these people, including the notable Chief Bigfoot, were residing in the area of Colbert and Lauderdale Counties.

The definition of the Creek Nation is "a confederacy of peoples chiefly of Muskogean stock formerly occupying most of Alabama and Georgia and parts of Florida."[13] Generally, the Creek males were taller than most Europeans, some standing more than six feet in height. Their females were smaller and many of them, according to early documents, were considered beautiful. Both sexes adorned themselves with ornaments. Claims by both the Creek and Shawnees were more or less eliminated by the 1814 Treaty of Fort Jackson.

North Alabama was the southwestern tip of the vast Cherokee domain. It included, with exceptions, all of Lauderdale County on the north bank and extended to Caney Creek, about six miles west of Sheffield, on the south side of the river.[14] However, there were not many Cherokee people at the Shoals when the first white settler arrived. A rather large village was located near the mouth of Blue Water Creek as early as 1790. It was presided over by the notorious Doublehead, one of the minor chiefs among the Cherokee. There are a number of other known town sites in the county that may have been of the Cherokee or, perhaps, of earlier tribes.[15]

White hunters and explorers first met the Cherokee along the Appomattox River in Virginia, although they had earlier lived in the northeast. Pushed southward by settlers and land promoters, they eventually settled along the Holston, Little Tennessee, and Tennessee Rivers, and even into South Carolina.

History tells us that the Cherokee were extremely proud people, even to the extent of looking down on the lower classes of whites. Although gentle and amiable to those they knew as friends, when they took to the warpath, total destruction became their war cry. They most often painted or stained their skin. The men were usually large and robust and the women were tall, slender, erect, and had features of perfect symmetry. The Cherokee, as well as the Creek, built their towns around a center square, in much the same way as did many of the early white settlers in the South. At about 1700, there were sixty-four towns in the Cherokee Nation. Yet, due to wars with the French, English, and neighboring tribes, this once great nation had been reduced to no more than 5,000 warriors by 1740.[16] On January 7, 1806, the Cherokee Nation signed away all of their land between Duck River in Tennessee to the Tennessee River in North Alabama.

The last of the Native Americas at the Muscle Shoals were the Chickasaw. They loved this land, were tenacious in trying to hold on, but in the end they fell victims to the avarice of the whites. Although they lost title to their lands in the Treaty of 1816, it was not until around 1840 that the last of these great people finally pulled up stakes in northwest Alabama and headed west.

Unlike the Cherokee who came from the east, the Chickasaw moved to this part of Alabama from the west. They were cousins to the Choctaw. In fact, some believe that in early times the Chickasaw people were part of the Choctaw tribe. The early Chickasaw Nation covered northern Alabama and Mississippi and western Kentucky and Tennessee. Their lands extended west to the Mississippi River and north to the Ohio River. Their earliest settlements east of the Mississippi River were situated near the Tennessee River in Madison County, Alabama. Later the center of their government was near the headwaters of the Tombigbee River in northeastern Mississippi. They were a relatively small tribe, with a population that ranged between an estimated 3,500 to 4,500.[17]

The Chickasaw warriors were raw-boned and slender, and most often their bodies would be inscribed with indelible ink. Europeans described the women as "beautiful and clean."[18] History records no group of people on any continent at any time who were cleaner than the Chickasaw. Some believe the reason these people chose to side with the English, as opposed to the French and Spanish, was their observation that the English were prone to bath more frequently than the other Europeans. At any rate, they became great friends to the English during the early development of Alabama and Mississippi.

The typical Chickasaw family owned two houses, one built beside the other. Their summerhouse was an oblong-shaped cabin, whereas, their winter quarters were of a circular form called the "hot house." On cold nights, fires were lit in the center of these winter houses without benefit of chimneys.[19] This may have been the inspiration for their daily baths. Their white neighbors were amazed to watch the entire family emerge from these smoke-filled rooms at daybreak and head to a nearby river or creek. Here they would break the ice, if necessary, so as to cleanse themselves.

Many interesting stories have been passed down by the early pioneers of Florence and Lauderdale County about their Chickasaw neighbors. James Simpson, whose father was a Florence merchant, told how the local Indians would come to town in groups to do their shopping. He wrote that they wore buckskin clothing and seemed to enjoy roaming over the store looking at everything.[20]

When the Chickasaw Nation ceded most of their Alabama territory during the Treaty of 1816, a small reservation in West Lauderdale County was set aside for Chief George Colbert. This rich farmland was deeded back to the federal government by Colbert in 1819. Yet this place was known as "The Reserve" long after the Colberts went to Oklahoma. As late as 1890 a post office called "Reserve" was established here.

The removal of the Historic Indian tribes to lands west of the Mississippi ended an epoch of time. For more than 10,000 years peoples of other and more ancient cultures had inhabited this place called the Muscle Shoals.

29. TWO LOCAL PERSONALITIES AMONG THE INDIANS

"Places affect people, and people affect places."
(source unknown)

The two most influential Native Americans to greet the white man at the Muscle Shoals were George Colbert and Doublehead. Colbert was a half-Scot and half-Chickasaw. Doublehead was a full-blood Cherokee. Both wore the title of chief. They were related by marriage. George Colbert's two wives, Salechie and Tuski-a-hoo-to, were Doublehead's daughters.[1]

Doublehead at one time or another made his home on both sides of the Muscle Shoals in what is now Colbert and Lauderdale Counties.[2] There are at least three springs that historically bear his name: one was located in West Colbert County and two in East Lauderdale County. A number of caves in Limestone County and Lauderdale County were said to have been the legendary hiding places for his treasures.

Doublehead's life was as his name implied – somewhat of a dual personality. He was at one time a fierce enemy of the white settlers. Near the end of his life he was considered the white man's friend.

As a minor chief at the Muscle Shoals, Doublehead became a power to be reckoned with following the assassination of his brother, Old Tassell, the principal chief of the Cherokee Nation in 1788.[3] His brother had been murdered under a flag of truce by a young white man in East Tennessee. Doublehead, whose villages were in the Muscle Shoals area, went on the warpath. Leading his warriors into middle and eastern Tennessee, he plundered, burned, raped, and slaughtered for some six years. Then, as if suddenly his revenge for his brother's death had been satisfied, Doublehead's way of life completely changed.

In 1806, a large tract of land between Cypress Creek and Elk River, covering a considerable part of East Lauderdale County, was set aside for the chief and became known as Doublehead's Reserve. Under the influence of John D. Chisholm, Doublehead leased thousands of acres of this land to white settlers who began moving into the area as early as 1807. However, these land holdings were not sanctioned by the Cherokee Nation or recognized by the United States Government. The presence of these people at the Muscle Shoals especially angered the Chickasaw Indians. Following official complaints made by Chief George Colbert, these settlers along with a number of squatters were evicted by the Army.[4]

Many of the Cherokee tribe resented Doublehead's dealings with the white man, and the circumstances relating to his reservation at the Shoals appeared to some as a form of bribery. This, perhaps more than anything else, lead to Doublehead's assassination at the hands of his own people on the Hiwassee River in the summer of 1807.[5] Logically it would seem that his burial would have occurred near where he fell. However, old legends persist that his body was returned to his village near Blue Water Creek in East Lauderdale County.

Chief George Colbert and a number of his brothers lived for a time in what is now Colbert County. These brothers were the sons of James Logan Colbert who, during his early age, found his way to the Mississippi and Alabama lands of the Chickasaw. He took unto himself three wives – two were full blood Chickasaw and the third of mixed blood. From these three wives he sired six sons and two daughters. James Logan Colbert's ancestry has never been fully established. Some historians claim that he came as a boy from Scotland in 1736. Others say that he was born in South Carolina and was reared as an orphan, connected in some way to an early settler of that state named James Logan. At least one writer suspects his name could actually have been Calvert, or some similar name, rather than Colbert.[6] James Logan Colbert soon became an established leader among the Chickasaw Nation and fought for the British during the American Revolution.[7] A number of his sons sided with the Americans during the War of 1812.[8] In November, 1784, James Logan Colbert, at the age of 64 years, made a trip to St. Augustine, Florida, in an attempt to persuade the Creeks to become allies with the newly formed American government. He was killed on this trip, some say by his horse. Others speculate that he was murdered by Caesar, his Negro slave.[9]

George Colbert operated a ferry and inn on the Natchez Trace at the Tennessee River. In 1801 he persuaded General James Wilkinson, who represented the Federal government, to move the river crossing on the Trace from the mouth of Bear Creek eastward to where the modern Natchez Trace Parkway crosses the river today.[10] This move was especially significant in drawing the attention of those who later were to cross the river as to the potential importance of the Muscle Shoals.

In the Treaty of 1816, George Colbert and his brother Levi were given a large tract of land in West Lauderdale County.[11] Known as Colbert's Reserve, and sometimes as "The Reserve," this prime farm land is known today as "The Bend of the River." George Colbert, or perhaps another Chickasaw with the same name, is said to have lived for a time on this land near a place called Savage Spring, which later was to become known as Woodland Spring.

No individual worked harder to keep the Chickasaw people from being evicted from their lands in Mississippi and Alabama than did George Colbert. One of his final efforts was at Tuscumbia where he made a passionate speech on the behalf of his people.[12] Within two years following the removal of the Chickasaw to new lands west of the Mississippi, old Chief Colbert was dead. He was buried in an unmarked grave at Towson, Arkansas, in early November 1839.[13]

Thus, the stories of Doublehead and Colbert are an interesting chapter in the history of the Lauderdale County. The legacy they left behind is forever woven into the very fabric of the land.

30. THE FIRST EUROPEANS AT THE MUSCLE SHOALS

"One who journeying along a way he knows not,
A place of drear extent, before he sees
A river rushing swiftly towards the deep,
And its tossing current white with foam ..."
(Homer)

Perhaps the name of the first European to see the spectacular Muscle Shoals will never be known. Historians generally agree that this honor probably belongs to an Englishman named Gabriel Arthur. The setting for this story is around 1673 – more than 130 years after de Soto's trip across Alabama. Arthur, who was working for Abraham Wood of Virginia, was captured by the Indians while on a trading expedition. As a prisoner he made a ten-day trip down the Tennessee River. Based upon his account of this journey, it appears that he came as far as the Muscle Shoals.[1]

Some twenty years later, in 1692, a renegade French trader, Jean Couture, made a canoe trip up the Tennessee River from its mouth to its upper reaches among the towns of the Overhill Cherokee. From there he made his way to Charlestown, South Carolina. There is no question but that Couture found it necessary to carry his canoe at least part way across the shallows and rapids that made up the barriers in the river called the Muscle Shoals. In 1700, this Frenchman served as a guide for a party of Carolina traders down the Tennessee to the Mississippi River.[2] This venture, in effect, opened up the Tennessee River as a principal trade route from the eastern colonies into the wilderness of the old southwest.

Colonel John Donelson was one of the first of the land speculators to become interested in the Muscle Shoals. He had known about this place since 1778, having learned about a trading post located here earlier in the century. A little over a year later he saw the place with his own eyes and became somewhat possessed with a dream to return and develop it. He did not live long enough to fulfill this vision. Yet, it is interesting that almost forty years later, his son-in-law, Andrew Jackson, and his grandson-in-law, General John Coffee, played key roles in establishing a town at the foot of the Shoals. Andrew Jackson's influence was "from afar," as a silent investor and promoter. It was John Coffee, Jackson's right arm in battle and nephew by marriage, who became one of the founding fathers of the new town of Florence.

Colonel John Donelson, with a crew of 40 men and 120 women and children passengers, left Fort Patrick Henry three days before Christmas in 1779. These were the families of the first settlers of Nashville who were to join the men who had made their way overland under General James Robertson. Donelson's initial plans were to disembark at the Muscle Shoals and travel by foot northward to Nashville. However, after searching in vain for a sign that Robertson was to have left at the Shoals, Donelson had no recourse but to continue his water journey to the mouth of the Tennessee and up the Cumberland to Nashville.

The Donelson fleet arrived at the Muscle Shoals on Sunday, March 12, 1780. The Colonel commanded the crude crafts from his flag boat, "Adventurer." In his journal he described his passage across these threatening rapids in the river: "... after running until about ten o'clock, we came in sight of the Muscle Shoals...When we approached them they had a dreadful appearance... the water being high made a terrible roaring...the current running in every possible direction. Here we did not know how soon we should be dashed to pieces, and all our troubles ended at once ... but by the hand of Providence, we are now preserved from this danger also. I know not the length of this wonderful shoal; it had been represented to me to be twenty-five or thirty miles; if so, we must have descended very rapidly ... for we passed it in about three hours. Came to, encamped on the northern shore, not far below the shoals, for the night."[3]

The next day they made an uneventful run and stopped again on the north bank across the river from the Indian town of Coldwater, now Tuscumbia. Alarmed by barking dogs during the night, they hurriedly broke camp and continued their journey down the river. Next morning Colonel Donelson sent a party back to the earlier camp to recover the things they had left behind. Here they found a Negro slave asleep beside one of the smoldering fires they had abandoned.[4] It is unfortunate that history does not record the name of this man for he was among the very first, if not the first, African American to visit the Muscle Shoals.

After settling near Nashville, Colonel Donelson became involved in what became known as the Muscle Shoals Speculation. He and an associate, Joseph Martin, while negotiating with the Chickasaw Nation for land on the Cumberland River, purchased from the Cherokee Indians land in the Bend of the Tennessee River. This curve in the river was sometimes referred to as the "Bent." They soon persuaded the Georgia legislature to organize a new county to include the land lying north of the Tennessee River reaching to the Tennessee line. Donelson, Martin, John Sevier, Lachlan McIntosh Junior, William Downes, Stephen Heard, and John Morell were appointed commissioners. Donelson was also appointed surveyor. In July, 1784, some of these men met at the Muscle Shoals, although the exact location is not known. Around this time attempts were made to establish settlements here. One story is that eighty men came with these commissioners to establish residence. Other sources indicate that this venture may have occurred a year later. However, they did not remain more than two weeks because of the hostile Chickasaw Indians who were vigorously guarding their claim. This opposition by these Native Americans was supported by the Spanish who had set up a trading post at the Shoals.[5]

During these futile years, Colonel Donelson made three hazardous trips to what is now Lauderdale and Colbert Counties, which kept him away from Nashville most of the time. The ambitious Colonel met his death April 11, 1786. It was reported that he was killed by the Indians, but his family said he knew too well the ways of the Native Americans to have fallen at their hands.[6] The Colonel's untimely death removed one of the prime leaders in the Muscle Shoals Speculation. However, at least one of his partners, General John Sevier, never lost sight of Donelson's dream. He tried again and again to launch a renewal of the efforts to develop the Muscle Shoals.

The year following the death of Donelson, his friend and neighbor at Nashville, General James Robertson, crossed the Tennessee River at the Muscle Shoals with 130 mounted men. They burned the Indian town of Oka Kapassa, or Cold Water, near what is now Tuscumbia. This village was being used as a French trading post. It was reported to have been the base for numerous raids by the local Indians on the white settlements along the Cumberland River. General Robertson reported many Indians killed, along with three French traders and a white woman. Five or six other Frenchmen were taken prisoners.[7]

All was quiet around Nashville for a month or so following Robertson's raid on Oka Kapassa. However, it wasn't long until small groups of Indians renewed their harassment of settlers in middle Tennessee. Some of these raids were led by a local Creek named Chief Bigfoot. The Cumberland settlement sent Captain David Shannon on a second raid which resulted in the death of Chief Bigfoot at what is now called McFarland Bottoms, a city park west of the Florence Indian Mound.[8]

As previously mentioned there were a number of attempts during the 1780's to establish colonies at this place on the Tennessee River. A town at the foot of the Shoals was recognized for its potential as a commanding commercial port for the foreseen trade that would connect with settlements on the French Broad, Holston, Cumberland, Ohio, Missouri, and Mississippi Rivers. Another advantage was the relatively short distance by land from the mouth of Bear Creek to the Tombigbee River and the Gulf of Mexico.[9]

An early promoter was Zachariah Coxe, one of the most energetic adventurers in the Southwest. He even envisioned a canal that would link the Tennessee and Tombigbee Rivers. Coxe was one of those who tried to occupy lands here as early as 1785. In 1789 he and his associates purchased three and one half million acres of land for $46,785 from Georgia. In March 1791, Coxe, his brother William, John Riddle, James Hubbard, Peter Bryant, and twenty-seven others, departed from the mouth of the French Broad River. Arriving at the Muscle Shoals in April, they immediately began construction of a blockhouse on one of the larger islands. Located near the present community of Center Star, it became known as Coxe Island. This historic site disappeared under the waters of Lake Wilson in 1925.

This effort to colonize the Shoals failed when Cherokee Chief Glass with sixty warriors from Nickajack on the upper Tennessee and nearby Melton's Bluff in what is now Lawrence County warned Coxe's party to peacefully withdraw or they would be put to death. Coxe and his settlers left the area. The ruins of his blockhouse on the island became the subject of much speculation for many years afterwards.

Coxe was not one to give up easily. In 1795, he and others again purchased from Georgia approximately the same lands, plus more, for $60,000. However, he was stopped this time by the U. S. Army. Both land acquisitions had been in violation of Indian treaties. The final demise of Coxe is not quite clear. Some claim that he was later arrested in Natchez for opening a land office, escaped, and captured again. Another source says that he died from being "hounded to death." A third source tells how he finally escaped into Spanish Territory where he was granted asylum. Further information speculates that a number of years later, Coxe was still talking about his proposed Tombigbee and Tennessee Canal as well as making plans for other adventures.[10]

Coxe's name remains very much a part of the business life of Florence. Cox Creek Parkway, a thriving commercial center east of the city, takes its name from Cox Creek, which, according to tradition, was named for Zachariah Coxe.[11]

By the turn of the century, much publicity had been given to the Shoals area. It is likely that isolated settlements of white people occurred not long after Coxe's expedition failed. These people perhaps traded with the Indians and lived in much the same fashion. By 1803, when the Natchez Trace was improved as a thoroughfare through this part of the country, there is evidence that more white intruders arrived. Silas Dinsmoor, Agent of the Chocktaw Nation, reported meeting a white woman at the Shoals in July, 1802. She was a daughter of a white man named Adams who was living here with a part of his family. Dinsmoor called them "a pretty dismal group – lazy and shiftless."[12] On March 15, 1804, it was reported that a Captain Campbell, commander of a garrison, was building houses and making large improvements within three miles of Doublehead's Village near the mouth of Blue Water Creek. Some believe this was the same man who established Campbell's Ferry near the present site of Wilson Dam. A white intruder by the name of Arnold died at the Shoals in 1806, leaving four horses, two saddles and bridles, one gold watch, a fowling piece, one rifle, and a trunk containing sugar, tea, and other condiments. A report from the Secretary War, dated April 2, 1806, shows that more than twenty families were living at the Shoals, in addition to Moses Melton who was residing at Melton's Bluff.[13]

The federal government did not approve of these intruders on Indian lands. Agents were ordered to begin evicting them as early as January, 1804.[14]

These first contacts by white adventurers and intruders during the seventeenth and eighteenth centuries constitute the beginning of the modern development of this land. It, likewise, is a continuation of man's life at the Muscle Shoals over a period of thousands of years.

31. EARLY YEARS IN THE WILDERNESS

"They shall drop upon the dwellings of the wilderness; and the little hills shall rejoice on every side."
(A Time To Remember, by the author)

The competing European powers were early to recognize the strategic importance of the great barrier in the Tennessee River called the Muscle Shoals. To varying degrees – dealing mostly with trading arrangements – England, France, and Spain became involved with the Native Americans who called this part of the wilderness their home.[1] It was not until after America won her independence that the influences of these sovereign powers of Europe subsided at the Muscle Shoals.

During the formative period of the United States, there was contention of ownership of this part of Alabama among several states. Georgia dated her claim as part of the original charter from King George I; this was not resolved until 1802, when they ceded all of North Alabama to the federal government in exchange for $1.25 million.[2]

Prior to 1802, South Carolina claimed a narrow strip of land reaching from the northern tip of that state to the Mississippi River. North Carolina, too, asserted her claim in 1780, by making provisions for awarding military bonuses to consist of 200 acres along with a slave; these small grants were located in the area west of the Cumberland Gap and north of the Tennessee River.[3] From 1784, until its demise in 1788, the ill-fated State of Franklin considered the Muscle Shoals of great importance for defense purposes.[4] The terrain and natural features of the counties on the north side of the Tennessee River seem much more related to the geography of the adjoining counties in south Tennessee than to the lower part of Alabama. Perhaps had not the earlier dividing line between the colonies of North and South Carolina prevailed at the time Tennessee became a state in 1796, this part of North Alabama would have been in Tennessee.

The Muscle Shoals was jealously claimed and guarded by Native Americans until the first part of the Nineteenth Century. This is one of the main reasons the development of the Muscle Shoals lagged some ten years behind Huntsville and Madison County. Although the Cherokee Nation relinquished their claims in 1806, the Chickasaw people held out for another decade. Even after both nations agreed to give up their lands, they managed to temporarily hold small reserves at the Shoals. One of the two Chickasaw reserves was in west Colbert County. Referred to locally as "The Nation," they finally gave up title to it in the Treaty of 1832.[5]

Their other reserve, known as "Colbert's Reserve," or sometimes, "The Reserve," was located in west Lauderdale County, opposite Colbert's Ferry on the Tennessee River. This prime land was provided for two Colbert brothers – George and Levi – by the Treaty of 1816.[6] During the latter part of 1818, the federal government negotiated with the Colberts for the release of this reserve.

When the Cherokee people ceded their land in 1806, they likewise held on to two reserves. One of these was wholly within what is now Lauderdale County, and the other overlapped into Limestone County. It was agreed that the first of these two reserves "... is to be considered the common property of the Cherokees who now live on the same, including John D. Chisholm, Atowe, and Checkout, and others."[7] These tracts, located between Cypress Creek below Florence and Elk River above Rogersville, became known as "Doublehead's Reserves,"[8] These holdings by Doublehead and his cohorts intensified the ongoing problems with the Chickasaw Indians whose claims included all of Lauderdale County. Chief George Colbert, the double-son-in-law of Chief Doublehead, maintained that Doublehead and his village had been allowed in the area only as the guests of the Chickasaw people.

Cherokee Chief Doublehead, who had been an enemy of the white man, now became a friend and landlord to these early intruders into Lauderdale County. Through his friend and agent, John D. Chisholm, Doublehead began to lease thousands of acres of land – with such leases for 99 years with renewable clauses for

900 years. Thus, begins an interesting story of the settlement of a number of families in the wilderness of Lauderdale County some eleven years before Alabama was admitted as a state. A document signed by Chisholm on August 3, 1807, shows 18 people with leases ranging in size from 100 to 12,000 acres. Two papers in 1809 give the names of 38 legal tenants and 39 intruders. A year later, yet another inventory identifies 107 residents living in the area between Cypress Creek and Elk River. Although some of the same names appear on more than one document, the sum of these numbers are fairly close to a total of 201 white settlers as reported in 1809 by the Cherokee Indian Agent.[9]

The early 1807 document includes the name of Captain John Johnson who leased 1,000 acres. Tradition has it that John and his wife Nancy were Florence first white settlers and that their plantation at one time or another was in West Lauderdale County near where the Natchez Trace crosses the river. They later moved to Colbert County where they established a plantation that eventually would become known as "Green Onion." Their daughter, Lucinda, was married to Major Lewis Dillahunty who had been sent into the territory south of the Tennessee River by President Monroe to prepare the minds of the Indians for the cession of their lands.[10]

The 1810 list includes such names as Samuel Burney, Senior; Samuel Anderson; Gabriel Butler; Amus Wilks; Samuel Craig; Israel Harmon; and others. Burney settled near the mouth of First Creek where he died sometime after 1840. Samuel Anderson carved out his place along Elk River near the mouth of Anderson Creek east of Rogersville. It is believed that Gabriel Butler is buried in the Butler Cemetery alongside Blue Water Creek near Elgin on land that was deeded to him in 1818.[11] Prior to the War of 1812, Amus Wilks had a blacksmith shop and trading post a few miles east of Florence.[12] Samuel Craig, a friend of Andrew Jackson, established a stage coach inn near the crossing of the Jackson Military Road at Shoal Creek.[13] Israel and Stephen Herman (or Harmon) settled near the mouth of Blue Water Creek. Stephen's son, Will, born about 1810, claimed to have been the first white child born in the county.[14]   Some point out that Mary "Aunt Polly" Richardson, who was married to Thomas Gresham, may have been the first in that she was born May 30, 1800.   There is a record, however, that shows her birth as being in Tennessee.   Her father and mother were John David and Catherine Stutts Richardson. Although not shown in any of the Doublehead Reserve lists, the Richardsons were among the first pioneers around Green Hill and Lexington.   It is said that they had intended to settle in the Mississippi Territory.   However, while traveling the Doublehead Trace out of Tennessee, they took the wrong turn and found themselves among friendly Indians at Richardson Creek near the bluffs overlooking Blue Water Creek.   Here they built their cabin and established their new home.   John, native of North Carolina, died about 1845.   His wife, Catherine, was born about 1771 in Pennsylvania.   They were married in Moore County, North Carolina.   Catherine died about 1871 at the age of 100 years.   Both are buried in the Granny Richardson Cemetery.[15]

Henry Davis Allen was one of the early squatters on Blue Water Creek between Lexington and Green Hill.   Allen is shown as a captain in the 27th Regiment in Maury County, Tennessee, as of January 28, 1813.   Some sources say he was in the War of 1812, although this has not been documented.   Traditions tell how the Allen family arrived at Blue Water Creek during a snowstorm and built a temporary hut covered with tree bark.   Another version says that Allen put up a tent made from animal skins until a more permanent dwelling could be constructed.   Meanwhile, Henry and his father, Rhody Allen, cleared enough land to plant a small crop the next spring.   It is believed that Rhody Allen was a Methodist circuit rider.   The Allens later erected a log house, barn, and other outbuildings.   There are a number of tales that have been handed down about this family.   One story is that Allen's wife, Polly, sometimes fed wolves from her back door ... until she caught one of these wild creatures looking at one of her babies.[16]

Both the Cherokee and Chickasaw Nations were unhappy about these white settlers and their leases of land from Doublehead.   Some historians believe the granting of these two reserves in Lauderdale County, and the subsequent leases of large acreages to the intruders, played an important role in the brutal assassination of Chief Doublehead at the hands of his own people in the summer of 1807. In March, 1809, Chief George Colbert of the Chickasaw Nation intimated that if these white intruders were not removed, he would himself evict them. In response, the Cherokee Agent, Colonel Return J. Meigs, was ordered to force these settlers to leave. On June 12, 1809, Meigs reported that his soldiers had marched over 400 miles in a campaign that took 51 days to evict 201 families from the Chickasaw lands.[17]

A number of these people returned along with others who were eager to carve out a home in the wilderness. This brought about so much pressure from the Chickasaw people that General Wade Hampton was ordered to establish a fort near the Shoals. Fort Hampton was built about 1810 approximately four miles from the mouth of Elk River. This was more of a garrison than a fort in that its mission was to keep the settlers out and not to fight the Indians. A Captain Smythe was its first commanding officer. He was later replaced by Captain George Washington Sevier, son of Tennessee's first governor, John Sevier. The August 24, 1810, edition of The Democratic Clarion and Tennessee Gazette, Nashville, Tennessee, reported this news item: "By a gentleman from the Muscle Shoals we have learned that Captain James McDonald's and Captain John Regan's companies had arrived at the Rifle Company a few miles from the mouth of Elk River, from the cantonment near Natchez. They were at present from the command of Major John Fuller; but Colonel Purdy from Hiwassee was expected there in a few days... The object for assembling soldiers is conjectured to be twofold: first to remove intruders on the Indian lands, and secondly to open a road to the Tombigbee... To effect the first object, Lieutenant Thomas Ramsey has left notices at several public places among the settlers requiring them to move off the land by the 15th of December next, otherwise the military were ordered to drive them off at the point of the bayonet..."

These soldiers at Fort Hampton made a series of raids. The first was in the early spring of 1811. Their mission was to destroy the homes and crops of the intruders and send them back across the Tennessee line. Years later, Will Herman recalled how these troops laid waste to everything his father had built, including their home, barns, and even the rail fences.[18]

Many of these early settlers returned again to this area of the Muscle Shoals. Some families, such as the Hermans and Allens, managed to reclaim their original homesteads. Others, such as Amus Wilkes, could not compete with the more prosperous land buyers. Instead, Amus chose some 240 acres alongside Cypress Creek near Cloverdale where he died sometime after 1844.[19]

It was not until December 14, 1819, that Alabama was admitted as the twenty-second state in the Union. From 1817 until 1819, this area was part of the Alabama Territory. Earlier, from 1798 until 1817, it was a part of the Mississippi Territory under the provisions of the 1787 Northwest Ordinance.

Thus ends the story of how it was in the wilderness of Northwest Alabama before the federal government legally acquired title to these coveted lands from the Native Americans. It didn't take long following the Huntsville land sales in 1818, for this part of the state to become a mecca for families who were eager to build their homes and establish their roots among the hills and hollows and in the rich and fertile river bottoms of Lauderdale County.

32. FIRST IT WAS HOUSTOUN AND ELK, AND THEN WE BECAME LAUDERDALE COUNTY

"Oh, we are weary pilgrims; to this wilderness we bring..."
(Puritan's Mistake)

Lauderdale County is almost a year older than the State of Alabama and some five weeks older than its county seat, Florence. Yet, as a local government entity its history goes back to the latter part of the eighteenth century and into the domain of Georgia, one of the original thirteen colonies.

Prior to 1804, Georgia claimed almost all of present Alabama and Mississippi as part of her original grant from England. Following the American Revolution, this state was quick to begin dealing with land speculators who were venturing into this vast wilderness. The Great Bend, or Bent, of the Tennessee River, and especially the Muscle Shoals, became the most coveted of these lands. This early activity led to the creation of Houstoun County, the first of the two counties which would become the ancestors of Lauderdale County.

In 1785 – four years following the surrender of Lord Cornwallis at Yorktown – Houstoun County, Georgia, was established by the Georgia legislature. This county in the wilderness took in all the Great Bend of the Tennessee River, including what is now Lauderdale County. The new county was named for the popular John Houstoun who served as governor of Georgia in 1778 and 1784. It was, perhaps, not incidental that Colonel John Donelson was one of the commissioners appointed by Georgia to organize Houstoun County.

Appeals were made for settlers who were adventurous enough to go into the wilderness. The Kentucky Gazette of Lexington carried the following advertisement in its December 19, 1789, edition: "The public were informed in the last paper, that a plan was in agitation for the settlement of the lands belonging to the State of Georgia, contained in the great bend of the Tennessee

River, commonly known by the name of the MUSCLE SHOALS COUNTRY... Any person who has a wish to assist in forming a settlement in that country may be informed of any particulars by application to the subscriber, who hereby engages to every able bodied man, two hundred acres land of the first quality in that country ... (signed) B. Gaines."[1]

The Native Americans who loved and coveted the Muscle Shoals even more than did the land speculators prevented Houstoun County from becoming a successful venture in the wilderness. Although attempts were made to establish settlements, these hostile Indians prevented such efforts. The new county had barely enough time to elect its own representative to the Georgia legislature, yet not enough time to see him properly seated. By 1804, it was all over. Georgia relinquished her claims to this part of the wilderness, and Houstoun County became only a footnote among the faded pages of history.[2]

Even though Madison County was established in 1808, it would take another eight years before the federal government could persuade the Indians to give up their claims to what would become Limestone and Lauderdale Counties. Meanwhile, all was not quiet within this part of the wilderness. The white people had seen or heard about the lands of the Muscle Shoals. It was hard to keep them out. It was not until the Treaty of 1816 that this area finally passed from ownership by the Indians to that of the federal government.

Within a year following this 1816 treaty held at nearby Colbert's Ferry, a second county government was born; it covered all of what is now Lauderdale and Limestone Counties on the north bank of the river between Madison County to the east and a line to the west that separated the Mississippi and Alabama Territories. This new entity was named Elk County for the river that flowed through it.

Elk County was created May 9, 1817, by the legislature of the newly established Territory of Alabama. In that there was a delay in the appointment of a governor for the new territory, Governor David Holmes of the Mississippi Territory signed the enabling proclamation which read in part: "... All that tract of country bounded on the north by the southern boundary of the State of Tennessee, and on the west and south by the river Tennessee, and on the east by Madison County, shall form one county to be called by the name of ELK: the courts of justice of which will be held at Fort Hampton..."[3]

Fort Hampton, the designated seat of government, was located on Elk River a few miles east of Rogersville. This military garrison had been established around 1810 by the federal government to keep white settlers out of the lands claimed by the Chickasaw and Cherokee. The fort was located near the center of the newly created county. Roads leading to the garrison had been cut through the forest from several directions by the soldiers which made it the most accessible point in this part of the wilderness.[4]

Officers for Elk County were commissioned on May 24, 1817. Thomas D. Crabb and George Wilder were jointly appointed as Justice of the Quorum. The Chief Justice of the Orphans Court was Thomas Bibb. Anthony Winston became Sheriff and William Rutledge was made Constable. Edmond Edmondson was appointed Clerk of the Court. The five Justices of the Peace were: Zedekiah Tate, Thomas Rinddish, Thomas Obannion, Nicholas P. Bond, and John Allison.[5]

Elk County existed less than a year. It was dissolved January 26, 1818, by the legislature for the Territory of Alabama as follows: "...a bill to be entitled an act to alter and fix the western boundaries of Madison County, and to divide the county of Elk.[6]

Eleven days later – February 6, 1818 – Lauderdale County was created by the legislature of the Territory of Alabama while meeting in the Douglass Hotel at St. Stephens, the seat of the territorial government. Lauderdale was one of eight counties established on that same date. It was named for Lieutenant Colonel James Lauderdale who died December 23, 1814, from wounds received in the Battle of Talladega. He was one of five brothers who fought as officers under Andrew Jackson in the War of 1812. The Lauderdales were early pioneers from Virginia who settled in what is now Trousdale County, Tennessee, around 1794.

James Lauderdale, born in 1780, was a surveyor before he entered the cavalry to serve under General John Coffee. This young soldier is buried in the Lauderdale Family Cemetery near Templow, Tennessee.[7]

There were no towns as such within the borders of Lauderdale County when it came into being. Only a few isolated houses could be seen here and there, although settlers were beginning to make their presence known in this part of the wilderness. This is noted by the wording of the act creating Lauderdale County: "And be it further enacted, that for the time being, the said courts in the said county of Lauderdale, shall be holden at the house commonly called `Col. Puler's place,' east of Cypress and near the creek, and may at the discretion of said Courts, for want of necessary buildings, be adjourned to some convenient place contiguous thereto."[8]

Historians have unsuccessfully sought the identification of Colonel Puler and the location of his home. It is believed that the place referred to was the home of Lauderdale County's first judge, William S. Fulton. The location of his home was perhaps in West Florence and near the Jackson Military Road that was under construction at the time.[9]

Officials of the new county were appointed in February 1818 as follows: Hugh McVay was made Clerk of the Superior Court, with Joel Rice as Sheriff and James Fyles as Coroner. Joseph Farmer became Treasurer and Charles B. Roundtree, Ranger. William Fanning and William McDonald were designated as Constables. Justices of the Peace were: James Bumpas, Zedekiah Tate, Andrew McMiken, Alex McDougal, Daniel Lance, and Joseph Farmer. Later in the year, John McKinley was made Chief Justice of the County Court and George Coalter Clerk of the Court.[10]

When these people came to the newly established Lauderdale County they found a veritable wilderness of virgin timber along with some open land as well as scrub brush and "barrens." One pristine grove near the present intersection of Court Street and Hermitage Drive had ancient trees with trunks that measured some five feet or more in diameter.[11] Lauderdale County was especially blessed with springs, branches, creeks, and rivers. These many waters were bountiful sources of fish and mussels. Because it had long been an Indian hunting ground, different parts of the county were crossed by ancient Indian trails. Wild game of almost every description was available for the hunter. These resources and the fertile lands in the creek and river bottoms and nearby valleys made The Muscle Shoals a paradise for those seeking new opportunities to begin anew. It is no wonder that the early settlers were eager to call this place their new home.

33. MAJOR ROADS AND HIGHWAYS

"The beaten road which ...with weary footsteps tread..."
(Percy Bysshe Shelley)

Early settlers found the Muscle Shoals area traversed with ancient Indian trails. A number of these were improved over a period of time to become roads and highways used today. Some of the first people to arrive here claimed they had to cut their way through the forests and thickets to find a place to stake their claims in the wilderness.

The best known, and perhaps the earliest of the wilderness roads, was the Natchez Trace in the western part of the county. This trail began as a buffalo run and was later used by the Indians. It was made into a roadway through the primeval forest by the United States Army between 1795 and 1835. This historic highway covered a distance of 500 miles between Nashville, Tennessee, and Natchez, Mississippi. It originally followed the high ridges through Lauderdale County and crossed the river near Waterloo.

However, in 1801, Chickasaw Chief George Colbert persuaded, General James Wilkinson, who represented the Federal government to move this crossing upstream to the present General John Coffee Bridge. In the early nineteenth century it was used by the military, mail carriers, and settlers into the southwest. Planters and merchants often floated their products down the Ohio, Cumberland, and Mississippi Rivers by flat boats and returned on foot by way of the Trace. Indians and outlaws made the journey hazardous. Some of the earliest settlers in the Muscle Shoals area arrived by the Trace. Use of this famous trail declined with the arrival of the steamboat as a safer and more convenient means of transportation. In 1934, Congress passed legislation authorizing a survey of the Natchez Trace. Today it is one of the most scenic national parkways in America.[1]

The Jackson Military Road quickly became the most important road leading into this area. It branched from the Natchez

Trace at Columbia, Tennessee, and entered Lauderdale County near the community of Green Hill. This route shortened the distance from Nashville to New Orleans by over two hundred miles. It followed original trails used by the Indians through this part of Alabama. Doublehead's Trace, which ran from Franklin, Tennessee, to the Muscle Shoals, became the main bed. This is documented by an early petition found in the minutes of Maury County, Tennessee, which stipulated, in part, as follows: "... Contemplating a Great Federal Highway from Nashville to New Orleans, gave orders or we are informed to General Jackson to cause to be laid out and cut out, a road from the most eligible point on the line of this state ... to intersect Double Head road at or near Doctor Farmers...[2]

Doublehead's Trace forked near the Tennessee line. One branch led to Doublehead's village near the mouth of Blue Water Creek; the other to Campbell's Ferry near the present site of Kendale Garden Subdivision. From the state line, the section of the Military Road into Florence followed an aboriginal trail from Buffalo River near Lawrenceburg to the mouth of Cypress Creek where there was a river crossing.

General Andrew Jackson's recommendation to the Secretary of War, dated December 17, 1815, led to the survey of this road. The actual construction was done by the troops under his command. Work began in May, 1817, and was essentially completed by May, 1820.[3]

There are legends that Jackson had used this trail during the War of 1812. A descendant of James Jackson, one of the founders of Florence and an early friend of the General, referred to a wooded area near the Military Road entrance to Bailey Springs as the site where his men camped on their return from the Battle of New Orleans.[4] No record of the use of this route for military purposes during the War of 1812 or the Indian Campaigns has been found. Jackson's main routes to New Orleans were by water and the Natchez Trace. His marches into South Alabama and Florida were mainly by way of Huntsville.

The Jackson Military Road became the main thoroughfare through Florence and Lauderdale County. One writer in 1821 described it this way: "The great Military road ... passes through this town, and the number of people who travel through it, and the numerous droves of horses for the lower country, for market, are incredible."[5] During the steamboat era, this highway became the southern terminus of the Zanesville Pike which began at Zanesville, Ohio, and ended at the port in Florence. It was heralded as the quickest way to get to New Orleans from the east. It reduced the delivery time for mail from Washington to New Orleans by at least a week.

The Jackson Military Road was not only used by those going south and west, it also was the major immigration route into the Muscle Shoals area for those who came here to establish new homes. In 1916, this pioneer road was designated as United States Highway 43, and was renamed Jackson Highway.

The historic Byler's Turnpike, Alabama's first state road, was established by the State Legislature in November, 1819. This road connected with the Jackson Military Road a few miles northeast of present St. Florian. From here it ran south to the Tennessee River where it crossed at the Bainbridge Ferry. The Byler Road facilitated travel from Nashville to Tuscaloosa. It became a way for early settlers into West Alabama from Tennessee, Virginia, and other states.

United States Highway 72 follows the early 1823 post road from Athens to Florence by way of East Port (or Bainbridge.) This road followed the present Snake Road between Cairo and Rogersville so as to cross the shallow ford over Elk River near the Salem community in Limestone County. The Florence to Huntsville Road, surveyed in 1829, generally followed parts of both the post road and an Indian trail from Ditto's Landing near Huntsville to Savannah, Tennessee.

A well-used pioneer highway into Florence was known as the Pulaski Pike. It was approved by Congress in 1832 as a post road from Florence to Pulaski, Tennessee, by way of Lexington. Only sections of it, such as Hough Road near Cox Creek Parkway, are in use today. The Pulaski Pike, and Lamb's Ferry Road at Rogersville, were supply routes connecting Pulaski with the Tennessee River during the years preceding the coming of the railroads.

Coffee Road was the original name for Cloverdale Road. It was named for General John Coffee whose plantation was on this road. It connected with the old Natchez Trace near the Tennessee line at one of its historic inns known as Cypress Inn. This early route funnels traffic from parts of Wayne County, Tennessee, into Florence. It also serves as a farm-to-market road from the communities around Underwood, Cloverdale, and Salem. Coffee Road was mentioned in the August 15, 1831, session of the county court when Samuel Brown was appointed to maintain one of its sections.

Savannah Highway was originally called Jackson Road in that it passed by the Forks of Cypress plantation of James Jackson. In 1831, Thomas Ticer was appointed supervisor of that section of Jackson Road from the state line to his home. Here this function was picked up by Perkin P. Pool to where it reached the farm of Samuel Young. This pioneer road has been re-routed a number of times and is now one of the major highways into Northwest Alabama from Hardin County, Tennessee.

Waterloo Road was at one time an alternate route from Florence to Savannah, Tennessee. However, the backwaters of Pickwick Dam covered that part leading west of Waterloo into Tennessee. A section of the earliest Waterloo Road ran south of its present route through the western part of the county. By 1831, this part was referred to as South Waterloo Road. The stretch of this road from Florence to Oakland was at one time called the Government Road. The eastern end of present Waterloo Road was at one time called Hood Road in that it passed by the James Hood plantation a few miles west of Florence.

Another important route leading from Florence was Cheatham's Ferry Road. It ran to a well-used river crossing near Smithsonia which was established by Christopher Cheatham around 1824. Many of West Lauderdale County's largest plantations were in this area. During the Civil War, the Confederate boat Dunbar was scuttled near the ford across Cypress Creek to avoid being captured by the Union Navy. It was later raised and repaired by the Confederacy. However, while it was under the water its gunwales were visible from the Cypress Creek ford. Thus, it became known as Gunwale Ford. Soon thereafter the old Cheatham's Ferry Road became the Gunwaleford Road.

Chisholm Road, now a part of Alabama Highway 157, was not built until around 1920. In August, 1919, a delegation from Florence attended a meeting in Collinwood for the purpose of building a pike to connect the two towns.[6] In earlier times Waynesboro and other nearby towns could be reached by the Natchez Trace or by using a series of connecting rural roads from Alabama into Tennessee. Chisholm Road runs close to the old Chisholm Place where John Chisholm, Senior, and other family members are buried. John was born in 1738 and was buried here in 1828. Others say this road was named for John's Son, Tolliver Chisholm. He was born in 1817, died in 1878, and is buried in the Florence Cemetery.

By 1844 thirty-two roads were listed in Lauderdale County. Only five of these were listed as first class roads: Huntsville, Savannah, Waterloo, Jackson Military, and Armistead.[7]

34. THEN CAME THE PEOPLE

"What is this, the sound and rumour? ...
Like the wind in hollow valleys when the storm is drawing near ...
'Tis the people marching on."
(William Morris)

They came in great numbers, these people from Tennessee, Kentucky, Georgia, North and South Carolina, and Virginia. The legal opening of the lands in Lauderdale County came with the federal land sales at Huntsville in early 1818. Previously, a few settlers and squatters had carved out homesteads in the wilderness, especially along Blue Water Creek and Elk River in the eastern part of the county and around the three branches of Cypress Creek in the northwest sections. Yet, the legal and binding land holdings could not be acquired until after the 1816 treaty with the Chickasaw Nation. Afterwards, it took almost two years for the government to set the stage, but the beginnings of the permanent population of Lauderdale County was then well on its way.

The government offered the open land in 160-acre tracts to be sold to the highest bidder. The buyers were required to pay one-fourth of the price at the time of the sale with the remaining balance to be paid in annual installments. The Cypress Land Company, which had purchased 5,515 acres for the purpose of establishing Florence, conducted their own promotions and sales. Some land in the county, considered as prime cotton acreage, sold for as much as $50 an acre. The average price for ordinary farmland was between $20 and $30 an acre. One farm sold for $78 an acre.[1] The wealthy planters and land speculators were especially interested in the rich river bottomlands of Lauderdale County.

People who were buying and seeking new homesteads made their way into Florence and Lauderdale County over such trails as the Natchez Trace and Andrew Jackson's Military Road. They came by horse back, in wagons, and many on foot. Some came down the Tennessee by flatboats and keelboats. There were instances of whole communities moving together. A settlement on Duncan Creek in Laurens County, South Carolina, moved to Lauderdale County in the early 1820's and took up farming in an area bordered by Waterloo, Murphy's Chapel, and Burcham Valley.[2] Sometimes large land owners would send slave teams, supervised by overseers, to clear the land and build temporary structures prior to moving their families to the area.[3] The population of Lauderdale County in 1820 totaled almost 5,000. It more than doubled by 1830. By the time of the Civil War the number of inhabitants had reached 17,420.[4]

The formative years for Florence and Lauderdale County were during the antebellum period. Many changes were brought about by the Civil War and Reconstruction and the advent of the Tennessee Valley Authority in the early 1930's. Other factors, as well, have helped modify the cultural heritage of the area; some of these include political changes, industrial, commercial, and financial developments, urbanization, and strong social forces.[5] All of these have assisted in forming the cosmopolitan structure of the Twentieth Century. Of interest is that a number of social traits identified with the earliest settlers of this part of the Tennessee Valley can still be observed among their 21st century descendants.

The salience of English, Scots, Welsh, Irish, and Scots-Irish family names among the early settlers of North Alabama, denotes the prevalence of those who came in such great numbers to the Muscle Shoals. These people were largely from two ancient cultures from the Old World: the Anglo-Saxons and the Celts. The Anglo-Saxons were Germanic people who invaded England in the 5th Century. In the early colonization of America these people became, in general, the inhabitants along the east coast, contributing to the cultures of the New England countryside, big cities, seaports, and the factories and workshops of the industrial East. Some historians have pointed out that the Anglo-Saxons became the leading influence in plantation life, with its social structure of slavery, which closely resembled the early feudalistic system of Europe. This might have been the case throughout most of the South, but not necessarily in Lauderdale County. A number of the wealthiest planters in and around Florence, such as James Jackson and John Simpson, were of pure Irish stock. There were a number of large plantations, especially in the Bend of the River and along the shoreline south of Center Star. However, most of the farms in Lauderdale County consisted of no more than 160 acres. Many of these small farmers were located in the upper lands of the county alongside hills or squeezed into narrow hollows. Generally, these lands were not considered good cotton or corn producers, especially in the area that became known as "the barrens," around Lexington and the Tennessee border. As a general rule, these "survival-type" farmers were descended from an ancient people known as the Celts.

The Celts were a division of an early Indo-European who pre-dated the Roman times and were the tribes who resisted, harassed, and refused to be conquered by the legions of Caesar. They were scattered all the way from Galatia in Asia Minor to Spain and the British Isles in Western Europe. These were the rugged Highlanders of Scotland, Wales, and Northern Ireland. No other race of people on earth was more suited to blaze a trail and populate the hills and hollows of North Alabama that these Scots, Scots-Irish, and Welsh. History records no people who were more self-sufficient, independent, or able to withstand extreme hardships than the Celts. It has been observed that the small crossroads community in Lauderdale County – with its store, cotton gin, and a church or two is about as Celtic in character as one can find even in the Highlands of Scotland.[6]

These were the pioneers who came in great numbers to Florence and Lauderdale County. They brought with them strains of ancient cultures that have left indelible influences on whom we are today.

35. EARLY EAST LAUDERDALE COUNTY

*"... where men are who know how to take care of
themselves, these are the cities and walls."*
(John Adams, 1776)

The settlement of East Lauderdale County – from the banks of the Elk to the waters of the Cypress – by families mostly from Tennessee, Kentucky, Virginia, Georgia, North Carolina, and South Carolina, commenced as early as 1807. First to arrive were the tenants who leased thousands of acres of land from Chief Doublehead. Interspersed here and there were the squatters who had no legal right to be here. Although poor and without a "tomahawk claim" they, too, were anxious to carve their niche in this part of Northwest Alabama. All but a few of these tenants and squatters were soon evicted by federal soldiers. This was still Indian Territory. Although the Cherokee Nation had signed away their claim in 1806, it was not until 1816 that the Chickasaw people finally and reluctantly gave up their ancestral home. Government land sales commenced at Huntsville in early 1818; thus began the influx of the hordes of people who would make this place their home.

The banks of Blue Water Creek, from its confluence with the Tennessee River all the way to the Tennessee line were among the first places to be settled. Doublehead's tenants and a few squatters had first discovered its fertile fields. A few of them managed to return after the 1811 evictions.

Among the first permanent settlers here were several families of McDougals, all of the same clan. These Scots had first settled near Dunn, North Carolina, after their arrival in America. The most prominent of this group was old Square Alexander McDougal . As a justice of the peace, he probably performed more marriage ceremonies than all the local preachers combined. His home became a meeting place for the first Methodists in this area until a church was built. By about 1834, the Square and his wife, Eleanor Garrett McDougal, had moved across the line into Wayland

Springs, Tennessee. His older brother, John McDougal, saw service in the Revolutionary War not long after the family had arrived in America. The McDougals were soon intermarried with other early families, among whom were the Smiths and Killens. James and Wesley Smith were reared in Chester County, South Carolina. Both brothers became Methodist preachers and moved to Texas. No name in the county is more well known than that of Killen. One descendant gave his name to the town of Killen when he became its postmaster in 1896. Other pioneers in the Blue Water Creek basin were the families of Walter Maxey, Rich McMahon, Joseph Robinson, John Minor, E. Sheffield, Daniel Troback, Cornelius Carmach, Samuel Shelburne, William Townsend, William Hickman, John and Moses Jones, Wilson Cage, Elisha Thomas, James Cocke, William Cornish, and John West.[1]

Rogersville

First known as "Rodgersville," this town came into being as a trading center near the intersection of three early thoroughfares. One of these is now U. S. Highway 72, a well-traveled route between Chattanooga and Memphis. A section of this road was originally an Indian trail leading from Ditto's Landing on the river south of Huntsville. Used by them as a by-pass around the Muscle Shoals river barrier, it forked at Center Star. The south branch led to Cypress Creek below Florence. The north fork terminated at the river near Savannah, Tennessee.[2]

Snake Road leads out of Rogersville into Limestone County. In the days before there was a bridge over Elk River, this highway allowed the traveler to go from Florence to Athens by way of a shallow ford across Elk River near the community of Cario in Limestone County.[3]

The third road to form a junction at Rogersville is the Lamb's Ferry Road. Around 1816, John Lamb and his son moved from Indian Creek in Giles County, Tennessee, to establish a ferry across the river south of the future town of Rogersville. This ferry soon became an important river port. Flatboats and keelboats from Knoxville and other points on the upper Tennessee River unloaded supplies here which were then hauled by wagons to the areas in and around Pulaski, Tennessee.[4] By 1836, Lamb's Ferry was referred to as Good's Ferry.

The Rogersville Post Office was established October 4, 1825, with Thomas Cunningham as postmaster. The town was named for Andrew and Patience Henderson Rodgers from Laurens County, South Carolina. The main business district is located on their eighty acres which was purchased on March 3, 1818, at the first Huntsville land sale. Andrew died in 1830, and is believed to be buried in an unmarked grave in the Old Liberty Cemetery. Afterwards, Patience Rodgers and her son, Thomas, sold this property to George Simmons. There were two other families by the name of Rodgers who lived in this area. William and Catherine Rodgers purchased 79 acres one mile east of town in 1831. About the same time, Samuel and Martha Rodgers acquired 160 acres south of Rogersville. By 1835, however, these two families had moved away.[5]

Archibald Fuqua, with his wife Sarah Clarke Fuqua and eight children, settled here in 1818. His ancestors, originally known as Fouquets, were from France. In May 1832, John P. Cunningham, Daniel Nancy, and William Sholars were appointed judges of the voting place at Rogersville for an election to be held in August. Other early settlers here were: William Kerley, George Clair, William Reed, Sam Barner, James Lotto, Gilbert Taylor, Robert Shaw, and Samuel Burney. Samuel Burney was here as early as 1810. A veteran of the American Revolution, he is believed to be buried in one of the unmarked graves in the Old Liberty Cemetery in Rogersville State Park. The original name for First Creek was "Burney Creek."

The first business was established along Cannon Branch, about a mile south of town. It wasn't until about 1828 that merchants began building in the present area of downtown Rogersville. Thomas Cunningham, George Simmons, Bayless Bourland, and Foley and Foster, were among the original merchants at this location. Other early merchandise houses were: McNeil, Harraway, Nance, Stamps, Martindale, Alexander, and Thomas J. Hurn. Captain Robert Shane made saddles and harnesses and Alexander Shields ran the cabinet shop. Peter F. Patrick operated two stagecoach lines. One route connected Lamb's Ferry with Pulaski; the other ran between Florence and Huntsville.[6]

Baptist minister Joshua James, Senior, was among the early settlers. According to legend, James was sent by a Baptist Church in Boston, Massachusetts, to work with the Indians. His family arrived on a flatboat at Lamb's Ferry around 1820. His daughter-in-law, Esther, organized the town's first school in a log house on Lamb's Ferry Road. Joshua James, Senior, is buried in the Liberty Cemetery in Rogersville. The graves of Joshua, Junior, and Esther are in the Jones-Hill Cemetery near Florence.

Another legend has it that the famed Methodist evangelist, Lorenzo Dow, preached at Rogersville at a very early date. This, perhaps, occurred about the time he was reported to have conducted a series of meetings at the Big Spring in Athens.

Another preacher of note was a former slave, the Reverend Harrison Ingram, who was born in 1856. Ingram was of the Presbyterian faith. He operated a limestone quarry directly across from the modern General Joe Wheeler State Park Lodge.

John Callahan, John Braly, and Joel Burrow, a veteran of the War of 1812, were early farmers north of the town. Daniel Nance, Chris Price, Archibald Fuqua, Sam Harraway, Samuel Craft, Thomas Davis, John Smith, Robert Cooper, Austin Sands, and John Cunningham were among those who owned land between Rogersville and the river.[7]

Lexington, Dugout, Porter Town, Belew, and Cotton Gin

The presence of a number of free-flowing springs in this part of the county attracted the early Indians as well as the white settlers who came later. Revolutionary War veteran Thomas Gresham received a land grant in 1816 just west of Lexington, although he was here as early as 1810. Gresham died in 1816, and was buried in the Gresham Cemetery. Thomas' brother John also entered land in the same section in 1818. Another veteran of that war, Benjamin French, is buried north of the town on the Old Mill Road. He arrived in Lauderdale County in 1830 and died in 1847.[8]

Beginning in March, 1818, the following families entered land in and around Lexington: Horatio Pettus, Edward Chambers, John Callahan, James Gage, Edward Poteet, Louis Marshall, Gutherage Masterson, John Miller, Rolin Brown, Thomas McCarley, Zachariah Johnson, Jacob Cody, Joseph Price, Benjamin Hagood, Mark Shelton, Wilson Collier, Robert Mitchell, John Finoler, James Hardin, William Hammond and Joseph McDonald.[9]

Lexington emerged first as a crossroads village, and later as one of the larger towns in East Lauderdale County. In 1832, Felix A. Westmoreland was appointed as its first postmaster.[10] In that same year Denis Springer, Robert Mitchell, and Zachariah Johnston were appointed supervisors of the voting place. Among the other early citizens were John W. Briggs, John W. Davis, William Derit, George Cox, and Edwin B. Westmoreland.[11] Derit, Westmoreland, and Davis were merchants. Briggs owned the town's tanning yard. Leather from this industry was used in Charles Clark's shoe shop. Samuel LeMay was Lexington's wagon-maker. During the early years of the Civil War, William Taylor operated a saddle shop. This must have been a thriving business because of the goings and comings of both the Union and Confederate Armies on the old Pulaski Pike. During one encampment, horses from a Union cavalry were allowed to roam about the town unattended. Evidence of this can be seen in the old Lexington Cemetery where a number of markers were broken.

One of the most influential leaders in Lexington was Andrew Lee Phillips who was born near Center Star in 1855. His general merchandise store was established at Lexington in 1888. He later owned a gin, gristmill, and flour rolling mill. He was responsible for the formation of the town's first bank in 1917. Phillips made significant contributions to the building of the Lexington School and the Methodist Church. He died in 1938 and is buried in the Old Lexington Cemetery.[12]

The present business district has been moved from its original location. Remains of the foundations of the earlier town were unearthed in recent years. It appears that the first stores were lined up in a row rather than scattered over the town area.[13] Some believe the town took its name from Lexington, Virginia. Others think that the patriotic remembrance of the American Revolution prevailed and that the town was named for Lexington, Massachusetts. This theory is reinforced by the presence of a number of veterans of that war who lived in this area.[14] Lexington was a popular name in those days. At one time there were two Lexingtons in Alabama as well as one in Tuscaloosa County which renamed itself New Lexington in 1836.[15]

Perhaps a forerunner of Lexington was Dugout. Established about 1820, this village came into being on the land holdings of Edward Poteet, a veteran of the American Revolution. He settled near the Alabama-Tennessee line in 1818. This once thriving community had a gristmill, blacksmith shop, general store, and later a cotton gin. Israel Price made shoes and had his own tanning vats just across the Tennessee line on the north side of Dugout.

Porter Town was also north of Lexington and near Dug Out. It was named for several Porter families who settled here from Abbeville, South Carolina, during the 1820s. Hugh and Sarah Bowie Porter were born in the early 1790s. Their son, James Gleen Porter, established a gristmill and blacksmith shop in this community. Hugh's nephew, Washington Porter, was also here as well as a widow, Rebecca Porter, who was born in 1780 in North Carolina. Her son, Andrew, was a native of South Carolina.

Belew was an early Blue Water Creek community near the Tennessee line, a few miles northwest of Lexington. Rainey Belew from South Carolina arrived here in 1818. He was married to Rebecca Johnson.[16] William M. Belew was appointed postmaster in 1889. This office was discontinued in 1907 when John W.

Richardson was postmaster. Somewhere in this area was the post office of Cotton Gin which existed between 1838 and 1843.

Anderson and Ingrum Hollow

Anderson is alongside Anderson Creek on the Lamb's Ferry Road between Rogersville and Pulaski, Tennessee. Of special interest are the abundance of primeval fossils found on the high ridges here. Most of these fossiliferous materials were, perhaps, deposited in some past geological age at the bottom of an ancient sea.[17]

The town was settled around 1825.[18] The Anderson Creek Post Office was established March 28, 1860, with Archibald D. Ray as postmaster. In 1896 its name was changed to Anderson when Benjamin C. Boston became postmaster. Anderson Creek, originally called Corn Creek, was named for James Anderson who settled a few miles south of the present town in 1818.[19] Of interest, too, was the presence of Samuel Anderson in this area as early as 1809. He is listed as a tenant on Doublehead's reserve that same year.[20] Indications are that he built his log cabin west of Elk River near the mouth of Anderson Creek. He was among those evicted in 1811 by federal troops. Prior to 1825, there were several families located north of Anderson: Thomas and Ashael Akers, Jesse Pratt, William and George White, Jacob Kinnemore, Coleman Hardy, Amos Waddle, Leonard Partin, Joseph Norman, Joseph Armer, and Walter Day.[21]

In 1835, Booker Foster built the water mill, race, and dam, which was known in recent years as "Dave Wright's Mill." It was located in what is called "Old Anderson." Foster, born in Virginia about 1795, listed his occupation as a farmer. His wife, Lucinda, was a native of South Carolina.[22] There are a number of old legends about this area of the county. One involves Jesse and Frank James who, according to a popular story, came to live with a relative during the winter of 1882.[23] A burial site in an old cemetery near Anderson, is still pointed to as "the grave of the daughter of Frank James."[24]

Ingrum Hollow is a few miles south of Anderson. The Ingrums moved their log house here from Calicoa in Giles County, Tennessee, a few years before Alabama became a state. They established a trading post alongside the Lamb's Ferry Road. This family found friendly Indians who taught the men how to save ammunition by hunting with bows and arrows. These Native Americans spoke of a great earthquake – perhaps the New Madrid Earthquake of 1811 – which caused a part of the nearby bluff to fall into Anderson Creek. William Franklin Ingrum, Senior, later built a gristmill, wool carding mill, rolling mill, blacksmith shop, and general store in Ingrum Hollow. During the Civil War they moved their log house to this hollow to escape the Yankees who were frequently on the road between Pulaski and Rogersville. A line of old trenches can be seen above this hollow. It is believed that they were placed at this strategic place to defend the approach from Lamb's Ferry Road.

Gourdsville, Arthur, Grassy, Powell, and Sugar

Grassy is north of Anderson. A schoolhouse was built on a grassy hillside in the summer of 1859. This is said to have been the reason the community was called "Grassy."[26] East of Grassy is the community of Powell. Powell School was located here. A large family of Powells settled in this area near the end of the Civil War; there were no girls in this family – all boys: Francis, Irvine, Charles, George, Robert, and Andrew. The youngest was born two years prior to the end of hostilities. Their mother, Elizabeth Powell, was a widow from Tennessee where all of her sons were born. This family name goes all the way back to the original pioneers of Lawrence County, Tennessee. According to family sources, the patriarch, Benjamin D. Powell, constructed his log cabin close to an Indian camp about two miles southeast of present Loretto, Tennessee, prior to 1824.

The old settlements of Gourdsville, Arthur, and Sugar were also north of Anderson. Legend has it that a local bootlegger sold his whiskey at 25 cents per gourd full. There was an Arthur Post Office from 1886 until 1906.[25] Sugar was alongside Sugar Creek in the extreme northeastern part of Lauderdale County. Confederate General Nathan Bedford Forrest fought a delaying action skirmish just north of Sugar on December 26, 1864, following Hood's retreat from Nashville. The post office at Sugar was established in 1882 and discontinued in 1905. This area was sparsely populated prior to the Civil War. John Fowler and Robert Armer were living in the vicinity of Arthur, Gourdsville, and Grassy before 1825. However, by 1860 a number of families had moved into this section of the county; a group arrived from Indiana during the mid 1880's. Others came around 1900 from Cullman and adjoining counties in Alabama.[27]

Eastep and Oliver

Eastep was located on Snake Road a few miles north of Rogersville. Solomon Estate, a Confederate veteran, was appointed postmaster here in 1890. He was a son of James and Winney Estep from North Carolina. The Esteps were originally from Scotland, having first settled in Virginia after coming to America. By 1902 this post office had been discontinued. The earliest settlers around Eastep were: John Callahan, Thomas Stanford, Zach Rose, Thomas Jenkins, John Chandler, Elijah Hussey, Charles Dement, William and James Romine, Thomas Banks, Robert Carleton, John Lemon, H. Minor, and Henry Minor.

Oliver is located on U. S. Highway 72 between Rogersville and Elk River. The first crossing at Elk River was by a ford east of here. Addison Binford was granted permission in 1835 to establish a ferry across the Elk at the mouth of Anderson Creek. He agreed to operate his ferry at times when the river could not be forded. He said that he would charge three cents per head for cattle, sheep, or hogs. His rate for a loaded wagon and team was seventy cents. A year later Terry Bradly was granted permission to establish his ferry across the Elk. In his petition he stated that no public ferry had been established within two miles of his proposed site.

The Oliver Post Office was authorized on March 27, 1894, with David Morrison as postmaster. It was discontinued in 1909. Early settlers in this area were: William Snoddy, Lem Mead, John Leak, James Lindsey, Nathan Strong, Joseph Crowsen, and Alex Turply.[28]

Springfield, Kingtown, and Comer

Springfield is located between Lexington and Elgin. It is named for the number of springs in the area and is said to be among the earliest settlements in Lauderdale County. There are records to show that at one time it was laid out as a town site. Several tenants leasing land on the Doublehead Reserve as early as 1810 were attracted to these numerous sources of water. During the early part of the Civil War, Confederate soldiers were trained under Captains John S. Dobins and "Big Bill" Weathers near one of these large springs. Sometime after 1825, a physician from Georgia named Butler purchased some 1,100 acres of land from the government. Here he built the town's first house – a two-story log dwelling without a porch either in front or in back. Dr. Butler later sold this place to Stephen Herman who had been a tenant on the Doublehead Reserve around 1810. Prior to the Civil War, this plantation was acquired by Moses Crittenden who worked a number of slaves here under his overseer, Kit Stein. This farm was sold in 1901 to Phee Jackson for one dollar an acre. In 1829, Obediah Brown was appointed overseer of a section of a road through Springfield which ran from Lamb's Ferry to Lawrenceburg, Tennessee. Four years later, Captain John West was made supervisor of a new road from the mouth of Blue Water Creek to Springfield. John White was placed in charge of a section of this road that ran from Springfield to Lexington. In 1832 William Butler, William Bradshaw, and Stewart Jackson were in charge of the voting place at Springfield. Four years later this responsibility was assigned to Benjamin Cross, Samuel Herston, and Samuel H. Richardson.

Kingtown is on Alabama Highway 101 between Springfield and Lexington. Gilford King and his wife, Selfa, were in this part of the county prior to the Civil War. Both were natives of North Carolina. This was also the area where the settlement of Comer was located. William and Polly Comer were in this general vicinity during the 1870's. Both were born in South Carolina about the time of the War of 1812. He was probably related to the Comers who settled near present Loretto, Tennessee, in the early 1800s. Robert T. Lanier was appointed postmaster of Comer in 1880; this office was discontinued in 1905. Among the earliest settlers in this section were: Silas Gilbert, Nathaniel Spears, William Allen, Tobias Rice, Thomas Barnett, Benjamin Cross, Thomas Brandt, and Rhodes Allen.[29]

Thornton Town, Good Springs, Whitehead and Toonersville

Thornton Town is near the intersection of U. S. Highway 72 and the Betty Ann Highway. This was originally a part of the land holdings of Benjamin Ingram. It was later purchased by Thomas J. Thornton who opened a general store on the Huntsville Road. Hence, the community was named for him. The Betty Ann Highway was named for Betty Ann Thornton of this family. West of Thornton Town was a community known as Good Springs. A Cumberland Presbyterian Church was established here in 1839 with Felix Johnson as pastor. The Good Springs Academy was located nearby. During construction of Wheeler Dam in the late 1930's, this church – now the Good Springs Baptist – and the business houses were moved up the hill nearer to Thornton Town. A large Indian Mound, once a part of Good Springs, can be seen today at the crossing of U. S. Highway 72 bridge and causeway over Second Creek.[30]

The community of Whitehead was named for the family of James Whitehead who purchased land at the Huntsville Land Sale on March 30, 1818. It is believed that Whitehead came originally from Franklin County, Georgia, and lived for a time in Lincoln County, Tennessee, before settling in Lauderdale County at the age of twenty-one years. He is buried in a small family cemetery in the Toonersville community.[31] The Whitehead post office was established in 1891, with George Whitehead as postmaster; it was discontinued in 1906.

Ancient remains of early flint mines are located near the community of Toonersville. Native Americans once gathered their hard flint rocks from these mines to make arrowheads, spears, and tools. One of the earliest white settlers in this community was Henry Newman from Boston, Massachusetts. He purchased four different tracts of land here in 1818. The south section of the Harvey Cemetery is located on one of these tracts. For some reason Newman soon disposed of his property and returned to Boston. Daniel White, who entered land near Blue Water Creek in 1825, also purchased a tract on Second Creek just west of Toonersville. Here was located White's Mill that served the area for many years. A general store was located near this mill.

Toonersville, originally known as Mt. Bethel, was named for a popular comic strip during the early years of World War II. A number of farmers in the community had taken defense jobs at Sheffield. They would catch a work bus at Lee Whitehead's store on the Betty Ann Highway. One of the local men, in jest, placed a sign at the bus stop that read "Toonersville."[32] Other early landholders in the areas of Thornton Town, Whitehead, and Toonersville prior to 1825 were: Wilson Coats, Ben Morris, Benjamin Ingram, Henry Minor, Drury Cox, William Stevenson, William Crittenden, and Thomas Barnett.[33]

Dutch Landing, Elgin, and Boston

Dutch Landing was on the Tennessee River south of Elgin between Second Creek and Blue Water Creek.[34] It served as a port for Chief Doublehead's village and, later, for the white settlers who leased land from Doublehead. Flatboats and keelboats loaded with supplies and trade items from East Tennessee landed at this place in the days before Alabama became a state. Years later, following the completion of the Muscle Shoals Canal, John Belew established a large warehouse here where cotton and grain were stored for shipment by steamboats. Belew also operated a blacksmith shop as well as a cabinet shop where he made coffins. Dutch Landing was a convenient place for receiving and shipping goods in that its shoreline was almost at water level with the river. Some think this natural feature, resembling the lowlands of Holland, was why it was called Dutch Landing. West of Dutch Landing – on the opposite side of Blue Water Creek – was a high and steep palisade overlooking the river known as "Doublehead Bluff."[35] Henry Newman of Massachusetts purchased Dutch Landing in 1818.

Doublehead's Village was located north of Dutch Landing along the east bank of Blue Water Creek. According to legend, Doublehead's home, a large two-story log house – built according to the style of the white man – overlooked this village. Here, based upon stories that have been handed down, Chief Doublehead was buried following his barbaric assassination in East Tennessee in 1807.[36]

Daniel White later purchased this place and operated Wayside Inn in this same log house. A number of his descendants believed that he – not Doublehead – built this structure.[37] Old Gabriel Butler, who had been a tenant on Doublehead's land, is buried near here.[38] William Roundtree, William Adair, John Anderson, William Cornish, and Shelton Standeford were early landowners between Dutch Landing and Elgin.[39]

Elgin was originally known as Ingram's Crossroads. Benjamin and Sarah Ingram, both natives of Virginia, purchased land a few miles east of here in 1818. Benjamin died in September, 1849, at the age of seventy years. His son, Benjamin Ingram, Junior, was a merchant at Ingram's Crossroads in 1850. George and Mose Ingram served at different times as postmasters for the community between the years 1849 and 1857. There was an early hotel near the intersection of U.S. Highway 72 and Alabama Highway 101. Both highways were major thoroughfares. Highway 72 was well traveled between Florence and Huntsville. The north-to-south route (Highway 101) connected the Jackson Military Road near what is now Loretto, Tennessee, with a ferry that crossed the Tennessee River near present Wheeler Dam. Ingram's Cross Roads underwent two name changes between 1890 and 1901. In the late 1880's, Thomas J. Crittenden was a member of the Board of County Commissioners and succeeded in having the name changed from Ingram Crossroads to Crittenden Crossroads. However, in 1901, when Richard M. Bolinger was appointed postmaster, he had it changed to Elgin Crossroads. The post office was located at the back of the Jackson and Bolinger General Store. It is said that Bolinger selected the name Elgin Cross Roads for Elgin, Illinois. Eventually the name was shortened to Elgin.[40]

Other early settlers in and around this crossroad were: Thomas J. Crittenden, Austin Sands, John West, William Baugher, David White, and Thomas Coffee, kinsman of General John Coffee.[41] William Butler and Aristidies Jackson were among those who came after 1825. They were joined by a number of other prominent families, including the Phillips, Lamars, Heltons, Herstons, McCanes, Joiners, Disons, Balchs, Walkers, Barnetts, and Williams.[42]

A community east of Blue Water Creek and west of Elgin was at one time referred to as Boston. It took its name from the Boston family. James McElren Boston purchased forty acres here from the Huntsville Land Office in 1831. Three years later, he and James Jones Boston – thought to have been brothers – paid $2,961 to Daniel White for 160 acres along the east bank of Blue Water Creek. Perhaps this was at the time Daniel White sold Wayside Inn. The Boston deed set aside an acre for a Baptist

Church and another acre for a burying ground which became known the Barkley Cemetery.

James McElren Boston was born about 1787 in North Carolina. As a justice of the peace, he performed marriage ceremonies and signed legal documents during the period 1831 - 1839. On June 3, 1836, he enlisted in the 2nd Alabama Volunteers during the Seminole War. He was soon elected the captain of a company in this unit which became known as Boston's Company." In early 1838, he served as a first lieutenant in Norwood's Battalion, a militia unit detailed to escort the Cherokee Indians along the infamous Trail of Tears from North Alabama into the Oklahoma Territory. Later that year, James M. Boston was seated in the Alabama House of Representatives from Lauderdale County.

James Jones Boston was born about 1780 in North Carolina. By 1805, he and his wife, Nancy, were in Tennessee where nine of their ten children were born. By 1824 they were in Lauderdale County. During the panic of 1837, James Jones Boston and his wife moved to Texas. A year later they were both dead. This family left a number of descendants in Lauderdale County.[43]

36. EARLY BEGINNINGS IN CENTRAL LAUDERDALE COUNTY

"The land was ours before we were the land's."
(Robert Frost)

The central part of the county is that area between Blue Water Creek and Shoal Creek. Prehistoric peoples were here thousands of years ago. As a part of the Doublehead Reserve, its earliest white settlements came about prior to 1810. This section was benefited by the Andrew Jackson Military Road constructed between 1817 and 1820. Large numbers of immigrants used this highway into what was then called the southwest. A number of its travelers decided to make their homes here. The three principal communities are Center Star, Killen, and Green Hill.

Center Star, Big Oak, Houstontown, and Bellview

Center Star is among the oldest communities in Lauderdale County. The early claims of both the Chickasaw and Cherokee Indians overlapped at this place which was near the dividing line between the two nations. Early settlers noted remains of an Indian village some two or three miles southwest of the community. Doublehead's Bluff lines the north bank of the Tennessee River on the west side of the mouth of Blue Water Creek. Old legends tell of Chief Doublehead's secret treasure cave which is thought to have been near Center Star. Evidence of more ancient habitation sites could be seen on the nearby islands before being covered by the waters of Wilson Lake. One of these, Coxe Island, was the site of an attempt by Zachariah Coxe in 1791 to establish a settlement at the Muscle Shoals. A few miles east of Center Star, near the mouth of Blue Water Creek, is where William Herman was born in 1810. A few members of the Herman family are buried here. Some 400 yards away is another pioneer cemetery where markers for two members of the Barnett family can be seen. The main stream of Blue Water Creek was once known as Blackwood Creek and its east fork was called Mill Creek.[1] In the early days a section of this stream was called "Granny's Creek," in that it ran close by the home of "Granny" Kate Richardson, a pioneer settler.

The land south of Center Star along the river was especially fertile and was sought after by cotton planters. One of its main attractions was the presence of large areas called "Old Fields" which had been cleared by the Indians.[2] It was soon laced with big plantations owned by prosperous farmers who built comfortable homes.[3]

The post office at Center Star was created April 15, 1850, with William T. Tapp, postmaster. It was discontinued in 1902. In 1914, it was temporary re-established to operate for almost a full year, with Virgil Larimore as its postmaster.[4]

The story of how Center Star got its name involves the history of the U. S. Postal Service. As railroads and steamboats appeared on the scene in the 19th century they were utilized to carry mail. Many communities were remote and had to be served instead by "star routes," so called because they were identified with stars on the Post Office Department lists. These routes were carried by private contractors using horses and wagons. This new post office was at the center of a "star route" for this section of east Lauderdale County. Thus, it became quite descriptive to name this place Center Star.[5]

Center Star was a rallying point at the beginning of the Civil War. Here, on May 26, 1861, Edward A. O'Neal organized his "Calhoun Guards," which was later designated as Company I, 9th Alabama Infantry Regiment.[6] On May 9, 1864, Center Star was the scene of a two-hour skirmish between Colonel William A. Johnson's Confederate Fourth Alabama Cavalry and a combined Union force made up of units from the 7th Illinois Cavalry and the 9th Ohio Regiment under Colonel Richard Rowett. Rowett reported that he drove Johnson back across the Tennessee River after capturing 35 prisoners.[7]

Among the earliest landowners around Center Star were: Brittain Farrow, William D. Bell, William C. Allen, Shelton Standifer, Wilson Cage, Thomas Bowden, Ephraim Moore, Hollingsworth Trudd, Nathaniel Evans, John McMahon, Lemuel and Samuel Mead, James Gordon, Brazell Forrow, and Benjamin Jones.[8]

South of Center Star are the communities of Big Oak, Houstontown, and Bellview. Josiah D. Fuller was at Big Oak in 1818. William Patton, who owned island property south of Rogersville, was at Big Oak during the same period. A partnership, Sam Hazard and Charles N. Baucher (or Parker), made purchases here in 1818.[9]

Houstontown, now called Pleasant Valley, took its name from Alabama Governor George Smith Houston of Limestone County, who lived as a boy near Gravelly Springs in West Lauderdale County. He purchased this prime farmland, consisting of 1,530 acres, from David Williams in 1880. Williams was an heir of Henry Williams who died in 1844. Houston was an absentee landlord, and this acreage remained in his family until sold at public auction in June of 1976. This community at one time was called Frog Pond. The early Frog Pond School was near what is now the Pleasant Valley Church of Christ. This one room facility was near a large pond where young boys enjoyed gigging for bullfrogs. This school served a number of religious faiths as a meetinghouse. General John Coffee, James Jackson, Thomas Kirkman, and General John Brahan were early landowners at Houstontown. Among its earliest settlers were: Samuel McDowell, John Lucas, William Crittenden, Moses and John Tomlinson, William Trousdale, James Gordon, Isaac Wallingsford, James Valent, and Demprey Deans. Later came J. N. Fritts, a riverboat captain, Carlisle Knight, a tanner, Patrick Comer, a maker of spinning wheels, Sampson Lanier, and Andrew McLaren.[10]

The early town of Bellview was at Doublehead Bluffs on the west side of the mouth of Blue Water Creek. Near these bluffs was Doublehead Spring. In the years before Alabama became a state, the low bottom land along the river on the east side of Blue Water Creek was known as Dutch Landing.[11] Prior to the coming of

Wilson Dam, the river here was shallow during low-water seasons. Old-timers remembered that it was an early ferry crossing and that they could walk almost half way across the river during dry summer months.

Bellview came into being during the building of the first Muscle Shoals Canal which commenced in 1836. There was an earlier lighthouse here to warn boats that they were approaching the treacherous shoals. One of the original locks was located here. Some forty years later, when the second canal system was under construction, it became Lock Three. A dam was built at the mouth of the creek to provide a pool of water for the operation of the lock.

During the building of the first canal around the Muscle Shoals two of the canal contractors, John R. and S. S. Henry, saw the mouth of Blue Water Creek as a promising site for a town. Thus, through their investment and promotion, Bellview was established. They also built a trestle bridge – almost two miles in length – across the river. This became the first bridge on the Tennessee in the vicinity of Florence. Hardly had the last span been completed when the entire structure collapsed into the swift and shallow rapids in the river below, scattering its timbers along its shorelines. The defeated Henrys gave up and moved away.[12] It wasn't long before the town they left behind began to wither and die. The migrant canal workers soon took over, many living in tent cities on the Houston Place. Saloons, gambling places, and houses of ill repute moved in. The former peaceful village of Bellview became known as Hell Town. When the first canal was abandoned sometime after 1838, it faded into an eerie ghost town on the Tennessee River.[13]

Bellview Road which runs between Bellview and Center Star was once known for its fine plantations. The early Phillips Place, home of Wilson Phillips and his wife, Mary Trousdale Phillips, was near the intersection of Houstontown and Bellview Roads. After they moved to Lexington, it became the Benjamin Taylor Plantation. Taylor's daughter, Susie Poke Taylor, refused to play the piano for Union soldiers who were camped there during the Civil War. This incident is now a part of the records in the National Archives.[14]

After the war, Susie was married to Captain Jonathan McDavid Cunningham, Junior. They inherited these vast acres which remained with their descendants for around one hundred years.[15] Benjamin Taylor and other family members are buried nearby in what is known as the William Henry Crittenden Cemetery.

Next to the Cunninghams were the two Douglass plantations; Abraham arrived in 1818 and James a year later. They were from Fairfield District, South Carolina. James' house was a two-story "I-style" structure with a porch. It had two large rooms and a hall, both downstairs and upstairs. A son, Dr. James A. Douglass, built a similar house nearby in 1867.[16] West of the Douglass farms were the William Trousdale Place and the Williams Plantation. Mary Cash Williams came with her son, Josephus, from Williamson County, Tennessee. A few miles south of Center Star on the Bellview Road was the brick mansion of John Hardin and his second wife, Susannah Appleton Hardin. Their son, Presley, was married to Mary Williams. The Hardin home was constructed of bricks with thick walls featuring six plastered columns in front. It was later used as a schoolhouse.[17]

Mitchell Town and Taylor Springs

Mitchell Town, located a few miles north of Center Star, was named for Captain John Robert Mitchell, planter and gristmill owner. He served in Company A, 35th Alabama Infantry Regiment during the Civil War. He was a son of Henry G. and Rebecca Richardson Mitchell. Henry's parents, Robert and Mary Collier Mitchell, arrived in Lauderdale County in 1820. Robert was a planter and merchant. His parents were William Mitchell and Lucy Hancock Mitchell of Brunswick County, Virginia. Captain John R. Mitchell's mother, Rebecca Richardson Mitchell, was born near Green Hill in 1815 when Alabama was a part of the Mississippi Territory. Her parents were John David and Catherine Stutts Richardson.

Captain Mitchell was married to Caroline Phillips, daughter of Jack Phillips and his wife, Suzanna Barnett Phillips. The Captain and his wife reared eleven children along with two adopted boys. Square dances were often held in their home. It was said that when their son, Henry, was married to Nora White that sixteen couples were seen dancing in the house during the same tune.

The second generation of Mitchells to operate a gristmill here was James Mason Mitchell, a son of Captain Mitchell. He later added a grocery store, blacksmith shop, saw mill, and cotton gin. James "Jim" Mitchell was first married to Emma Elizabeth Butler and there were eight children. After her death, he was married to Lizzie Davis and there were five children. Following Lizzie's death, Jim was married to Alta Sherrod and they had one child. Jim operated his business complex at Mitchell Town from about 1899 to 1915. Following a few years in Oklahoma, he returned to Alabama and operated a store in North Florence until his death in 1951.[18]

Stewart and Californy Rust Wilson settled at Mitchell Town in 1830, purchasing their first forty-acre tract in 1834. Two years later, they acquired adjoining land from Stewart's brother, Robert Wilson, where they built their large two-story dwelling made of poplar logs. Stewart and Robert Wilson were sons of Irish immigrants who first settled in North Carolina. The Wilson home was ransacked several times during the Civil War. Stories handed down through the family tell how on one occasion, they managed to save some meat from the smokehouse by hiding it in a sage field near the family cemetery. In this area can be found evidence of Civil War earthworks.[19] Other early landowners near Mitchell Town were: Samuel Herston, Elish Thomas, James Cocke, and Ralph Graves.[20]

Early maps show two Taylor Springs in this part of the county. One is at Brush Creek northwest of Killen and the other is northeast of Killen near the bridge over Blue Water Creek on County Road 71.[21] Both springs are mentioned a number of times as campsites by the Union and Confederate Armies. It is believed that these two springs were at one time or another owned by members of the Taylor family. Goodwin Taylor's plantation was near Killen, Benjamin Taylor's was at Center Star, and Gilbert Taylor owned land near Rogersville.

Antioch, Parkertown, and Arnot

Antioch is located north of Center Star. The Antioch Church of Christ is located here. The old Antioch School served this area as early as 1920. Antioch is a Biblical name associated with the beginning of Christianity. Early landowners around Taylor Springs and Antioch were William Townsend, William Hickman, Samuel Shelburne, and William and Henry Williams.[22]

Parkertown is north of Killen at a rural intersection on Bridge Road (County Road 25.) It is named for Doctor Oliver Parker and his descendants. His son, Lonzie Parker, operated a general store in this community. This merchandise business was continued by Dewey Parker following his brother Lonzie's death in the 1930's.[23]

Atlas is a few miles west of Parkertown. No one seems to know how it received its name which comes from the ancient Greeks and their mythology. In 1920 there was an Atlas School located here. Also the Atlas Church of Christ is a part of this community. A post office was established in 1890, with John Liles as postmaster. It was discontinued in 1906, when John C. Thigpen was postmaster.[24] John Stewart acquired land near this place in 1819.

Arnot was located between Shoal Creek and Green Hill near the modern Lone Cedar Church of Christ. William H. Quillen was appointed postmaster here in 1902. Two aboriginal paths crossed near this community. One of these connected the Tennessee River below Huntsville to the lower section of the river at Savannah, Tennessee. The early crossing of this trail over Shoal Creek is still called Savannah Ford. The other path became the Jackson Military Road after 1817. This intersection was the site of Samuel Craig's Stagecoach Inn, believed to have been established as early as

1810. Seven log huts were used to accommodate the guests.[25]
Craig and Andrew Jackson were said to have been friends.
Legend has it that Jackson and his wife, Rachael, spent the night
here on their way back to Nashville after the Battle of New Orleans.

About 1819 a Revolutionary War veteran, Hamilton
Reynolds, settled at Savannah Ford. One source claims that
Reynolds later moved to Pruitton where he was buried in 1845.
Others say that he moved to McNairy County, Tennessee, about
1849. Another veteran of that war, Lewis Markham, or Marcum,
lived near Arnot for several years prior to his death around 1845. A
native of Virginia, Marcum attained the rank of Sergeant Major, and
was in the Battle of Cow Pens.

Green Hill and Cow Pen

It has been said that the soldiers of Andrew Jackson, while
passing through this area, liked what they saw and returned
another day to claim it. According to one family story, two of these
soldiers, Nicholas and John Wright, drew crude maps that would
someday guide them back to this area.[26] Another version of this
tale is that these two brothers, along with Captain Henry D. Allen,
were helping to clear the way for the Jackson Military Road
between 1817 and 1820. While camped at the site of Old
Tabernacle Methodist Church, they made plans to return as
settlers.[27] Other soldiers of the War of 1812 who settled at Green
Hill were: John Chisholm from Virginia, Captain John W. LeMaster
from South Carolina, and Joseph Gist and David Lancaster from
North Carolina.

Zella Garrard, who was born in Tennessee in 1815, told
fascinating stories about early life in Green Hill. One time a pack of
wolves chased her across the Blue Water hills. On another
occasion some Indians came to her home located near Blowing
Cave in search of a cave they believed to have been the hiding
place for two deerskins that were filled with Doublehead's money.

Green Hill was named for the Mexican War hero, Captain Green Berry Hill, who died in 1852 at Green Hill from wounds received in Mexico. Immigrants from Greenville County, South Carolina, they were early settlers of Lauderdale County. This community, which consists of Upper Green Hill and Lower Green Hill, was first known as Cornish. John and James Cornish were among its first settlers. A post office by that name was established March 30, 1830, with George Kennedy as postmaster. Kennedy was a neighbor to the Cornish families. In 1841, the name was changed to Cherry Grove with Charles McCluskey as postmaster. McCluskey relocated the post office to his brother-in-law's store, and on June 25, 1850, its name was designated as Green Hill. The proprietor of this store, James Hill, was the brother of Captain Green Berry Hill.[28]

In its early history Green Hill was the "gun manufacturing center" for Northwest Alabama. This area was ideally located on the Jackson Military Road used by pioneers going into the new west who needed well-made weapons. Hiram Kennedy established a gun plant at Green Hill sometime after 1823. His father, David Kennedy, joined him around 1836. David had been a gun-maker in upper Moore County, North Carolina. His father, Alexander Kennedy, had made the long rifle during the Revolutionary War, first in Pennsylvania, and later in North Carolina. In 1840, eighteen men were employed at the Kennedy Gun Factory in Green Hill; slaves were used in molding the barrels. In that year, a total of 428 small arms were produced.

Other gunsmiths were soon in business at Green Hill, including some who arrived with the Kennedys. Jacob "Drummer Jake" Stutts shipped rifles by wagons and boats. James Calvin Myrick's farm and gun shop were near Happy Hollow on Shoal Creek. A veteran of the War of 1812, his first wife was said to have been a full blood Indian. Old Alexander Higgins from South Carolina later moved his small plant to Waterloo. There were two groups of McDonalds who made long rifles near their homes: Archibald McDonald was from North Carolina and John McDonald was from South Carolina. At least two of John's boys – Joseph and

Elias – continued making guns after the Civil War. Ephraim McDonald, whose shop was alongside the Military Road, was placed in charge of this highway's upkeep at Green Hill during the 1830s. Other local gunsmiths were: William Davidson, Thomas White, and Asa and David Richardson. The demand for Kentucky Rifles faded after the old flintlock gave way to the modern precision-tooled weapon at which time Green Hill became basically a farming community.[29]

Because of its location on the much traveled Military Road, Green Hill had a number of stagecoach inns in addition to Craig's Inn at Arnot. Holland's Stagecoach Inn was north of Green Hill near the banks of Little Blue Water or Roaches Creek. Harrison Holland and his wife, Isabelle Wiley Holland, were the innkeepers. Across the road from this inn was a general store and stagecoach repair shop owned by Elias M. McDonald. Here he made buggies, wagons, and long rifles.[30] One of Elias' sons, Fernanda Socrates "Bud" McDonald, was married to Lydia Harrison, daughter of the innkeepers; the McDonalds later inherited the Holland Inn.

Lane's Inn at Green Hill was operated by Samuel Clairborn Lane from about 1849 until around 1880. This large two-story log house was originally the home of John and Susannah Richardson Killen.[31]

Some of the early stagecoach drivers were: Thomas Mattlock, John Gannon, Henry Carr, and William and James Angel. These Angels perhaps lived near the Holland Inn where a large source of water is still known as "Angel's Spring."

There were a number of early water-powered mills around Green Hill. Duncan Smith, Berry McDonald, Thomas Ross, Isham Richardson, and Enoch Raleigh Kennedy had gristmills on Cow Pen Creek. Duncan McDougal, and the Wright brothers – Nicholas and John – had mills on O'Possum Creek. Along Richardson Creek were the mills of David and Henry Richardson, James Roberts, James and William Danley, and John and Amos McDonald. At Big Blue Water Creek were mills operated by John D. Richardson, John Robinson, and Asa Q. Robertson. Wolfe Creek had a large number of these operations owned at various times by David Heffington, William Mark Rickman, Senior, William Nabors Hill, Daniel McDougal, George Atwell, Thomas Choate, George Grisham, John McKinney, and John Carter. About 1828 Thomas Grisham established his gristmill on Hurricane Creek. Ironically, it was destroyed by a storm around 1860 - the source of the creek's name. About fifteen years later, one of the Killen brothers, either Dan, Tom, Henry, or Duncan; operated a mill here.

About fifteen years prior to the Civil War, the thriving Brazil and Adams Distillery was established on Little Blue Water Creek north of Green Hill. About 1875, Garrett (or Gahara) Beumer and John Berendesen purchased this business. Beumer was from Prussia and Berendesen is believed to have been a native of either Holland or Germany. Farmers at Green Hill and in nearby Lawrence County, Tennessee, planted vineyards and apple orchards for processing in this industry.[32]

Other early settlers and landowners in and around Green Hill prior to 1825 were: Loving Ross, A. Traughbaugh, Joshua Smith, Thomas Gresham, Robert Moore, William Adams, Joseph Farmer, and James and John Killen.[33]

Cow Pen is a community around Cow Pen Creek and near Goose Shoal on Shoal Creek, and is about a mile west of Green Hill. There is evidence of prehistoric Indian villages and campsites, especially near Goose Shoal. Some of the county's earliest white settlers made this place their home. A number of them came from Spartanburg and Greenville Counties, South Carolina, giving rise to the belief that they named this place "Cow Pen" for the 1781 Revolutionary War battle fought at Hannah's Cowpens, South Carolina. Geographically, the battle site was an area of open wood in a loop of the Broad River frequently used by herdsmen to graze their cattle. There are a number of loops in nearby Shoal Creek which may in some measure be remindful of Hannah's Cowpens. However, the best guess is that this name was chosen because of the battle and not its terrain features.

There were two water-powered mills along Cow Pen Creek in 1828. The community is best remembered for the woolen factory erected here in 1850 by Isaac and Samuel Milner, Judge William

Basil Wood, and John Wren. The Milners were from England. Isaac was a Methodist preacher. Nearby Milner's Chapel United Methodist Church was established by this family. Gray cloth was produced at the woolen mill for Confederate uniforms during the Civil War.[34] The Foster, Simpson, and Company Cotton Mill was also in this area. Duncan Smith's Store was a fixture in this community as early as 1840.

Joseph Emory McDonald's blacksmith shop was located next to McDonald Spring which was across the road from the modern Stutts Road Church of Christ. Here he made wagons, buggies, and long rifles. His home was at the crest of the hill east of his shop. Nearby were the farms of his brothers, Amos and Matthew. Their parents, John and Margaret Emory McDonald from South Carolina, settled near Cow Pen Creek in 1834. Other farmers here prior to the Civil War were: William and John R. Stutts, Jordon and Thomas Hamm, Duncan Smith, Gilbert Prince, Jessie Mitton, Alston Hill, William Liles, John Spinks Kennedy, John C. Bradley, Thomas Ross, John L. Warren, Joseph L. Warren, and Reuben R. Warren. Landowners prior to 1825 were: David Heffington, Samuel Craig, Joseph Gist, James Bright, Elisha Melton, William Higginbottom, William Howe, Urish Nanny, Randolph Palmer, Richard MaMahon, John Watkins, and Marion Bradley.[35]

Atlas, Mecca, Robertson, Franklin, and Happy Hollow

Atlas is about three miles south of Green Hill. A post office was established here in 1890 with John Liles as its postmaster. No one seems to know why this community chose to be identified with a meaning of the name Atlas: "one who bears a heavy burden." The nearby North Carolina Church of Christ is said to have been named for the native state of a large number of early settlers in the community. Established about 1826, it served as a community school and house of worship for the Baptists and Methodists as well as the Church of Christ for more than fifty years. About 1880 a controversy brought an end to this arrangement. The Baptists moved out and built their own nearby Union Grove Baptist Church. The Methodists relocated to Center Hill to their new Ebenezer Methodist Church. Near the community of Atlas is the historic Hill Cemetery named for James and Catherine Stutts Hill, early settlers from Moore County, North Carolina.

Mecca was located about three hundred yards east of Cow Pen Creek and less than two miles west of Green Hill. A post office was established here in 1889, with Jesse W. Stutts as postmaster. Stutts is said to have chosen the name "Mecca" because he considered it a focal point for people with a common interest.[36]

Robertson was a community located almost on the Tennessee line northwest of Green Hill. It gets its name from John Tyre Robertson who arrived from South Carolina in 1818. Robertson, who was married three times, had twenty-one children who lived to be grown. A number of his sons served in the Confederate Army. Captain John Tyre Robertson, Junior, was one of his sons. He was commanding officer of Company A, 35th Alabama Infantry Regiment.[37]

Franklin was near the confluence of Shoal and Cow Pen Creeks. A post office was located here in 1890 with William J. Stutts as postmaster. Dr. Wiley W. Richardson was appointed in 1891 and sorted the mail in the same building where he practiced medicine.[38]

Happy Hollow is at the east end of the Shoal Creek bridge on the old Jackson Military Road (now County Road 47.) The modern Arrow Head Shores Subdivision is located here. A short distance north of the present bridge was an early ford used by Native Americans and, later, by travelers on the Jackson Military Road. There is evidence that people of the Woodland Culture lived here perhaps as early as 2,000 B.C. Old-timers claimed that at one time an ancient Indian mound was located in this area.[39] Both ceremonial and burial mounds were used by these Woodland people.

On the opposite bank of Shoal Creek was the Lauderdale Cotton Factory and village. It was built in 1845, by George Washington Foster and his brother Thomas Jefferson Foster. This mill was purchased in 1860 by John Spinks Kennedy, Jesse G. W. Leftwich, William H. Hayes, and Richard B. Baugh. Baugh owned a plantation in Happy Hollow although his home was near the intersection of Locust Street and West Irvine Avenue in Florence. He managed the operations of the mill. Hence, it became known as the Baugh Factory. His name was also connected with the nearby ford. The mill village was made up of about forty cottages along with a church, store, and a free school for the children.

There were a number of skirmishes in and around this mill as well as across the creek at Happy Hollow during the Civil War.[40] At least a part of the Lauderdale Factory was moved to Tuscaloosa following a flood in March of 1862. A year later the U. S. Army under the orders of Colonel Florence M. Cornyn set fire to the factory. However, there is evidence that a grist and flourmill were operating here in 1864 when General Hood crossed Shoal Creek on his way into Tennessee.

Wilson English's farm overlooked Baugh Ford on Shoal Creek from the top of the hill on the west bank. He acquired this land in 1818. He was a son of Matthew English whose homestead was located in a nearby fertile bottom on Shoal Creek. Matthew's name shows up as a resident on Indian Lands in Alabama in 1810. He came to Alabama from North Carolina by way of Tennessee. Among other early landowners in this area were: John Cantrell, Joseph Robertson, Henry Garrard, Robert Reece, Joseph Mason, John Coffee, Thomas Kirkman, Austin Sands, and Samuel and John Craig.41

Arkdale, Center Hill, McGhee, Stutts, Posey, and Bailey Springs

Arkdale is the location of the modern Allen Park alongside the east bank of Blue Water Creek about four miles east of Green

Hill. This was where Captain Henry D. Allen built his log cabin on Indian lands before Alabama became a state. Born in 1782 in Edgecomb County, North Carolina, he was a son of Rhody and Mary Emily Ranson Allen. Rhody was descended from Robert Allin who came to America from Ireland in 1690 on the ship "Charles."[42]

Captain Henry Allen's first wife, Polly, has been heralded as a pioneer heroine. She was home alone with her children when the federal troops arrived in the spring of 1811 with orders to evict the white settlers from Indian lands. Through kindness she saved her home by cooking a sumptuous meal for the hungry men. Although they set fire to her cabin, two of these well fed soldiers slipped back to extinguish the flames. Born as Mary Barnes in 1787, she was a daughter of Joseph and Selah Deloach Barnes. Following Polly's death, Captain Allen was married to Marcy Mayfield Robinson, widow of John Robinson. One of the Allen daughters, Mary, was married to William Washington Pettus who served as a First Lieutenant in Company E, 27th Alabama Infantry Regiment, C.S.A. He died in 1882 and is buried in the Pettus Cemetery west of Lexington. Another daughter, Margaret, was married to Benjamin Franklin Chisholm, a Second Sergeant in Company A, 35th Alabama Infantry, C.S.A.

Both Captain Allen and his first wife, Polly, are buried in the Allen Cemetery at Arkdale. His second wife, Marcy, rests in the Granny Richardson Cemetery. Arkdale in earlier times had its own general store. Among its storekeepers were: John Davis, Jesse Minton Wilcoxson, and William Pettus.

Center Hill is located on County Road 64 southeast of Green Hill. It has a commanding view from the center of a large hill overlooking Blue Water Creek. Perhaps this is why it was named Center Hill. Its earliest landowners were John Gresham, John and Daniel McDougal, John Richardson, and Joseph Robinson (or Robertson.) Robinson purchased land here in 1818, and is buried in the nearby Robinson-Stutts Cemetery. John Robinson, perhaps a son of Joseph, built his home at Center Hill in 1842. Carved in one of the chimney stones were these words: "J. Robinson 1842 by J. Chism." John W. McDonald, a son of Archibald McDonald from

North Carolina, sold his farm just west of Center Hill in 1854. He was married to Catherine Stewart whose father and mother were Duncan Stewart and Catherine Wright Stewart. The Stewarts are buried in the Scott Cemetery. Also buried here are Duncan and Ann Campbell McDougal who were born in Scotland.[43]

The Ebenezer Methodist Church was erected at Center Hill about 1880 by Hiram I. Richardson and his wife, Julia Ann Young Richardson. It was torn down sometime after 1936. Richardson was teaching at North Carolina School in 1861 when he entered the Confederate Army. The Richardsons later moved to Waterloo where they built a hotel and gave the community the Richardson Chapel Methodist Church.

Early court records indicate that Center Hill may have originally been called McGhee; if not, McGhee was in the proximity of this community. In 1832, Alexander McDougal, James A. Smith, and Allen Stewart received appointments as judges to preside over the voting place at McGhee. In 1836, these appointments were given to Jacob McGhee, Hiram Kennedy, and John Richardson. Perhaps the community took its name from the family of Jacob McGhee. Descendants of this family have changed the spelling of their name to McGee.

The Stutts community was located about three miles southeast of Green Hill. It was named for Leonard Stutts and his many descendants. He was the father of the well-known Green Hill gunsmith Jacob "Drummer Jake" Stutts. This family is said to have originated in Germany where their name was spelled as Stultz or Stutz. They came to America by way of Holland. Settling first in Pennsylvania, they later moved to Moore County, North Carolina. Court records show the appointments of John Richardson, Hiram Kennedy, and Jacob Stutts as supervisors of the voting place at Stutts for an election to be held in September, 1837. It is believed that this voting placed served the entire Green Hill area. A post office was established at Stutts in 1899, with John W. Beavers as postmaster.

Posey is located about two miles south of Center Hill and Arkdale. The Posey plantation was located here. Amanda F.

Posey was appointed postmaster in 1894. This office was discontinued the following year when the mail was consolidated with the Green Hill post office.[44]

Bailey Springs was a popular antebellum resort near Shoal Creek about nine miles northeast of Florence. A post office was established here in 1854, with Jonathan Bailey as postmaster. It was discontinued in 1901 when the mail was sent to Saint Florian. According to family sources, Jonathan Bailey was in Lauderdale County as early as 1813.[45] Land records show that he first purchased land near this site in 1818.[46] In 1831 and 1832, he acquired 200 acres and in 1846, bought the adjoining property where the mineral springs were located and where he established his famous resort. For several generations Bailey Springs was a well known healing, recreational, and entertainment retreat for the aristocracy of the South. During the Civil War it was used as a campsite by both the Union and Confederate Armies, and on at least one occasion a skirmish was fought here.

In 1893, the Bailey Springs University was established for the education of women. Mainly because of its remote location, the institution was never a commercial success, and finally, in 1900 its doors were closed.[47] Some of the other landowners in this area prior to 1825 were: Matt Watson, Leroy Pope, John Coffee, Hubbard Black, William Farris, Henry May, John Brahan, Joseph Hough, William Wallace, and Cris Tate.[48]

Brush Creek, Masonville, Lock Six, Kingman, and Killen,

It could be said that the communities of Brush Creek, Masonville, Lock Six, and Kingman were the predecessors of the modern town of Killen. In early times Brush Creek, which takes it name from the stream that meanders through this valley, was at the intersection of two major highways from the east: the Huntsville Road and the Pulaski Pike. The Huntsville Road, originally called the Florence to Athens Road, was surveyed through here in 1829.[49] Yet, it existed earlier as a series of local roads.

The Pulaski Pike was a major supply route between the river at Florence and Pulaski, Tennessee. Harrison Chapel United Methodist Church is located at the site of this early intersection and village. A store, mill, school, and two churches served the community. Several large springs can be found nearby. One of these is shown on old maps as Taylor Spring, although there is another spring by that name between Killen and Lexington. Goodwin and Gilbert Taylor believed to have been connected to the Taylors of Scotland – owned land in this part of the county as early as 1818, although their original tracts did not include either of these two springs.

The presence of Indian artifacts around these water sources indicate their use by prehistoric peoples. Also, both armies camped near these springs during the Civil War. Because of the strategic intersection of the two major roads here plus an abundant water supply the Federal Army set up a large field hospital at Brush Creek, perhaps during the last years of the Civil War. Burial pits for amputated arms and legs as well as discarded medicine bottles and other equipment have been uncovered by farmers in the area.[50]

Among the earliest settlers here were the Harrisons; Middleton Harrison purchased land here in 1818. Other landowners were: Carroll Martin and William Roundtree.[51] Among those arriving later were: Willie and Olive Cox of North Carolina, Wesley Grigsby and his wife Ventie Richardson Grigsby, John D. Tidwell and his wife Derendia Ann Billingsley, and George and Mary Grigsby Haygood.[52]

The first Haygood to arrive in America from England was Francis Haguewood; he left a will dated 1676, which was probated in Surry County, Virginia.[53] Poplar Spring, known for its earlier school and voting precinct, is near Brush and Shoal Creeks.

Masonville was located near Six Mile Branch at the intersection of U.S. Highway 72 and the Old Lexington Road (County Road 71). This is where Joseph Mason settled in 1824. Two years later he was appointed the first postmaster of Masonville. Until the early 1950s there were a few businesses at this intersection, including a grocery, service station, and the Shady Rest Motel. At one time a gristmill was a part of this community.[54] Until recent years a landmark known as the Tom Bethune House was located nearby.[55]

Another source refers to the community of Masonville as being located ten miles east of Florence. At one time a road sign was located near the front of the original Killen Methodist Church which gave the distance from that point to Florence as ten miles. Perhaps this would have placed a later post office under either James Coulter or John Harrison who were succeeding postmasters near the top of the hill a few miles west of Six Mile Branch.[56]

In 1855, Samuel W. Barr became Masonville's postmaster. His home was located a mile or so east of Six Mile Branch. Barr's wife is buried in the small Barr Family Cemetery a short distance north of Elm Street at this location. It is believed that Barr moved the post office to this area where it remained until it was discontinued in 1866.[57]

In the May 9, 1832, session of the Lauderdale County Court, D. B. King, Littleberry Harrison, and Lemuel Farrow were appointed judges for the voting place at Masonville. Luke Harrison, John C. McMahan, and Otha Tharp were appointed three years later. In 1836, John Donahoo, Littleberry Harrison, and Hugh B. King were given the same responsibility. James Valiant and Otha Tharp served with Hugh B. King the following year.

Lock Six, now under water, was not a town. Yet, its status as the center of activity for the operation and maintenance of the nine locks on the old Muscle Shoals Canal made it a significant community. Designated as Lock Six Reservation, it consisted of a sizable acreage near the mouth of Six Mile Creek. There were a number of buildings located here, including operations and maintenance shops, two large barracks for the workers, two homes for the families of the engineer and his assistant, stables for the mules and horses, and other structures. Its shipyard had a number of buildings and a dry dock where barges were built and launched. This was also the headquarters for a small railroad which operated between the stretch of locks from near Florence to near

Rogersville. The grounds of Lock Six became a favorite picnic and visiting area for people from Florence. Author, historian, and university professor emeritus, the late, Joshua Nicholas Winn, III, who spent his youth in one of the engineer's houses here, often referred to Lock Six as "the Garden of Eden."[58] The era of Lock Six ended with the completion of Wilson Dam when the backwaters of Lake Wilson hid forever the beauty of what once had been.[59]

The Kingman Post Office was established July 26, 1899, with Preston G. Curtis as its postmaster; he picked up the mail at Lock Six. Curtis was also proprietor of a general store located just outside the main entrance to reservation. Kingman was named for Major William Rice King, one of the early construction engineers on the lock who was a combat engineer during the Civil War. Following his tenure at Lock Six, he was appointed commanding officer of the Army Engineering School, and later, was designated as district engineer in Chattanooga. The post office was discontinued in 1914.[60]

Killen is a prosperous and growing town east of Florence. It, no doubt, is an outgrowth of early Masonville which was located a few miles to the east and Brush Creek located a few miles to the west. When Huntsville Road (U.S. Highway 72) was re-routed into Florence, the small community of Brush Creek gradually disappeared. About the same time an up-to-date business district began to form alongside the new thoroughfare, with stores carrying the names of Cox, Liles, and McPeters. Reinforced by the government work on the canal, and nearby Lock Six and Kingman, a town began to emerge that became Killen. The late Professor Joshua Nicholas Winn III, in his book, Muscle Shoals Canal ... Life With The Canalers, says that "Killen, according to old-timers, when a smaller community a long time ago, had no name."[61] However, it became necessary for it to have a name when a post office was located here on August 22, 1896. James S. Killen became its first postmaster; hence, the town was named for him. He was descended from James and Ann Nancy McDougal Killen, early settlers from North Carolina. Family sources say the earliest Killens in America migrated from Ireland, and the name was probably derived from O'Killeen.[62] This family name is also associated with Scotland where there is a small and lovely hamlet named Killen.

The town of Killen is located almost in the center of what had once been an antebellum plantation known as "Locust Grove." This was the home of John Donohoo who is buried in the Killen Cemetery. Early documents show the location of Donohoo Spring as being on South Bridge Road, southeast of the present business district. His home is believed to have been near this spring. County records show the survey of the road from Florence to Athens in December, 1829. Later, John Donohoo was given $4.00 by the court to purchase a hammer to break rocks at the bridge on Shoal Creek. However, it was stipulated that ownership of the hammer would revert to the county upon completion of the bridge.[63] His obituary appeared in the September 1, 1847, issue of a Huntsville newspaper.[64]

Goodwin Taylor arrived in this area in 1818 and built his home near the mouth of Four Mile Creek, south of Killen. The high steep banks overlooking the Tennessee River here were once known as Taylor's Bluff.[65] In 1831, Taylor was placed in charge of the section of Huntsville Road from Shoal Creek to Donahoo's plantation. Other landowners here prior to 1825 were: William Cowden, Henry Minor, John Chisholm, John Welch, Charles Best, Payton R. Gill, William Cauden, Joseph Scott, Malcolm Gilcrist, William Roundtree, and Thomas Bibb.[66]

Wilson's Crossroads and Saint Florian

During early years the place now called Saint Florian was known as Wilson's Crossroads. Two large antebellum plantations, owned by the Wilson brothers, John and Matthew, joined near this place. The farm of Samuel Wilson, an older brother, was located south of here near the Four Mile Branch community east of Florence. These Wilsons were from Botetourt County, Virginia. John and Anna Brewer Wilson built their home on the south side of

Jackson Military Road across from the present intersection of County Roads 47 and 30. Wilson Spring at the foot of the hill below their home site is a landmark today. A rare photograph of their home published in the June 22, 1902, edition of the Montgomery Advertiser, shows a two-story structure with weatherboards covering the original logs. There was an elegant portico at the front entrance similar in style to those seen in early Virginian architecture.[67] The home of Matthew and Eliza Wilson was located near Wilson's Creek west of Wilson's Crossroads and closer to the Mars Hill Road. This house was similar in appearance to the John Wilson home.[68] The total land owned by John and Matthew Wilson in and around Wilson's Crossroads amounted to 3,380 acres, including 1,200 improved acres for cultivation. In 1860, Matthew owned 50 slaves and John owned 60. This number did not include Christopher Brewer and his wife, who were the maternal grandparents of W. C. Handy, Florence's famous "Father of the Blues." When John Wilson was married to Anna Brewer, these two slaves came to live with them. Although John and Anna gave them their freedom prior to the war, they preferred to remain with the Wilsons as trusted servants.[69]

Other landowners in the area prior to 1825 included: Joseph Farmer, Henry Minor, Hugh Campbell, Hunter Peel, Andrew Burns, George Simmons, Jason Hopson, James Brickell, Malcolm Gilchrist, and two McDonalds – William and Thomas.[70]

Three roads – Jackson Military Road, Butler Creek Road, and Middle Road intersected at Wilson's Crossroads. These routes followed early Indian trails. The Jackson Military Road followed an old path from Buffalo River near Lawrenceburg to a river crossing at the mouth of Cypress Creek below Florence. The Butler Creek Road and the Middle Road were originally one extended wilderness path leading from Middle Tennessee to a crossing of the Tennessee River known as Campbell's Ferry (near present Kendale Garden Subdivision.) This was sometimes called the Campbell's Ferry Road. In the first attempt to survey the Military Road, known as the Major Butler Survey, the crossing of the Tennessee River was perhaps to have been at Campbell's Ferry.

The September 30, 1817, compendium for this proposed highway, known as the H. Young Survey, shows the river crossing to be the mouth of Cypress Creek a marked advantage for the future town of Florence![71]

The land around Wilson's Crossroads bears evidence of peoples who lived here before the white man arrived. According to legends a prehistoric village and a man-made mound may have been located near the Henry Stumpe Spring. Several uncovered holes in this area suggests that there may have been burials here. Old stories have been handed down that tell of an Indian battle nearby. Hundreds of small flint chips have been uncovered near this spring; this may have been where early man chipped stones into tools or weapons. It is believed that hard, blue flint stones were mined from nearby Shoal Creek and brought to this workshop. Andrew Jackson is said to have camped a few miles north of Saint Florian on his march back to Nashville following the Battle of New Orleans. This was in a wooded area near where the Bailey Springs Road joins the Military Road.[72]

Hopewell Church, one of the area's earliest Methodist Churches, was located on the Matthew Wilson plantation near the modern intersection of Cox Creek Parkway and County Road 47. Confederate soldiers on their march to the battles of Franklin and Nashville removed a large pew from this church as they passed by on the morning of November 21, 1864. Membership of this antebellum congregation included both whites and blacks. After the Civil War, this meetinghouse became the property of the Church of Christ. Following the relocation of their congregation to Mars Hill, the old Hopewell Church was vacant until 1875, when it was purchased and made into a home by William Mecke who had brought his family here from Poughkeepsie, New York. The African-American members of old Hopewell built their own Hopewell African Methodist Episcopal Church on the back part of the Wilson plantation facing the Middle Road.

John S. Wilson, then an old man, was cruelly tortured and murdered on April 30, 1865, by local Civil War outlaws headed by the notorious Tom Clark. John's brother Matthew Wilson died nine years later. A short time prior to Matthew's death, his land was sold to Father Houser of the Catholic Church who had been responsible for bringing Catholic colonies to nearby Lawrenceburg, Loretto, Saint Joseph, and Saint Marys. In May, 1873, John Wilson's heirs sold the remaining part of his plantation to Father Houser. Thus, begins the story of the founding of Saint Florian in the early 1870's.

Father Houser laid out the Wilson lands in lots as small as two acres and in farms from forty to eighty acres. These parcels were then sold to German Catholic families for prices ranging from $8.00 to $15.00 per acre. These people came from Michigan, Pennsylvania, Ohio, Wisconsin, Illinois, New York, and other states. The first of these colonists to arrive were the families of Florian Rasch, John Kasmeier, Senior, Frank Breidainger, Adam Zulauf, and Theodor Woltering. According to local historians, the town was named for Florian Rasch who donated the first bell to be placed on the church. Others who arrived soon afterwards included the Grossheims, Lockers, Bufflers, Schmildkofers, Iagners, Stumpes, Meckes, Eckls, Ecks, Schauts, Bernaeurs, Gusmuses, Kriegers, Speckers, and numbers of others who came even later.[73]

Stories have been handed down about how the neighbors felt sorry for these German settlers who were trying to make a living on worn-out red clay land that had been almost washed away by large gullies. However, before long it became obvious that these hard working and ingenious people had not only built up the land, but had become seemingly more prosperous than their neighbors. One old-timer said that his father knew he had found the answer to their success when he observed that these German farmers always went to town with full wagons and came back with empty ones; here as, their Protestant neighbors would go to town in empty wagons and return home with their vehicles loaded with all kinds of store bought supplies.[74]

Saint Florian's first place of business was Adam Zulauf's Store. Appointed postmaster on July 25, 1879, Zulauf made the post office a part of his store. By 1881, he had built a two-story, eight room brick building, with a hotel addition for travelers and boarders. In the same year John Schaut opened a general merchandise. In 1888, when Peter Schaut became postmaster, he moved the post office to Schaut's Store. Other postmasters were: Katie Schaut (1896), Robert B. Kilburn (1897), and Maggie Kilburn (1899). This office was discontinued in 1904.

Edward Rasch was also an early merchant. Peter Stenz was the town cobbler who at times employed as many as five men in his shop. The local funeral director was John Beumer, a carpenter by trade. Other early wood workers were George Locker, Henry Stumpe, and John Ultsch. Pete Hollander and Frank Peters were the blacksmiths. Grossheim's blacksmith shop on the Middle Road also made wagons for the local farmers. The Aigner family made and sold bricks locally using the rich red clay from the land.[75]

One of the area landmarks is Saint Michael's Catholic Church at Saint Florian. The walls, roof, and tower of the present sanctuary were completed in 1918. The beautiful windows, with their ecclesiastic art, were manufactured in Munich, Bavaria, during the 1920's.[76]

North Bainbridge, Four Mile Branch, and Jacksonburg

North Bainbridge was also known as Bainbridge Ferry. It is now the location of the Kendale Gardens Subdivision. The early town of Bainbridge was on the opposite bank of the river in what is now Colbert County. This was where Byler Road, Alabama's first designated state highway, crossed the river. It connected with the Jackson Military Road north of Bailey Springs. From there it crossed the river at Bainbridge Ferry on its was to Tuscaloosa. A few stores were once located on the north bank of the river. Also nearby was a distillery owned by one of Florence's early mayors, Zebulon P. Morrison. Bainbridge Ferry was the crossing place for General John Bell Hood's defeated army following the disastrous battles of Franklin and Nashville. Evidence of Hood's defensive earthworks here were recently destroyed by bulldozers. The earliest landowners at North Bainbridge included James Jackson, John Donelson, and the Cypress Land Company.[77]

Near the entrance to the modern Indian Springs Subdivision on U.S. Highway 73 East is the pioneer Cain and Middilton Cemetery. Three of the early graves here are: William James Middilton who was born in 1831 and died 1846; Elizabeth Cain, wife of John Cain, Esquire, born in 1796 and died in 1837; Elmirah who died in 1844 at the age of thirteen years.

Four Mile Branch was a small community situated around the ford at Four Mile Branch on the well-traveled Huntsville Road a few miles east of Florence. Wagons would stop in the middle of this ford so as to thoroughly soak their wheels. This helped to tighten these wooden circular frames around the axles. A beautiful waterfall was located at the mouth of Four Mile Branch. This once popular swimming place for boys is now under Wilson Lake. The hill leading from the ford was so steep that it was difficult for early automobiles to ascend it without turning around and backing up the grade. D. Garrett's Grocery was located at Four Mile. During the construction of Wilson Dam, Garrett moved his store to the Wilson Dam Road.[78]

Four Mile Branch was first known as Raccoon Branch. On February 1, 1836, James Letsinger was appointed overseer of that part of Huntsville Road from the city limits of Florence to "Racoon Branch." This same James Letsinger was allowed ten dollars and six and one quarter cents by the county court on February 1, 1836, for furnishing a shroud and digging a grave for the burial of Henry Copenhouer. Landowners in or around Four Mile community prior to 1825 were: Samuel Wilson, Reuben Huff, Dabney Morris, Andrew Burne, Jonathan Estill, John Craig, John Coffee, and John Jackson.[79]

Jacksonburg is located about seven miles north of Florence near the Chisholm Road and the L&N Railroad. It was named for Joseph W. Jackson who was appointed its first postmaster in 1889. Other postmasters who served here were Marvin F. Jackson and John Zahand. The Zahands were Swiss settlers in this area. The original landowners at Jacksonburg were: John Learduce, John Chisholm, Malcolm Gilchrist, and Edward and Andrew Williams.[80]

According to legend there was an early attempt made to establish a Morman community in the area of Jacksonburg and Blackburn. However, no record has been found to substantiate this story.

37. IN NORTH CENTRAL LAUDERDALE COUNTY

"There are souls like stars that dwell apart ..."
(Sam Walter Foss)

North central Lauderdale County is mostly made up of hills and hollows between Florence and the Tennessee line. It has a scenic beauty interlaced with cold and swiftly flowing creeks supplied by its many gushing springs. In the early times, its forests were especially noted for wild game of all kinds, from the small squirrel to the roaming deer and bear. There is evidence of its preference by early tribes of Native Americans. One of its numerous streams of water still carries the colorful name of Indian Camp Creek named for the native village located near its confluence with Butler Creek in the long ago. Generally, this part of the county was settled by white pioneers later than the more fertile lands located to its east and west. Many of these families crossed into Alabama from Wayne, Lawrence, and other neighboring counties in Tennessee.

Pruitton, Hines, Webster, and Big Cut

Pruitton is the official designation of this North central Lauderdale County community, according to the archives of the Post Office Department. However, its earliest name was Pruitt Town. It was named for Pruitt Town, South Carolina, home of the Pruitts who migrated from Virginia. The Thomas Pruitt Plantation was located at this place along Butler Creek about six miles south of Iron City, Tennessee. A standing landmark as late as 1996 is the Lizzie Liles place, believed to have been built during the late 1880's. This family may have been connected with the Lyles of Newberry County, South Carolina, who were active patriots in the Revolutionary War.

The Butler Creek Road, which runs from the Tennessee line through Pruitton, was originally an Indian Trail that led to the Tennessee River near the present Wilson Dam. In 1888, a railroad, later known as the L&N, passed through the Pruitt farm on its way from Columbia, Tennessee, to Florence. For a number of years a passenger station was located here. Thomas Pruitt, who settled near Cloverdale in the early 1820's, is said to have been the first of this family to arrive in Lauderdale County. He was born in 1783 in Virginia, and moved as a young boy with his parents to South Carolina. His brother, Henry Palmer Pruitt, migrated to North Alabama in 1833.

On a high hill overlooking Pruitton lived Hugh Riah (Uriah) Reynolds, a veteran of the War of 1812. General Nathan Bedford Forrest and Colonel Jacob Biffle spent the night in Reynolds' log house November 21, 1864, on their way to the Battle of Franklin. Reynolds' wife was Elizabeth Ham, daughter of John and Phoebe Blassingame Ham. They had fourteen children. Hugh Riah Reynolds, born in Pendleton County, South Carolina, was a son of Revolutionary War Veteran Hamilton Reynolds whose home was at the nearby Savannah Ford on Shoal Creek. The Reynolds Cemetery is located on a hill near Sour Branch.

North of Pruitton at the Tennessee line was the large plantation of John Dickie Wade, native of Halifax County, Virginia. Originally known as the "Johnson Place," Wade named this plantation "Egypt," because, he said, it always produced a bountiful crop of corn. Around 1838, John and his brother, William, contracted with John R. and S. S. Henry to built a trestle bridge across the Tennessee River at Bellview near Center Star. It was made of wood with wooden piers. This was the first bridge across the river in the Muscle Shoals area.[1]

Dr. Maurice Wade Pruitt, a descendant of both the Pruitts and the Wades, wrote accounts of Pruitton in his book, Bugger Saga. His stories tell about the notorious outlaw "Mountain" Tom Clark, as well as other gangs who raped, robbed, plundered, and murdered local citizens during the final years of the war. The post office at Pruitton was established in 1883, with Edmund Myrick as postmaster. Its second postmaster was Thomas D. Pruitt. His son, Thomas L., was appointed to this office in 1914. The last to serve in this capacity at Pruitton was Albert S. Goad. The mail was discontinued here in 1921.[2] The earliest landowners in this area were: John Coffee, Moses Terry, James and Thomas McBride, Luke Huggins, James Bright, William Higginbotham, and Joseph Gist.[3]

The community of Hines was originally known as Webster. The name change came about in 1892, following the appointment of Joab G. Hines as postmaster at Webster in 1890. This area is part of an early Native American settlement. Indian Camp Creek flows through this area. Hines is also located on the old L&N Railroad. One of its landmarks – until demolished during the 1970s – was a large two-story log house known as the Bretherick Place. A few years before the Civil War, William M. Bretherick of England came to Lauderdale County as a machinist for the Lauderdale Cotton Factory on Shoal Creek. He and his wife, Sarah, had a big family, with the older children all born in England. Following the Civil War, Bretherick and several sons operated a grist and wool-carding mill near Hines. James Allen Patterson was made postmaster in 1905. He held this office until 1921 when Henrietta Patterson was appointed. The mail was collected, sorted, and delivered from Patterson's Store. Later, it was moved to the Patterson home which also served as the polling place for the Blackburn Beat.[4]

Big Cut Station was on the L&N Railroad directly north of Hines. In fact, the postmaster at Hines would meet the train at Big Cut to pick up the mail delivery. Because of the high and steep hills in this part of the county, it was necessary for the railroad to cut its way around some of these barriers. The largest of these "cuts" occurred at this site around 1888. Hence, it was named for this man-made feature.[5]

Zip City, Little Cypress, Bethel Grove, Hope, and Blackburn

Zip City is an old community with a modern "automobile age" identification. Alonzo Parker is credited with giving this unusual name to his community. During the 1920s, Parker's General Merchandise faced the busy Chisholm Highway (Alabama 17). During that era of prohibition, he often remarked that cars were "zipping" through so fast on their way to Tennessee where liquor could be purchased that the community should be named "Zip City."[6]

This area is sometimes referred to as the Wilson Community. Phillip Wilson was an early settler. The creek that flows through the eastern part of this community is named for this family. Also, the Wilson School near Zip City is on land donated by Green Wilson. William Bayles, Levi and Rutledge Todd, Henry Butler, and John Pickens were among the earliest landowners in this area.[7]

A few miles west of Zip City is the site of a pre-Civil War wool and card factory known as the Darby, Benham, and Company Mill. Henry Jackson Darby, who was married to Mary Sue White, was one of its proprietors. This factory, located near the crossing of County Road 8 over Little Cypress Creek, is believed to have been destroyed in 1863 by the Union Army.

Lorenzo D. Fowler's gristmill was also located here. Fowler and his wife, Mary, were first cousins, being grandchildren of Joshua Fowler of Pickens County, South Carolina. Joshua was a corporal in the 6th South Carolina Regiment during the Revolutionary War.[8] Cave Hole, a deep place in Little Cypress Creek below Fowler's mill, was the scene of one of the horrendous crimes committed during the Civil War by the local outlaw Tom Clark. Here he captured and assassinated three Confederate soldiers from Colonel Biffle's 19th Tennessee Cavalry. One of the victims was Wesley W. Fowler, age twenty-one, of Company B, and a son of the local miller. The other two were John Gilliam, age twenty, and George Washington Golightly, age eighteen. Their families resided near Fowler's Mill. John was a son of Bennet Gilliam, a carpenter who came from Virginia. George's father was Madison Golightly, a son of Henry Golightly, native of South Carolina, who was born in 1778. "Mountain" Tom Clark refused to permit the removal of the bodies of these victims of his crime for several days. After Clark finally went away, it became the task of the women and old men in the neighborhood to bury the dead. These three soldiers were placed in a common grave in the nearby Parsonage Chapel Cemetery. This site is now marked by a marble stone and three Confederate markers.

In early times Parsonage Chapel Methodist Church served as "headquarters" for about twenty preaching places on the large Cypress Circuit. Here was the parsonage where the circuit rider lived. His churches were scattered over parts of Lauderdale County as well as sections of adjoining counties in Tennessee. This church was later moved closer to the creek and its name changed to Hillsdale Methodist.[9]

Berry Adams was the first to enter land in 1818 near this section of Little Cypress Creek.[10] Next came Isaac Thornton in 1831, followed by Joseph P. Bourland, Abraham James, and Robert S. Miller in the early 1850s. In addition to these early people, the 1850 census shows the following families living near Fowler's Mill: Josiah Fowler, John, James, and Owen Obriand, B. W. O'Neal, Samuel Tilman, W. Marshal, C. L. Henry, Thomas and C. L. Pruett, Holman Bird, Absalom Jeans, E. G. and William Phillips, Joseph Beddingfield, Thomas Stewart, Dennis House, and Thomas W. Young.

There was a community called Little Cypress located near the conjunction of Gray and Lyles Branches and Little Cypress Creek. In more recent times this area is often referred to as Clear Creek Community. Samuel O. Johnson, native of Kentucky, was appointed postmaster of Little Cypress on February 22, 1856. However, within three months this office was discontinued. The Nolen Family Cemetery is located here. As early as 1818 the following men purchased land in this area: James Bright, Henry M. Rutledge, William Bayles, and Levi Todd.[11] There is a well preserved foundation of what appears to have been a pioneer mill hidden under the waters of the creek at this site. It is believed that the bed of Little Cypress perhaps changed its course during a high flood, causing the mill to fall into the newly created bed of the stream.

Bethel Grove is located on Jim Olive Road west of Chisholm Highway and near the confluence of May Branch and Middle Cypress Creek. This settlement is a few miles west of the Little Cypress community and near the Tennessee line. In fact, a study of the census records indicates that the communities were so close that they could have been considered as one settlement. Bethel Grove takes its name from an early Methodist Church established in a grove of trees. The Methodists called it Bethel in recognition of the ancient Biblical city known as a holy place in central Palestine. Charles Littleton, veteran of the Revolutionary War, was one of the organizers of this church. It was this old soldier who built the pulpit. According to descendants of Phillip Darby, an early settler at nearby Salem, the Darby family attended Bethel Grove before the Salem Methodist Church was organized.

Littleton was granted 160 acres of bounty land here in 1818. His single pen one-and-a-half story log house was torn down in 1977. He was born in Frederick County, Virginia, in 1760. His father, Solomon Littleton, was an Englishman who sided with the American cause. In revenge, the British captured Solomon and placed him in a smallpox hospital at Ninety-Six, South Carolina. This confinement caused his death. Land owned by Solomon Littleton later became part of the District of Columbia.

In 1776, Charles Littleton enlisted as a private in the South Carolina Militia. He was in the Snow Campaign and later saw action in the Battles of Stono, Rocky Mount, and Hannah's Cowpens. In August, 1795, he was married to Elizabeth Henderson in Newberry County, South Carolina. They reared a family of eight children. Littleton died March 29, 1848, and was buried near his home.[12] His widow was living near Bethel Grove at the time of the 1850 Census, as were her sons, David Lee Littleton and Dr. Samuel Holbrooks Littleton.

282

Another historic church here is the Bethel Berry Church of Christ. It was organized June 21, 1868, as the Middle Cypress Congregation and known as the Bethabara Church. This name comes from the Book of St. John 1:28: "These things were done in Bethabara beyond Jordan, where John was baptizing." However, by 1888, its name had been changed to "Bethel Berry," influenced perhaps by the nearby community of Bethel Grove. The deed to the property is recorded as the Bethel Berry Christian Church.[13]

The earliest landowners around Bethel Grove were: John Swearingam, Sam Brown, William and Thomas Williams, and William McKee.[14] Some of the families living here in 1850 were: George Fifer, James Hughs, Elilugh Jeans, Richard Quaser, Henry Pruett, Sr., Henry Pruett, Jr., James O'Briand, Rody Duff, Mary Duckett, and Jabus Beard.

In 1893, Bethel Grove underwent a name change and became known as Hope. This was an inspirational and symbolic name selected by a community with great hopes of becoming a thriving town when the proposed Mineral Belt Railroad was being planned to connect East Florence with the ore fields in the nearby Tennessee counties. Unfortunately, this did not materialize. The postmasters who served at Hope between 1893 and 1904 were: Henry Fowler, George M. McMullan, and John N. Keeton.[15]

Blackburn is on the L&N Railroad near Indian Camp Creek. Beginning in 1888, there was a passenger station located here. The L&N also built a number of company houses along the railroad track for their maintenance crews. The community was named for William and Mary Blackburn who came from South Carolina.

The early Piney Grove Cemetery is located here. Reuben Huff purchased land a mile or two east of Blackburn prior to 1825.[16] During the last year of the Civil War there were a number of atrocious crimes committed in and around Blackburn by ruthless gangs of lawless men, including the notorious outlaw "Mountain" Tom Clark.

Mars Hill, Petersville, Underwood, and Brandon's Factory

Mars Hill takes its name from Acts 17:22, which reads: "Then Paul stood in the midst of Mars' hill ..." This section of Florence is the home of the Mars Hill Bible School, which has one of the highest rated scholastic programs in the nation. It is owned and operated by the Churches of Christ and is located on a campus of some 100 acres. This is the site where in 1871, Theophilus Brown Larimore founded his academy for young preachers and Christian workers. Later, this institution became the Mars Hill College which operated successfully until 1887.[17] The original college building, which was also the Larimore home, is an area landmark listed on the National Register of Historic Places. The historic Gresham Cemetery is located across from the Mars Hill campus. The Gresham home once stood near the cemetery. Indications are that this log structure was built in the late 1820's by Philemon Gresham, who was born in 1800 in Wilkes County, Georgia. Esther Gresham, wife of T. B. Larimore, was born here. Mars Hill was also the home of former Alabama Governor Hugh McVay who settled here before Alabama became a state. McVay, son of a Revolutionary War soldier, was born in South Carolina. He is buried in the family cemetery near the home site.[18] On the original McVay land is King's Spring, one of the city's largest springs as well as one of its most scenic places. It takes its name from a later owner, Phillip King. In prior years King's Spring was a popular picnic area.

One of North Alabama's early iron foundries was located at Mars Hill. Established in 1835 by William P. Johnson, it was purchased and expanded by James Wright and William T. Rice in 1853. Various kinds of equipment were manufactured here, including sawmills, cotton gins, steam engines, textile machinery, farm equipment, and small household items. During the Civil War they made shells, guns, and other items for the Confederacy. In May, 1863, this foundry fell victim to a raid by the Union Army. A mission of Florence's First Methodist Church met at this factory for preaching and Bible lessons. Later, this small congregation erected Moore's Chapel Methodist Church across the road from the foundry. The Mars Hill Church of Christ is located near the foundations of the Wright and Rice Foundry. After the L&N Railroad was built, beginning in 1888, there was a passenger station at Mars Hill which served the community.[19] In addition to Governor McVay, some of the other early landowners were: George Gresham, William Ward, Lewis Allen, John Brahan, William Donelson, John McGregor, Green K. Hubbard, Elsey West, William Lovelson, and William and Thomas McDonald.[20]

Petersville is a modern and thriving suburb of Florence located on the Cloverdale Road. Its history dates back to the end of the Civil War. A number of former African-American slaves from the Peters Plantation on Gunwaleford Road established a small settlement in tenant houses here and were joined by some of the freed slaves from General Coffee's place which was located nearby. They worked on farms as well as at a nearby cotton gin and saw mill owned and operated by Frank Rasch.[21] Sometime around 1914, a family from St. Florian by the name of Peters moved to this area.[22] Bert Berkey opened the first business here. Later, Ringlestine's Store was located nearby. In addition to the plantation of General John Coffee, other early landowners were: Malcolm Gilchrist, Hanson Thrasher, George A. Pinchon, James McCartney, and John P. Cunningham.[23]

Underwood joins Petersville to the north on Alabama Highway 157. It gets its name from William A. Underwood who bought a farm on the Stony Point Road around 1890. He built a one-room log school for the children in this area. Later, a frame building known as Underwood School was built on land donated by John Phillips. This is where the modern Underwood School is now located. William A. Underwood was born in Mississippi. His parents were William and Nancy Underwood. They had fourteen children. This family arrived at the Cypress Cotton Mill village north of Florence between 1853 and 1857. They came from Itawamba County, Mississippi, near the Bay Springs Cotton Mill in Tishomingo County, Mississippi. This Bay Springs factory had been established by George Gresham who moved to Tishomingo County from Mars Hill community near Florence in 1838. A number mill hands in the Bay Springs Factory moved to the Cypress Mills near Florence prior to the Civil War. The Cypress Cotton Factory was destroyed by the Union Army during the Civil War. Afterwards, William and Nancy moved from the mill village to a farm. This is reflected in the 1870 census where William had changed his occupation from "factory" to "farming." Another son, David Pinkney "Pink" Underwood, became a well-known farmer in the Underwood community. Pink was married to Flora Sharpton, whose family had also been workers in the Cypress Cotton Mill.[24] Other settlers in or near the Underwood community were: Will Lindsey, Henry Richardson, Frank Wilkes, John Bailey, William Smith, and Henry Miles. Will Call and Joe Sharp established the first businesses in the community. Prior to 1825, most of the land here was owned by Malcolm Gilchrist of Lawrence County, Alabama. Gilchrist operated a fleet of flatboats and keelboats and became one of the largest landholders in this part of the Tennessee Valley.[25]

Brandon's Factory was a cotton mill and adjoining village on Little Cypress Creek southwest of Zip City and about eight miles from Florence. The land for this mill was purchased in 1871 from the minor heirs of Henry Jackson Darby by James B. Irvine and Washington M. Brandon. There had been a small mill at this site, known as Duckett's Mill, established by John Duckett in 1836. Henry Jackson Darby had been a partner in the Darby, Benham, and Company Wool Mill located a few miles upstream near the Parson Chapel Methodist Church. Descendants of the Darby family believed there was either another Darby and Benham operations here or, perhaps, an auxiliary to the upstream factory. Also, it is thought that there may have been a family connection between the Darbys and John Duckett.

The Brandon Mill boasted 1,800 spindles and an annual consumption of 500 bales of cotton. The yarn produced was for the Philadelphia market. The mill village housed forty employees.[26]

The Brandon Factory was later purchased by John H. Young and his wife, De La Young. In 1886, the Youngs sold two-thirds interest in this plant, along with other mills and operations, to W. K. Embrey and his son, John M. Embrey. At this time, the mill became known as the Embrey, Son, and Young Factory. This firm now included an auxiliary operation located upstream at the site of the former Darby, Benham, and Company Wool Factory.[27] The old Kernachan Mill at the confluence of Wilson Branch and Indian Camp Creek also became a part of this enterprise.[28] Altogether, there were 30 looms and 2,500 spindles producing cotton yarns and jeans for the New York market.

There was a company store in the mill village owned and managed by Embrey and his son. John Scruggs McDonald, Sr., operated a grist and wool carding mill on the creek below the factory. His brother, Thomas Anderson McDonald, was the village blacksmith.[29] These McDonalds were sons of John and Margaret Emory (Embrey) McDonald who settled at Cow Pen in 1834. They were related to the Embreys who owned two-thirds interest in the factory.[30]

The history of the Stony Point Church of Christ near Underwood is connected with the early Brandon Cotton Factory. Established as a Methodist Church as early as 1845, the original building was located on Chisholm Creek until 1884, at which time the Methodists erected a church nearer to the Brandon Mill. The Church of Christ relocated to the top of the hill where they continue to serve as one of the area's historic congregations.[31]

At some point in time after these mills were closed and the community of workers moved away, David Allen Sharp established a thriving gristmill just above the original dam. David was a son of Charles and Matilda Anglin Sharp who were early settlers from Virginia. There are colorful legends about David Sharp and his mill. One tells of his distrust of banks. It was said that periodically David would bury his gold in the nearby woods for safekeeping rather than use the financial institutions.[32]

About 1939, Arlin and Otis White established a mill here and developed the lake and grounds into a beautiful picnic and swimming resort. The Whites used junk cars as reinforcement for the concrete in their new dam at this site. They were descended from Sherwood White who built an early mill on Second Creek in East Lauderdale County.[33]

A few miles northeast of Brandon Mill was the early home of John Chisholm father of Tolliver Chisholm for whom Chisholm Highway was named. The Chisholm Cemetery is located on the old homestead. Other early landowners prior to 1825 were: Ed Williams, John Wilkes, John Deck, William Griffin, and Eli Kerr.[34] They were followed later by Darius A. Butler, Joseph Ijams, William A. Wason, and Stephen Townsley.[35]

38. SETTLEMENT OF WEST LAUDERDALE COUNTY

"And a new people takes the land..."
(G. K. Chesterton)

West Lauderdale County is a place of hills, hollows, and some of the most fertile bottomlands that can be found anywhere in the Tennessee Valley. It is rich in the lore of its people. No place in the county can claim an earlier history of man's habitation. A study of the Tennessee Valley Authority's archaeological maps shows numerous early village sites and prehistoric mounds. Some of these date back some 4,000 years to the Woodland and Copena civilizations. Recent excavations in Dust Cave, a few miles west of Florence, show evidence of earlier inhabitants here more than 10,000 years ago. Significant findings have likewise been unearthed in nearby Smith Bottom Cave. It is expected that other caves in this area will yield additional testimony. The historic Natchez Trace Parkway cuts through this part of Lauderdale County. The original bed of this road ran along the ridgelines and crossed the Tennessee River at Waterloo. In 1801, Chief George Colbert of the Chickasaw Nation persuaded General James Wilkinson, a representative of Federal government, to relocate this ferry to where the new Natchez Trace Parkway crosses the river. Long before Alabama became a state, many people traveled this road from Nashville, Tennessee, to Natchez, Mississippi. A number of these wayfarers liked what they saw and returned later to become a part of the land.

Sullivan's Crossroads and Central Heights

Sullivan's Crossroads was named for Dr. Charles W. Sullivan, a popular physician, who made his home here. A son of Dr. Oen Boyce Sullivan at Waterloo, he was born in 1854, and died in 1886. The earliest of the Sullivan family in Lauderdale County was Charles Sullivan who settled on 600 acres of land along

Burcham Creek. Here he built his two-story log house with two stairways, four fireplaces, and a kitchen which was located at the rear of the main structure.[1] A native of Virginia, born in 1781, he was a school teacher and excelled in his instructions of the English language. There are also a number of references to him being an early land surveyor for the county. Other landholders in this area prior to 1825 were: Thomas Shannon, James Boroughs, John Roberson, John Walker, and William Wallace.[2]

New life was breathed into Sullivan Crossroads in 1912 when Dave Murphy moved from nearby Murphy's Crossroads. His general merchandise store soon became the center of Sullivan's Cross Roads. Old timers remember a post office being located for a time in the rear of Murphy's Store, although no official records have been found. Elmer Koonce, it is said, was the first postmaster. He was succeeded by Roy Blackburn who later moved this mail center to his home. Koonce and Murphy established a nearby cotton gin in 1918. Morris Drug Store and Burt Patterson's Blacksmith Shop soon became fixtures in this community. Following Murphy's death in 1923, his sons, Cecil and Clyde Murphy, took over the cotton gin and general store. They expanded the mercantile business through a system of rolling stores that covered a radius of fifteen miles.

The name Sullivan's Crossroads evolved into a new name Central Heights around 1928. This was a time when small rural schools were being consolidated. Sullivan's Crossroads was selected as a central location for such a school. Sam Haddock gave the land and the large consolidated Central School System came into being. Thus, the name Central Heights seemed a more appropriate name for the newly vitalized community.[3]

Huggins, Wesley Chapel, Burcham Mills, and Young's Crossroads

Huggins was one of the earliest settlements in the county. It is better known today as the Wesley Chapel Community because of the nearby historic Wesley Chapel United Methodist Church and Cemetery. John Huggins settled here in 1818. A year later he was married to Sarah Faires, a daughter of the Reverend Alexander Faires, one of the county's first pioneers.

Two Faires brothers, Alexander and Richard, were here as early as 1816. Their father, Richard Faires, Senior, died in 1819 at the age of 96 years. Both of these brothers were farmers and local preachers. They established the Methodist Church here in 1818, although they began holding preaching services in the community soon after their arrival.[4] By 1825, there were four more of the Faires family located here: Elias, James, John, and William. Some of the other landowners of this period were: Sam Savage, Henry Kilpatrick, William Smart, Jacob Castleman, Joseph Haddleton, Sam Grimes, Joseph South, James Brooks, Jackson Stanfield, Joseph German, and James and Ebenezer Young.[5] Early 1837 court records show John Spain, Thomas McBride, and John Cantrell as election holders at Huggins.

Burcham Mills was located on the old Savannah Highway where it crossed Burcham Creek. A cotton gin, gristmill, and blacksmith shop were located here. Its original owner was said to have been Jack Simmons. One of its superintendents was Jesse Newton Parish. Among the workers were Oscar Gresham, Johnnie Haddock, and a man by the name of Anderson. Following World War I, part of the gin was moved to Threet's Cross Roads by Harper Austin and his brother. William Q. McKelvey was appointed postmaster here 1880. A native of South Carolina, McKelvey was born in 1826. John A. Anderson was serving as postmaster in 1897 when the post office was discontinued. Early landowners near Burcham Mills prior to 1825 were: James McKnight, Matthew Benthall, George Murphy, Thomas Perry, John and J. L. D. Smith, Richard Purdom, George Roach, Alfred and Robert Watkins, David and Jacob Reeder, William Birdsong, Valentine Calahan, and John Copeland.[6]

Another early settlement in this area was Young's Crossroads. It was located where the Natchez Trace crossed Savannah Highway. John and Samuel Young settled here in 1818.

Samuel Young was appointed postmaster on January 29, 1830. Five years later, Thomas K. Young was appointed to this office. Thomas held it until it was discontinued in 1845.[7] Other early settlers around this crossroads were: Ezekiel Lindsey, George Roach, Thomas McBride, John Brown, and James and William Waldrip.[8]

Lovelace Crossroads and McGee Town

Lovelace Crossroads is a small community at the intersection of the original Savannah Highway (old Alabama Highway 20) and Mud Road (Lauderdale Road 16). Prior to the Civil War, several members of the Lovelace family arrived here from Newberry County, South Carolina: William and his wife Elizabeth Whitmire; Hazel and his wife Alma; and Francis who was a widower at the time of the 1850 census. George Hughes, who lived nearby, was also from South Carolina. He was married to Mary Ann Lovelace, daughter of William Lovelace and his wife Elizabeth. Included in the household of Francis Lovelace were three sons: John, Hazel, and George W. In the same census were listed three ladies of the Lovelace family living together: Mary, age 60, Margaret, age 55, and Rebecca, age 45. Near this neighborhood were the homes of Moses and George Duncan from South Carolina; John and Elijah Rhodes from North Carolina and Maryland; Nathaniel Hughes from South Carolina; Mathius Munn from New Jersey; Thomas Skipworth from Tennessee; Bennett Pope and William Powers from South Carolina; and Jesse Cook from Kentucky.[9] Several small grocery stores and gasoline stations were located here in more recent years whose proprietors were: Floyd Lovelace, George McCorkle, William Ervin McDonald, and Charles Wesley Porter. Prior to 1825 a landowner from Courtland, Malcolm Gilchrist, owned property here, as did James Jackson, James Irvine, James Lockridge, Harmon Beasley, John Williams, J. L. D. Smith, Thomas Bibb, and John Donelson.[10]

McGee Town, one of this area's more recent communities, is located on the old Savannah Highway a mile or two south of Lovelace. The Anderson Rosenwald School for African-American children was located in this area. Julius Rosenwald, born in Springfield, Illinois, in 1862, was a merchant who exercised a creative influence on philanthropy throughout the world. In 1917, he established a fund to better the condition of Negroes through education. Lucian Anderson donated the land for this school that bore his name.

McGee Town grew up around Edgar McGee's General Store and small subdivision during the early part of the Twentieth Century. Following Edgar's death, his son, Lloyd, operated this business.[11] Lewis Edgar McGee was a son of John Luther McGee and his wife Cynthia Carolina Adams McGee. They are buried in Wesley Chapel United Methodist Church Cemetery. John was born in Wayne County, Tennessee, in 1855. He was a son of Samuel Washington McGee who was born in 1823, near the Natchez Trace Parkway in Wayne County. Samuel's father, Micajah McGee, was born about 1800, in South Carolina. The McGees were of Scots-Irish origin.[12]

Kendell, Threet's Crossroads, Murphy's Crossroads, and Stewartville

Kendell is northwest of Cloverdale and near the Tennessee state line. It is believed that its name came from the family of Louis C. Kendell. His wife, Elizabeth Adalet Walker, was born near this place in 1859. She was a daughter of William Carroll Walker who was born in 1823 on Forty-Eight Creek in Wayne County, Tennessee. One source indicates that Louis and Elizabeth Kendell moved to Norman, Oklahoma, where Elizabeth died in 1881. They had two children, Anna and Clyde. Clyde Kendell was a veteran of the Spanish-American War.[13] A post office was established at Kendell in 1890 with John W. Wallace as postmaster. It was discontinued ten years later when James E. Phillips was in charge of that office.

Joseph Terrell entered land near here in 1824. A native of Lancaster County, South Carolina, he was born in 1792. Terrell was a veteran of the War of 1812. He was married to Tabitha Hilton, also of Lancaster County, South Carolina. Joseph's father was William Terrell, veteran of General Francis Marion's Militia during the Revolutionary War. Other early landowners in this area were: James Lockridge, William Halbert, James Hill, Joshua Hodges, Joseph Young, David Mabray, Richard Darby, and Robert McKnight.[14] Threet's Crossroads was originally known as Russell's Crossroads. It is located a few miles south of Kendell and a few miles north of Cloverdale. John Perry Threete, born near Kennedy, Alabama, in 1826, was an early settler here.[15] He was a son of Joshua Threete. John was married to Margaret Terrell. The Threets are believed to be descended from, or related to, John Thweatt of Virginia who became an early settler of Newberry County, South Carolina. It was written of John Thweatt that he was "beyond doubt one of the most witty men who ever lived in this land."[16] A post office was established at Threet in 1893, with James C. Bevis as postmaster. It was discontinued thirteen years later.[17] At sometime around World War I, before or after, the cotton gin at Burcham Creek was moved in part to Threet's Crossroad, perhaps on Lindsey Creek.

Robert Austin purchased land here from the Federal Government on March 1, 1854. He shod horses at his blacksmith shop during the Civil War. Family sources claim that Robert, born about 1819, was the first white child born in Florence. John Austin, who was born about 1789, was living near Threets Crossroads in 1850. He was a native of Virginia. His wife, Martha, was born in South Carolina. Austin Cemetery is located on the Robert Austin homestead where members of this family are buried. A number of Threets are also buried here. Other early burials include: Dr. S. O. Paulk, born in 1842, and died in 1916; Reverend J. H. McCorkle, born in 1826, and died in 1919; Nellie Adeline Bevis, born in 1823, and died in 1892; and John T. Darby, born in 1831, and died in 1902.

Liberty Baptist Church, one of the country's historic congregations, is located in this community. Originally organized in 1852 as Liberty Baptist Church of Christ on a knoll near the Natchez Trace, it was moved to its present location in 1893.[18]

Murphy's Crossroads is located in the Chapel Beat at the intersection of Savannah Highway and County Road 8. East of this junction is Murphy's Chapel Freewill Baptist Church which was originally a Methodist Church. The Methodists began meeting in a brush arbor a mile or two east of this place and later erected their building at the present Murphy's Chapel site. The earliest church burying ground was located behind the old brush arbor. This cemetery was abandoned when the present Murphy's Chapel Cemetery was established. However, there are a number of graves in the arbor cemetery, including those of Charles and Matilda Anglin Sharp, natives of Virginia, who were among the earliest settlers in this area.[19] Charles died in 1865 at the age of 88 years.

Murphy's Crossroads was named for Dave Murphy who owned and operated a general merchandise store here. In 1912 he moved his business to Sullivan's Crossroads near the present community of Central Heights. There were several Murphy families living around Murphy's Crossroads and nearby Dart during the 1840's. John and Alice "Alley" Murphy were from South Carolina. He was born in 1801, and died in 1863. Alley was born in 1806, and died in 1887. Of Irish descent, the Murphy family settled in South Carolina prior to the Revolutionary War. John Murphy, Junior, a son of John and Alley, was captured at Fort Donelson in 1862. He did manage to escape, however, and suffered wounds a couple of months later in the Battle of Shiloh. One of his sons, Jesse Marion Murphy, born in 1864, was married to Josephine Wallace, daughter of John Welsey Wallace of the Chapel Beat. Wallaces were from South Carolina where their ancestors had arrived from Scotland during the Colonial period. The Murphys and Wallaces left many descendants in Lauderdale County.[20]

The oldest marked grave in the Murphy's Chapel Cemetery is that of E. F. Terry, who died in 1857 at the early age of eighteen. The earliest birth recorded in this cemetery is that of John McKelvey who was born in 1795 and died in 1880.

Stewartsville is on the Savannah Highway a few miles south of Murphy's Crossroads. William H. and Siani Stewart settled here around 1850. Their son donated the land for the Stewartsville Church of Christ.[21] Lindsey Creek, which flows just east of Murphy's Crossroads and Stewartsville, is named for Ezekiel Lindsey, one of the earliest settlers in this part of Lauderdale County. Other landowners who were here prior to 1825 were: John Brown, George Roach, Thomas McBride, James Lockrigde, James and William Waldrop, and Sam and John Young.[22]

Dart, Johnson Crossroads, Salem, and Cloverdale

The community of Dart is located on Savannah Highway near the Tennessee state line. Its name was provided by the U. S. Postal Service when the post office was established in 1899. Before this office was discontinued four years later, three men had served in the role of postmaster: John L. Dearen, John B. Young, and S. Lovelace. It was not unusual for newly appointed postmasters to designate their newly established post offices with their own last name. This leads to speculation that perhaps the name "Dearen" could have been misspelled by the postal service and it came out as "Dart." Another theory is that this community was named for Henry Hart who settled near here prior to 1850, and the spelling somehow came out as "Dart." Henry Hart, born in 1810, was a farmer from North Carolina. He was married to Ann Turner from Virginia who was born in 1828. There were no landowners or settlers in the area prior to 1825.

Johnson Crossroads is located less than four miles northeast of Cloverdale on County Road 139. This community is named for Stephen Johnson, his wife Martha, and their children: Martha, Carolina, Thomas, Rachel, Levi, and Mary. Stephen

Johnson, born in 1821 in Kentucky, was the oldest son of Thomas and Elizabeth Johnson who settled near here about 1826. Elizabeth was a daughter of Brigadier General Levi Casey, a militia leader during the American Revolution from Newberry County, South Carolina. The other children of Thomas and Elizabeth were: Samuel, Rachel, Allen, Caroline, and Thomas H. Caroline, known as "Callie," was married in 1834 to Joshua Darby. Thomas H. Johnson died in 1872, and is buried in the Littleton Cemetery near the Bethel Grove community. Some other members of this family are buried in this cemetery, although their graves are not now marked. Thomas H. Johnson, Callie Darby, and her husband Joshua, are buried in the nearby Littleton Cemetery.

The Johnson Crossroads Baptist Church is located in the community of Johnson Crossroads. The original acre of land where this church is located was deeded by the following heirs of Stephen Johnson (who is identified as Dr. Johnson): Betty Olive, Callie Johnson, Mary Johnson, Rachel Johnson, Levi Johnson, D. F. Johnson, and Martha Johnson. The first worship service for this congregation was held under a brush arbor in the summer of 1904. Button Johnson, Polk and Wesley Raines, Madgie and Mattie Cox, Lady Spires, Mollie McDaniel, and Bell Rhodes were probably among its charter members. Mamie Johnson was a clerk in this church. Other early leaders were: John Price, Ethel Cagle, and Elmer and Etta Borden.[23]

The Paulk Cemetery is located in an isolated wooded area near Johnson Crossroads. Jonathan Paulk and his wife, Elizabeth, are buried here. He was born in 1801 and died in 1870. She was born in 1805 and died in 1880. They came from Virginia during the 1850's. The oldest grave in this cemetery is that of Richard Darby from South Carolina, who was born in 1777 and died in 1834.[24] Records show that Dennis Houselap purchased land here prior to 1825.[25] The community of Salem can be traced back to 1818 when families from Tennessee, South Carolina, and Kentucky built their cabins here and began to clear the land. They named the new community for the place of which Melchizedek was king as found in the Book of Genesis. An early Methodist Church was organized in a one-room log building believed to have been burned during the final years of the Civil War. It was replaced in 1868. On September 20, 1873, Elizabeth McKnight and Andrew and Amanda Kelley deeded the two acres around the church to the Methodist Episcopal Church, South. A new and larger building called New Salem Methodist Church was erected here in 1882. The present church was completed in 1956.[26] Robert McKnight of Kentucky, Richard Darby of South Carolina, Joseph Young of Tennessee, and Alfred Miller of North Carolina were among the first to settle in or near Salem. Stories handed down through the Darby family tell how members of these first families had to blaze their way through the forest to find their land claims. This same source also relates how the Darby family traveled to Bethel Grove Methodist Church near the Tennessee line for worship before the Salem Church was established.[27]

Cloverdale is an old settlement, located about fifteen miles north west of Florence. It is said that in the early days this was a wild game paradise. Also, it became a place where hunters and trappers brought their raw hides to trade for other items[28] It soon developed into one of the largest tannery centers in North Alabama with patrons reaching into middle Tennessee. Thus, almost from its beginning, the community became known far and wide as Rawhide. Jonathan Paulk established a tannery here in the 1850's. This industry was so important to the Confederacy that its destruction was one of the major objectives assigned to Colonel Florence M. Cornyn during his raid into North Alabama in May 1863.[29] A number of other mills were also located in the area of Cloverdale.

There is evidence to indicate that long before the white man arrived, the local Indians were tanning hides here.[30] Archaeological findings in recent years indicate the presence of a number of early Native American villages and camp sites in and around Cloverdale.

Liberty Camp Ground, one of the largest religious meeting sites in Northwest Alabama, was located on Little Cypress Creek south of Cloverdale. In some records it was referred to as the Christian Camp Ground. As early as 1834 roads were opened to provide access to this popular camp from both the Waterloo Road and a road that intersected with the Cloverdale Road. An attempt was made to change the name of Rawhide to Waveland in 1872, when Stephen E. Rice was appointed as its first postmaster. This was apparently not a popular move; within two years the official name was designated by the U. S. Postal Service as Rawhide, Alabama.[31]

In the Simmons Family Cemetery south of Cloverdale is the grave of Vachel Ijams, soldier of the American Revolution. He died February 20, 1833, at the age of 74 years. His first service was as a private in a militia battalion raised during 1781 in Queen Anne County, Maryland. He later became a sergeant in the Maryland State Troops. Nearby is the grave of Ijams' son-in-law, George Herndon, from Orange County, Virginia. Herndon purchased land here in 1818. Also, south of Cloverdale is the small Casey Family Cemetery. Elizabeth Duckett Casey and other family members are buried here. Elizabeth, who died in 1839 at the age of 80 years, was the widow of General Levi Casey, a South Carolina militia leader.

Some of the earliest landowners around Cloverdale were: John Coffee, Patrick Hulton, Aaron Cunningham, James Brooks, Barden Darby, Levi Howell, Andrew McMackin, Sam Hazard, John Walker, William White, William Berry, William Duberry, Stephen and Jesse Jennings, David Reeder, John West, Ephraim Welbourne, Zebulon Jenkins, Azon and Valentine Vanhouse, Jackson Standfield, and James Faires.[32]

Cloverdale became the home of a settlement of Finnish people in the later part of the nineteenth century and the early years of the twentieth century. These immigrants from Finland were seeking freedom from oppression and looking for a place that would provide a better way of life. Most of these pilgrims who ended up at Cloverdale came from the north central part of Finland and lived for a brief time in Wisconsin and Michigan. For a period of twenty-seven years from 1885 until 1912 – some eight to ten families, totaling about sixty people, arrived to settle on farms located generally along what is now Renegar Road. William and Louisa Keranen were among the first of these families. Among the others were the families of Joseph Ilves, Matt Haataja, Olli Seppanen, William Isaac Abramson, and Stefanus and Jacob Hakola.[33]

On May 29, 1889, the old community of Rawhide became officially Cloverdale, Alabama, as designated by the United States Postal Service. William B. Young, who had been postmaster of Rawhide, continued to serve in this office until he was replaced in October of that year by Charles S. W. Paulk. One popular story about this name change involves a young girl believed to have been either Lavenia or Mary South, daughters of Wash and Mattie South. This young lady, according to the legend, was so inspired by the beautiful clover blossoming along the roadsides in Rawhide that she wrote a song entitled "Cloverdale." Thus, a petition was circulated among the community and the people agreed to change the name from Rawhide to Cloverdale.[34]

The Bend of the River and Colbert's Reserve

There are many bends in the serpentine course of the Tennessee River. Almost all of the northern tip of Alabama was referred to in early territorial papers as "the Great Bend," or sometimes as "the Bent." This defines the "U" shape of the river as it turns at Guntersville to flow northwestward across the state until it reaches Mississippi where it swings northward and heads toward its confluence with the Ohio River.

Locally, within the confines of West Lauderdale County, there is a bend within the Great Bend known as "the Bend of the River." Captain Robert Andrews, who once owned a large plantation here, spoke eloquently of the Bend of the River during its dry and hot summer months as "that lazy bend which affords all the blessings that a hard working cotton farmer could ever hope to need."[35] Geographically, this bend perhaps should be defined as that area along the north bank of the river between the mouth of Cypress Creek on the east and the community of Wright on the west. Locally, however, the term "Bend of the River," or sometimes

"River Bend," is more restrictive, especially for the folk who live here, or have lived here. As they define it, the "Bend of the River" seems to include only that fertile land along the north bank of the Tennessee which is several miles in depth. It begins a mile or so west of Cypress Creek and stretches westward to within sight of the Natchez Trace Bridge. This vague description includes Woodland and Smithsonia and the farms, streams, caves, ponds, springs, and islands in and between.[36] It is rich in Indian history and lore. The Tennessee Valley Authority's salvage archaeology excavations, carried out just prior to the completion of Pickwick Dam, confirm the presence of peoples here over a period of thousands of years. Mounds, villages, and campsites were found throughout this area. Among the prehistoric artifacts uncovered were those from what is known as the Southern form of the Copena Culture identified with the Hopewell Civilization in the Ohio River Valley. Artifacts found in more recent years near the entrance to Key Cave indicate the presence of man during the Late Paleo Period or earlier.[37] Excavations made at Dust Cave in the summer of 1996 reveal that prehistoric peoples were fishing in the Bend of the River at least 10,000 years ago. A few of the small ponds, including Walker Pond, have been dated to the time of the Ice Age.[38] Included in and near the general description of the Bend of the River is an area known locally as "The Reserve." It was originally made up of about 30,000 acres measuring some three to four miles in depth in a distance of about twelve miles up and down the north bank of the Tennessee River opposite Colbert's Ferry. It takes its name from a private reservation that was set aside for Chief George Colbert and his brother Levi in 1816. This was one of the provisions of the treaty with the Chickasaw Nation when they were persuaded to convey all of their claims north of the Tennessee River to the United States. According to legend, George Colbert lived here for a time following his dealings with Generals Andrew Jackson and John Coffee in the Treaty of 1816. It seems there were some of his own people who believed he had betrayed them. During the presidential campaign of 1828, Jackson's political enemies made use of this private deal with the Colberts to support charges of corruption against him. This reservation remained in possession of the Colberts until 1818, when it was sold by way of James Jackson, one of the founders of Florence, to the Federal Government for $ 20,000.[39]

General Andrew Jackson recommended as early as November 12, 1816, that a military depot be located in this area of West Lauderdale County. More specifically, the east boundary of this proposed ordnance site was to be about one-half mile west of the mouth of Cypress Creek.[40] Efforts to promote the selection of this site along Cypress Creek as a military arsenal were continued by General John Coffee well into the decade of the 1820's.

The 1850 Census described the Reserve, with its poplar, oak, ash, walnut, hickory, and mulberry timber, as a good land. This farmland, perhaps the richest in the Tennessee Valley, was bought up by a few wealthy men after it was acquired from the Colberts. The Reserve and the Bend of the River, thereafter, became known for large cotton plantations. Among the early planters along or near Cheatham's Ferry (Gunwaleford) Road were: Henry D. Smith, Dr. Neal Rowell, Dr. William Koger, William H. Key, John Peters, Wyatt Collier, Nathan Boddie, Dr. Jonathan Beckwith, William O'Neal Perkins, Colonel Samuel Savage, Dr. James Stewart, Edmond Noel, John Simpson, Abram Kernachan, Sarah Hanna, Andrew Jackson Donelson, and Captain Alexander Donelson Coffee. Teachers here in 1850 were Amous L. Daron, Rish Griffit, and Lucious Lorance. Nathan Richards was a blacksmith and James Harwick was a miller.[41]

Canaan United Methodist Church is a Bend of the River landmark. Built prior to 1840, it is one of the few remaining plantation churches in Alabama. It suffered damage during a Civil War skirmish. In early 1865, it was one of the few churches in the area of Gravelly Springs not dismantled and used for the housing of cavalry troops and horses. This area was the training camp for Union General James Harrison Wilson's Corps prior to their invasion of South Alabama and Georgia. During this encampment, the Canaan Church was used as a hospital by the Federal Army.

Reserve, Havannah, Savage's Spring, and Woodland

There was a community known as Reserve located immediately east of the Colbert Reserve. This settlement was approximately nine miles west of Florence, about eight miles east of Colbert's Ferry, and some twenty miles east of Waterloo. A post office was established here in 1890, with Aaron S. Lanier as postmaster. There was a rapid succession of appointments to this office over the next ten years: Robert T. Call in 1892; George W. Maury in February, 1894; William L. Hurst in November, 1894; Robert T. Call in 1900; William Adair in February, 1901; and in May, 1901, Hezekiah N. Call became the last postmaster. Afterwards, the mail for Reserve was routed to Ponder Station believed to have been located on the south bank of the river.[42]

Havannah was the original name for the community later called Reserve. It was one of the earliest towns laid out in Northwest Alabama, and was only about four months shy of being as old as Florence. A newspaper article in 1818 announced that lots in Havannah were to be sold at public auction on October 26 and 27 of that same year. This article played up its potential status as a shipping port for cotton at the head of navigation below the Muscle Shoals. Also mentioned was its ideal location at the lower end of Long Island (Seven Mile Island) which they claimed was a good site for a ferry across the river.[43] This river crossing became known at different times as Foster's Ferry, Pride's Ferry, and Savage Ferry. High expectations for the development of Havannah never materialized. Its trustees were: E. J. Bailey, George Coalter, Hugh Campbell, Samuel Ragsdale, and Joseph Farmer.[44]

Following the failure of Havannah as a town on the Tennessee River, this community became known as Savage's Spring. Colonel Samuel Savage, native of South Carolina, was one of Lauderdale County's earliest landowners. Arriving in 1818, he and his wife, Ann, built their home on a high elevation overlooking the spring now known as Woodland Spring. They called their plantation "Savage Spring." General Andrew Jackson stopped overnight here on February 4, 1821, while making his way back to

Tennessee. Samuel and Ann Savage had a son, Charles Savage, who became a promising Florence attorney, but died at an early age. Two daughters, Sallie and Hetty, were married into the prominent Dillahunty family of Lawrence County, Alabama. A third daughter was married in 1819 to James Hammond. In 1833, the county court appointed Samuel Savage, James Nail, James Perry, Joseph Garrett, Benjamin Darby, Samuel Garner, and Nig Robertson as reviewers of a road being laid out from Pride's ferry to Brown's Ferry Road near Wesley Chapel Methodist Church. This route was to pass the Zion Church and Benjamin Darby's shop.[45] It continues to be known as Pride's Ferry Road. Savage's Spring was associated with early Native American history. According to legend, this is where Chief George Colbert lived while in hiding following the Treaty of 1816.[46]

Woodland was the third designation for the original town of Havannah. Some say this was in recognition of an early Woods family who lived here. Others claim that it took its name from the antebellum plantation of George Washington Foster. Foster's home, a sizable one-and-half story frame house overlooking Woodland Spring, burned during the 1960's. Prior to the Civil War, one of Foster's mills was located about half way between Woodland and Smithsonia. In 1855, Foster built "Courtview" at the head of Court Street in Florence. The Woodland Cemetery, once on the grounds of the Woodland Methodist Church, holds the graves of some members of the following families: Wisdom, English, Hays, Darby, Hollis, McDougal, Burrow, Cody, Cook, Burt, and Adair.[47]

Near Woodland is the mouth of Sinking Creek, another interesting feature of this part of the river bend. This creek has two heads located about two miles apart south of Mud Road near the Central Heights community. These two branches form one main stream about three miles south of their heads. In its southward course this creek disappears underground for a distance and then reappears before it reaches the river near Woodland. An antebellum plantation, "The Sinks," owned by William O'Neal Perkins and his wife, Pocahontas Bolling Perkins, was named for this creek that flowed through it. Two daughters from this family married two of the sons of James Jackson James Jackson, Junior, and George Moore Jackson. Afterwards, The Sinks became the home of Colonel James Jackson, Junior, and his family.[48]

The plantations of John Simpson, Nathan Boddie, and Abram Kernachan were near Woodland. Prior to 1860, a canal known as Lassiter's Ditch, was constructed by slave labor near Woodland at a cost of $12,000. A man by the name of Lassiter was the contractor. The purpose of this drainage ditch was to handle the overflow of Sinking Creek during flood seasons. Remains of this canal show erosion through many years. In some places its depth is some thirty feet with widths of about fifty feet.[49]

William H. Key's nearby 2,800-acre plantation was worked by 130 slaves. During the Civil War, one of his laborers reported to the Yankees that Key had used the large Key Cave along the banks of the Tennessee River to hide his corn. While removing this grain, the soldiers discovered that the Key family had also secluded their dining room silver here along with the corn. However, when the colonel learned that his men were in possession of these household items, he had all of it collected and returned to the owner's family. He also conveyed a suggestion that in the future they keep such valuables in their house and not in a cave.[50]

The old community, known at various times as Havannah, Savage's Spring, Reserve, and Woodland, has all but faded into the category of an abandoned ghost town. Its original site has now been inundated by Pickwick Lake. Among its original landowners were: Samuel Savage, David Hubbard, Thomas Kirkman, Abram Kernachan, Sam Hazard, John H. Smith, John Donelson, and James Jackson. Jackson's holdings included most of Seven Mile Island, as well as a number of smaller ones now under the backwaters of Pickwick Dam. Other nearby islands were owned by John McKinley, J. L. D. Smith, Dabney Morris, Christopher Strong, Peter Armistead, and Samuel Savage.[51]

Cave Spring, Cheatham's Ferry, and Smithsonia

Cave Spring was a community that grew up around a large outflow of water from the mouth of a huge limestone cave. It was also known as Cheatham's Ferry because of the well-known river crossing here that connected with Newport on the south bank of the Tennessee. Christopher Cheatham, born in Hartford County, North Carolina, was an early resident of Huntsville where he owned and operated Twickenham Hotel. He was also part owner of Bell Tavern. In 1824, Cheatham bought 1,000 acres at Cave Spring. Here he built a simple log house and established the ferry which he operated until 1837.[52] His daughter, Martha Ann, was married in 1832 to Dr. Neal Rowell, a physician. Cheatham died in December 1839, and the Rowells came into possession of his plantation, "Alba Wood," along with the prosperous ferry operations. They built a substantial brick home on a knoll overlooking the Gunwaleford Road. It remained for more than a century until it was pushed over by a bulldozer, resulting in the loss of one of the area's most treasured landmarks.

Although now submerged under Pickwick Lake, Cave Spring was originally located at the base of a cliff about a quarter of a mile from the riverbank. In the summer of 1926, a teacher from Waterloo, John Lincoln Hall, Senior, along with several companions, explored the cave in a row boat. Hall estimated that they went back at least several miles in what he described as an underground river. The cave was made up of a number of chambers, a few of them named for their different features as well as for local legends associated with the cave. A big flat ledge not far inside the mouth of the cave was used by the local young people as a popular place for parties and dances.[53]

Cheatham's Ferry was a few miles upstream from the earlier Colbert Ferry operated by Chickasaw Chief George Colbert at the crossing of the Natchez Trace over the Tennessee River. In January 1833, Henry Smith advertised that he had established a new ferry at this site and would charge nothing for the first three months. Three years later he was given permission by the local court to move his ferry to about a half mile above the established ferry. In his will, Smith referred to his ferry site as "Point Smith," although it is not clear as to whether he meant the north or south bank of the river. His home and plantation were on the north bank just east of the Natchez Trace. He acquired this land, known originally as the John Johnson Place, in 1822. Smith became one of the county's largest landowners. Following his death in 1846, his industrial land holdings near the mouth of Sweetwater Creek in East Florence were advertised as the "Sweetwater Lands." Smith often referred to himself as "Henry Smith of Sweetwater"; his signature appeared this way on his last will and testament. He was first married in 1814 to Mary A. Smith in Southhampton, Virginia. His second marriage was to Rebecca Beckwith, a sister to Dr. Jonathan Beckwith of West Lauderdale County; this occurred in 1842, just four years prior to Smith's death. Henry Smith's daughter, Mary Amanda, was married in 1838 to Joseph H. Darnell. Henry had a brother, Joseph Lawrence Dawson Smith, who was married to a sister to James Jackson of the Forks of Cypress Plantation. These two wealthy Smith brothers had a nephew, Henry D. Smith, whose plantation was on the Gunwaleford Road a few miles west of Florence. The Smith Bottom Cave and the large Smith Pond were once a part of his land holdings.[54]

Henry D. Smith, born in 1803 in North Carolina, arrived in Lauderdale County about 1828. He served in the Alabama House of Representatives for twelve years. He died in 1869, and was buried alongside his wife, Martha, and other family members in an isolated family cemetery located on the site of his early plantation. A military map in the National Archives, drawn during the encampment of General James H. Wilson at Gravelly Springs in 1865, shows a "Connor's Landing" at or near the site of Smith's Landing. Neither the 1860 nor the 1870 census records show a Conner living in this area. However, the families of two former slaves, Jack Conner and a neighbor Lucy Conner, were located near this landing in 1870.

Garner's Ferry was located between Smithsonia and Woodland at the site of one of Foster's mills.[55] R. M. Garner owned land here around 1900.

Smithsonia, the modern name for Cave Spring and Cheatham's Ferry, was named for one of the most successful Lauderdale County entrepreneurs during the second half of the 19th Century. Columbus Smith, who as far as is known was not related to the earlier Henry, Henry D., and J. L. D. Smiths, began with practically nothing to build what could almost be compared with a small feudal kingdom in the Old World. He did this during the Reconstruction Period when a vast majority of the people in the South were struggling to survive. Not much is known about the origin of Columbus Smith. Some say he was born in Tennessee while others think he was born in Alabama.[56] In 1903, a reporter wrote that Smith, as a young boy, operated a ferry across the Tennessee River during the Civil War.[57] Another source indicates that he may have roamed the country as a young man, and that this was how he received his nickname "Pad."[58] Smith and his stepfather, John Richards, purchased Cheatham's Ferry in July, 1863, from D. C. Oats who had acquired it from the Rowells. This was during the turbulent Civil War period. It wasn't long until Smith became sole owner of both the ferry rights and the adjoining seventy-five acres of land. This was the beginning of his economic domain as well as a new name "Smithsonia" for the earlier Cave Spring and Cheatham's Ferry community. Smith's next venture was a small country store. By 1868, it was necessary for him to erect a larger building for his expanding business.[59] His commercial complex soon included a grist mill, cotton gin, and related shops. Smith's wharf extended across to nearby Koger's Island where he shipped his cotton and other goods. Before the completion of Pickwick Dam, Koger's Island was separated from the north bank of the Tennessee by only a small-segmented stream of the river's flow.[60]

Smith's first residence was a modest two-room structure. In 1871, his family was moved into a newly built six-room frame house. His third home, completed in 1889, was a mansion made of solid stone, three floors in height, overlooking the river as well as his business empire below the bluff. A post office was established in 1886, with Smith as postmaster. It was discontinued in 1926 when John S. Sloan held this office. At the apex of Smith's "Smithsonia," he owned some 10,000 acres, including 6,500 acres under cultivation. Columbus Smith's gravestone in the cemetery behind the Canaan United Methodist Church reveals May 14, 1832, as the date of his birth. He died July 9, 1900. John Thomas Reeder who was married to Smith's daughter, Bessie, managed the estate following his father-in-law's death. Reeder was a riverboat captain who invested in several steamboats, including the "J. T. Reeder," which made regular runs between Smithsonia and Florence.[61]

Smithsonia is now a lonely and beautiful place overlooking the vast Pickwick Lake which covers what had once been one of most enterprising agricultural communities in the Tennessee Valley. As with the other sections of the Bend of the River, it is one of the earliest inhabited areas of the Tennessee Valley. Nearby Koger's Island, known earlier as Colbert's Island, was once the center of an ancient civilization known as the Koger Island People. They were of the Mississippian Culture who arrived around 800 B.C. and remained until about 1,550 A.D.[62] An earlier people called "Gatherers" of the Archaic Period were on this island and on these shores perhaps some 10,000 years ago, as evidenced by a number of small shell mounds they left behind.[63]

After the conveyance of Colbert's Reserve to the U. S. Government in 1818, the following men became the early landowners around Smithsonia and the nearby islands: James Jackson, Peter Armistead, Obediah Jones, Christopher Cheatham, Abram Kernachan, Newton Neal, John Wiseman, George and James Erwin, Thomas Mayfield, Jonathan Beckwith, William Koger, Edmund Noel, Peter Booker, John Martin, Major and Thomas Harroldson, Samuel Bennett, David Hubbard, Henry Smith, Joseph Riley, Hardy Clements, Reas Bowen, Josiah Parker, Thomas Walles, Gabriel Bumpass, John Coffee, David Brown, Thomas Walles, and Thomas Hawkins.[64]

Oakland, Kimbrough Crossroads, and Rhodesville

Oakland sits astride the Waterloo Road between Florence and Waterloo. This road was originally laid out as the Government Road. The original road from Florence to Waterloo was located south of Oakland; later it was referred to as the Lower Waterloo Road. Prior to the removal of the Indians there was a government commissary at Oakland.[65] This community was named for its unusually large oak trees.

Turner Walston, an early planter, first acquired his land from Chief George Colbert.[66] His deed, with Colbert's signature, became a family heirloom. Walston, born in 1783, was a native of North Carolina. His wife, Elizabeth, was a Virginian. There were two well-known Methodist preachers in this family – John and James Walston. Both were Oakland planters. Reverend John Walston's daughter, Eliza Jane, was married to Henry Barbee Lindsey, a son of William Madison Lindsey and Mary Belew Lindsey. William Madison Lindsey was a grandson of John L. Lindsey and Rebecca Anderson Lindsey early settlers of Cypress Inn, Tennessee. John L. Lindsey, along with his father, Captain Samuel Lindsey, and three uncles, served in the American Revolution from their home in Newberry County, South Carolina. The Walston Cemetery is one of the county's pioneer cemeteries. Across the road from this burying grounds was the early Vaughn Cemetery which no longer exists.

South of Oakland is Evans Spring, believed to have been named for Jesse Evans an early landowner. County records show that his estate was settled in 1825. Evans Spring flows from under a rock ledge at the base of a small knoll to form one of the most scenic ponds in the Muscle Shoals area. It was at one time owned by Andrew Jackson.

The business area of Oakland was established prior to the Civil War. This community became known as a center for cotton ginning. James and John Vaughn established the first of this industry here. At one time there were two gins adjacent to each other along with a blacksmith shop and a general store. R. C. "Bob" Smith, one of the gin owners, built a large Victorian-style house across from his business in 1909. Other business leaders were: Arthur Smith, Lawrence H. Rickard, Thomas Reeder, and Percy Wright. Among the other families were: Will Vaughn, J. H. Olive, Gwelford Winburn, F. M. Rhodes, Betty Hewitt, F. P. Hall, David Jones, and the Cantrells and Peersons.

The original schoolhouse and the Methodist Church at Oakland were made from hewn logs. The church was burned during the Civil War. Miss Tellie Lindsey, a daughter of Caleb Lindsey, was one of its teachers.[67] Following the Civil War, Eleven Grove and Galilee Churches were built by former slaves at Oakland. Prominent members of this early African-American community were: Henry Barnett, Lula Johnson, Ben Gilbert, Bama Bryant, Lizzie Clemmons, and Lizzie Martin.

Samuel Vaughn was appointed postmaster in 1850. In 1897, after almost fifty years in operation, this office was closed and the mail routed to Florence.[68] Among the original landowners were: J.L.D. and John H. Smith, James Jackson, Thomas Bibb, Thomas Perry, Edmund Bailey, Turner Walston, John Jackson, Andrew Jackson, Bowling Gordon, Matthew Watson, John Pope, John McKinley, Thomas Percy, Bowling Gordon, and George Murphy.[69]

Kimbrough Crossroads is a twentieth century designation of an old community located a few miles east of Oakland. Around 1930, Lee Bother Kimbrough built a store and a number of rental houses at this intersection of the Waterloo and Kimbrough Roads. Following his death in 1949, John and Josie Jones operated a general store on the south side of this same intersection. Lee Kimbrough's brother, Richard Arthur Kimbrough, owned a store a few miles south of here at the junction of Kimbrough and Gunwaleford Roads. Richard was a county commissioner when his untimely death occurred in 1934. Kimbrough Road was named for him. Their parents, Richard Thomas Kimbrough and Fannie Miranda Rikard Kimbrough, moved across the river from Mhoonton in November, 1905. Their farm was located between Waterloo and Gunwaleford Roads. This was a large family. Four daughters were married into prominent families in this section of the county: Rebecca Elizabeth Kimbrough was married to Ray Wright; Beulah Mae Kimbrough was married to Luther L. Whitten; Minnie Miranda Kimbrough was married to George Milton Jones; and Velma Ida Kimbrough was married to William McKinley Hill. The Kimbroughs were descended from John Kimbrough who, with his wife Mary Douglas Kimbrough, entered Port Tobacco, Maryland, in 1666. Also on board this ship from England were two sons and a daughter. One of these sons, Marmaduke Kimbrough, was the direct ancestor to the Kimbroughs at Kimbrough Crossroads. They arrived in Alabama by way of Virginia, North Carolina, and Tennessee.[70] Among the landowners near this community prior to 1825 were: Stanton Flint, William Griffin, John McKinley, Miles Watkins, Frances Crow, and William Donelson.[71]

Rhodesville is west of Oakland at the intersection of the Waterloo Road and County Road 5, near the confluence of Colbert and Fowler Creeks. It is named for the Rhodes family. Spencer Rhodes, born in 1818 in Newberry County, South Carolina, operated a store, blacksmith shop, and mill here. In 1889, a steam cotton gin was in operation. A post office was established in 1889. Mitchell Malone was postmaster. He was a son of the Reverend Mitchell Malone, an early planter and Methodist preacher. The senior Malone was from North Carolina, and his wife, Susan, was born in Virginia. Two years later, Columbus Spencer Rhodes was appointed postmaster. The office was discontinued in 1907.[72] Columbus Rhodes and his wife, Mary Copeland Rhodes, are buried in the Gravelly Springs Cemetery; Columbus was a son of John W. Rhodes. Elijah Rhodes, born in Maryland in 1791, migrated to Lauderdale County by way of Newberry County, South Carolina.[73] The early landowners at Rhodesville were: John Coffee, William Ragsdale, Hardy Hightower, Joseph Thompson, Peter Armistead, Thomas Whitson, William Strawn, Charles and Christopher Strong, Jesse Hendrick, Mark Cockrell, Craven Belsha, James Benford, Alfred Anderson, and Gabriel Bumpass.[74]

Gravelly Springs, Barton, Willet, and Bluff Creek

Gravelly Springs, Barton, Willet, and Bluff Creek are names that have been used for the same community at various times over a span of many years. This was a refreshing watering hole on the old Natchez Trace. It no doubt served the Indians in much the same fashion. They, too, followed this same route, although in its beginning it was no more than a buffalo trail that eventually evolved into an Indian path. Nearby Bluff Creek Cave may well have been a shelter for earlier peoples. Perhaps the spring and adjoining hollow may have been one of the hideouts for the infamous highwaymen who plundered the "Devil's Backbone," as the Trace has been called. One of its earlier paths can be seen at the top of the hill above the spring. The original Waterloo Road that descended the hill from the Trace to Gravelly Springs was nearer to the Gravelly Springs Baptist Church and Cemetery.

Relatively speaking, the spring is a small outpouring of water from the base of Bluff Creek Hill, producing some five gallons a minute.[75] However, its cold stream and tree-shaded surroundings continue to appeal to the passing wayfarer on the road from Florence to Waterloo. Boiling Spring, another local landmark, is located about two miles west of Gravelly Springs.

Bluff Creek, which passes through this community, is noted for the abundance of gravel in its bed and along its banks, especially where the spring branch enters the creek. This natural feature gave its name to the community in early times. Of interest, too, was the community of Gravelly Hill in South Carolina during the period of the American Revolution. Some of the early settlers of West Lauderdale County came from that area of South Carolina.

There are records of settlers being at Gravelly Springs as early as 1818. Some of these same families were identified with this community for more than a hundred years. Of interest, too, is that a number of them were related either by blood or by marriage.

Two of the earliest settlers were William Barton and Francis Willet. Both entered land in 1818. The first post office at what is now Gravelly Springs was established as Barton, Alabama, in 1830 with James E. Matthews as postmaster.[76] Willet was designated by the court as the voting place for this area of the county from 1831 through 1844. However, in 1843 – and again five years later this beat was called Bluff Creek.[77] Election officers at Willet in 1832 were David Houston, Ephraim D. Read, and Clark Thomas. In 1835 they were David Houston, Samuel Brumley, and Simon Kirk. The following year Richard H. Willet replaced Simon Kirk. In 1837, Moses White and Ross Houston were named to assist Samuel Brumley in these duties.

Francis Willet died in 1825 leaving a number of minor heirs. His widow Polly and a neighbor, John Webb, were named administrators.[78] Simon Kirk, listed as an election officer in 1835 at Willet, was born in Virginia in 1803. Kirk was married in 1836 to Hulda Belsha in Lauderdale County. They later moved to West Point, Texas. Simon's father, Thomas Kirk, was a sergeant in the Continental Army during the American Revolution. Afterwards, he served five years as an Indian scout at Eaton Station. Thomas Kirk was married to Nancy, widow of Simeon Webb; they had at least seven children. Thomas Kirk, the old soldier and Indian scout, died in 1831. His unmarked grave is located alongside an earlier roadbed of the Natchez Trace about halfway between Gravelly Springs and the river.

One of the earliest plantations near Gravelly Springs was established by Rachel Thomas in 1822. Josiah Thomas, perhaps a son of Rachel, was listed in the 1850 census. A native of Kentucky, he was born in 1801. Jabez Cannon and his wife, Sarah Reeder Cannon, arrived here in 1820. They were natives of Newberry County, South Carolina. Two sons from this family, William J. and Jabez Pugh, served in the Confederate Army. William Cannon was a captain in the 9th Alabama Infantry Regiment. Following the war, he became a successful businessman in Sylacauga, Alabama. Jabez Pugh Cannon was a private in Company C, 27th Alabama Infantry Regiment. He kept a diary of his service in that unit which

314

was published after the war. He was married to Kate Carroll of Gravelly Springs. Following the war, Dr. Jabez Cannon practiced medicine in McKenzie, Tennessee.[79]

One of the Cannon daughters, Rachel, was married to Elijah Graves Chandler, a native of Virginia. Chandler, born in 1814, became a merchant at Gravelly Springs. Their daughter, Ella Mae, was married to Jesse Reeder Thomas.[80]

Another general store at Gravelly Springs was owned by the Carrolls for a number of generations. Jesse Carroll from Culpepper County, Virginia, purchased land here in 1821. William Carroll, perhaps a son or brother, was married in 1827 to Eliza Barton, daughter of Francis and Polly Barton. Their son, Wilson Carroll, was married to Mary Jane Baker who was a daughter of William Baker, native of Virginia. James Baker, who served as Secretary of State under President George Bush, is a descendant of this family.[81]

Wildwood Plantation at Gravelly Springs was the boyhood home of Alabama's 25th Governor, George Smith Houston. This vast acreage of fertile land was a mile or two east of Gravelly Springs. David Houston of County Tyrone, Ireland, settled here around 1825. The Houston family arrived in America in 1760, settling first in Newberry County, South Carolina. David was married to Hannah Pugh Reagon, who was of Welsh descent. They were the parents of thirteen children. The Houstons built a Georgian two-story brick mansion near the present crossing of the Natchez Trace Parkway and the Waterloo Road. A large reservoir on the roof supplied rainwater for the kitchen and bathroom. The author T. S. Stribling remembered that the Houston house was far back in a grove of trees. He wrote that a traveler could only catch glimpses of its splendor through the leaves as he passed along the Waterloo Road. The thing that impressed the opulence of this manor house upon the visitor, according to Stribling, was a little painting under a round glass lens, about eight or ten inches in diameter set on top of the newel post in the hallway.[82]

Jane, a daughter of David Houston, was married to Phillip Jacob Irion from Rockingham County, North Carolina. There were three Irion brothers in Gravelly Springs at an early date: Phillip, Frederick Augustus and Thomas C. The first two arrived in the late 1830's. Thomas stopped off in Tennessee before settling at Gravelly Springs in the early 1840's. The father of these brothers was Frederick Witt Irion, native of Culpepper County, Virginia, who was born in 1766. His father, Phillipp Jacob Irion, Junior, was born in 1733 in Lichtenau (Baden) Germany. His wife, Barbara Regina Heyler, was also a native of Germany. One or more branches of this family changed their name from Irion to Irons after settling in Alabama.[83]

The Youngs have been associated with this community for many generations. James and Cornelia Young – both born about 1800 in South Carolina – reared a large family who were later intermarried with other families in the area.

Temple Turnley, another Virginian by birth, was born in 1796. He was a son of John and Elizabeth Turnley. It is said that this family opened their home as a preaching place to the first Methodist preacher in Spottsylvania County, Virginia. Temple Turnley was first married to Mecca B. Harris of Summer County, Tennessee, a niece of the famed Methodist Bishop William McKendree. Following Mecca's death, Turnley was married to the widow, Elizabeth Britt. After her death, he was married to the widow, Elizabeth Hammond. Temple was a grandson of John Turnley who was at Valley Forge with Washington. He was also at the Siege of Mud Island, the Battles of Brandywine, German Town, Trenton, and was at Yorktown when Cornwallis surrendered. Temple Turnley's son, Wesley, was killed in the Battle of Frayser's Farm, in June 1862, as a member of Company D, 9th Alabama Infantry.

John Perryman, who purchased land at Gravelly Springs in 1818, arrived in Alabama from Kentucky. He was born in 1804, and was married to Martha "Patsy" Waters, native of Tennessee. John was a son of the Revolutionary War soldier John Perryman who was born in Charles County, Maryland. He later resided in North Carolina, Virginia, Kentucky, and Fayette County, Tennessee. This veteran was with General Horatio Gates in the

Battle of Camden. Later in the war, he was in the campaigns around Richmond and Williamsburg.[84]

Pettypool Hill is the dividing line on the Waterloo Road between Gravelly Springs and the backwaters of Pickwick Dam. This ridge is named for John Pettypool from Virginia and his wife, Susan, from Tennessee. Their son, David Jones Pettypool, served in J. B. Sleeth's Scouts, Fourth Alabama Cavalry. After the war ended, this old soldier entertained the community with his tales about being a horse soldier. One of his stories was about being wounded on the south bank of the river near Riverton in Colbert County.[85]

Pettypool Hill is remembered as the place where the Civil War outlaw, Tom Clark, was captured on September 4, 1872. Clark and two companions were overtaken here by Sheriff Blair and his deputies from Florence. It is believed that they were on their way to Waterloo where they had planned to escape by steamboat to the West.

The Gravelly Springs Post Office was established in 1842, with Ross Houston, Junior, as postmaster. It was discontinued in 1906 when Jessie T. Carroll was postmaster. James and Frank Carroll had previously served in this position.[86] The other landowners who were in or near Gravelly Springs prior to 1825 were: Christopher Robinson, Jesse Kindrick, David Brown, Jesse Hendricks, Ebenezer Lounge, Robert Byars, William Curtis, Christian Strong, Malcolm Gilchrist, Sam Warrick, Serkin Nolan, Hardy Hightower, Samuel Johnson, Samuel Wilks, Craven Belsha, and Gabriel Bumpass.[87]

The area around Gravelly Springs became a training camp for the largest cavalry force ever assembled in the western hemisphere during the winter of 1865. This corps was under the command of U. S. Major General James Harrison "Harry" Wilson who was only twenty-seven years of age. He made his headquarters in the Houston mansion at Wildwood Plantation. Wilson's troops attempted to live off the land, but soon discovered that this area had suffered so much hardship during the war that there was very little available in the way of food and supplies.[88]

Almost every barn, outbuilding, and church structure in the area were dismantled for use in the construction of billets and stables for his men and horses.

Pulitzer Prize winner Thomas Sigismund Stribling wrote that as a boy he wintered in Tennessee and summered in Alabama. He was referring to Clifton, Tennessee, and Gravelly Springs, Alabama. His grandfather, James Waits, native of South Carolina where he was born in 1801, settled near Gravelly Springs. His blacksmith shop was on the opposite side of the road from his house. Stribling said that his grandfather worked like a giant in his forge until he acquired another slave or two. He then quit work and never lifted another hammer or tongs again.

The Pulitzer Prize winner described the Waits place as an isolated farm with a rail fence around the double log house. This house, he said, did not face the road, because in South Carolina the old houses faced each other's backs "with gables lifted in disdain for the passer – by."[89] He wrote that his grandfather was a Yankee, although his two sons, Shelton and Leonidas, fought for the South.

Waterloo

It would be difficult to name a place in North Alabama that is richer in Native American history than the area around Waterloo. Archaeological surveys of the Pickwick basin, made in the late 1930's, indicate that this place must have been a metropolis for peoples during the Mississippian and the earlier Woodland Periods. Evidence of the presence of the Copena Culture was also found.

This prime river site was sought after by eager land speculators of the early 1800's. One of the first to become interested in Waterloo was Dr. Edward Gabriel Bumpass, physician, postmaster, author, and investor. It is said that he had his eye on this place as early as 1807.[90] It is fitting and proper for Gabriel Bumpass to be called the father of Waterloo. It was under his guidance that the Articles of Agreement to establish the town was signed at Pulaski, Tennessee, in March, 1819. He became one of Waterloo's first citizens. Beautiful Bumpass Creek bears his name.

Dr. Bumpass was born in Person County, North Carolina, about the year 1770. He and his brother, James, also a physician, headed a colony of fifty or more immigrants out of South Carolina. These people became the first settlers of Giles County, Tennessee, although they were delayed about a year in Nashville waiting for the Indians to cede their lands in that part of the state. Finally, around 1810, they began the task of cutting a road through the wilderness. This highway from Columbia to Pulaski became known as the Bumpass Trail.

When the Huntsville Land Office opened in 1818, Dr. Bumpass began investing in hundreds of acres of land in Lauderdale County. He was a large man weighing more than 300 pounds, but quite agile. He was also rather eccentric. Many stories have been told about his long life at Waterloo. One was about a man caught stealing corn from the Doctor's cribs. Upon learning that the poor man and his family were without food, Dr. Bumpass invited him to a hearty breakfast, filled his sack with grain, and told him to come back at any time to get more. During his advanced years he lived with his daughter, Camilla, and her husband, Captain John Till. It was said that every morning after breakfast, he could be seen sitting on the porch of the town's hotel reading one of his many books until time to walk back home for supper. Bumpass was one of the leaders in the early Republican Church near Florence – a forerunner of the historic Stony Point Church of Christ. He died sometime after 1870, and was buried in the Witherspoon Cemetery located near the confluence of Bumpass and Second Creeks. In 1937, the Tennessee Valley Authority relocated his grave to the Richardson Cemetery so as to make way for the backwaters behind Pickwick Dam. One of his daughters, Elvira, was married to William Witherspoon, a brother to Major James Witherspoon.

Another daughter, Martha, was married to Ross Houston, brother to George S. Houston, Alabama's 25th Governor. One son, Robert Weakley Bumpass, was a state senator in Tennessee.

The other founders of Waterloo were Tyree Rodes, Maximilian H. Buchanan, German Lester, and John McCracken, all of Giles County, Tennessee. There were fifty-one original shareholders, including Alexander McDonald, John Webb, Thomas B. Haynes, Micajah Ellis, and Charles Parker. There were 100 shares of two acres each; fifty of these were allotted to Dr. Bumpass. Each original share was to be divided, making a total of 400 shares. Bumpass employed Bib Cooperman as the town surveyor. The total land sales in 1819 amounted to $9,525.50.

The background for the naming of the town has been lost in the archives of time. Some have pointed out that it was established about four years following the famous Battle of Waterloo in Belgium and, probably, this was the source of its name. A romantic notion is that Waterloo's founding fathers may have been influenced by the mighty river at its door, as well as the nearby scenic creeks, streams, and springs, as a poetic meaning for the name of Waterloo. Actually, the town was first laid out in the lowland at the riverbank, a site which is now under the backwaters of Pickwick Dam. In the beginning Waterloo was referred to as "The Landing." It was incorporated in 1832, making it among the oldest towns in Alabama to establish its legal entity.

Because of its early location alongside the river, Waterloo was threatened by floods almost every spring season. A big one came in 1847. Thirty-five houses as well as warehouses and boats were either swept away or destroyed. Most of the families and businesses moved to where the present town is, although it was known then as the plateau. Yet, a few determined souls remained at the old site. For the next twenty years there were two sections of town – the old one near the river and the new town on the plateau above the river. The next big flood hit in 1867 at which time all that remained in the old town was washed away. The choice lots on the plateau were owned by Dr. Bumpass who was then nearing his eightieth birthday. These prime pieces of property on today's Main

Street were purchased by James Humphrey, Elijah Chandler, and Major Witherspoon. It was thirty years later – March, 1897 – when the worst of all previously recorded floods swept over the Tennessee Valley. At this time the high water mark exceeded the 1867 disaster at Waterloo by some twenty inches. Fortunately, its people by then had moved to higher ground.

One source says that although land was granted to the trustees of the town in 1819, the first settlers did not arrive until 1824.[91] Another reference states that John Webb and Jack Briscoe arrived around 1816, and were followed by Dr. Bumpass, and James and William Witherspoon. A little later two men, Hussey and Limerick, settled here, although not much is known about them.[92] The former is believed to have been George Hussey, native of North Carolina, who later moved to Green Hill. A shoemaker by trade, he was born in 1805. Yet another source indicates that by 1832 there was little if any development of the town proper. In that year a boatman described it as "a town without houses at the foot of the Muscle Shoals."[93]

Major James H. Witherspoon was said to have established the first merchandise business here in 1824. A native of North Carolina, Witherspoon from the beginning was the leading merchant in Waterloo. Soon he was boasting a merchant house made of bricks which were molded by slaves from the red clay. He built a cotton gin, gristmill, and saw mill on Second Creek. Witherspoon was also a Methodist minister who was credited with organizing the church in Waterloo which is one of the earliest Methodist congregations in the county. Witherspoon's home was a landmark for more than a hundred years. It was a large two-story log house, later covered with clapboards, with both upper and lower porches in front. Major Witherspoon was born in 1808 and died in 1883. His wife, Jane, who was born in Ireland, preceded him in death by eight years. Their graves were relocated to the Richardson Cemetery in the late 1930's.

Not long after Witherspoon built the first business, another merchant, James Johnson, formed a hotel, general store, and a cotton gin here. James R. Humphrey, son of a veteran of the Battle of New Orleans, arrived around 1829. A native of Kentucky, Humphrey lived at Huntsville before coming here. As a man of some means – and with a belief in the future of this river town – he made rather extensive investments. He purchased a line of keelboats from a man named Drum. These vessels operated between Waterloo, Eastport, Southport, Tuscumbia, and Florence. He built a hotel, storehouses, warehouses, and one of the most prosperous tan yards in the area. His son, John Thomas, and his grandsons, James B. and Thomas W., all became leading citizens of the town.[94]

Soon after 1850 James Lathem, native of South Carolina, became a town merchant. About the same time, Thomas T. McCorkle came with his father, James, from York District, South Carolina, and opened his combination merchandise and drug store, a business that survived in this family for more than one hundred years. The elder McCorkle was born in 1770 and died in 1866. The McCorkles were excellent record keepers. Their store ledgers and papers reveal an interesting story of life in early Waterloo.

Other early settlers at Waterloo included E. T. Chandler, R. H. Rawlings, P. H. Cunningham, John Hinderman, George Waters, and Bill Petus. Among those who invested in land prior to 1825 were: Dabney Morriss, Anthony and John Winston, William Berry, Samuel White, Jesse Evans, Stephen Hightower, Richard Baugh, William S. Barton, Thomas Kirkman, James Jackson, Charles N. Baucher, Samuel Hazard, John Webb, Tyree Rodes, Eli Kerr, Phillip J. Irion, William Parker, and James Madison.[95]

Alexander Higgins was a pioneer gunsmith at Waterloo. He first settled near Green Hill about 1818, coming from the Old Ninety-Sixth District, South, Carolina. He established his blacksmith and gun shop on Bumpass Creek Road east of the town. Here he made and sold the Higgins Long Rifle. This accurate and well-made gun had been introduced by the Higgins Clan of Laurens County, South Carolina, and later manufactured in Butts County, Georgia, and Chambers County, Alabama. Josiah Higging, born in 1811 in Laurens County, South Carolina, purchased a farm near Wrights Crossroads on Brush Creek in

1836. In 1848 he began acquiring tracts of rich bottom land on the west bank of Second Creek where he built his large home which was completely encircled by a porch. Josiah was married to a full blood Chickasaw Indian named Chealty (pronounced as "Che-aul-tie") Smith on January 1, 1830. The ceremony was performed by Alexander H. McDougal near Green Hill. Many of Josiah's and Chealty's descendants continue to live around Waterloo. Michael Higging, who was also a gunsmith, moved to Mississippi. Alexander as well as Josiah, Chealty, and their daughters, Martha Jane Lindsey and Ellender Elizabeth Tune, are buried in the Simpson/Whitten Cemetery overlooking Second Creek.

Around 1850, Jesse Lucy operated a general merchandise at the foot of Lucy Hill, which later became known as Town Hill. Lucy's business included a saloon where men could drink and gamble. Joel Childress was murdered here one winter evening while playing a game of "Seven-Up." He had accused his partner of cheating.

Joseph Bishop's blacksmith shop was at the top of Lucy Hill where Richardson Cemetery is now located. There was a large distillery at Boatman Spring where both whiskey and brandy were made from corn, apples, and peaches. Other merchandise houses during this period were listed as: Hargrave Barsew; Carter Madry; James Humphrey; West and Jones; and Witherspoon and Harrison.

The post office at Waterloo dates back to April 1827 when Thomas Pate was appointed as its first postmaster. Sixteen months later it was moved to Barton, a community now known as Gravelly Springs. However, it was re-established at Waterloo in 1828 with Edmund F. Wills as postmaster. In the early days the mail arrived by boat. Later, a horse-drawn vehicle was dispatched from Waterloo to Florence to pick up the mail. One of the last of these carriers was Green Berry Lindsey, Senior. He would go to Florence one day and return with the mail the next. In addition to his mail delivery, Lindsey sought passengers who wished to ride to and from the county seat. His father, Sylvester B. Lindsey, preceded him in this business. His newspaper advertisements ran as follows: "Attention Travelers! During low water in the river, I will leave Waterloo, with my nice spring wagon, every Monday, Wednesday and Friday at 9 a.m. through to Florence by 5 p.m. Returning, I will leave Florence on Tuesday, Thursday, and Saturday, at 9 a.m. and get to Waterloo at 5 p.m. Charge for passenger and 50 pounds baggage, $ 2.00 each way... Sill B. Lindsey."[96] Sylvester Lindsey had served in the Fourth Alabama Cavalry. He often told of fighting in the Battles of Little Bear Creek and Town Creek. He boasted of being at Shiloh under Fighting Joe Wheeler and of riding with Forrest in the capture of Colonel Abel Streight in his famous raid across Sand Mountain. Lindsey was married to Hannah Lee, a distant cousin to General Robert E. Lee.[97]

Waterloo has been called "the town of beloved physicians." Among those who served the community over the years were Gabriel Bumpass, Oen Boyce Sullivan, John W. Lee, A. H. Powers, and Rubin Weston.

Dr. Sullivan erected a small office on the corner of Waterloo Road and Main Street around 1844. He later built his large two-story home adjacent to it. Dr. Sullivan was a circuit-riding physician with a territory that extended across the line into Tennessee. He also used the ferry to visit patients around Riverton in Colbert County. He was born at Sullivan Crossroads in Lauderdale County. The Sullivans came from Ireland to Virginia and then to Laurens County, South Carolina, before settling in Alabama.

Waterloo was a thriving river port during the steamboat days on the Tennessee River. Situated at the lower end of the Muscle Shoals fall line, it served as the nearest deep water port to Florence. It became a gateway to places such as New Orleans and St. Louis, as well as a receiving point for supplies from other parts of the country. During low water seasons, smaller transport boats and large wagon trains ran from Waterloo to Florence on a regular basis.[98] However, for a period following the end of World War I, the federal government, in dredging the river, made it difficult for deep – draft boats to enter the Waterloo dock. On one occasion, caskets that had been ordered by the McCorkle Drug Store had to be unloaded at Riverton and later ferried across to Waterloo.

The Haynes family was involved in both building and repairing steamboats. Weathersby Haynes, native of North Carolina where he was born in 1850, was a tar maker. Henry Harvey Haynes, a Tennessean who was born in 1822, was a cooper by trade. His wife, Nancy Turpin, was a native of Kentucky. Years later, their son, Robert Henry Haynes, cut crossties that were shipped from Waterloo by steamboats.

Around the turn of the century, the timber industry became a big economic factor for Waterloo and the surrounding area. In 1897, within a twelve-mile radius there were seven saw and planing mills owned by A. V. Bevis, John Sheppard, Kinney Crow, R. H. Haynes, L. A. Ranson, Keel and Haynes, and Sheppard and Franklin. These mills turned out vast quantities of lumber annually for markets in St. Louis, Missouri, Evansville, Indiana, and East Florence. Crossties were big items. In 1897, their average market price amounted to $20.00 per hundred. A total of 121,550 ties were cut and shipped that year from around Waterloo.

Waterloo has been a river crossing point from early times. The first commercial ferry was established here about 1798 by Chief George Colbert. This was the original crossing of the Natchez Trace prior to being moved upriver to the present General John Coffee Bridge on the Natchez Trace Parkway. In 1832, Dr. Gabriel Bumpass was granted ferry rights which he held for many years. A newspaper advertisement in 1851 heralded the ferry at East Port, Mississippi, that crossed to Waterloo as "The nearest and best way from Middle Tennessee to North Mississippi."[99] Large holding pens for cattle and hogs were located at both ends of the ferry crossing. As late as the 1920's the Methodist ministers at Waterloo used the ferry on Sundays to hold services in the Riverton Church.[100]

An early school at Waterloo was taught by Carrie Sullivan, daughter of Dr. O. B. Sullivan. There is an existing early document called "Article of Agreement" between this teacher and her patrons in the town "to teach a subscription school at Waterloo, Alabama" for the term of five months for the sum of $1.25 per month "for each subscribed pupil."[101] In the late 1890's, this young lady crossed the river daily to teach at the Riverton School. She also a taught music to the young ladies in Waterloo. In the late 1890's Donald J. Edwards established a "Certificate School." Homer L. Reeder was listed as the co-principal.[102]

Waterloo played an important role in the tragic Trail of Tears during the early part of the Nineteenth Century when Native Americans were forced to leave their ancient homes to be relocated on reservations west of the Mississippi River. These people were transported by water, and some by land, to Waterloo. Here they were collected in camps until they could be placed aboard deep-water vessels and transported to their new lands. Some died and others escaped into the hills while waiting for their boats.[103] A number of people in the area trace their heritage back to these Native Americans.

Because of its strategic position on the river, Waterloo became a key port for both the Union and Confederate Armies during the Civil War. Union gunboats shelled the town in the summer of 1862 following an incident when older men of the community fired on the U.S.S. Cottage, one of their transport vessels. This occurred near the end of July. A number of these elderly men, led by Josiah Higgins, were arrested and sent to a federal prison in Alton, Illinois. Later, they were transferred to a makeshift confinement facility at McDowell College in St. Louis, Missouri. Here John Thomas Humphrey, a riverboat captain, died on October 16, 1862. His companion, Josiah Higgins – then 51 years of age – was released. When Higgins arrived in Waterloo he was carrying his friend's prison hat and handwritten diary which he presented to Humphrey's widow.[104]

Union General William T. Sherman crossed the river at Waterloo in October 1863 on his way to Chattanooga. He used Dr. Sullivan's home for his headquarters until he marched his army to Florence. During the winter of 1865, Union General James Harrison Wilson trained some 22,000 cavalrymen in this area. Wilson's First Division under Brigadier General Edward McCook was located at the Waterloo Landing. The proud Chicago Board of Trade Artillery Battery was stationed just north of the downtown area. This unit, commanded by Captain George Robinson, was a part of Brigadier General Eli Long's Second Division which was encamped at Gravelly Springs. One historian wrote that, although Wilson had been ordered to burn Waterloo, "he succumbed to the charm of the Southern ladies and spared the town."[105]

Bumpass Creek Road was said to have been one of the main routes used by Confederate bushwhacker Bert Hayes.[106] According to legend, Hayes was responsible for the deaths of a number of people in this area, although this has never been documented.

The advent of the Tennessee Valley Authority Act in 1933 became a mixed blessing to the people at Waterloo. They soon learned that the proposed Pickwick Dam on the Tennessee River near Savannah, Tennessee, would form a lake to cover all the rich river bottom farms in and around this area of Lauderdale County. Some of these farmers who lost their land moved to Mississippi and to other places such as Indiana. Others merely relocated to higher ground. James "Jimmy" Haynes was one of the larger planters. After Pickwick Dam was completed, he turned his porch chair around to face the front of his store so he wouldn't have to look at the lake that covered former fields of bountiful corn.[107]

There are a number of success stories told about young people who left Waterloo for other places. One of these involves Ezra Lee Culver who migrated to the North a good many years before there was a Tennessee Valley Authority. After establishing his own enterprise, he built a number of notable landmarks, such as the Lincoln Tunnel, Yankee Stadium, and the Waldorf-Astoria Hotel in New York, the state capitol buildings in Charleston, West Virginia, and the Florida Key bridges. Culver is a son of George Washington Culver, Junior, and his wife, Virginia Haynes Culver. She was a daughter of Robert Henry Haynes and his wife, Jane Barrier Haynes. An ancestor, John Culver, served in the Revolutionary War under General Washington. The first Culver in America arrived in 1635. Mrs. E. L. Culver donated the historic Newman House to Waterloo a few years prior to her death. In 1995, Ezra Lee Culver restored this house and established the

Edith Newman Culver Memorial Museum in it which he gave to the town in memory of his late wife.

Pickwick Lake which flooded the lowlands brought new life to Waterloo. It has become a fisherman's paradise. The nearby forests are filled with game for the hunter. It is now one of the most scenic natural attractions in Alabama and the South.

The hills around Waterloo and the folkways of its people are mindful of the beautiful Appalachian Mountains that stretch from Maine to Alabama. Even the local names given to its terrain features seem as quaint and colorful as those found among the Blue Ridge and the Great Smokies; among the places located north, east, and west of Waterloo are: Salt Hollow, Hardtimes Landing, Dykes Hollow, Pea Ridge, Lindsey Hollow, Panther Creek, Shaw Hollow, Shaw's Landing, Union Hollow, Caney Hollow, Cedar Fork, Chigger Chapel, Backbone Hollow, Bitter Branch, Sunday Creek, Graveyard Hollow, Sheppard Hollow, Dry Creek, Sharp Hollow, Johnny Hollow, Scott Hill, Chapel Beat, Landrum Hollow, Fords Mill, Cedar Fork, Turpin Hollow, Manbone Ridge, and Manbone Creek.

Human bones were found in Manbone Cave by early settlers. Some people believed that this cave may have been used as a hideout by Joseph Thompson Hare, a notorious outlaw on the nearby Natchez Trace.[108]

Haddock, Shaw's Landing, and Spains

Haddock, Shaw's Landing, and Spains were names for a settlement north of Panther Creek in the Waterloo area. This was near the Alabama, Mississippi, and Tennessee state lines. Much of this section was evacuated in the late 1930's prior to the inundation of Pickwick Lake. One old-timer remembered the bottomlands in Spains Beat as being, "the most productive farming area around Waterloo."[109]

Haddock takes its name from the family of John A. Haddock who became its first postmaster on October 10, 1890. His parents, Alexander and Mary Haddock, were settlers near the Central Heights community. Alexander's father was James H. Haddock who was born in North Carolina in 1795. James was married to Acenah Paulk, who was born in South Carolina. They were married in 1816 and came to Alabama by way of Cypress Inn, Tennessee.

Charles Shaw and brothers operated a store, cotton gin, and gristmill in this community for many years. In fact, these businesses were in operation when the Tennessee Valley Authority purchased the lands for Pickwick Lake in 1937. Robert Shaw, native of Tennessee, was living on Panther Creek as early as 1834. George W. Shaw, born in 1825, was a prominent farmer in the community in 1870.

The name Spains was used sometimes for a community and officially as one of the county precincts. John W. Spain and his brother, J. Wesley Spain, were well-to-do farmers here. Published reports show that in 1896 John Spain raised 1,740 bushels of corn. The previous year he reported a meat production of 2,750 pounds. Wes Spain produced 2,500 pounds of meat that same year.[110] Ruffin Spain, a Virginian, settled on Panther Creek prior to 1850. He was born in 1782. His wife, Jimmina, was a native of North Carolina. A will was filed for Marshall D. Spain in 1825, with Solomon D. Spain listed as one of the administrators. Other members of this family living in the Spains Beat in 1850 were: Newel and Louisa Spain, and Hardy Spain and his wife Martha. One of the twentieth century bishops of the United Methodist Church – Robert H. Spain of Nashville, Tennessee was a descendant of the Spains of Lauderdale County.

Gatewood "Gator" Qualls was an early settler in Spains. He was born about 1798 in Virginia and died in Arkansas. His father and mother were John Qualls and Millie Jerusha Ferris Qualls. Gatewood Qualls was married to Millie Ann Bolden from Henry County, Virginia. She was a daughter of Tyler Bolden. Other early landowners here were Richard Baugh, and Stephen Hightower.[111]

Wright's Crossroads

County Road 8, which traverses the width of Lauderdale County, terminates at the Waterloo Road a few miles east of Waterloo. At this crossroads is the community of Wright, also known as Wright's Crossroads. Ancient civilizations have lived here. A number of the most interesting of the Tennessee River Indian mounds are located near the mouth of Brush Creek and on nearby islands, although most of them are now covered by Pickwick Lake.

Wright's Crossroads was named for an early settler, Moses Wright, who came here around 1832. While traveling the Natchez Trace as a post rider from Nashville, he saw this area and returned to make his home here. A native of North Carolina where he was born in 1799, Moses, with a number of slaves, cleared the land and built his log house along with cabins, barns, and other farming-type buildings. One of his grandsons, George Moses Wright, established a general store which remained in the family for about one hundred years.[112]

Land buyers in this area prior to 1825 were John Webb, John Jackson, and Nathaniel Harrison, with adjacent islands owned by James Jackson, William Strawn, and Ben Price.[113] Barton Branch, which flows through the community, was named for William Barton who lived in Gravelly Springs. He perhaps owned land alongside this stream sometime after 1825.

In 1855, Phillip Lindsey acquired two tracts of land at the spring near the head of Barton Branch. He was a son and grandson of Revolutionary War veterans, John L. Lindsey and Captain Samuel Lindsey of Newberry County, South Carolina, respectively. Phillip's great-grandfather, Colonel John Lindsey, was a Colonial militia officer in Frederick County, Virginia, prior to the Revolution. He is mentioned in one of Washington's reports soon after the French and Indian Wars. Phillip Lindsey's wife, Frances, was a daughter of Charles and Matilda Anglin Sharp who were early settlers in West Lauderdale County. Both Charles' and Matilda's parents were from Virginia, and both of their fathers served in the American Revolution.

Phillip Lindsey was one of the area farmers raided in 1865 by the soldiers of General Wilson camped at Gravelly Springs. In a claim filed with the federal government after the war, Lindsey wrote:

"... I farmed all during the war; was present and saw all the property taken by General Hatch's command camped about three miles from me."[114]

A 750-acre plantation, Hunter's Hall, owned by Thomas A. Lansford, was located a mile or two east of Wright's Crossroads. There is a watering hole at this site called Lansford Spring. A large part of Lansford's farm was in the rich bottomland alongside the river. A native of North Carolina, Lansford died in 1856 at the age of 42 years. His wife, Annie, was born in Tennessee in 1826. Both are buried in the family cemetery on a hill overlooking Waterloo Road.

Wright's Crossroads was caught up in the timber industry at the same time as was its neighbor, Waterloo. The Wright family recorded some happenings around these businesses. They noted that wagons loaded with crossties would sometimes be lined up two miles along Brush Creek Road waiting to be loaded onto boats at Wright's Landing. They marveled at the strength of one African-American who "could pick up a tie in each hand and place them in the chute to be loaded onto the boat."[115]

In 1900, there were three stores, a mill, and gin at Wright's Crossroads. One merchant, Samuel H. Emerson, also handled large quantities of "boop poles and cross-ties."[116] A post office was established February 20, 1891, with David M. Waters as postmaster. Others who held this office until it was finally discontinued in 1911 were: David Jones Pettipool, Thomas J. Wilson, and Samuel Emerson.[117]

A POSTSCRIPT IN CLOSING

"...we must all thank God that we have been allowed .to play a part in making these days memorable in history of our race."
(Winston Churchill, 1941)

This postscript serves as a transition between the past and the future. It signals the ending of an epoch involving the people and places of yesterday. It marks, too, the beginning for a future historian who will someday link together what has been, what now is, and that which is yet to be.

Time-wise, Part Two of this volume begins with the legacy of the Tennessee River which first made its way across Northwest Alabama in some forgotten eon of time. Significantly, Part One ends with the advent of the Tennessee Valley Authority which literally conquered this once wild river. This watercourse now flows through the valley through a series of the most beautiful and the most placid man-made lakes in the world. The once treacherous river obstacle called the Muscle Shoals is now covered by three of these scenic lakes-Pickwick, Wilson, and Wheeler. Never has a region and people been more bountifully blessed by nature and the genius of man.

As our generation has been the recorder of that which has been, we look to our children and grandchildren to be the historians who will tell our story tomorrow. Perhaps they, too, will be guided by the wisdom as expressed in the words of Henry Wadesworth Longfellow:

"they who walk in history only seem to walk the earth again."

FOOTNOTES AND RESOURCE REFERENCES

Chapter 1

1. McDaniel, Mary Jane, article "Land Sales Gave Birth to Florence," Times Daily, Florence, Alabama, November 19, 1992.
2. Simpson, James, "Reflection of Florence," The Florence Times, August 9, 1918.
3. Davidson, Donald, The Tennessee, Volume I, (Rinehart and Company, Incorporated, New York, 1946.)
4. Johnson, Kenneth R., "Celebration A Good Time To Look Back," Times Daily, March 18, 1993.
   Leftwich, Nina, Two Hundred Years at Muscle Shoals, (Multigraphic Advertising Company, Birmingham, Alabama, 1935.)
5. Wright, Milly, unpublished paper, "Early Land Buyers and Settlers, Florence and Lauderdale County, Alabama" (1989.)
   General John Coffee Papers, Collier Library, The University of North Alabama, 1994.
6. McDaniel.
7. Wright.
   Wiltshire, C. R., "Trials and Triumphs of Florence," The Tri Cities Daily, June 21, 1948.
8. Wiltshire.
   McDaniel.
9. Watts, Charles Wilder, Sheffield, Alabama, private papers.
   Rice, Turner, "Andrew Jackson and His Northwest Alabama Interests, The Journal of Muscle Shoals History, Volume III, (The Tennessee Valley Historical Society, 1975.)
   Darby, Kathleen A., "Historic Sketches of Lauderdale County" The Journal of Muscle Shoals History, Vol. XI, (1986.)
10. Simpson, James, The Florence Times, August 9, 1918.
11. The Gazette, Florence, Alabama, May 19, 1849.
12. Royall, Anne Newport, Letters From Alabama 1817-1822, (University of Alabama Press, University, Alabama, 1969.)

13-15. Harraway, William E., "The Long Ago," <u>The Journal of Muscle Shoals History</u>, Volume XI, (The Tennessee Valley Historical Society, 1986.)

16. Johnson, Anne Rowell Hood, Dothan, Alabama (interview with the author, August 19, 1954.)

17. Wiltshire.

18. Douglass, Hiram Kennedy, in an interview with the author March 12, 1958.

19. Wright, Milly, "Forming A `Body Politic' at Florence, <u>Times Daily</u>, December 10, 1992.

Chapter 2

1. Durant, Will, The Story of Civilization, Part II (Simon and Schuster, New York, 1939.)

2-3. Chappell, Gordon Thomas, "The Life and Activities of John Coffee," an unpublished paper (Vanderbilt University, 1941.)

4. O'Neal, Elizabeth Kirkman, The Forks of Cypress, (Memphis, Tennessee, 1966.)

5. Russel, Dr. Darrell A., "James Jackson of the Forks of Cypress: Will and Inventory, Natchez Trace Traveler, Vol. 13, No. 1, February 1993.

6. Axford, Faye, "The Forks of Cypress," an unpublished paper, 1964.

7. Hamilton, Cherovise, "The Forks of Cypress," (University of North Alabama History Paper, July, 1978.)

8. Sherwood, Waring, The Story of James Jackson of "The Forks," (Published at Memphis, Tennessee, 1978.)

9. Hicks, Jimmie, "Associate Justice John McKinley: A Sketch," The Alabama Review, Vol. XVIII, No. 5, July, 1965.

10. Royall.

11. Simpson.

12. Wright, Milly, "Fathers of the Founders or Kinship in the Shoals," an unpublished paper dated September 12, 1988.

13. Nashville Whig, September 11, 1819, and Tennessee Gazette and Mero District Advertiser, Nashville, March 27, 1805.

14. Simpson.

15. Wright.

16.   Watts.

17.   Edwards, Cris, and Axford, Faye, The Lure and Lore of Limestone County, (Portals Press, Tuscaloosa, Alabama, 1978.)

Chapter 3

1.   General John Coffee Papers.

2.   Coppock, Paul R., "Ferdinand Sannoner, Native Son of Florence," The Commercial Appeal, Memphis, Tennessee, January 27, 1974.

3-4.   Lewis, Oscar, "Ferdinand Sannoner," an unpublished paper.

5.   Douglass, interviewed May 1956.
        Warren, Billy Ray, interviewed July 12, 1997.

6-7.   Lewis.

8.   Coppock (Those attending the placing of the marker were George Alfred McCroskey, Oscar Lewis, Jim Odum, and William L. McDonald of Florence, along with James Jackson of Memphis who was a descendant of one of the founders of Florence.)

Chapter 4

1.   Johnson, Kenneth R., "Some Aspects of Slavery in the Muscle Shoals Area, The Journal of Muscle Shoals History, Vol. II, 1974.

2-3.   Gibson, Arrell M., The Chickasaws (The University of Oklahoma Press, Norman, Oklahoma, 1961.)

4.   Royall.

5.   McCurtain Gazette, Idabel, Oklahoma, November 25, 1914.

6.   McCurtain Gazette, January 13, 1917.

7.   Cresap, Bernarr, "The People at the Muscle Shoals," Journal of Muscle Shoals History, Vol. VII, 1979.

8.   Rogers, William Warren; Ward, Robert David; Atkins, Leah Rawls; and Flynt, Wayne, Alabama, The History of A Deep South State, (The University of Alabama Press, 1994.)

9.   Schweninger, Loren, James T. Rapier and Reconstruction, (The University of Chicago Press, 1978.)

10.   McDaniel, Mary Jane, "Large Plantations in Lauderdale County, Alabama, 1860," Journal of Muscle Shoals History, Vol. VI, 1978.

11.   Furnas, J. C., Goodbye To Uncle Tom, (William Sloane Associates, New York, 1956.)

12.   Armistead, Robert, interviewed May 23, 1986.

13. Weeden Papers, notes made by the author during the period 1947-1972, courtesy of John D. and Jessie Weeden, Sweetwater Plantation, Florence, Alabama.

14. Jackson Papers, notes by author 1959-1994, interview of James Jackson, Memphis, Tennessee.

15. Carter, Edward L. Sr.; Carter, Guy R.; Carter, Bessie I.; and Vessell, Blanche Carter interviewed between 1945 and 1954.

16. Ehrlich, Walter, <u>They Have No Rights - Dred Scott's Struggle for Freedom,</u> (Greenwood Press, Westport, Connecticut, 1979.)

17. Davis, William C., <u>A Way Through The Wilderness,</u> (Harper Collins Publishers, New York, 1995.)

18. Garrett, Jill K., <u>A History of Florence, Alabama</u> (Columbia, Tennessee, 1968.)

19. Schweninger.

20. <u>Times Daily,</u> Florence, Alabama, news release received from Associated Press on November 5, 1992, (author has copy.) Johnson, Kenneth R., "Shoals Native Made History In Congress," <u>Times Daily,</u> July 10, 1997.

21. Handy, W. C., <u>Father of the Blues,</u>" (The Macmillan Company, New York, 1947.)

Chapter 5

1. Wood, William B., from speech made at Florence, Alabama, on July 4, 1878. Also see National Archives Microfilm Publications: Records of the Cherokee Indian Agency in Tennessee 1801-1835, Microcopy 208, Roll 4. Correspondence and Miscellaneous Records 1808-1909, No. 2311. W. S. Hoole Special Collections, Library, University of Alabama.

2. Wiltshire
   Wood, William B., "History of Lauderdale County, A Historical Address," <u>The Journal of Muscle Shoals History,</u> Vol. V, 1977.

3. Wright, Milly, "Early Records of Lauderdale County, 1818-1822," (published in 1993.)

4. McDaniel, Mary Jane, "Rapier Was Instrumental in Starting Barge Traffic," <u>Times Daily,</u> June 9, 1994.

5. Simpson.

6. Wood. History.

7.   Simpson.

8.   Wood. History.

9-10. Simpson.

11.   Rice, Turner, Birmingham, Alabama, letter to author September 4, 1971.

12.   "The Early Settlers of Florence and Vicinity," <u>The Florence Daily News</u>, May 22, 1921.

13-20. Wood. History.

21.   Wright, Early Land.

22.   Wood Family Papers in author's collection.

23-24. Garrett, Jill Knight, <u>A History of Lauderdale County</u>, Alabama, (Columbia, Tennessee, 1964.)

25.   Patton Family Papers in author's collection.

26.   Kelso, Mrs. Thurman M., <u>A History of the First Presbyterian Church, Florence, Alabama</u>, (1968.)

Chapter 6

1.   Royall.

2.   Watts.

3.   Garrett.

4.   Bedford Family Papers in author's collection.

5.   Moser, Harold D., Hoth, David R., and, Hoemann, George H., <u>The Papers Of Andrew Jackson</u>, Volume V, (The University of Tennessee Press, Knoxville, Tennessee, 1996.)

6-7.   Wood. History.

8.   Simpson.

9-10. Wood. History.

11.   Wright, Milly, interviewed June 10, 1997.

12.   Sheridan, Richard C.; "Chemistry at Old La Grange, Alabama's First College," Journal <u>of Muscle Shoals History</u>, Vol. VII.

Chapter 7

1-3.   Garrett.

4-6.   Wood. History.

7.   Brewer, W., <u>Alabama, Her History and Resources</u>, 1540 -1872, (Montgomery, Alabama, 1872.)

8.   Wood. History.

9.   Garrett, Jill K., and McClain, Iris H., <u>Some Lauderdale County, Alabama, Cemetery Records</u>, (Columbia, Tennessee, 1970.)

10-11. Wood. History.

12. Brewer. History.

13. Wood. History.
     <u>Memorial Record of Alabama</u>, (Brant and Fuller, Democrat Printing Company, Madison, Wisconsin, 1893.)

14-15. Memorial Record of Alabama

16-17. Tease, J. Edward, private papers.

18. Edwards and Axford.

19. Wood Family Papers.

Chapter 8

1.   McDaniel, Mary Jane, private papers.

2.   McDaniel, Mary Jane, Historic Muscle Shoals: Buildings and Sites, <u>Journal of Muscle Shoals History</u>, Volume X, 1983.

3.   Kelso.

4.   Young, Robert A., <u>Reminiscences</u>, (Publishing House, Methodist Episcopal Church South, Nashville, Tennessee, 1900.)

5.   McDaniel. Historic.

6.   Edwards and Axford.

7.   Lindsey, Leonard, interview May 31, 1954.

8.   Wilson, James Harrison, <u>Under The Old Flag</u> (New York, 1912.)

9-10. Edwards and Axford.

11.   DeLand, T. A., and Smith, A. Davis, <u>Northern Alabama, Historical and Biographical</u>, (1888.)

12. Warner, Ezra J., <u>Generals in Gray</u>, (Louisiana State University Press, Baton Rouge, Louisiana, 1959.)

13. McDaniel, Mary Jane, "Biographies Of O'Neal Tend To Hide Prison Link," <u>Times Daily</u>, February 8, 1996.

14. <u>Confederate Veteran</u>, Vol. XVIII, No. l, (January, 1910.)

15. Garrett and McClain.

16. Roulac, Mrs. George Erwin, interview May 15, 1954.

17-18. Edward Asbury O'Neal Papers, University of North Carolina Library, Chapel Hill, North Carolina.

19.   O'Neal, Elizabeth K., and Vaughn, Susan K., <u>Scattered Recollections</u>, (Birmingham Printing Company, Birmingham, Alabama.)

Chapter 9

1-2.   Watts.
3.   Holcombe, Hosea, Philadelphia, Pennsylvania, <u>History Of The Rise and Progress Of The Baptists In Alabama</u>, 1840. (Collection of Charles Wilder Watts, Sheffield, Alabama.)
       Sheridan, Richard C., "The Shoals Creek Baptist Association And Her Alabama Churches," <u>The Alabama Baptist Historian</u>, July, 1984.
4.   Maness, Mrs. George H., <u>The First Baptist Church, Florence, Alabama, 1888-1963, A History</u>, Florence, Alabama, 1963.
5.   Braden, Guy B., "The Colberts and the Chickasaw Nation," <u>Tennessee Historical Quarterly, Vol. XVII, No. 3</u>, 1958.
6.   Kelso.
7.   Lancaster, Mary Holland, <u>Gathering Up Our Sheaves With Joy, A History of Trinity Episcopal Church, 1824-1976</u> (Williams Printing Company, Nashville, Tennessee, 1985.)
8.   Kilpatrick, Wayne, "History of The Church of Christ in Northwest Alabama, 1823-1861," <u>The Journal of Muscle Shoals History</u>, Volume XI, 1986.
9.   Davis, Derrel, "Historical Sketch, Stony Point Church of Christ," (date unknown.)
10-11. Kilpatrick, Wayne, "History of The Church of Christ in Lauderdale County, 1866-1880," <u>The Journal of Muscle Shoals History</u>, Volume XI, 1986.
12.   Historical marker located at the Wood Avenue Church of Christ.
13.   Kilpatrick. History. 1866-1880.
14.   <u>Times Daily</u>, February 10, 1985.
15.   Kerby, Dr. Otis, Tuscumbia, Alabama, private papers.
16.   <u>Times Daily</u>, February 10, 1985.
17.   Lovett, Rose Gibbons, Catholic <u>Church In The Deep South</u>, 1981.
18-20. Gremillion, Terry, "The History of St. Joseph's Parish," (a college history paper compiled April 15, 1987.)
21.   Lovett.

22. <u>Times Daily</u>, February 10, 1985 (a survey of area churches.)
     Shoals Area Directory, South Central Bell, and June 1994.
23. Muhlendorf, Beatrice; Siegel, Betty; and Levi, Doryce, interview
     August 26, 1996.
24. Miller, Elroy, Dayton, Ohio, in a statement to the author during the
     summer of 1955.

Chapter 10

1. <u>Alabama Republican</u>, Huntsville, Alabama, April 18, 1818.
2. McDaniel, Mary Jane, "Sweetwater Was Site Of Early Mill
    Enterprise," <u>Times Daily</u>, Florence, Alabama, June 25, 1992.
3. Perry, Robert, "Florence Should Take Steps To Recognize
    Martin," Times Daily, Florence, Alabama (date not shown)
4. Sheridan, Richard C., "Civil War Manufacturing In The Tennessee
    Valley," a paper presented before the Alabama Historical
    Association on April 24, 1987.
5. <u>The Florence Journal</u>, February 7, 1866.
6. Sheridan. Civil War.

Chapter 11

1.   Wright, Milly, "Florence Developed Culturally, Physically," <u>Times
     Daily</u>, January 28, 1993.
2.   <u>North Alabama Newspaper</u>, April 11, 1845.
3.   Sheridan, Richard C., notes to author, dated August 14., 1992.
4.   Sheridan. Civil War.
5-6. <u>The Florence Gazette</u>, April 21, 1825.
7.   <u>The Florence Gazette</u>, December 3, 1830.
8.   Sheridan. Civil War.
9.   Sheridan, Richard C., private papers.
10. Lindsey, Leonard, interview March 31, 1954.
     Wallace, Dan, interview on November 1, 1988.

Chapter 12

1. McDaniel. Rapier - Barge Traffic.
2. Teuton, Frank L., "Steamboating On The Tennessee," <u>The Journal
    of Muscle Shoals History</u>, Volume V, 1977.

3.   Kitchens, Ben Earl, <u>Gunboats And Cavalry</u>, (Thornwood Book Publishers, Florence, Alabama, 1985.)

4-5. Teuton, Frank L., "Steamboating On The Tennessee."

6.   Kitchens.

7.   Teuton.

8.   Lindsey, Leonard, interview on May 30, 1955.

9-11. Johnson, Kenneth, "Stages May Have Run In The Shoals As Early As 1817," <u>Times Daily</u>, April 28, 1994.

12.   McDonald, Jesse William, interview on January 19, 1947.

13.   Garrett. History – Florence.

Chapter 13

1.   Abramson, Inah Mae Young, private papers.

2.   Cole, Magnolia Johnson, interview on May 23, 1951.

3.   McDaniel, Mary Jane, "John Coffee Initiated First Female School in Florence," <u>Times Daily</u>, August 27, 1992.

4.   Lewis, Oscar D., private collection.

5.   Crozier, Edwin, "The Life of Caroline Lee Hentz," <u>Old Shoals Journal</u>, (date not shown.)

6.   Kelso.

7-8. Isom, Jay, "Before The Florence City School System." <u>Shoals Community Magazine</u>, February, 1991.

9.   McDonald, Elizabeth Womack, "History of the Florence City Schools," Board of Education, Florence, Alabama.

10-12. McDonald. Elizabeth. Womack. History.

13.   Garrett. History - Lauderdale County.

14.   McDonald. Elizabeth Womack. History. Schools," Board of Education, Florence, Alabama.

15-16. McDonald, Thomas Glen, Guidance Counselor, Florence City School System, October 19, 1996.

17.   McDonald. Elizabeth. Womack. History.

18.   Rogers, Donna Haynes, private collection.

Chapter 14

1.   McDonald. Elizabeth. Womack. History.

2.   Kelso.

3.   McDonald. Elizabeth. Womack. History.

4.   Douglass, Hiram Kennedy, interview on April 19, 1955.

5.   Johnson, Ronya, Communications Coordinator, International Bible College, in a letter to the author, dated December 3, 1996.

6.   Sheridan, Richard C., "The Baptist University of Florence, Alabama," a private paper published in April 1970.

7.   McDonald. Elizabeth. Womack. History.

8-9.   Johnson, Kenneth R., "Urban Boosteism and Higher Education In The New South," <u>Alabama Historical Quarterly</u>, Volume XLII, 1980.

Chapter 15

1-2.   Lawrence, B. J., "The Great Bend Of The Tennessee River and The Shoals," Decatur, Alabama, a private paper, 1994.

3.   Winn, Joshua Nicholas III, <u>Muscle Shoals Canal ...Life With The Canalers</u>, (Strode Publishers, Inc., Huntsville, Alabama, 1981.)

4.   Lawrence.

5.   Winn.

6.   <u>Historic Muscle Shoals: Buildings and Sites</u>, (Tennessee Valley Historical Society, 1983.)

7-8.   Winn.

9.   Winn, Joshua Nicholas III, interview on September 21, 1976.

Chapter 16

1.   Garrett. History - Florence

2.   Kitchens

3.   Warner. <u>Generals In Gray</u>

4.   <u>The Florence Gazette</u>, March 19, 1862.

5.   Lindsey, Lucy Johnson, interview on April 6, 1939.

6.   <u>The Florence Gazette</u>, April 9, 1862.

7.   Kelso.

8.   Lindsey, Leonard, interview on December 3, 1956.

9.   <u>The Nashville Union</u>, July 30, 1862.
       <u>The Memphis Appeal</u>, August 2, 1862.

10-11. Garrett. History – Florence

12.   Hoole, William Stanley, <u>Alabama Tories, The First Alabama Cavalry, U.S.A., 1862-1865</u>, (Confederate Publishing Company, Incorporated, Tuscaloosa, Alabama, 1960.)

13.   Warner. <u>General in Blues</u>.
14.   Kitchens.
15.   Garrett. History – Florence.
        Watts, Charles Wilder, private collection.
16-18. Watts.
19.   "Beginnings of the University of North Alabama," by author, (Birmingham Printing and Publishing Company, 1991.)
20.   Watts.
21.   Garrett. History – Florence.
22.   <u>The War of Rebellion: Official Records of the Union and Confederate Armies</u>, Series 1, Vol. 23, Part 1, (Washington, D.C., 1880-1901.)
23.   Vanderboegh, Micheal, private papers. Frederick, Lorene, "Man Uncover Old Cover-Up," <u>Times Daily</u>, October 28, 1986.
24.   Deny, Eva, "Waterloo, A Town on the Tennessee," <u>History and Folk-lore of West Lauderdale County</u>, (Muscle Shoals Area Basic Education Program, Muscle Shoals, Alabama, 1979.)
25.   Patton Family Papers.
26.   <u>Tennessee Historical Quarterly</u>, September 1962.
        Eliza Coffee Papers (a copy in the collection of author.)
27.   Romine, Mack H., private Civil War collection.
28-29. Weakley, Eliza, private journal.
30-31. Garrett. History - Florence
32.   Bennett, John and Bobbie, Cincinnati, Ohio, private papers.
33-35. Garrett. History - Florence.
36.   Weakley.
37.   Watts.
38.   War Department, <u>The War of the Rebellion: A Compilation of the Official Records of the Union and Confederate Armies</u>. Series I, Volume XXXVIII.
39.   Johnson, Kenneth R., "Confederate Forces Arrive In The Shoals," <u>Times Daily</u>, September 7, 1995.
40-41. Dunnavant, Robert, Junior, <u>Railroad War</u> (Pea Ridge Press, Incorporated, Athens, Alabama, 1994.)
42.   Weakley.
43.   Johnson. Confederate Forces.

44.   Sword, Wiley, <u>The Confederacy's Last Hurrah</u>, (University Press of Kansas, 1992.)

45.   Rogers, William Warren; Ward, Robert David; Leah, Rawls Atkins; and Flynt, Wayne, <u>Alabama, The History Of A Deep South State</u>. (The University of Alabama Press, 1994.)

46.   Rainey, I. N., <u>The Civil War Experiences of I. N. Rainey</u>, privately published, 1965.

47-48. Jones, James Pickett, <u>Yankee Blitzkrieg</u>, The University of Georgia Press, 1976.

49.   Jones, James Pickett.

Chapter 17

1.   Garrett, Jill K., "Colonel Jacob Biffle - Second Only To Forrest," <u>The Valley Featurette</u>, Athens, Alabama, January 29, 1971.

2.   Pruitt, Wade, <u>Bugger Saga</u>, P-Vine Press, Columbia, Tennessee, 1977.

3.   Garrett. History - Florence

4.   Sherman, W. T., <u>Memoirs of W.T. Sherman</u>, Literary Classics of the United States, Inc., New York, 1990.

5.   <u>Nashville Union</u>, Nashville, Tennessee, February 17, 1864.

6.   Daniel, Earl, in an interview on December 1, 1968.

7.   <u>War of Rebellion, Official Records</u>, Series I, Volume 49, Part 2, page 751.

8.   Byler, Edgar D., "Captain William Burton (Bert) Hayes, Company H., Wilson's 21st Regiment, Tennessee Cavalry, C.S.A., <u>Wayne County Historian</u>, Volume 2, Number 3, September 1989.

9.   Cannon, Jabez Pugh, Inside of Rebeldom, <u>The National Tribune</u>, Washington, D.C., 1900.

10.   McDaniel, Buildings and Sites.

11.   Pruitt, Wade, <u>Bugger Saga</u>, P-Vine Press, Columbia, Tennessee, 1977.

12.   <u>The Florence Times</u>, December 24, 1897.

13.   Weeden, Mattie Patton, private papers in the Patton Family Papers. These papers were at one time stored at the Sweetwater Plantation. Their location today is unknown, although some copies are in the collection of the author.

14.   <u>Nashville Dispatch</u>, May 13., 1865.

15. Garrett. History - Florence.
16. <u>Nashville Union</u>, February 4, 1865.
17. Garrett. History - Florence.
18. <u>Nashville Dispatch</u>, May 16, 1865.
19-20. <u>Nashville Union</u>, May 18, 1865. (Dr. Wade Pruitt, in his book, <u>Bugger Saga</u>, credits Captain Risden DeFord with the apprehension and execution of Campbell and Oliver.)
21. Pruitt. In a letter to the author dated January 11, 1969.
22. Literary Index, Florence, Alabama, March 26, 1868.
23. Koonce, Herbert F., interviewed on April 21, 1968.
24. Pruitt. McDonald, Elizabeth Womack, interviewed on December 21, 1961.

Chapter 18

1. Cole, Magnolia Johnson, in a interview with the author on May 19, 1948. (Mary Ellen McCuan Johnson was her mother.)
2-3. Rogers, Ward, Atkins, and Flynt.
4. Dendy, Eva, "History of Waterloo, Alabama," private papers.
5. Garrett. History - Lauderdale County.
6-7. Schweninger.
8. Metcalf, Doris, "Rapier Became Black Leader, Distinguished Congressman," <u>Times Daily</u>, November 26, 1992.
9-10. Schweninger.
11. <u>North Alabamian and Times</u>, November 17, 1868.
12. Schweninger.
13-14. Metcalf, Doris, "Bureau's Most Lasting Effects Can Be Found In Education," Times Daily, December 7, 1995.

Chapter 19

1. Wright, Milly, private collection of historical papers.
2. McDaniel. Sweetwater - Early Mill.
3. Shelton, Mason Bradford, Florence, Alabama, Memoirs, a private paper (copy in the collection of the author.)
4. Leftwich, Nina, <u>Two Hundred Years At Muscle Shoals</u>, Multigraphic Advertising Company, Birmingham, Alabama, 1935.
5. <u>Sheffield, City On The Bluff</u>, 1885-1985, (Friends Sheffield Public Library, 1985.) \

6-7.   Shelton, Mason Bradford, Memoirs.

8.   "The History of Martin Industries," <u>On The Backburner</u>, February and March, 1980, (The Foundry, Florence, Alabama.)

9-10.   Johnson, Franklin Pierce, mill supervisor, private papers.

11.   Hillis, G. W., interview on March 22, 1997.

12.   Staggs, L. D., Jr., private papers.

13.   Lewis, Oscar D., private papers.

14.   Hamm, Jane Johnson, <u>East Florence Church of Christ</u>, 1997.

15.   Melton, the Reverend Henry, interviewed on June 14, 1997.

16.   Hill, Estella Wilkes, private papers.

17.   Nichols, G. C., private papers. 18.

18.   Potts, Irma Matthews, interviewed on May 5, 1990.

19.   Hill, Estella Wilkes, private papers.

Chapter 20

1.   McKnight, Mrs. Lula Lanier, interviewed on March 21, 1949.

2.   Wright, Milly, "Forming A Body Politic At Florence."

3.   1928/29 Telephone Directory for Florence, Sheffield, and Tuscumbia.

4.   Cole, Mrs. Magnolia Johnson, interviewed on May 9, 1954.

5.   McDaniel. Buildings And Sites.

6.   Garrett. History - Lauderdale County.

7.   <u>Florence Times</u>, June 30, 1899.

8-9.   McDaniel, Mary Jane, "Water Tower A Remnant Of City's Boom," <u>Times Daily</u>, October 17 and 24, 1996.

10.   Young's Business and Professional Directory (Florence, Sheffield, and Tuscumbia, 1900,) Nashville Public Library, Nashville, Tennessee.

11-12.   Garrett. History - Lauderdale County.

13.   Isom, Jay, "In The Beginning: The Founding Of The Florence City Schools," <u>School News</u>, 1991.

14.   McKnight, James Howard, private historical collection.

15.   Wright, Milly, interviewed with Robert James Armstead on August 16, 1986, when he was 100 years old. He was a grandson of Lewis Armstead.

16. <u>A History of The Church of Christ at Poplar Street and Wood Avenue, Florence, Alabama, 1886-1986</u> (Country Lane Printing, Florence, Alabama, 1997.)
17. Maness.

Chapter 21

1. Clary, Martin, <u>The Facts About Muscle Shoals</u>, (Ocean Publishing Company, New York, City, 1924.)
2. Watts.
3. Burt, Reynolds B., "Shoals, Site Attractive for Beauty, Water Power," <u>Times Daily</u>, June 18, 1993.
4. Young, Ronald D., and Brown, Earl H., "TVA's National Fertilizer Development Center at Muscle Shoals — Its Historic Role In Times of Emergency and Peace," 1976.
5. Garrett. History - Lauderdale County.
6. District Office, U. S. Corps of Engineers, Nashville, Tennessee.
7. Construction of Aqua Claudia at Rome the begun in 38 A.D.
8. Burt, Reynolds B., "Worthington Was Truly A Shoals Man," <u>Times Daily</u>, November 11, 1993.
9-12. Johnson, Leland R., Engineers On The Twin Rivers, U. S. Army Engineer District, Nashville, 1978.

Chapter 22

1-2. Young and Brown.
3. Rosenbaum, Alvin, <u>Usonia</u>, (The Preservation Press, National Trust For Historic Preservation, Washington, D.C., 1993.)
4. Vessel, Floyd E., interviewed on December 21, 1954.

Chapter 23

1. Rogers. Ward, Atkins, and Flynt.
2. Udall, Stewart L, <u>The Quiet Crisis</u>, 1963.
3-4. Johnson, Kenneth R., "Community Sensitive To The Destitute," <u>Times Daily</u>, December 26, 1996.
5. Johnson, Kenneth R., "Mass Poverty Considered A Problem To Resolve," <u>Times Daily</u>, January 9, 1997.
6. Hall, James F., Senior, in an interview with the author on October 3, 1965.

7. Johnson. Community Sensitive.
8. Archives, First United Methodist Church, Florence, Alabama.
9. Johnson, Kenneth R., "Compassion For Suffering Took Positive Form In Area," Times Daily, January 2, 1997.
10. Johnson. Mass Poverty.
11. Watson, Acy L., interviewed on August 9, 1955.
12. Johnson. Mass Poverty.
13. Rogers, Ward, Atkins, and Flynt.
14. Rickard, Hunter, interviewed on March 4, 1948.

Chapter 24

1. Hamby, Reverend G. Mack, interviewed on August 12, 1950.
2. As witnessed by the author on January 21, 1933.
3. Hubbard, Preston J., Origins of the TVA, Vanderbuilt University Press, Nashville, Tennessee, 1961.
4. Currey, Alma Jean Sharp, interviewed on January 21, 1994.
5. Henry, Waits G., interviewed on September 12, 1956.
6-7. Young and Brown.

Chapter 25

1. "A History of Navigation on the Tennessee River System," House Document No. 254, 75th Congress, 1st Session.
2-4. Davidson, Donald, The Tennessee, Vol. One, (J.J. Little and Ives Company, New York, 1946.)
5. House Document No. 254, 75th Congress, 1st Session.
6. "Geological Formations and Fossils of Northwest Alabama," Science Department, State Teachers College, Florence, Alabama (Author and date not shown.)
    Jones, Douglass, "The Early Gateway to Alabama," Nature South, (Judge David Enslen Collection, Fayette, Alabama, date and publisher not shown.)
7. Davidson, Donald. Jones, Douglass.
8. Dooling, Dave, "Ancient Treasure Under Our Feet," Huntsville Times, Huntsville, Alabama, May 6, 1979.
9. Appenzeller, Tim, "Travels," Discover Magazine, September 1996.

10.   Paper, <u>Geological Formations and Fossils in Northwestern Alabama</u>.

11.   Deland, T. A., and Smith, A. Davis, <u>Northern Alabama, Historical and Biographical</u> (publisher unknown, 1889.)

12.   Davidson, Donald.

13.   Sherer, Dennis, "Hooked On Digging," <u>Times Daily</u>, Florence, Alabama, August 5, 1996.
"Lauderdale Cave Is Archaeological Bonanza, "<u>East Lauderdale News</u>, Rogerville, Alabama, August 1, 1996.

14.   <u>House Document No. 254, 75th Congress, 1st Session</u>.

15.   Jackson Family Papers, courtesy of James Jackson, Memphis.

16.   The Tom Hendrix Indian Collection, Florence, Alabama.

Chapter 26

1.   Hubbert, Charles, University of Alabama, <u>Florence Times - Tri Cities Daily</u>, July 14., 1978. Moore, Charles E., Florence, Alabama, private papers.

2.   Neel, John, "Prehistoric Alabamians", <u>EnviorSouth</u>, April, June, 1980.

3.   Sherer, Dennis, "Hooked On Digging," <u>Times Daily</u>, August 5, 1996.

4-5.   Pounds, Virginia, and Owens, Laurella, <u>The World of the Southern Indians</u>, (Beechwood Books, Birmingham, Alabama, 1983.)

6.   Neel. (see note 2.)

7.   Pounds and Owens.

8.   Florence Indian Mound Museum displays and texts showing the Copena artifacts found at the Muscle Shoals in Northwest Alabama. (Florence, Alabama.)

9.   Bureau of American Ethnology, Bulletin Number 120, 1938. (Tennessee Valley Authority Library, Muscle Shoals, Alabama.)

10.   Walthall, John A., <u>Prehistoric Indians of the Southeast</u>, (The University of Alabama Press, Tuscaloosa, Alabama.)

11.   Index Map of Pickwick Reservoir Archaeological Findings, Tennessee Valley Authority, Map Branch, Chattanooga, Tennessee.

12. Moore, Charles E., Florence, Alabama Archaeologist, Private Papers. "Archaeologists Believe Mound is Older Than Previously Thought," East Lauderdale News, May 30, 1996.
13. Kitchens.

Chapter 27
1. Griffith, Lucille, History of Alabama 1540-1900, (Colonial Press, Northport, Alabama, 1962.)
2. Pounds and Owens. (see note 3, Chapter 1.)
3. Blue, Matthew P., manuscripts on Lauderdale County, Alabama (Department of Archives, Montgomery, Alabama, early 1850s.)
4. "Archaeologists Believe Mound Is Older Than Previously Thought," East Lauderdale News, May 30, 1996.
5. Vega, Garcilaso de la, Recollections of the Explorations of Hernando de Sota (Tennessee Public Library, Nashville.)
6. Hudson, Charles, The Southeastern Indians, (The University of Tennessee Press, 1976.)
7. Walthall, John A, Prehistoric Indians of the Southeast (see note 7, Chapter 2.)
8. Pounds and Owens. (see note 3, Chapter 1.)
9. Moore, Charles E. (see note 8, Chapter 2.)
10. Blue.

Chapter 28
1. Milfort, General Le Clerc, History of the Muscogees, (Paris, France, 1802.)
2. Neel, John, "How Alabama Got Its Name," EnviroSouth, Vol. 4, No. 2, (April and June, 1980.)
3. Pounds and Owens.
4. Sheffield, City on the Bluff, 1885-1985. (Friends of Sheffield Public Library, Sheffield, Alabama, 1985.)
5-6. Cotterill, R. S., The Southern Indians, the Story of the Civilized Tribes Before Removal, (University of Oklahoma Press, Norman, Oklahoma, 1954.)
7. Mooney, James, The Siouan Tribes of the East, Bureau of American Ethnology Bulletin Number 22.
8. Hudson.

9-10.   Cotterill.

11.   <u>Sheffield, City on the Bluff</u>, 1885-1985.

12.   Cotterill.

13.   <u>Webster's Seventh New Collegiate Dictionary</u>, (Rand McNally and Company, Chicago, 1961.)

14.   <u>Sheffield, City on the Bluff</u>, 1885-1985.

15.   Moore, Charles E.

16.   Pickett, Albert James, <u>History of Alabama</u>, (republished in 1962 by the Willco Publishing Company, Tuscaloosa, Alabama.)

17.   Cotterill.

18.   Gibson.

19.   Adair, James <u>History of the American Indians</u>, (1775).

20.   King, F. R., private papers, Public Library, Leighton, Alabama.

Chapter 29

1.   Martini, Don, "A Genealogical Study of the Colbert Family of Chickasaw Indian Fame, I" (Natchez Trace Parkway Library, Tupelo, Mississippi, date not shown.)

2.   Brown, John P., <u>Old Frontiers</u> (Southern Publishers, Inc., Kingsport, Tennessee, 1938.) Malone, Henry T., <u>Cherokees of the Old South</u> (University of Georgia Press, 1950.) Garrett. History - Lauderdale County.

3.   Malone.

4.   Axford, Faye, "Elk County," <u>Limestone Legacy</u>, Vol. 3, No. 3, (Athens, Alabama 1981.)

5.   Clairborne, J. F. H., <u>Life and Times of General Sam Dale, The Mississippi Partisan,</u> (copy in University of Mississippi Library.)

6.   Colbert, Richard A., <u>James Logan Colbert</u>, (Birmingham, Alabama, 1995.)

7-8.   Martini, Don, <u>Chickasaw Empire</u>, The Story of the Colbert Family (Ripley, Mississippi, 1986.)

9.   Kappler, Charles J., <u>Indian Affairs, Laws, and Treaties</u>, Volume II (Washington, D.C., 1892-1913.) Phelps, Dawson A., "The Natchez Trace in Alabama," <u>Alabama Review</u>, Vol. VII, No. l, January, 1954.

10.   Martini.

11.   Garrett. History - Lauderdale County.

12. Leftwich, Nina, Two Hundred Years at Muscle Shoals, (Press of Multigraphic Advertising Company, Birmingham, Alabama, 1935.)

13. Army and Navy Chronicle, Vol. X, No. 4, January 23, 1840 (Private papers of Richard C. Sheridan, Sheffield, Alabama.)

Chapter 30

1. Watts, Charles Wilder, The Journal of Muscle Shoals History, Vol. VII, (Tennessee Valley Historical Society, 1979.)

2-4. Davidson, Donald.

5. Johnson, Kenneth R., "A History of Franklin County, Alabama, With Emphasis on the Cedar Creek Area," Journal of Muscle Shoals History, Vol. XIII (Tennessee Valley Historical Society, 1993.)

6. Davidson, Donald.
Carter, Clarence Edwin, The Territorial Papers of the United States, Vols. IV, V, VI, and XVIII (U.S. Printing Office, 1936.)
Collection of General John Coffee Papers at Collier Library, University of North Alabama.
Cotterill.

7. Burt, Reynolds B., Times Daily, September 17, 1992.

8. Ramsey, J. G. M., The Annals of Tennessee (Charleston, 1853.)
Pickett.

9. Haskins, Charles H., "The Yazoo Land Companies," Papers of the American Historical Association, Volume V, 1891.
Watts, Charles Wilder, Sheffield, Alabama, private papers.

10. Watts.
Carter, Vol. IV, Southwest Territory.

11. Garrett. History - Lauderdale County.

12-14. Watts.

Chapter 31

1. Cotterill.

2. Rogers, Ward, Leah, and Flynt.
Watts, Charles Wilder, "Our Heritage from the Muscle Shoals," The Journal of Muscle Shoals History, Vol. VII, (The Tennessee Valley Historical Society, 1979.)

Johnson. History - Franklin County, Alabama,

3.   Watts. Our Heritage.

4.   Davidson, Donald.

5.   Leftwich.

6-8.   Garrett. History - Lauderdale County.

9.   National Archives Microfilm Publications: Records of the Cherokee Indian Agency in Tennessee 1801-1835, Microcopy 208, Roll 4. Correspondence and Miscellaneous Records, 1808- 1909, No. 2311. W. S. Hoole Special Collections, Library, University of Alabama.
Axford, Faye, article "Elk County," <u>Limestone Legacy</u>, Vol. 3, No 3, Athens, Alabama (1981.)

10.   James, J. L., <u>Colbertains, A History of Colbert County, Alabama, and Some of the Pioneer Citizens Before 1878</u>. (Reprinted by the Natchez Trace Genealogical Society, 1980.)
Gentry, Dorothy, <u>Life and Legend of Lawrence County, Alabama</u>, (Nottingham-SWS, Inc., Tuscaloosa, Alabama, 1962.)

11.   <u>Cemeteries Of East Lauderdale County, Alabama</u>, (Published by Friends of the Rogersville Public Library, 1996.)

12.   Wood, William B., from a speech made at Florence, Alabama, on July 4, 1878 (copy in collection of author.)

13..   Garrett. History - Lauderdale County.

14.   Wood, William B. from a speech made at Florence, Alabama, on July 4, 1878.

15.   Carter, Marymaud Killen, <u>Fifteen Southern Families</u>, (Polyantos, New Orleans, 1974.)
Johnson, Fred, Lexington, Alabama, interviewed on July 13., 1996.

16.   Allen, Granville, O., <u>Our Allens From Maryland To Muscle Shoals Via The Mid-West</u>, (Gregath Publishing Company, Cullman, Alabama, 1995.)

17.   Axford, Faye, <u>Limestone Legacy</u>, Vol. 3, No 3.

18.   Herman, William, "Old Times in Lauderdale," <u>Florence Gazette</u>, Florence, Alabama, April 19, 1884.
Wood, William B., from speech made on July 4, 1878.

19.   Wright. Early Land Buyers.

Chapter 32

1. The Kentucky Gazette, Lexington, Kentucky, December 12, 1789.
2. Brewer, W., Alabama, Her History and Resources, 1540-1872 (Montgomery, Alabama, 1872.)
   Axford, Faye, Elk County, (Limestone County Historical Society, Athens, Alabama, 1978).
3-4. Axford.
5. Mississippi Department of Archives and History.
   Wallace, Katherine T., "Notes and Documents: Elk County, Alabama," Alabama Review, July, 1968.
   Jones, Frank, Birmingham, Alabama, private papers, 1950.
6. Journal of the House of Representatives of the Alabama Territory at the First Session of the First General Assembly in the Forty-Second Year of American Independence (St. Stephens: Thomas Eastin, Printer to the Alabama Territory, 1818.)
7. Lewis, Oscar, Florence, Alabama (private papers.)
8. Brewer.
   Lewis, Oscar.
9. Lewis, Oscar.
10. Garrett. History - Lauderdale County.
11. Douglass, Hiram Kennedy interviewed on May 10, 1956.

Chapter 33

1. McDaniel. Buildings and Sites.
2. Minutes of the Court, Maury County, Tennessee, Box of 1817-1818 Papers, copied by the author August 24, 1970.
3. Smith, William, Florence, Alabama, private collection.
4. Jackson, Elizabeth McCulloch, "Historic Trees In And Around Florence, Alabama," Family Record, March 1965 by James Jackson, Memphis, Tennessee.
5. Royall.
6. The Florence Herald, August 14., 1919.
7. Garrett. History - Lauderdale County.

Chapter 34

1. McDaniel, Mary Jane, "Our Heritage from the Land," <u>The Muscle Shoals Heritage, Journal of Muscle Shoals History</u>, Vol. VII, (The Tennessee Valley Historical Society, 1979.)

2. Reeder family papers in the possession of Mrs. James Price, Florence, Alabama.

3. Furnas, J. C., <u>Goodbye to Uncle Tom</u>, (William Sloane Associates, New York, 1956.)

4-5. Cresap, Bernarr, "The People at the Muscle Shoals," <u>The Journal of Muscle Shoals History</u>, Vol. II, 1979.

6. McWhiney, Grady, <u>Cracker Culture</u>, (The University Alabama Press, Tuscaloosa and London, 1988.)

Chapter 35

1. Wright. Location of Land Buyers.

2. Hill, William Q., Florence, Alabama, private papers.

3. McGee, Helan Starkey, Oklahoma City, Oklahoma, interviewed on May 17, 1984.)

4. Carter, Clarence Edwin, <u>The Territorial Papers of the Mississippi Territory</u>, Volumes I - IV (U.S. Government Printing Office, Washington, D.C., 1938.)
Garrett. Notes to the author, August 21, 1957.

5. Kimbrough, Mildred, and Barnett, Muriel, "Some History of Rogersville, Alabama," <u>East Lauderdale News</u>, September 5, 1991.

6. Harraway, William E., "The Long Ago," <u>The Journal of Muscle Shoals History</u>, Vol. XI, 1986.
Department of Archives and History, Montgomery, Alabama, article entitled "Town Sketches of Lauderdale County."

7. Wright. Location of Land Buyers.
Waddell, Mrs. Oswald, "Early History of the First Baptist Church," an unpublished paper, date unknown.
Kimbrough, Mildred, memorandum to author, September 29, 1995.

8. Historical marker near the site of his grave.

9. Wright. Location of Land Buyers.

10. Hill, William Q., "Post Offices and Postmasters of Lauderdale County."

11. Kizer, Sallie Mae, "A Student's History of Lexington," included in I'm From Lexington, by Fred Johnson.

12. Hall, Mary Turner Kelly, granddaughter of Andrew L. Phillips, interviewed on June 28, 1997.

13-14. Kizer.

15. Foscue, Virginia O., Place Names in Alabama, (University of Alabama Press, 1989.)

16. Johnson, Fred, I'm From Lexington.

17. From the author's files on fossils unearthed in 1966.

18. Williams, Morris Lee, History of Anderson, Alabama, (1979.)

19. Wright. Location of Land Buyers.

20. Pruitt, Maurice, collection of documents, Collier Library, University of North Alabama, Florence, Alabama.

21. Wright. Location of Land Buyers.

22. Williams, Morris Lee, History of Anderson, Alabama.

23. Cagle, Willa Jean, "The Story of the James Brothers," (published in the History of Anderson, Alabama, by Morris Lee Williams, 1979.)

24. Ingrum, James, Florence, Alabama (interviewed June 19, 1995.)

25. Ingrum

26-27. Hammond, J. M., "History of Grassy School," in the History of Anderson, Alabama, by Morris Lee Williams.

28. Wright. Location of Land Buyers.

29. Truitt, Vernice C., "The History of Springfield," East Lauderdale News, January 11, 1973.
Wright. Location of Land Buyers.

30. Springer, Lee, Florence, Alabama, interviewed on October 22, 1956.

31. Whitehead, Lizzie, Rogersville, Alabama, interviewed on January 5, 1956.
Kimbrough, Mildred, memorandum to author, September 29, 1995.
32. Meredith, Eugene, Rogersville, Alabama, interviewed on November 17, 1954.

33. Wright. Location of Land Buyers.

34-35. U.S. Engineer's Drawings, 1829 Proposed Canal, State of Alabama (B. J. Lawrence Collection, Decatur, Alabama.)

36. Butler, Kit, Killen, Alabama, interviewed on August 2, 1953.

37. White, Patrick B., Senior, Rogersville, Alabama, interviewed on September 19, 1957.

38. Grave marker located in the Butler Cemetery near Elgin in East Lauderdale County.

39. Wright. Location of Land Buyers.

40. Foscue, Virginia O., <u>Place Names in Alabama</u>.
Kimbrough, Mildred, memorandum to author, September 29, 1995.

41. Wright. Location of Land Buyers.

42. <u>The Florence Herald</u>, November 27, 1973.

43. Boston, Hollis B., Colonel, Montgomery, Alabama, letter to author, dated February 19, 1992.

Chapter 36

1. Wood, William B., "History of Lauderdale County," <u>Journal of Muscle Shoals History</u>, Volume 5, 1977.
Map of North Alabama, published in 1848.
Carter, Marymaud Killen.

2-3. Douglass, Hiram Kennedy, in an interview with the author on December 22, 1954.

4. Hill, William Q., Post Offices.

5. Douglass, Hiram Kennedy, interviewed on December 22, 1954.
<u>Encyclopaedia Britannica</u>, Volume 18, London, 1973.

6. Coffee, Eliza, private papers (collection of the author.)

7. Garrett. History - Lauderdale County.
Weakley, Eliza, private papers (University of North Alabama.)

8-9. Wright. Location of Land Buyers.

10. Garrett. History - Lauderdale County.
Wright. Location of Land Buyers.

11. Map, U. S. Engineer's Drawing, 1829 Proposed Canal, State of Alabama (B. J. Lawrence Collection, Decatur, Alabama.)
Map of North Alabama, 1848 (a copy on file with the author.)

12. Wood, William B., "History of Lauderdale County."

13-14. Douglass, Hiram Kennedy, interviewed on December 22, 1954.

15. Cunningham, Wells Rutland, interviewed on February 2, 1959.

16-17. Douglass, Hiram Kennedy, interviewed on December 22, 1954.

18. Gean, Martha, family records.

19.　　Cochran, Bill, Attorney, Florence, Alabama, interviewed on August 9, 1992.

20.　　Wright. Location of Land Buyers.

21.　　Topographic Map Showing Forest Cover, Bear Creek Watershed (Tennessee Valley Authority, August, 1961.)
Map of Lauderdale County, Alabama, (published by The Hudgins Company, Atlanta, Georgia, 1907.)

22.　　Wright. Location of Land Buyers.

23.　　Mitchell, Mrs. Elba Parker, interviewed on February 9, 1996.

24.　　Hill, William Q., Post Offices.

25.　　Hill, William Q., interviewed on February 21, 1993.

26.　　Hill, William Q., <u>A History of Green Hill and Some Surrounding Communities in Lauderdale County, Alabama</u>, (1978.)

27.　　Allen, Granvile O., <u>Our Allens From Maryland to Muscle Shoals Via The Mid-West</u>, (Gregath Publishing Company, Cullman, Alabama, 1995.)

28.　　Hill, William Q., History - Green Hill.

29.　　Wallace, Dan, Cypress Inn, Tennessee, interviewed on May 6, 1993.

30.　　McDonald, Elias M., original ledger owned by Wynell Davis, Lawrenceburg, Tennessee.

31-32.　　　　Hill, William Q., History - Green Hill.

33.　　Wright. Location of Land Buyers.

34.　　Sheridan, Richard C., "Shoals Area Industries Aided Army in Civil War," <u>Times Daily</u>, May 28, 1992.

35.　　Wright. Location of Land Buyers.
Hill, William Q., interviewed on May 23, 1991.

36-38. Hill, William Q., History of Green Hill.

39.　　Henken, Frank, interviewed during the Summer of 1954.
Hill, William Q., interviewed on May 23, 1991.

40.　　<u>The Official Records of the Union and Confederate Armies of the War of Rebellion</u>, 61 volumes.
<u>The Confederate Veteran</u>, December, 1896, and March, April, May, and June, 1897.
Pierce, Sergeant Lyman B., <u>History of the Second Iowa Cavalry</u>, Hawk-Eye Steam Book, Burlington, Iowa, 1865.

41. '　　Wright. Location of Land Buyers.

42. Allen, Granville O., Our <u>Allens From Maryland To Muscle Shoals Via The Mid-West</u>, Gregath Publishing Company, 1995.

43. Rumble, Vickie Regina, <u>Guardian Angels, A History of the Killen Family.</u>

44. Hill, William Q., History of Green Hill.

45. Lewis, Oscar, Florence, Alabama, private collection.

46. Wright. Location of Land Buyers.

47. Sulzby, James F., Junior, <u>Historic Alabama Hotels and Resorts,</u> (University of Alabama Press, 1960.)

48. Wright, Milly, "Location of Land Buyers."

49. Wright, Milly, private collection.

50. Tidwell, Mrs. Alice, interviewed on October 23, 1973.

51. Wright. Location of Land Buyers.

52. Wilson, Regina, and Love, Judy, <u>History of The Harrison Chapel United Methodist Church</u>, (Killen, Alabama, 1976.)

53. Owens, Colonel Robert J., <u>The Whitmires of Whitmire, S.C., and Kin, Volume 2</u>, (Chandler, Arizona, 1990.)

54-57. Pettus, Ronald, Killen Historian, interviewed on February 5, 1996.

58-59. Winn, Joshua Nicholas III, <u>Muscle Shoals Canal...Life With The Canalers</u>, (The Strode Publishers, Inc., Huntsville, Alabama, 1978.)

60. Hill, William Q., Post Offices.

61. Winn. Muscle Shoals Canal.

62. Rumble. Guardian Angels.

63. Wright, Milly, private papers.

64. Pettus, Ronald, Killen Historian, interviewed on February 5, 1996.

65. Lawrence, B. J., "The Great Bend of the Tennessee River and the Shoals," (Decatur, Alabama, 1994.)

66. Wright. Location of Land Buyers.

67. Alabama Archives, Montgomery, Alabama.

68. Bernauer, Marianne, "A History of St. Florian,: (a private paper dated 1965.)

69. Handy, W. C., <u>Father of the Blues</u>, (The Macmillan Company, New York, 1947.)

70. Wright. Location of Land Buyers.

71.   Smith, William E., Junior, (private papers related to the nomination of the Jackson Military Road to the Alabama Register of Historic Places, prepared in 1996.)

72.   Bernauer. A History of St. Florian." Jackson, Elizabeth McCulloch, "Historical Trees Around Florence," (published by the D.A.R. about 1934.)

73.   Bernauer. A History of St. Florian.

74.   McDonald, Jesse William, interviewed on October 31, 1940.

75-76. Bernauer. A History of St. Florian.

77.   Wright. Location of Land Buyers.

78.   Jaynes, Edward T., interviewed on November 12, 1995.

79-80. Wright. Location of Land Buyers.

Chapter 37

1.   Wade, Sam, "The Wades And Their Slave Sandy," The Journal of Muscle Shoals History, Volume V, 1977.

2.   Hill, William Q., Post Offices.

3.   Wright. Location of Land Buyers.

4.   Patterson, Jim, "City Serving Two States," Florence Herald, October 23, 1978.

5.   Pollard, Jean Watkins, interviewed on January 16, 1996.

6.   Foscue.

7.   Wright. Location of Land Buyers.

8.   Fowler, Floyd, Severn, Maryland, private papers.

9.   Fowler, Carver, Florence, Alabama, interviewed on July 19, 1954.

10-11. Wright. Location of Land Buyers.

12.   Jones, Kathleen Paul, and Gandrud, Pauline Jones, Alabama Records, Volume 104, (Blewett Company, Columbus, Mississippi, 1980.)

13.   Sockwell, Sandra McGrady, The Place Names of Colbert and Lauderdale County, Alabama.

14.   Wright. Location of Land Buyers.

15.   Hill, William Q., Post Offices.

16.   Wright. Location of Land Buyers.

17-18. The Journal of Muscle Shoals History, Volume IV, 1976.

19.   Jaynes, Edward T., interviewed on October 26, 1995.

20.   Wright. Location of Land Buyers.

21.   Jaynes, Edward T., interviewed on October 26, 1995.

22.   Sockwell, Sandra M.,

23.   Wright. Location of Land Buyers.

24.   Underwood, Robert Milton, Austin, Texas, private papers. Early <u>Florence Herald</u> and <u>Courier Journal</u> newspaper clippings in the collection of the author (date unknown.)

25.   Wright. Location of Land Buyers.

26-27. Wilhelm, Dwight M. <u>History of Cotton Textile Industry in Alabama 1809 to 1950</u> (Montgomery, Alabama, 1950.) The General John Coffee Papers, Tennessee State Archives, Fowler, James, interviewed on February 2, 1989.

28.   Deed Book 22, page 340, Lauderdale County Courthouse.

29.   McDonald, Sr., Jones Emory, Florence, Alabama, interviewed on April 15, 1956.

30.   McDonald, Jesse William, Florence, Alabama, interviewed on June 26, 1943.

31.   Davis, Derrel, "Historical Sketch, Stony Point Church of Christ," (date unknown.)

32.   Sharp, Mary Threet, Florence, Alabama, private papers.

33.   White, Patrick, Rogersville, Alabama, interviewed on September 14, 1955.

34.   Wright. Location of Land Buyers.

35.   Tract Books, Lauderdale County, Alabama.

Chapter 38

1.   Henderson, Lois, Florence, Alabama, research notes dated November 26, 1993.

2.   Wright. Location of Land Buyers.

3.   Lewis, Oscar D., historical papers (clippings from the <u>Florence Herald</u>, dates unknown.)

4.   Abramson, Inah Mae Young, <u>History of Wesley Chapel United Methodist Church</u> published in 1976.

5-6.   Wright. Location of Land Buyers.

7.   Hill, William Q., Post Offices.

8-10. Wright. Location of Land Buyers.

11.   Collum, Barbara Lovelace, interviewed on January 10, 1996. 12-13. Rains, Robert, and Berry, Allen, <u>Wayne County, Tennessee,</u>

      <u>1817-1995, History and Families</u>, (Turner Publishing Company, Paducah, Kentucky, 1995.)

14. Wright. Location of Land Buyers.

15. Sharp, Mary Threet, Florence, Alabama, private papers.

16. O'Neal, John Belton, <u>The Annals of Newberry County, South Carolina, Historical, Biographical and Antecdotal</u>, (Aull and Houseal, 1892.)

17. Hill, William Q., Post Offices.

18. Sharp, Mary Threet, Florence, Alabama, private papers.

19-20. Dowdy, Johnnie Sharp, Lauderdale County, Alabama, interviewed on August 9, 1958.

21. Sockwell.

22. Wright. Location of Land Buyers.

23. Horton, Mrs. Leland, "History of Johnson Crossroads Baptist Church, Cloverdale, Alabama," August 5, 1994.

24. Irons, Orlan, <u>Cemetery Records, Lauderdale County, Alabama</u>, Volume I, (Natchez Trace Genealogical Society, 1990.)

25. Wright. Location of Land Buyers.

26. McCorkle, Clyde F., interviewed on April 5, 1996.

27. Darby, Mrs. A. W., "Name and Places in Lauderdale County Taken From The Long Ago," (unpublished paper, 1962.)

28. Garrett. History – Lauderdale County.

29. <u>The War of Rebellion: Official Records of the Union and Confederate Armies</u>, Series 1, Volume 23, Part 1.

30. Lowe, Seth, interviewed on September 9, 1989.

31. Hill, William Q., Post Offices.

32. Wright. Location of Land Buyers.

33. Duke, Milka, paper, "Immigrants From Finland Had `Sisu' To Face Unknown" (1995.)
Gray, Hilda Hakola, paper, "History of the Finns of Cloverdale, Alabama" (date unknown.)

34. <u>Florence-Picture Newspaper</u>, "Rawhide Blossoms into Cloverdale," (author and date not known.)

35. McDonald, William Ervin, in reminiscence of his Uncle Robert Andrews, as told to the author over a period of many years.

36. Darby, Mrs. Andrew, interviewed on December 5, 1959.

37. Lyon, Edwin A., A New Deal For Southeastern Archaeology (The University of Alabama Press, Tuscaloosa, Alabama, 1996.) Moore, Charles E., interviewed on March 13, 1996.

38. Hubbert, Charles, University of Alabama, July 14, 1978, <u>Florence Times</u> and <u>Tri Cities Daily</u>.

39. Garrett. History - Lauderdale County.

40. Watts. Private papers.

41. Darby, Mrs. Andrew, interviewed on December 5, 1959.

42. Hill, William Q., Post Offices.

43. <u>The Clarion and Tennessee State Gazette</u>, Nashville, Tennessee, July 14, 1818.

44. Watts, Charles Wilder, Sheffield, Alabama, "Town of Havannah," <u>Natchez Trace Traveler</u>, Volume 12, Number 4, 1992.

45. Lauderdale County, Alabama, Court Records. Moser, Harold D., Hoth, David R., and Hoemann, George H., <u>The Papers Of Andrew Jackson, Volume V, 1821-1824</u>, (The University of Tennessee Press, Knoxville, 1996.)

46. Garrett. History - Lauderdale County.

47. Irons.

48-49. Darby, Mrs. Andrew J., in a lecture to the Tennessee Valley Historical Society, November 22, 1959.

50. Watts, Charles Wilder, private papers.

51. Wright, Milly, <u>Early Land Buyers, Lauderdale County, Alabama, 1818-25</u>, (Natchez Trace Genealogical Society, 1989.)

52. Darby, Mrs. Andrew J., in a lecture presented to theTennessee Valley Historical Society, May 6, 1962.

53. Hall, John Lincoln, Senior, interviewed on May 25, 1950. Murphy, Glenn, interviewed on June 2, 1994.

54. <u>The National Banner</u>, Nashville, Tennessee, January 2, 1833. Lauderdale County, Alabama, court records. Wright, Milly, interviewed on June 17, 1997.

55. Lauderdale County, Alabama, court records.

56. McDaniel, Dr. Mary Jane, "Columbus Smith, The Early Days of Smithsonia," <u>Shoals Community Magazine</u>, 1991.

57. <u>Smithsonia, Alabama</u>, a publication, dated 1903, found among the papers of the late Joseph Hines by the author (publisher unknown,

but believed to have been either the <u>Florence Times</u> or <u>Florence Herald</u>.)

58. McDaniel, Dr., Mary Jane, Columbus Smith.

59. Mosakowski, Martha Reynolds Smith, granddaughter of Columbus Smith, private papers.

60. Murphy, Glenn, interviewed on June 2, 1994.

61. Mosakowski, Martha Reynolds Smith, private papers.

62. "Mysteries of the Ancient Americans," (The Reader's Digest Association, Inc., Pleasantville, New York, 1986.)

63. Webb, William S., and DeJarnette, <u>An Archaeological Survey of Pickwick Basin in the Adjacent Portions of the States of Alabama, Mississippi, and Tennessee</u>, Smithsonia Institute, Bureau of American Ethnology Bulletin 129 (U.S. Printing Office, Washington, D.C. 1942.)

64. Wright. Location of Land Buyers.

65. Murphy, Glenn, interviewed on June 2, 1994.

66-67. Lindsey, Rivers, Senior, interviewed on October 31, 1959.

68. Hill, William Q., Post Offices.

69. Wright. Location of Land Buyers.

70. Terrell, Judith, private papers.

71. Wright. Location of Land Buyers.

72. Hill, William Q., Post Offices.

73. Rogers, Donna Haynes, private papers.

74. Wright. Location of Land Buyers.

75. Sockwell.

76. Hill, William Q., Post Offices.

77. Sockwell.

78. County Court Records, Lauderdale County, Alabama.

79. Daniel, Earl, Chattanooga, Tennessee, private papers.

80. Thomas, Laura, Florence, Alabama, private papers.

81. Crouch, Carroll H., Senior, Colbert County, Alabama, private papers.

82. Stribling, T. S., <u>Laughing Stock</u>, edited by R. K. Cross and J. T. McMillan (St. Luke's Press, Memphis, Tennessee, 1982.)

83. Irons, Orlan K., private papers.

84. Rogers, Donna Haynes, private Papers.

85. Daniel, Earl F., interviewed on May 7, 1965.

86. Hill, William Q., Post Offices.
87. Wright, Milly. Early Land Buyer.
88. Jones, James Pickett, <u>Yankee Blitzkrieg</u>, (The University of Georgia Press, Athens, Georgia, 1976.)
89. Stribling, T. S., <u>Laughing Stock</u>, edited by R. K. Cross and J. T. McMillan.
90. Wright, Milly, "Gabriel Bumpass and the Wonderful Town of Waterloo," (November 6, 1996.)
91. Hill, Thomas F., <u>Birmingham News</u>, July 23, 1969.

Index

N

Nabors, B. L., 167
Nail, James, 304
Nance, Daniel, 238
Nancy, Daniel, 237
Nanny, Urish, 261
Napoleon, 3, 17
Neal, Newton, 309
Negley, Albert, 104
Negley, James Scott, 104
Nelson, A. H., 167
Nelson, William "Bull", 104
Newman, Henry, 246, 247
Nichols, G. C., 159
Noel, Edmond, 302
Noel, Edmund, 309
Nolan, Serkin, 317
Noland, Matilda F., 41
Nolke, W. C., 79
Norman, Joseph, 241
Norris, 178, 184
Norris, George W., 183
Norris, George Washington, 178
Northcross, 82
Norton, H. B., 85
Norton, John W., 147
Norwood, 249
Nye, Shadrack, 58

O

O'Briand, James, 283
O'Neal, B. W., 281
O'Neal, Basil Wheat, 51
O'Neal, Edward, 50
O'Neal, Edward A., 45, 51, 251
O'Neal, Edward Asbury, 50, 51, 52, 111,
    144
O'Neal, Edward Asbury, Jr., 52
O'Neal, Emmet, 45
O'Neal, Emmett, 50, 52, 53
O'Neal, Olivia, 111
O'Neal, Olivia Moore, 52
Oats, D. C., 308
Obannion, Thomas, 224
Obriand, James, 281
Obriand, John, 281
Obriand, Owen, 281

Old Tassell, 207
Olive, Betty, 297
Olive, G. W., 160
Olive, J. H., 311
Oliver, Charles, 136
Oliver, Daniel and Jane Rose, 136
O'Neal, Alfred, 51
Overton, John, 11

P

Paddleford, Joseph, 58
Paine, Robert, 90
Palmer, Randolph, 261
Parish, Jesse Newton, 291
Parker, 252
Parker, Alonzo, 280
Parker, Charles, 320
Parker, Dewey, 256
Parker, Josiah, 309
Parker, Lonzie, 256
Parker, Oliver, 256
Parker, Roma Harrison, viii
Parker, William, 322
Partin, Leonard, 241
Pate, Thomas, 323
Patrick, P. F., 76
Patrick, Peter F., 238
Patterson, 167
Patterson, Burt, 290
Patterson, Henrietta, 279
Patterson, James Allen, 279
Patterson, Josiah, 43, 109
Patterson, Malcolm, 53, 109
Patterson, Malcolm R., 43
Patton, 113
Patton, Mary, 28
Patton, Robert, 48, 49
Patton, Robert and Jane, 48
Patton, Robert M., 135
Patton, Robert Miller, 34, 48, 49, 80, 84,
    141, 145
Patton, William, 23, 48, 252
Paulk, Acenah, 329
Paulk, Charles S. W., 300
Paulk, Elizabeth, 297
Paulk, Jonathan, 72, 297, 298
Paulk, R. E., 155
Paulk, S. O., 294

Pruitt, Maurice Wade, 278
Pruitt, Thomas, 277, 278
Pruitt, Thomas D., 279
Pruitt, Thomas L., 279
Pugh, William J. and Jabez, 314
Puler, 6, 225
Purdom, Richard, 291
Putteet, A. T., 180

Q

Qualls, Gatewood, 329
Qualls, Gatewood "Gator", 329
Qualls, John, 329
Qualls, Millie Jerusha Ferris, 329
Quaser, Richard, 283
Quillen, William H., 256

R

Ragsdale, Samuel, 303
Ragsdale, William, 312
Raines, Polk and Wesley, 297
Ramsey, H. M., 180
Ramsey, Houston, 180
Ramsey, Houston M., 160
Ramsey, Lawrence, 159
Ramsey, Thomas, 220
Rankin, 33
Ranson, L. A., 325
Rapier, James, 143
Rapier, James and John, 142
Rapier, James T., 25, 142, 143
Rapier, James Thomas, 142
Rapier, John, 22, 25
Rapier, John H., Sr., 21
Rapier, Richard, 21, 22, 28, 74
Rapier, Suson, 22, 143
Rasch, Edward, 274
Rasch, Florian, 273
Rasch, Frank, 285
Rawlings, R. H., 322
Ray, A. D., 81
Ray, Archibald D., 241
Ray, Mattie, 83
Read, Ephraim D., 314
Reagon, Hannah Pugh, 315
Redd, Uhland O., III, 150
Reece, Robert, 263

Reed, Lizzie, 81
Reed, William, 237
Reeder, Brown, 169
Reeder, David and Jacob, 291
Reeder, Homer L., 326
Reeder, John Thomas, 309
Reeder, Lucy, ix
Reeder, Thomas, 311
Regan, John, 220
Reynolds, Clay, 158
Reynolds, Hamilton, 158, 257, 278
Reynolds, Hugh Riah, 278
Reynolds, Hugh Riah (Uriah), 158, 278
Reynolds, Thomas H., 158
Reynolds, Welton, 85
Rhodes, Bell, 297
Rhodes, Columbus, 312
Rhodes, Elijah, 312
Rhodes, F. M., 311
Rhodes, John and Elijah, 292
Rhodes, John W., 312
Rhodes, Mary Copeland, 312
Rhodes, Spencer, 312
Rice, 33
Rice, Joel, 225
Rice, Neander, 143
Rice, Neander Hickman, 30, 31
Rice, Septimus Primus, 81, 91
Rice, Stephen E., 299
Rice, Tobias, 245
Rice, W. P., 169
Rice, William T., 72, 284
Richards, H. G., 86
Richards, Henry Grady, 86, 168
Richards, John, 308
Richards, Nathan, 302
Richardson, 73, 150, 219
Richardson, "Granny" Kate, 251
Richardson, Asa and David, 259
Richardson, David and Henry, 259
Richardson, Henry, 286
Richardson, Hiram I., 265
Richardson, Isham, 259
Richardson, John, 264, 265
Richardson, John D., 259
Richardson, John David and Catherine
    Stutts, 219, 254
Richardson, John W., 240
Richardson, Julia Ann Young, 265
Richardson, Mary "Aunt Polly", 219

V

Valent, James, 252
Valiant, James, 268
Van Buren, Martin, 39
Van Dorn, 110
Van Dorn, Earl, 108
Vanhouse, Azon and Valentine, 299
Vanlier, Samuel, 72
Vaughn, James and John, 310
Vaughn, Samuel, 311
Vaughn, Will, 311
Veid, J. J., 154
Vestal, E. M., 148
Vigus, 79

W

Waddle, Amos, 241
Wade, John Dickie, 278
Wade, William Henry, 135
Waits, James, 318
Waldrip, James and William, 292
Waldrop, James and William, 296
Walker, 248
Walker, Elizabeth Adalet, 293
Walker, John, 290, 299
Walker, L. P. and R. W., 44
Walker, Leroy Pope, 44, 59
Walker, Richard Wilde, 44
Walker, William Carroll, 293
Wall, William Spencer, 79
Wall, William Spenser, 59
Wallace, 71
Wallace, John W., 293
Wallace, John Welsey, 295
Wallace, Josephine, 295
Wallace, William, 266, 290
Wallace, Young A., 82
Walles, Thomas, 309
Wallingsford, Isaac, 252
Walston, Eliza Jane, 310
Walston, Elizabeth, 310
Walston, John, 310
Walston, John and James, 310
Walston, Turner, 72, 310, 311
Walthall, 127
Ward, Edward, 65
Ward, William, 285

Ware, Helen, 83
Warren, John L., 261
Warren, Reuben R., 261
Warrick, Sam, 317
Warson, W. B., 137
Washburn, Cadwallader Colden, 120
Washington, 316, 327
Washington, Martha, 15
Wason, William A., 288
Waters, Bettie, 81
Waters, David M., 331
Waters, George, 322
Waters, Martha, 316
Watkins, 125
Watkins, Alfred and Robert, 291
Watkins, John, 125, 261
Watkins, Miles, 312
Watson, Matt, 266
Watson, Matthew, 311
Waul, Thomas Neville, 80
Weakley, Eliza, 117, 122
Weakley, James H., 9
Weakley, Samuel, 112
Weakley, Samuel D., 66, 101
Weathers, "Big Bill", 244
Webb, Ezra, 69
Webb, Ezra, Jr., 32
Webb, John, 314, 320, 321, 322, 330
Webb, Simeon, 314
Weeden, John D., 86, 173
Weinbaum, H. A., 64
Welbourne, Ephraim, 299
Welch, John, 270
West, 323
West, Elsey, 285
West, John, 236, 244, 248, 299
Westmoreland, Edwin B., 239
Westmoreland, Felix A., 239
Westmoreland, Martha, 38
Weston, Rubin, 324
Wharton, John A., 104
Wheat, Rebecca, 50
Wheeler, "Fighting Joe", 171, 185
Wheeler, Fighting Joe, 324
Wheeler, Joseph, 107, 119
Wheeler, Joseph E., 128
White, Arlin and Otis, 287
White, Chillon, 78
White, Daniel, 246, 247, 248
White, David, 248

389

Wood, Margaret, 70
Wood, Samuel, 70
Wood, Sterling Alexander Martin, 33, 46
Wood, W. B., 147
Wood, William B., 146
Wood, William Basil, 33, 45, 46, 70, 146, 260
Wood. William Richardson, 33
Woodall, 81
Woodall, Margaret, 34
Woodcock, John H., 37
Worthington, John Warren, 174
Wren, John, 70, 261
Wright, 331
Wright, James, 72, 284
Wright, John, 259
Wright, Moses, 330
Wright, Nicholas, 259
Wright, Nicholas and John, 257
Wright, Percy, 311
Wright, Ray, 312
Wyatt, Zula, 167

Y

Yarbrough, William L., 32
Yeamans, John, 13

Yeiser, E. R., 142
Young, 167
Young, De La, 286
Young, E. M., 158
Young, H., 272
Young, Jacob, 57
Young, James, 60
Young, James and Cornelia, 316
Young, James and Ebenezer, 291
Young, John B., 296
Young, John and Samuel, 291
Young, John H., 286
Young, Joseph, 294, 298
Young, Julia, 81
Young, Robert A., 49, 52, 91, 111
Young, Sam and John, 296
Young, Samuel, 230, 292
Young, Stephenson, 169
Young, Thomas K., 292
Young, Thomas W., 281
Young, William B., 300

Z

Zahand, John, 275
Zulauf, Adam, 273

Published by

Bluewater Publications is a multi-faceted publishing company capable of meeting all of your reading and publishing needs. Our two-fold aim is to:
1) Provide the market with educationally enlightening and inspiring research and reading materials and to
2) Make the opportunity of being published available to any author and or researcher who so desires to become published.

We are passionate about preserving history; whether it is through the re-publishing of an out-of-print classic or by publishing the research of historians and genealogists, Bluewater Publications is the publisher you need.

To learn more about the Dr. William Lindsey McDonald or for information about how you can be published through Bluewater Publications, please visit:

www.BluewaterPublications.com

Confidently Preserving Our Past,
Bluewater Publications.com
Formerly Known as Heart of Dixie Publishing

CPSIA information can be obtained
at www.ICGtesting.com
Printed in the USA
BVHW011504300122
627553BV00004B/79